Straw Sandals

LU HSÜN

CHINESE SHORT STORIES
1918-1933

Straw Sandals

Edited by
HAROLD R. ISAACS

Foreword by
LU HSÜN

The MIT Press
Cambridge, Massachusetts, and
London, England

This book was set in Baskerville
by Publishing Systems, Inc., Athens, GA. 30601,
printed on Finch Textbook Offset,
and bound in G.S.B. S/535/11 "Grey"
in the United States of America.

Library of Congress Cataloging in Publication Data

Isaacs, Harold Robert, 1910– comp.
  Straw sandals; Chinese short stories, 1918–1933.

  1. Short stories, English—Translations from Chinese. 2. Short stories, Chi-
nese—Translations into English. I. Title.
PZ1.I75St [PL2658.E8]   895.1'3'01   73–12853
ISBN 0–262–09014–7 (hardcover)

". . . [These intellectual aristocrats] took possession of the old Chinese literary garden, walking in with their shiny, leather boots. Now they sit tight inside and refuse entry to those who would walk in wearing straw sandals."

—Lu Hsün

Foreword

Fiction was never thought of as literature in China. It was held in low esteem, and no novels of any merit have appeared since the *Dream of the Red Chamber*, written at the end of the eighteenth century. The appearance of the writer of fiction in the field of Chinese literature coincides with the beginning of the "literary revolution" in 1917 and continues until now. This has come about partly as a response to the social demands of the time and to the influence of Western literature.

The new fiction, however, has had to wage an unceasing struggle to survive. Advocates of the literary revolution began by trying to free men from encrusted tradition. They believed that if they could do away with the old order, they would restore natural man and a good society. But they met with repression and persecution from the conservatives. After some ten years, as progressive writers became advocates of

The Chinese original of this foreword remained in its place in Lu Hsün's file of his writings and duly appeared in his collected works, entitled *Lu Hsün Ch'uan-chi* (People's Literature Publishing Co., Peking, 1958), vol. 6, pp. 16–17.

Foreword

the literary revolution, this oppression became ever more severe. Publications have been banned. Books have been burned. Writers have been executed. Many of our young writers work in this darkness and many pay with their lives for what they do.

This volume represents a selection of short stories written during the fifteen years or so of our literary revolution. Since we are only starting on new experiments, it is only natural that there is some immaturity. Still, these stories can be seen as young plants growing under a large rock. They cannot grow straight and strong but, twisting this way and that, they grow nevertheless.

In recent times there have probably been more books written about China by foreigners than by Chinese. All of these books are unavoidably written from a foreign point of view. We have an old saying: "If the lungs and viscera could only speak, the doctor's diagnosis would be put to shame." I think that even if they could speak, what they had to say would not necessarily always be reliable. Still, they would report things no physician could find, unexpected things, absolutely true to life.

Lu Hsün

Shanghai
August 15, 1934

HAROLD R. ISAACS

Introduction

This collection of translated Chinese stories was assembled in
1934. It was put together to present and to illustrate the development of the literary revolution in China, at that time
underway for barely more than fifteen years. The stories
were chosen with the guidance and counsel of Lu Hsün, one
of the makers and the premier creative writer of that revolution, and his younger friend and associate, Mao Tun,
thought at that time to be the foremost among the writers
after Lu Hsün himself. The intent was to trace, through examples, the passage of the new literary movement in China
from the humanistic or romantic concerns of its beginning to
the intensely political and ideological cast it took on under
the pressure of the great events that swept the country in
those years.

As Lu Hsün points out in his foreword, another purpose
was to introduce to Western readers the work of writers suffering the heavy-handed repressions of Chiang Kai-shek's
Kuomintang regime. Lu Hsün himself occupied a position of
such unassailable fame and prestige that the regime, ruthless
toward so many, did not dare to touch him, though it did

what it could to limit his influence. Lu Hsün had come slowly to a position of sympathizing support for the Communist movement. As he indicates in the biographical note he supplied for use in this volume, he was deeply shaken by the wanton massacres that marked Chiang Kai-shek's conquest of power in 1927. His hostility to the Kuomintang regime moved him toward a more active association with the Communists when he joined in 1930 in the founding of the League of Leftist Writers. By 1934, Lu Hsün had become the model and the mentor, indeed often the supporter and protector, of a group of writers who were either members or followers of the Communist Party. But from the standpoint of the Party apparatus, Lu Hsün was a prickly kind of supporter to have. He never accepted the identification of literature with politics, much less the idea of political control over a writer's work and thought, a matter over which he had been in open conflict with Communist critics during these years. Lu Hsün stubbornly insisted on the autonomy of the creative process, the freedom and independence of the writer. In those days of Kuomintang power, this meant in the first place challenging a regime which suppressed publications, arrested, imprisoned, and executed writers who opposed it. That is why the original working title of this collection—finally named *Straw Sandals* from a line in one of Lu Hsün's essays—was *China's Stifled Voices*. The events and transformations of the many years that have passed while this manuscript lay unpublished in the files now give a peculiarly heavy weight of irony to that title. The war against Japan was fought and won, the Kuomintang regime collapsed, and the long struggle to put the Communist Party in power in China ended in victory. For writers, however, and particularly for some of the writers represented in this collection, the struggle for their own freedom and independence went on, and on, and on.

Introduction

Lu Hsün himself died in 1936, the last year of his life filled with stubborn and exasperated resistance to Communist Party functionaries who were seeking to impose an abrupt change of "line" on the writers who supported their cause. It had to do with the shift to a new "united front" with the Kuomintang to pursue the war against Japan, a goal with which Lu Hsün certainly had no quarrel but a tactical reversal which he found very difficult to accept. He was not schooled in that rubbery flexibility with which all true Communists learned to handle their changes of "line" and was not prepared to yield up or mask the feelings or ideas to which he had come with so much deliberate pain. But what was much more to the point, he did not believe writers should take orders—to about-face or anything else—from anyone. Lu Hsün died soon enough so that he could be enthroned not long thereafter by Mao Tse-tung as the reigning hero-spirit, after Mao himself, of the Communist literary world. But in the very process of raising the late Lu Hsün to the status of hero of the new Communist culture, Mao Tse-tung, in his famous Yenan "Talks on Literature and Art" in 1942 served notice on all writers that Lu Hsün's style of satirical attack on the society was appropriate to his time and place but did not fit at all the needs of a Communist-led society. Lu Hsün was "entirely right," Mao said, to attack the "dark forces" of harmful reaction, but in the Communist regions, "where democracy and freedom are granted in full to the revolutionary writers and withheld only from the counterrevolutionaries, the style of the essay should not simply be like Lu Hsün's. Here we can shout at the top of our voices and have no need for veiled and roundabout expressions which are hard for the people to understand."[1] Mao went

1. Mao Tse-tung, *On Literature and Art*, Foreign Language Press, Peking, 1967, pp. 32–35.

on to lay down the doctrines and rules by which the Party would thereafter guide and govern all literature and art and decide what and who was "revolutionary" or "counterrevolutionary."

During the years that followed, Lu Hsün's most intimate friends and associates played the most prominent roles— ultimately as targets and victims—in the long series of collisions that took place between writers and the literary apparatus of the Party intent upon bringing them under its total control. These went on at intervals, in the Yenan period, during the war with Japan, and on down through the years of Communist power, in the Hundred Flowers campaign of the mid-1950s, and the Cultural Revolution of the late 1960s. Had he lived, it is clear, Lu Hsün could never have yielded to the Party's inevitable demand for his total submission. As it was, he remained iconized in name, but not in works. Along with almost all other books, including most of those published by the regime itself, the works of Lu Hsün were taken off the shelves by the cultural revolutionists in 1966, and in their multivolume bulk they have remained unreprinted and unavailable up to now; only some of his stories have just begun to reappear. Indeed, not only were the writers and the books removed, but so was the Party apparatus which ruled them. The machinery governing the domain of literature, education, information, and propaganda itself became the principal target of the Cultural Revolution. It was totally demolished, all its leading figures and even its minor functionaries disappearing in their turn into the limbo to which they had previously banished all who in one way or another did not totally conform to the Party's fiats.[2]

2. For detailed and documented studies of this history, see Merle Goldman, *Literary Dissent in Communist China*, Harvard University Press, Cambridge, 1967 (paperback, Atheneum, New York, 1971); also her "The Fall of Chou Yang," *China Quarterly*, July–September 1966, 132–148; Tsi-An Hsia, *The*

Introduction

This history in all its stages is mirrored in the fates of the sixteen writers represented in this book. The details for each one will be found in outline in the biographical notes that follow this introduction. By the time this collection was put together in the early 1930s, five of them were already dead, three killed by Kuomintang executioners in 1931, one dead of illness that same year, one murdered by Kuomintang plainclothesmen during an attempted kidnapping in 1933. Lu Hsün died of tuberculosis in 1936. Two were killed by the Japanese in the 1940s. Two who became officials in the Communist regime died, presumably of natural causes, in the 1950s or later, but neither had done any writing for many years. Of five others, three became members of the literary apparatus that was dismantled during the Cultural Revolution and nothing has been heard of them since; and two—the most prominent among them all as writers—Mao Tun and Ting Ling, were purged and sent into obscurity, Ting Ling in 1957 and Mao Tun when he was dismissed as Minister of Culture in 1965. Of the sixteen, only one, the aging Kuo Mo-jo, the senior literary official of the regime and intimate of Mao Tse-tung, remains. From his lonely eminence, he presides over a realm from which all the writers with whom he shared this history in the pre-Communist years and since, are gone, all gone, dead, banished, out of view, in any event writing no more, silenced, stifled. The literary scene in China that once moved and pulsed to the beat and the spirit of the men and the woman who appear in this book and others like them, is today a dim wasteland where not much moves and, as far as one can learn, nothing pulses at all. There

---

Gate of Darkness, Studies on the Leftist Literary Movement in China, University of Washington Press, Seattle, 1968.

is only the simple harmony built around Mao's Thought, or there is silence.[3]

Such is the ironic and paradoxical history that is brought into some fresh focus, I hope, by the resurrection and publication of this book of stories. To give more of the history of this book itself, however, I have to begin by filling in something more of the history of which it is part. I have to do this especially for those who may come to this whole subject new or perhaps approach it from some nearer threshold and therefore with some foreshortened view of the setting and the circumstances in which this work of writing was done.

The history of the beginning of China's emergence from its past is much written and still needs much to be studied. Foreign Christians began scratching at least four hundred years ago at the polished surfaces of Chinese thought and belief. Western guns did not begin blowing holes in the walls of old China until 1840, but Western power thereafter swiftly and forcibly imposed itself on the country's political and economic systems. In a guise that few Western Christians could or would recognize or acknowledge, Christian influence of a kind turned up in the first serious response to this Western assault, the messianic and antidynastic Taiping rebellion that almost toppled the Manchu throne in the 1850s–1860s. In the next decades, the Western powers reduced the Manchu regime to complete helplessness and came close to dismembering the country and transforming their spheres of influence into actual colonies. Only when Western military and economic domination was nearly complete, in the last few years of the century, did Western ideas and literature really begin to undermine the surviving structure of Confu-

3. For translated samples of the post–Cultural Revolution "literature" now deemed fit to print in China, see *The Seeds and Other Stories*, Foreign Language Press, Peking, 1972.

cian traditionalism. The process was hastened when a group of intellectuals tried unsuccessfully in 1898 to do in China what had been begun so successfully in Japan in 1868, to effect swift reform from the top, to absorb and adapt change, to modernize in order to save their society from complete collapse and their country from colonization. K'ang Yu-wei and his band of reformer-intellectuals were checked after a hundred days by the doughty Empress Dowager and, like so many who came after them, some paid with their lives for trying to convert the new ideas for a more open society into the actualities of politics. But the breach in the system was opened, not to be closed again until new and stronger defenders of a different orthodoxy came along half a century later.

The span of this latest phase of Chinese history is still shorter than the span of a single long lifetime. Lu Hsün was seventeen years old, Kuo Mo-jo was six, and Mao Tse-tung was five when K'ang Yu-wei tried to modernize China by imperial decree. In the following decades, great waves of intellectual and political change rolled over China. New ideas poured in from Europe, from America, from both via Japan where, after the defeat of China in the first Sino-Japanese War of 1894–1895, thousands of Chinese went to study, among them Lu Hsün and Kuo Mo-jo. Among them also Chiang Kai-shek.

Among them too was Ch'en Tu-hsiu, son of an Anhwei Mandarin family who had gone to Japan after the downfall of the Manchus in 1911 and who had come back to found, in 1915, the most famous of all the revolutionary journals of the time, *New Youth*, in which the passionate iconoclasm of this new generation found its most intense expression. Thus Ch'en's opening manifesto, the charter of what came to be known as the Chinese Renaissance:

Introduction

We must break down the old prejudices, the old way of believing in things as they are, before we can hope for social progress. We must discard our old ways. We must merge the ideas of the great thinkers of history, old and new, with our own experience, build up new ideas in politics, morality, and economic life. We must build the spirit of the new age to fit it to new environmental conditions and a new society. Our ideal society is honest, progressive, positive, free, equal, creative, beautiful, good, peaceful, mutually helpful, toilsome but happy and felicitous for the many. We look for the world that is false, conservative, negative, restrained, inequitable, hidebound, ugly, evil, torn, cruel, indolent, miserable for the many and felicitous for the few, to crumble until it disappears from sight.

In the name of democracy and science, the new youth "must attack Confucianism, the old tradition of virtue and rituals, the old ethics and the old politics . . . the old learning and the old literature."

In January 1917, Ch'en published in the *New Youth* Hu Shih's historic essay, "Suggestions for the Reform of Chinese Literature," in which this young scholar, still finishing his studies in the United States, launched the movement to replace classical literary Chinese, the *wen yen*, with the vernacular common speech, the *pai hua*, as the medium for modern Chinese literature. This was a revolution in itself which accumulated its own complexities as *pai hua* became the medium for the freer passage of foreign ideas and vocabularies into the currency of the Chinese language. Ch'en took it as the starting point for the development of a new revolutionary literature:

Preparation for the literary revolution has been long in ferment. My friend Hu Shih has lifted the standard against the old-school Chinese scholars. I raise now the banner of revolt on which three cardinal principles are inscribed: (1) Down with the artificial, flattering, "aristocratic" literature; for the establishment of a plain, expressive, people's literature.

(2) Down with the threadbare overelaboration of the classics; for a fresh, honest, realistic literature. (3) Down with the obscure, difficult mountain-and-forest literature; for a clear, popular, social literature.

In 1918, Ch'en published in the *New Youth* Lu Hsün's "Diary of a Madman." It came as the first stunning realization of everything he had summoned forth, the use of the vernacular in a new way in a new medium (it marked, among other things, the first use of the modern short story form in Chinese) to assail the character and the values of the old society. It was, moreover, a work of art that launched Lu Hsün from this first appearance as the most gifted of all the writers to appear in China in this time of transformation. Lu Hsün was thirty-eight years old when he began to write fiction. He had come to it slowly. The roots of his anger, irony, bitterness, and humor have only just begun to be explored.[4] As T. A. Hsia so sharply observed, Lu Hsün saw himself from the beginning as the one whose job it was to shoulder up "the gate of darkness"—an allusion to a T'ang legend— in order "to give unimpeded passage to the children so that they may rush to the bright, wide-open spaces and lead happy lives henceforward as rational human beings."[5] Instant fulfillment seemed to await prophecies in that bursting time: on May 4, 1919, students stormed the official residence of the foreign minister in Peking in protest against yielding to the decision at Versailles that gave power in the province of Shantung to Japan. The children rushed through in great numbers, not quite yet into any bright wide open spaces and happy lives as rational human beings, but into two decades

4. See T. A. Hsia, "Aspects of the Power of Darkness in Lu Hsün," in *The Gate of Darkness*, pp. 146–163. Leo Ou-fan Lee, of Princeton University, is at work on a psychohistorical study of the life of Lu Hsün.
5. Quoted from Lu Hsün's 1919 essay, "What is Required of Us as Fathers Today," in *Gate of Darkness*, pp. 146–147.

of tumult, of rebellion and upheaval in individual lives, of revolution and war in the history of the people and the country.[6]

There are at least two aspects of this experience that have to be stressed to fit the people and the stories of this book into their place and their time. The first is the enormously explosive character, the eruption-like quality of everything that happened to these individuals, in their own lives, in their creative work, in their politics. The second is the shortness of their time, the speed with which all these breakouts of people, of emotions, of every meaningful individual experience, were caught up in the surge of massive historical events. Barely five years after May 4, every individual's choices and actions became a matter of life and death for each one.

The new writing that flowered so profusely in those first years tended to be realistic, in the spirit of Lu Hsün, or romantic, in the spirit of Kuo Mo-jo. The realists, grouped around the Society for the Study of Literature, included Cheng Chen-to, Yeh Shao-chün, Chou Tso-jen—Lu Hsün's brother, a critic and translator of considerable note himself—Shen Yen-ping, later to acquire his own fame as Mao Tun, and others, deeply influenced by the tradition of Chekhov, Dostoevsky, and Balzac. They wrote stories that dissected the traditional society, stories about common people caught in its ancient webs of belief, superstition, and exploitation. The romantics located themselves around Kuo Mo-jo's Creation Society, whose members were the Chinese heirs of Shelley, Goethe, and Nietzsche, whose works they translated and in whose spirit they wrote. Lu Hsün did not have a high opinion of these writers; he once called the Creation

6. See, as a starting point for further exploration, Chow Tse-tung, *The May Fourth Movement: Intellectual Revolution in Modern China*, Harvard University Press, Cambridge, 1960.

Society a band of "wits and vagabonds," also more sharply translated as "dilettantes and rogues." They wrote, however, mainly about themselves, about the rending conflict between young and old, the heavy strain of the break from deeply rooted family mores, of resistance to the demands of filial piety, all the restrictions which kept men and women from freely choosing and loving each other. Their work reflected, as in Yü Ta-fu, the despair, the grief, and the confusion, and the breakdowns to which these conflicts led so many of them. The writers of this May 4 generation—and writing was very much the popular mode among the young people—moved among all these themes in these intensively lived years. But they were not given much time to keep trying to search themselves out as individuals responding only to their own individual needs and feelings. Challenging the old society soon ceased to be only a matter of choosing how to express themselves in new ways. It became a matter of choosing whether and how to participate in a new kind of demanding politics that promised a revolutionary transformation of the whole system they opposed.

In the stream of ideas that had flooded into China after 1900, Mill and Spencer and Huxley were soon followed by Bakunin and Marx and, after 1917, by Lenin and the political shock waves of the Russian revolution itself. Ch'en Tu-hsiu went on to found the Chinese Communist Party in 1921. Under Russian guidance in 1923, that Party moved to join the moribund Kuomintang of Sun Yat-sen in an effort to launch a new national revolution. Its object was to overcome the warlord armies that ravaged the country and to expel the foreign imperialists who held it in thrall. Swift fulfillment waited on these prophecies too and within barely two years the new movement, centered in Canton, was sweeping northward. The men and women of 1919 found themselves dividing into its two streams, the conservative

Kuomintang intent on keeping control of events, and the Communists promising revolution while marching obediently under the Kuomintang banner. The young people soon found their individual concerns telescoped by these intense pressures, and they were marching in political armies, in fighting armies, in propaganda brigades, carried by high and fast-moving waves into the larger business of history. Among the writers, realist and romantic alike were caught up in the new vision, in the belief that the issues of the individual plight and rebellion could be solved only on the scale of the larger social conflict. The slogan became: "From the literary revolution to revolutionary literature!"

Kuo Mo-jo, who underwent a characteristically dramatic conversion to Marxism in 1924—not through reading Marx but upon reading a Marxist work by a Japanese author—issued this typical call to writers in April, 1926:

Young men! Young men! . . . if you want to write, tighten up your nerves and grasp quickly the spirit of the times. Become revolutionary spirits, do not lag behind! This is to the whole nation's advantage, not only your own. No thoroughgoing individual liberty is possible under the present system. Don't think that the wine you drink makes you romantic, the poetry you write makes you a genius! You must fulfill your lives by going among the soldiers, the people, and into the factories. Know the new literary current. . . . The literature we need now is socialist, realist literature. . . . Our demand must be the masses' demands. History has taught us this. Let us struggle on!

Lu Hsün, for his part, moved soberly and slowly toward the arena of politics and never did yield the pursuit of literature to political dictation. He went south to teach, first to Amoy and then to Canton. On April 8, 1927, a few days before Chiang Kai-shek seized power at Shanghai, Lu Hsün gave a talk in Canton at the Whampoa Military Academy, the principal training center for Kuomintang army and propaganda cadres. In the light of events about to happen, and others still far in the future, there was a somberly prophetic touch to some of Lu Hsün's words that day about the relation between men of literature and men of power. Literature, he said, is made up of the words of people without power. "Those with real power do not open their mouths, but they kill people. . . . In nature it is also like this. When the hawk catches the sparrow, the hawk is silent, the sparrow shrieks little cries. When the cat catches a mouse, the cat is silent, the mouse squeaks. In the end, it is the one which opens its mouth that gets eaten by the one that doesn't open its mouth."

The main purpose of his talk, however, was to warn against the idea of submitting the creation of literature to the discipline of politics. He said:

> Writers at this revolutionary center are probably inclined to emphasize that there is a close bond between literature and revolution, that literature should be used to propagandize, to advance, to incite, to help carry out the Revolution. But I think this kind of writing will be without effect because good writing has never been produced under orders from other people; good writing is free, an expression of the natural outpouring of the heart. If you first hold a thesis and then try to illustrate it accordingly, your writing will be just like the eight-legged essay. It will have literary merit, but no effect on the readers. So, for the revolution's sake, let's have more workers for the revolution and not be in a hurry for "revolutionary literature."

What history soon taught all those who plunged into these events is a complex matter that is not easy, again, to summarize briefly.[7] The essence of it is that the contradictions of the Kuomintang-Communist relationship in the move-

7. A starting point for further inquiry: Harold R. Isaacs, *The Tragedy of the Chinese Revolution*, 2nd rev. ed., Stanford University Press, Stanford, 1961; paperback edition, 1972.

ment—little realized or heeded by the ardent fighters who joined its ranks—finally exploded in the violent climax of Chiang Kai-shek's Shanghai coup on April 12, 1927. Chiang, commander-in-chief of the victoriously advancing Kuomintang armies, turned on his Communist allies, beginning the mass slaughters in Shanghai and in the Yangtze Valley by which he won and kept power at his new capital in Nanking. Between late 1927 and 1930 the Communists, now under the leadership of Li Li-san, went into a convulsive reaction, staging hopeless and costly insurrections, summoning up the "new revolutionary wave" that never appeared. The Communist movement was hounded from the cities, but the Communist Party apparatus survived, torn by factional strife, functioning sporadically and ineffectually. This apparatus was almost entirely separated from the surviving Communist forces in the remoter hinterland, where Mao Tse-tung was establishing new bases at the head of guerrilla peasant armies and beginning the new career that ultimately led, via Yenan and the Japanese invasion, to a different ending.

It was in the period from the collapse of the revolution at Chiang's hands in 1927 to 1933 that writers who were Communists or Communist sympathizers went through the experience reflected in the work that appears in the latter half of this collection. Some had fled, like Kuo Mo-jo, who went into exile in Japan and did not return to China until 1937. Some went inland to join the Communist-led bands in Kiangsi and Hunan. Others, as the biographical notes of so many of these authors show, moved in and out of Shanghai, to Wuhan and back again, looking for new ways to pick up the threads of their personal and political lives. Lu Hsün returned north to Shanghai to resume his writing career as best he could. He devoted himself all but singlemindedly thereafter to the encouragement and support of the young writers who came to seek his counsel. At the founding meeting of the League of Leftist Writers in 1930, he said:

Revolution is suffering mixed with dirt and blood. It is never so perfect and fascinating a thing as the poets imagine. Revolution is life and activity. It demands of us all the low, menial, tedious work which is left unmentioned in the romantic flights of the poets. Revolution is constructive as well as destructive. Destruction is pleasing but construction troublesome. Those who cherish romantic fantasies about revolution will quickly find disillusionment and disappointment when they come into contact with the reality of it and the progress it brings and the tasks it imposes upon us.[8]

---

8. It was also during this time, in 1932, that Lu Hsün wrote the lines that appear on the cover design of this book, much quoted as a couplet:

Eyebrows raised, coolly I face a thousand pointing fingers
Head down, like a willing ox, I serve the children.

These were the children, again, for whom in his 1919 allusion he had seen himself shouldering up that gate of darkness. But this couplet was part of a poem that Lu Hsün wrote in the course of an exchange with friends, including Yü Ta-fu and the poet Liu Ya-tzu, and there is more to be glimpsed in the allusive and elusive meaning of these lines:

Coming upon my good fortune, what more do I ask of fate?
I cannot move or turn around without bumping into it.
A tattered hat to cover my face as I pass through the marketplace
A leaky boat and some wine as I drift into the main current.
Eyebrows raised, coolly I face a thousand pointing fingers
Head down, like a willing ox, I serve the children.
Hiding in my tiny garret, achieving my own "unity,"
Not caring whether it be winter or summer or spring or autumn.

Lu Hsün called this poem "Tzu-ch'ao," "Self-Mockery." This translation is made from the renderings of several translators, each one striking a different balance of choices among the various possible meanings of some of these words and lines. The word *hua-kai*, translated as "good fortune," actually means the brightly colored canopy or umbrella under which a high official would go forth into the city. It is also, in Lu Hsün's local dialect, a homonym for the lid of a cooking pot, hence also suggesting "ill-starred fate" or "misfortune." Thus the poet can be saying that his good fortune is his misfortune, and he may have borrowed from Yü Ta-fu the lines in which he seems to be wishing he could escape it in that tattered hat, in a leaky boat, drinking wine, and drifting into midstream. But his abrasive defiance reasserts itself against those pointing fingers. The "unity" in the next to last line

Introduction

But Lu Hsün and the younger men who tried to learn from him very soon found themselves caught between pressures they could not escape. The Kuomintang inflicted upon them suppression of their work, imprisonment, and death. The Communist Party, caught in the bind of Kuomintang terror and its own weaknesses and failures, inflicted on these writers the effects of its violent internal conflicts and its demand for total and subservient conformity. They all became, as we have seen, victims of the one, or, ultimately, of the other.[9]

---

is a mocking use of a term much employed in Kuomintang political propaganda at the time. The final reference to "spring or autumn" is the use of the title of an old historical chronicle to say that the poet does not care what historians may say about him. .

9. Jaroslav Prusek, a Czech Communist scholar who established a notable center of Chinese studies in Prague, and who himself became a major authority on this period of Chinese literature, concluded an article in 1968 with these judgments: "We should bear in mind that during this short time not one of the writers named had ever any considerable period for peaceful work. . . . This explains much of the apparently fragmentary nature of some of the work, the relative lack of care and even the dilettantism to be seen in the work . . . Nor can we guess how all these new forms would have developed after the short period which brought them into the world was over. The war which followed and particularly the absolutism of the regime brought into power by the revolution slowed down and put an end to further development of any kind. The field was cut before the grain could ripen. There are few phases in human history that give us such a feeling of tragedy as this short period of the history of modern Chinese literature. The tragedy lies in the fact that while this literature came into being to help the revolution forward and to help free man from his bonds, the revolution as it grew swept this literature from the scene and often swept away the people creating it as well." —"A Few Notes on the Literary Aspects of the May Fourth Movement in China," in *The May Fourth Movement in China*, Major Papers Prepared for the XXth International Congress of Chinese Studies, Prague, 1968.

Prusek himself, who could apparently function in what might be called the Czech equivalent of the Hundred Flowers blooming period, could not survive the sequel to the Soviet invasion in 1968 and the reestablishment of hard-line Communist control in Czechoslovakia. He is reported to have been purged, his program liquidated, his students scattered. It is clear that

Introduction

The experience of being jammed between those closing
gates of darkness is perhaps most poignantly illustrated by
the case of five young writers who were executed by the
Kuomintang at the Lunghua Garrison Headquarters just
outside of Shanghai on the night of February 7, 1931. Much
has been written about these five, mourned and celebrated
by the Communists as the Five Martyrs, their remains exhumed and reburied in a place of honor, their works collected and published, their life stories told and their last days
chronicled in many memoirs.

Now it so happens that the fate of the Five was a link in
the circumstances of my own life, one of the links that led
me to begin publishing a small newspaper in Shanghai
called the *China Forum*, almost exactly one year after they
were arrested and killed. The first issue, on January 13,
1932, devoted a whole page to pictures of the Five, the story
of their arrest, *"together with nineteen others"*—an appended
phrase to which we shall have to return in this account—
and details of the international campaign of denunciation
and protest by writers and intellectuals that had been gener-
ated by the Communist International in America and Europe. The second issue of the *China Forum*, on January 20,
included an English translation of a story by one of the five
writers, Hu Yeh-p'in's "Living Together," which appears in
this collection. Fourteen more stories by various writers appeared in translation in the *China Forum* during the next
year and a half, including "Slave Mother," by Jou Shih, at
thirty the oldest of the Five; and there was a poem by Yin
Fu, at twenty-two the youngest. The other two of the Five
were Feng K'eng, a girl who had actually only written a
little poetry years before, and Li Wei-seng, who was much

despite the powerful nationalist "contradictions" that divide the world Communist camp, certain characteristics remain common to all Communist cul-
tures.

more prominent as a veteran trade union functionary of the Party than as a writer—another significant detail to which we will have to return. Along with these five, the material in that first issue of the *Forum* also listed the name and picture of a sixth, Tsung Hui, who had been executed half a year earlier, in mid-1930, aged twenty-one.

I shall have to come back to the subject of the Five Martyrs and their end because it is not only the most poignant but perhaps also the most mordant symbol of the experience reflected in the lives and the stories of the people who fill this book. The linkage between the fate of those five young people I had never met and my own experience gives me reason to stop here to say that I too was just twenty-one when I began publishing the *China Forum*. I had already been in China then for more than a year, working first as a reporter or editor for two of the city's English-language dailies, the *Shanghai Evening Post* and the *China Press*; then wandering up the Yangtze Valley and deep into western Szechwan almost to Tibet, coming back downriver to Shanghai late that summer amid the many deaths and unattended mass miseries of the great Yangtze flood of 1931. Only days later, on September 18, 1931, the Japanese opened the first action of their new war against China, taking the city of Mukden and beginning the occupation of Manchuria. The Nanking Government, bearing down hard with all its forces on its opponents at home, announced a policy of nonresistance to the Japanese invasion. The effects of all these exposures, the shocks, the encounters, the learning of that year came together for me not long thereafter when Communist friends and friends of Communists I met in Shanghai suggested the possibility of my starting up a paper of my own. I took them up with alacrity and the result was the *China Forum*.

The *Forum* suffered a variety of interruptions and difficulties. The day after the appearance of its third issue, on January 28, 1932, the Japanese attacked Shanghai and met with surprise resistance from the Nineteenth Route Army, which fought back in defiance of its orders from Nanking. The battle lasted for thirty-four days. It introduced the world to terror-bombing—Chapei was the forerunner of Guernica, Coventry, Dresden, Hiroshima, and Viet Nam— and taught me more about the shapes that death can take. When I could resume publication that March, there was official and unofficial harassment, printers frightened off, mail intercepted—all the problems of functioning overground when so much about the enterprise was forced to stay underground. Some of the interruptions were for days, one lasted for several months. Still the *Forum* kept appearing for thirty-nine issues, the last sixteen of them issued in both Chinese and English, set by hand and printed on a small platen press in a tiny shop of our own. Its last issue appeared on January 13, 1934, exactly two years after its first. The end came abruptly, not because the Kuomintang or the Shanghai foreign authorities had finally succeeded in suppressing it but because mounting disagreements between me and my Communist friends came to a head and the paper could not survive our break. It became my own small version of the experience of being caught, or nearly caught, between those same two gates of darkness. That was when we moved from Shanghai to Peking, my wife Viola and I, and took as our first task there to complete the assembling and translating of these stories, counseling by mail as we did so with Lu Hsün and Mao Tun in Shanghai. There can be no room here for more than these few lines of my own autobiography, but I do need to introduce this much of it because it does have to do with the making of this book and because in a minor and infinitely less endangered way I shared with some of the people of this book enough of the experience of that time, the early 1930s in Shanghai, to tell a little of what it was like.

Shanghai was very much the creature of its peculiar history, with its foreign-ruled enclaves, the International Settlement and the French Concession, and the sprawling Chinese city of millions that grew up around all the licit and illicit sources of work and wealth that they provided. Treaty-protected foreigners enjoyed extraterritorial "rights"—independent political status in the country, freedom from Chinese legal jurisdiction or taxation—and foreign traders enjoyed the advantage of a five-percent limitation on China's power to tax the imports that entered the country through these foreign-controlled treaty port establishments. These rights and privileges were guarded by the foreign powers with fleets of warships and garrisons—speedily enlarged in times of trouble, as in 1927 when the British Concession at Hankow was overrun and Shanghai seemed threatened in the same way—and with their own police forces and courts to maintain their own rule and control over their own space.
The sizeable numbers of Chinese who lived in these foreign enclaves were in effect like colonial populations, the "natives" of a regime complete with all the trappings of the European colonial system, including the discriminations, exclusions, and racial attitudes practiced by the foreign masters and the submissive acceptance of the "treaty port mentality" by great numbers of Chinese in their role as subjects. Indeed, it was the older, more deeply rooted Chinese chauvinistic pride that fueled the nationalist drive that challenged this state of affairs in the 1920s. Even after he had blunted that drive, Chiang Kai-shek had to keep pressing the nationalist demand for abrogation of the "unequal treaties" and rendition of the foreign concessions, a demand, incidentally, to which his foreign friends and mentors did not yield

until long after they had been deprived of their "rights" and driven from the treaty ports by their rivals the Japanese. The United States did not sign a new treaty relinquishing extraterritoriality—its first-ever "equal" treaty with China— until 1943.

Society in Shanghai in the 1930s was made up of the familiar colonial pieces: foreigners of the treaty powers a privileged caste; an upper class of treaty port Chinese grown immensely wealthy as participants, adjuncts, agents—"compradore" was the China coast word—of foreign enterprise; a large class of Chinese white-collar employees and workers making their living in both foreign and Chinese establishments; and a great mass of helot-like poor that kept flocking in from the ravaged and impoverished countryside, providing an endless supply of the laborers, human beasts of burden, beggars, prostitutes, criminals, and ultimately helpless people who left some 50,000 dead babies on the streets of the city each year—there was a philanthropic organization whose sole activity consisted of picking up and disposing of these tiny corpses. Greater Shanghai in 1930 was a city of more than three million with about 50,000 foreigners, half of them Japanese.

The French Concession existed largely as a base for the operations of criminal gangs rooted in the old network of Yangtze Valley secret societies. They controlled the opium smuggling, gambling, prostitution, and assorted other rackets which were such a large part of the life of the city. These gangs had begun by 1927 to play a cardinal political role and became agents of the Kuomintang government in dealing with unions, radicals, and other opponents of the regime. Their principal leader, Tu Yüeh-sheng, was treated with deference by both the foreign and Kuomintang authorities and was invariably referred to in the Chinese and foreign press as "a prominent merchant" and "philanthropist."

These were the elements that provided much of the atmosphere and incident of the Shanghai of Malraux's *Man's Fate*, a novel built—with great fidelity to the main facts—around the events of Chiang Kai-shek's takeover in Shanghai in 1927.

In the British-dominated International Settlement (Americans, Japanese, and some token Chinese also sat on the Municipal Council), a characteristically more elaborate structure of formal legality was maintained to support the idea that the Settlement was a rock-like island of Anglo-Saxon justice in the chaotic sea of Chinese lawlessness that swirled around it. As such, the Settlement had provided asylum over the years for varieties of political "outs," especially those in whose survival foreigners had an interest or by whom they did not feel threatened. Faction-fighting warlords and politicians of high and low order were safe inside the foreign boundary. In the 1930s, Shanghai was full of such refugees from the conflict of cliques and persons in and around the new Kuomintang regime of Chiang Kai-shek. In its Shanghai version, the British "rule of law" could be stripped down to its barest pretenses and still provide some shred of cover, some limited freedom of movement and even of publication, for opponents of the regime. What was dangerously "illegal" outside remained at least "semilegal" or even "legal" inside the Settlement boundaries. Where real or alleged Communists were concerned, however, these margins of difference narrowed and all but disappeared. From 1927 on, the task of ferreting out and disposing of these more dangerous enemies became a shared concern of the foreign and Kuomintang authorities. The Shanghai Municipal Police had its own "Special Branch" to deal with political matters and, like the Kuomintang, it recruited defectors and informers from among the Communists. The legal system was readily bent to these special needs. Extradition of Chinese criminals from Settlement to Chinese jurisdiction required proceedings in a Settlement court to prove that there was a "prima facie" case against them. This was observed with moderate care when the accused had done nothing worse than steal or kill; it became a swift and farcical procedure when it had to do with individuals arrested as "Communists." Between 1930 and 1932, the Settlement courts handed over 326 real or alleged "Communists" to the Kuomintang. Most of them, like the five writers and those nineteen others arrested that January night in 1931, went to their deaths at the hands of Kuomintang executioners waiting just beyond the Settlement limits.[10]

Some narrow openings remained in this system through which much did pass. The foreign areas did provide some protective covering for those who could stay "legal" or stay successfully hidden, and quite a few did. The police were not as efficient as they wished to be, never as efficient as the equivalent Communist policing of a later day. Things went on in Shanghai then under the British, the French, and the Kuomintang that would be quite inconceivable in Shanghai today. An Indochinese Communist leader named Nguyen Ai-quoc, later better known as Ho Chi-minh, lived underground uncaught in Shanghai for more than a year, near enough overground for me, highly visible as I was, to meet him quite often at the Chinese YMCA, walking distance from police headquarters in the Settlement. The Communist Party, battered and fragmented and lacking popular following and contacts, nevertheless could and did hold its secret meetings and the little groups under its auspices managed to carry on a semipublic semisecret life of their own. In September 1933, an "Anti-War Congress" was publicly announced but conspiratorially held right in the heart of the

10. Cf. "Extradition: Theory and Practice," *China Forum*, April 13, 1933.

city, and even though it was attended by a group of European Communists who had come openly to Shanghai for the purpose and a number of Chinese Communists who had secretly come from Kiangsi, the affair came off without a hitch. The extraterritorial system itself, of course, made it possible for the *China Forum* to exist quite openly. When the Kuomintang authorities formally filed a bill of particulars against me on a series of charges—most of which carried the death sentence under Kuomintang law—the United States attorney at the consulate general asked me why I did not waive my extraterritorial rights. When this suggestion became known, a shocked cry of alarm went up from some of the most conservative spokesmen in British Shanghai who came stoutly to the defense of my "rights" while, to be sure, feeling quite different about my use of them.

There were also in Shanghai certain highly visible and important Chinese figures who were able to give voice to political opposition from relatively protected positions. One such, in the purely literary field, was Lu Hsün. His prestige as China's foremost writer protected him from arrest, if not from suppression of some of his work and repeated anonymous threats against his life. Lu Hsün carried on bold and often quite public activity, continuing to write his biting short essays—the *tsa wen*, which he established as his own most characteristic medium of criticism and attack—and sponsoring and supporting writers' groups and publications and giving as much personal protection as he could to individuals who sought his help and guidance. Another was Soong Ching-ling, widow of Sun Yat-sen, founder of the Kuomintang. In 1925–1927, she had supported the radical wing of the Kuomintang and after the split had remained an uncompromising foe of Chiang Kai-shek, breaking with her family—her sister became Chiang's second wife and her brother his finance minister and right-hand man—to maintain her own unique place in the Chinese political scheme of things. One wonders whether the subject of the life of this striking and unusual woman will ever find its author. Now nearly eighty and holding an honorific vice-presidency in Peking, she is still—presumably—the untouchable figure. I have seen nothing to indicate where, if anywhere, she has fit into the murky picture of leadership struggles in Peking in recent years, but it is unlikely, even if she were moved to do so, that she could or would speak out as freely in Peking as she did so often and so boldly in Shanghai.

From her home on Rue Molière in the French Concession—the same house, a Sun Yat-sen shrine, that was invaded and vandalized by Red Guard or other hoodlums during the Cultural Revolution—Mrs. Sun would issue stinging attacks on the Nanking government's policies and actions. With Lu Hsün and the aging Tsai Yuan-pei, another major figure beyond reach of any ordinary attack—he was head of Peking National University in the May 4 period and was now head of the Academia Sinica in Nanking—Mrs. Sun sponsored the China League for Civil Rights. Their sponsorship made it briefly possible for a number of liberal Chinese writers, educators, and editors to join in a campaign against the system of repression. Soong Ching-ling led them a good deal further than most of them wanted or dared to go, intervening vigorously on behalf of arrested individuals, issuing public reports on cases of the terror, and even taking a delegation right into a Nanking prison to visit some of those held there, including a prominent Communist, Lo Tunghsien, who had fallen into Settlement police hands and been extradited.[11] Mrs. Sun was counterattacked by the Kuomintang press and grotesquely slandered by the so-called "mosquito press" that dealt in gossip and sensation, and she re-

11. *China Forum*, April 13, 1933.

ceived frequent threats against her life. But the regime could not actually move against her or against Dr. Tsai except by moving against their friends. On June 18, 1933, Yang Chien (Yang Hsing-fo), assistant to Tsai Yuan-pei at the Academia Sinica and one of the most active figures in the China League for Civil Rights, was murdered by thugs on the street outside his office in Shanghai.

The murder of Yang Chien was one of a series of murders and kidnappings that occurred in Shanghai that spring. They were part of a deliberate campaign undertaken by Chiang Kai-shek's semiprivate, semiofficial anti-Communist organization that came to be known as the Lan I-shang, variously translated as Blue Jackets, Blue Shirts, or Blue Gowns. Chiang's apparatus in Nanking had begun to adopt and adapt some of the styles and methods of the new Nazi rulers of Germany and one result was the creation of a highly politicized band of agents, spies, and thugs who opened a drive against Chiang's opponents, especially among the intellectuals. They engaged in intimidation, beatings, kidnapping, torture, and murder, invaded and smashed offending bookstores, film studios, and publishing houses. They began at the same time to turn out newspapers, magazines, and films of their own. This campaign was carried quite openly into the Settlement and French Concession. Blue Jacket agents made "illegal" raids, seizing their victims and taking them out of the foreign areas without bothering to go through the flimsy procedure of operating through the foreign police and the extradition system.

On May 4, Blue Jacket thugs kidnapped the girl writer Ting Ling from her room in the Settlement, and the writer Pan Tzu-nien, who was visiting her when they broke in. A few hours later waiting agents seized Ying Hsu-jen, another writer, and when he offered resistance threw him to his death on the pavement below. In the following months episodes of this kind became frequent, almost commonplace. One individual, half-victim, half-participant, actually witnessed the taking of Ting Ling, and his own detailed account of the affair appeared in the *China Forum*. Other accounts were sent in by individuals who had been fast enough to evade capture after being pointed out to waiting thugs by ex-comrades. These reports make it hard to read some of the stories in this collection simply as crude and not very skillful attempts by fledgling writers filled with revolutionary ardor. Ting Ling's "One Certain Night" reads like such a story, but the reader has to know also that such a group—the five writers and the nineteen others—*was* executed on one such certain night and that one of them was Ting Ling's husband, father of her new baby.

In his 1933 story "Death," which appears in this collection, the young writer Shih Yi describes a girl caught in this way on a Shanghai street and tortured until she died. No one should mistake the characters of his story for creatures of his imagination. Ex-Communist defectors *were* walking the streets to spot ex-comrades. Sadistic jailers and torturers *were* operating in Kuomintang jails and headquarters in and around Shanghai. Young people like his heroine *were* fearfully resisting or ultimately yielding, dying, or living somehow to die another day. And so it was, soon, with Shih Yi himself. In the *China Forum* of September 18, 1933, this item:

Liu [sic] Shih Yi, a youthful writer of stories, poems, brochures, articles, an active member of the League of Leftist Writers, was kidnapped sometime Saturday night after 5 P.M. . . . Liu left his home in the Dixwell Road district to visit a friend in the French Concession. He left this friend's home toward 5 P.M. Since then he has not been seen or heard from. His young wife is without news of his whereabouts. Sunday morning two secret police agents of the Blue Jackets called at his home but fortunately found no one there. Liu has undoubtedly been made the latest victim of the barbarous Blue Jacket terror in Shanghai. From all indications, he was kidnapped in the streets. Will his fate be that of Ting Ling, murdered, or abandoned to the darkness in some filthy dungeon cell?

These were all events I learned about, some at first hand, others at close enough quarters. I was able to move about myself with a peculiarly isolated freedom. My high visibility was an advantage, even a safeguard of a kind. It was also a severe handicap. The normal rules of conspiratorial behavior were redoubled for me. Written material usually reached me by messenger or some other indirect means. It did not do for any vulnerable Chinese to be seen openly in my company. Whenever I did meet such friends, it was always after the most torturously careful precautions and even then, at such encounters no one ever mentioned names. I did not even know the real names of the young Chinese who worked at such risk for the *Forum*, not even one of them who lived and worked sequestered in our Shanghai apartment for months at a time. If I ever did meet any important Communist figures in Shanghai in those days, I never knew who they were. What one did not know, one could not tell. The business of this ardent young foreign sympathizer was to get out the *Forum*, to write about the outside world and the large politics, Japan, the Powers, the war, about the Kuomintang regime, its rule and its terror, not to learn—or have any chance really to know—about what was going on in the Communist Party, its internal conflicts or even about the tensions between it and writers like Lu Hsün and Mao Tun, whom I did know and see from time to time, though never to talk about such matters as these.

My own slowly gathering conflict with the Communist friends and supporters of the *China Forum* is a longer story than can or need be told here. It began, meaningfully enough, in a politically untutored resistance to untruth and exaggeration, not about the Kuomintang and its terror, which could hardly be exaggerated, but of Communist claims about their own policies and achievements. This began at the very beginning when I discovered the difference between Communist accounts abroad of the anti-Japanese resistance in the battle of Shanghai and what I had seen and learned myself during the weeks of that now forgotten bloody episode. Indeed, the report I gave in the *Forum* about that affair was later "criticized" in a long and reproachful letter which I duly published. Of affairs elsewhere and other issues relating to the Communist movement, I had begun to read and question enough to develop many complicated doubts. In what turned out to be my crowning misdeed, I published an anniversary article about the Russian revolution in November, 1933, without mentioning, much less adulating, Stalin. The chill in my relations with my underground friends turned into a freeze. When I formally refused to rectify—confess?—it was all suddenly over, and my way led me, still naïve, out of their circle for good.

But it was not until after we had gone to Peking, indeed after we had finished the work on *Straw Sandals*, that we began to fill in some of the painfully wide gaps in our knowledge. We embarked in the middle of 1934 on the slow task of trying to sort out the recent history of the Communist movement in China. This was the work that eventually became *The Tragedy of the Chinese Revolution*. It involved the painstaking translation of Communist Party documents and other source material with a friend who was himself a veteran of these struggles and through whom I came to be able to study a thousand pages or more of such texts and notes. It was only in this way that I began to learn for the first time of what had been going on in the Chinese Communist movement during the years of my brief but intense political apprenticeship. It was in the course of this work, then, one day late in 1934, that I first learned something more about that meeting in Shanghai on January 17, 1931 where the five writers—and the *nineteen others*—were arrested.

Again, summary is not simple, but the main points for our purpose are clear enough. The meeting in Shanghai on that January 17 was an episode in a bitter factional struggle which had just come to a head inside the Communist Party leadership. The adventurist policy under Li Li-san had run its futile course and by mid-1930 this had become plain even to the Comintern. A great struggle of factions and persons had been going on for months around the issues of policy and a new leadership for the Party. This was seen then, I might mention again, as a leadership based on the cities in Kuomintang China, not on the hinterland peasant forces that Mao Tse-tung was gathering around him on his way to taking ultimate command of the whole movement himself. The Central Committee and the Politbureau of the Party were still located in Shanghai, still able at least to exist and meet there. In Shanghai on January 7, 1931, a meeting that was called the Fourth Plenum of the Central Committee was held under the eye and the control of the Russian representative of the Comintern, Pavel Mif. The old leadership under Li Li-san was brusquely deposed and Mif's own protégé, the Moscow-returned student Chen Shao-yu—better known later in Comintern journals as "Wang Ming"—was put in his place. Chen and his band of newcomers had spent the turbulent years of the revolution in Moscow and had only recently come back. They now shouldered aside the opposition of a group of veteran Party militants led by Ho Menghsiung, whose history in the movement dated back to its beginnings. The Fourth Plenum decisions were met by indignant opposition in the Communist apparatus and its various affiliated groups and committees in Shanghai. It was Ho Meng-hsiung and a group of his comrades and followers—

including the five writers—who met at that hotel on the night of January 17. They were the *nineteen others* who were taken with the five writers to Lunghua to die, always mentioned but never named during the international campaign of protest then mounted by the Comintern over the execution of the five.

Most of those present that night have never been identified. Of the five writers, only Li Wei-seng was an important Party figure with a history and a standing in the movement no less long or impressive than that of Ho Meng-hsiung, and he was obviously at the meeting in this capacity and not as a "writer." The other four were much junior to him in Party experience. They were all members of sections and groups, all followers of the old Party leadership now so suddenly unseated by the Fourth Plenum switch. There is actually no hard evidence of the actual intentions of those who met together that night and no hard evidence of how or by whom the meeting was betrayed to the police. There are only the circumstances that had preceded it and the curious and cynical way in which the Communists handled the matter afterward.

This episode was recently given its most exhaustive examination by the late T. A. Hsia in his study, "The Enigma of the Five Martyrs," first published in 1962.[12] He combed every available source and sifted all the evidence with a careful and knowing hand. This evidence strongly supported, without ultimately proving, the presumptions (1) that the meeting was held to consider how to react to the sudden unseating of the Party leadership, whether to submit or to split and (2) that to liquidate its opposition at a stroke, the new Party leadership itself betrayed the meeting to the Shanghai

12. No. 2 in the Research Series, Center for Chinese Studies, Institute of International Studies, Berkeley, 1962, reprinted in *The Gate of Darkness* in 1968.

police. This was the substance of my own reference to the matter in *The Tragedy of the Chinese Revolution*,[13] which T. A. Hsia cited, along with much other material not then available to me. Perhaps most mordantly suggestive in his account is a passage from a review of this bit of Party history made much later by Mao Tse-tung himself in which he speaks of the "excessively severe blows" that were struck at some of the comrades involved in this affair. Hsia could ask but found he could not firmly answer from the evidence: *what blows?* But the evidence, as any reader can find it spread in T. A. Hsia's pages, leaves very little doubt. The blows struck hard enough at those who died that night as the gates of darkness closed in on them at Lunghua. Exhumed now and honorably reburied, the "twenty-odd"—it was said only twenty-three, not twenty-four bodies were found at the spot—need a monument to *all* the kinds of terror that lay in their encounter with history.

For my own part, the full impact of those blows came at me in a quiet room in Peking from the examination and clarification of material I had a chance to study only after my own lesser brush with these events. I can feel still the sensation of being hit hard by truths I had not known were there when I moved among them. Unlike the victims at Lunghua, my experience cost me not my life but only a piece of my youth, some of the naïveté they had paid so heavily to keep. I can only hope that this volume, appearing after this interval of so many years and read now in the light of all that has happened since, will add meaning to their story.

About the making of this book, the original editor's preface, written in 1934, said:

13. Pp. 334–335.

"The collection is designed to give a consecutive picture of the development of the new Chinese literature in the last fifteen years. This could be done with short stories because this form has been predominant throughout this period. With this purpose in mind, the original list from which the selection was made was drawn up by Lu Hsün and Mao Tun. Valuable supplementary suggestions were made by Professor Cheng Chen-to. . . . Although the final choices were made with the constant advice and instruction of his friends, the editor must himself assume responsibility for them. . . .

"The bulk of the rough translation work was carried by Miss Yang Chi-sen, who also checked the final drafts and made innumerable suggestions and criticisms which are largely responsible for any degree of success which the translations can claim. Mistakes there must be, and these must be checked to the editor's debit. The stories translated by Sze Ming-ting required no editing as they were finished works. All of them were published in the editor's *China Forum* during the spring of 1932. The first draft of [this translation of] 'Spring Silkworms' was done by Feng Yu-sing; of 'Land of Snow' and 'On the Threshing Field' by Yang Chao. The originals of most of the stories were first published in magazines which have since been suppressed."

A word of interest can now be added about "Sze Ming-ting." That name was a pseudonym for the late George A. Kennedy, then a young teacher of Chinese in a Settlement school. George was very far indeed from having any serious interest in the politics of that time in Shanghai, but even those who did not get to know George Kennedy until his later years as a distinguished Chinese language scholar at Yale will almost be able to hear the mockingly diffident tone in which he explained his choice of name: "If Stalin can be 'steel' and Molotov can be 'hammer,' " he said, "I can be 'cement'!"

Early in the *Forum* days a well-known New York publisher
had expressed interest in a book of the stories we were publishing but between the time he first offered his encouragement and the time I finally delivered the manuscript, the
situation had changed. His enthusiasm evaporated when he
discovered that I had become an "enemy of the people" or
worse, and that he would be unable to depend on that "special support" which the Communist movement in New York
used so well in those days to make its impact felt in book
publishing; it could guarantee the sale of enough copies of
any book that any ordinary commercial publisher was willing to bring out, to assure a break-even outcome for a book
whose popular appeal was doubtful. Whether because this
"special support" was lacking in my case—as one publisher
bluntly informed me in his letter of rejection—or because
these stories were not then seen as commanding publishable
interest for their own sake, *Straw Sandals* was turned down by
publisher after publisher during the next two years. When in
1936 a collection of Chinese stories did appear under the
editorship of Edgar Snow, who did not suffer from my hand-
icaps, our discouragement was complete and *Straw Sandals*
was put regretfully away, among our souvenirs.

It rested there all this time and would be resting there
probably still, if we had not gone to a party in Cambridge
last December in honor of a visiting Chinese friend. There
Viola Isaacs happened to talk with Professor Patrick Hanan,
who teaches Chinese literature at Harvard, and the conversation led her to remember and to mention *Straw Sandals*.
Hanan's surpise and interest reignited our own and that evening we went hunting in old filing cabinets and found *Straw
Sandals*, along with folders containing some of Lu Hsün's and
Mao Tun's letters about it, and a sheaf of publishers' rejec-
tions. Michael Connolly of M.I.T. Press, member of a differ-

ent generation, had a different opinion; his interest was instant, and here it is.

Many of the stories in this book will obviously not be as "new" to some Western readers as most of them would have been in 1934. Some of Lu Hsün's work, of course, had already been translated even then, and much more has been published in various Western languages since. Several other collections by various writers were published in English translations in the 1940s but have not remained in print. The regime in Peking published a great deal that has since been removed from circulation and has not been reissued. In the present collection a number of stories, like Ting Ling's "Diary of Miss Sophia" and several by the less well-known writers of the 1930–1933 period, do appear in English here, as far as I know, for the first time. In any case, this collection is offered for its own sake and for the perspective that time has given to our view of this period in modern Chinese literature and of the fate of these writers in the unfolding of the history they helped to make. It is possible that *Straw Sandals* is a more meaningful book now than it would have been had it appeared as it was meant to, in 1934. Some books, like some ideas, have their time, and the time for this book may, after all, be now.

My main acknowledgments are still the original ones, to Lu Hsün and to Mao Tun. Lu Hsün is long since gone. Mao Tun, if he is still living somewhere in China, would be 76 years old now, thinking who knows what thoughts about all that has passed since he lived and worked so close to Lu Hsün in Shanghai long ago.

For the resurrection of this book, and for sharing in the new work connected with it as she did the old, I have to thank Viola R. Isaacs, with whom I have shared it all, then and since, all that went into the writing of both this new and more complicated introduction and into the first much simpler essay it replaces, an underpinning continuity that happily has nothing to do with politics.

I owe great thanks for much help in the re-editing process. Professor Merle Goldman of the East Asian Research Center at Harvard put at my disposal material which helped me update the biographical notes on the authors which follow this introduction. I have also profited from her 1967 work, *Literary Dissent in Communist China*, and other papers, and from the late T. A. Hsia's essays in *The Gate of Darkness*. I learned much from a brief exposure at the Harvard China Seminar to Leo Ou-fan Lee's ongoing study of Lu Hsün and have had the benefit of his comments on this introduction. These scholars are helping to ensure that the history of literature and politics in China in these years will not go down the memory chutes but will remain in view, open to the continuing scrutiny of all.

A considerable effort has been made to correct errors and improve the fidelity of the translations, especially those not done originally by George Kennedy. This effort was limited for various reasons, including in the case of four of the stories the unavailability of Chinese texts. On about half of this manuscript, this work of correction was generously and painstakingly done by Donald and Loretta Gibbs, who also checked and provided a number of references and made other useful suggestions. I am even more indebted to A. L. Chin for reducing error in much of the remainder, and most particularly for a full retranslation of Ting Ling's "Diary of Miss Sophia." I have also had from this same source indispensable help in checking out numerous details of fact, translation, and romanization, and was especially glad to be led to the use of the couplet by Lu Hsün which appears as part of this book's jacket design and the poem of which it is part—in the translation of which, incidentally, almost every-

one mentioned here took some part—and to the discovery
that Lu Hsün included the original of his foreword to *Straw
Sandals* in the collection of his works that was eventually
published in Peking. I have also to thank Ezra Vogel for a
useful comment on this introduction. For a careful check of
the manuscript in all other respects, I must also thank the
staff at M.I.T. Press. I trust it is obvious that all errors that
remain—and there must still be many—have to be strictly
my own.

And speaking of Lu Hsün and romanization, I have to report a conflict which I am not sure I have rightly resolved.
Lu Hsün himself romanized his name as "Lu Sin." He made
rather a point of it, in fact, this version of his name in roman letters appearing even on the covers of some of his
works in Chinese editions. In one of his letters that I still
have, written in English by a friend or secretary but signed
by him, he signed it written as one word run together, "Lu-
sin." (It was a note, incidentally, demurring at accepting the
$22.50 I tried to send him, the payment received for the ap-
pearance of his story, "Gust of Wind," in *Story*, where it was
published—by "Lu Sin"—in September 1935.) My first impulse in the present case was to respect the preference of
"Lu Sin" more than the rules of Messrs. Wade and Giles.
But then I was pressed to think of all the catalogues and in-
dexes and bibliographies and all the avid students and readers consulting them, and all the confused obstacles to knowledge about China that Messrs. Wade and Giles worked so
hard to reduce. In the end, knowing that "Lu Sin's" own reaction would be an amused smile under a raised eyebrow, I
gave in to the needs of posterity instead of heeding my own
conscientiousness about my own recollections of Lu Sin. He
gave me the picture of him that serves as a frontispiece for
this book and since, happily, he signed it in Chinese, it will
not look down on me from the wall hereafter as a reproach

for the choice I made in the rendering of his name in this book. I hope that in all other respects this volume in its own way will serve the purpose he put first, the shouldering up of those gates of darkness to let some light in.

Harold R. Isaacs

Newton, Massachusetts
April 10, 1973

About the Authors

LU HSÜN (Chou Hsu-jen) (1881–1936)

At the time of the preparation of this volume in 1934, two years before his death, Lu Hsün supplied the following biographical note for this book:

"I was born in 1881 into a big family in Shaohsing, Chekiang province. My father was a scholar who passed the second degree examinations. My mother, whose surname was Lu, was a country girl who taught herself to read, and she eventually became able to read works of literature. The family had inherited some forty or fifty *mow* from my grandfather, but even before my father died, all the land had been sold. I was then thirteen or fourteen, but despite all our difficulties, I was able to continue studying Chinese for three or four years more.

"Lacking money and needing to find a free school, I went to Nanking and, after living there for a little over six months, passed the entrance examinations for the Naval School. I was assigned to the engine department, and when I realized I could not hope to get up on deck, I left the school. Subsequently I entered and completed a course at the Mining and Engineering School and was sent to Japan for further study. There, once again, my plans changed and I found myself studying medicine. I remained in this field for two years before I began to develop an interest in literature. I read literary works, translated some, and also wrote some essays and tried to get them published. I returned to China in 1910 only because my mother had no means of support. My first year home, I was an assistant at the Hangchow Normal School and the next year became superintendent of the Shaohsing Middle School. After the revolution of 1911–1912, I became headmaster of the Shaohsing Normal School.

"However, the leader of the 'revolutionary army' at Shaohsing had originally been a bandit and I didn't like his behavior. Since he announced his intention to have me killed, I left for Nanking where I worked in the Education Ministry. I later went to Peking and was promoted to be head of the Second Division of the Social Education Bureau.

"In 1918, the 'literary revolution' began, and I started writing short stories under the pseudonym Lu Hsün, which were published in the magazine *New Youth*. I continued to publish stories and critical essays while also serving as lecturer at Peking National University, at the Normal College, and at Women's Normal College.

"Because of my critical essays, the number of my enemies increased. When Ch'en Yuan, a professor at Peking National University, began to spread the word that 'Lu Hsün' and I were one and the same person, Marshal Tuan Ch'i-jui dismissed me and threatened to arrest me. I had no choice but to leave Peking, and I joined the faculty of Amoy University. But before six months had passed, my ideas led me into conflict with the president and a number of professors, so I left Amoy to become dean and professor at Chungshan (Sun Yat-sen) University in Canton.

"After about six months, when it became clear that the Kuomintang's Northern Expedition (1926) was going well, a number of professors from Amoy University also came over to Canton. But soon afterward (1927) the 'Party Purification' took place. There was a slaughtering such as I had never in all my life seen before; I resigned my position and returned to Shanghai, thinking I could make my living doing translations. However, because I joined the League of Struggle for Freedom, word reached me I had been placed on the Kuomintang's wanted list and I had to go into hiding. After this, I joined the League of Leftist Writers and the League for Civil Rights. Up to the present time, all my works published after 1926 have been banned by the Kuomintang authorities.

"Apart from translations and edited work, as creative work I have written two collections of short stories, one collection of prose-poems, a volume of personal reminiscences, one collection of essays, eight collections of critical essays, and a short history of Chinese fiction."

"Diary of a Madman," which opens this collection, marked many beginnings. Its appearance in Ch'en Tu-hsiu's journal *New Youth*, founded only three years earlier, introduced the modern short story in *pai hua*, vernacular Chinese. It began the use of this new medium in literature to attack both old literary conventions and the mores and values of traditional Chinese society. Three examples of this same genre follow, "Medicine" and "K'ung I-chi," written in 1919, and "Gust of Wind," in 1920. These and other stories of his first years as a writer of fiction placed Lu Hsün in the preeminent position he occupied for the rest of his life, at a height, indeed, that no other Chinese writer approached during his lifetime or since. Lu Hsün was unromantic, unblinking, always sharp and hard, abrasive, humorous, sardonic, ironic. He also had—as a fourth story in this collection shows ("Remorse,"

1925), a soft, sad, even a loving touch for the people about whom he wrote.

"Medicine" and "K'ung I-chi" were translated by George A. Kennedy and first appeared in these English renderings in the *China Forum* on March 25 and May 21, 1932.

KUO MO-JO (1892–   )

Kuo Mo-jo was born in Kiating, Szechwan. He studied in Japan, beginning, as did Lu Hsün, in the field of medicine. He began writing from Japan in 1919. With a group of fellow writers, he founded the Creation Society in 1921 and edited a series of its publications in ensuing years. In 1924, Kuo Mo-jo experienced a conversion to Marxism (upon reading a Marxist work by a Japanese author) and under his leadership the Creation Society and many of its members began trying to transfer their strongly romantic concerns from the arena of the individual and the drives of love and sex to the arena of the society and the drives of politics and revolution. In 1926 Kuo Mo-jo led a group of his fellow writers to Canton to engage in teaching and revolutionary propaganda work. When the revolutionary movement was halted by Chiang Kai-shek's repressions in 1927, Kuo fled to Japan. He returned to China upon the outbreak of full-scale war between China and Japan in 1937 and thereafter became an increasingly influential figure in Communist literary circles, identifying himself closely with whatever became the official party line in the fields of literature and culture. When the Communists came to power in 1949, he was named to high posts, vice-premier in the government, vice-chairman of the People's Political Consultative Conference, chairman of the All-China Federation of Literary and Art Circles, and president of the Academy of Sciences.

Kuo Mo-jo's career thus spans the full half-century of his generation's literary and political experience. His prolific writings—poems, plays, novels, essays, autobiographies—always remained, despite successive renunciations and self-criticisms, in the romantic vein which he, more perhaps than anyone else, opened for modern Chinese literature, and with which he is most closely associated. As a writer, Kuo Mo-jo broke through many of the rigidities and frigidities of traditional Chinese mores and literature. He opened the way for writers to deal boldly with relations between men and women, problems of love and conflict in individual lives, with the pursuit of new dreams and new forms of self-realization in the modernizing frameworks of Chinese life. It seems to be a commonly held view, however, that Kuo's large body of work has more historic than literary distinction.

On the other hand, if Kuo Mo-jo did not become the premier literary figure of his generation, he did become its premier literary politician, thanks to his adaptability, his suppleness, and his unfailing ability to follow the Communist Party line wherever it has gone during these many years. These virtues have produced their own rewards. The aged Kuo today is not only the most prominent literary figure in China, intimate of Mao Tse-tung (with whom he has exchanged many admiring poems over the years); he is also the *only* important writer, indeed the only cultural official of important repute, still on the scene after all the appearances, reappearances, and disappearances of these turbulent decades. He is the only one who was there before the Cultural Revolution who is still there now. At least as of this writing, he is the only visible survivor of that remarkable group of men and women of the May 4 and post–May 4 generation in China who wanted to change their world by what they wrote.

Kuo himself seems always to have retained some fleeting sense of the incompatibility of his writing and his politics. In the famous 1924 letter in which he proclaimed his conversion to Marxism, he wrote: "I have found the key to all the problems which appeared to me self-contradictory and insoluble. It cannot be helped if this means the death of my poetry; I only hope it would sooner die." In 1952, during one of the periodic convulsions of policy and purge in the literary milieu, Kuo confessed the persistence of his "petty bourgeois sentiments" and his "blind ignorance." In 1966, at the outset of the turmoil of the Cultural Revolution, Kuo, from his height as senior literary figure of the regime, proclaimed: "Strictly speaking, according to the standards of today, all I have written should be burned."

If this was not some kind of strangled cry of protest, it was his ultimate verdict on his own creative work. It would almost seem that inwardly and in his own fashion, Kuo Mo-jo has always shared the opinion of his writing held by most of those—Lu Hsün prominently included—who never had any political or personal need to be counted among his admirers. This opinion may perhaps be reflected in the selection of the work that represents him here, an excerpt from a 1923 play about a rebellious woman, shifted from the then-present—when many such conflicts were taking place—to a scene set in a time long past. This play seems fairly to suggest the kind of preoccupation and the quality of style that marked Kuo Mo-jo in the early years and in the early work on which his best repute as a writer is based.

YÜ TA-FU (1894–1945)

Yü Ta-fu was born in Fuyang, Chekiang. He studied in Japan for ten years, earning a degree in economics from Imperial University in Tokyo. His first collection of stories, *Sinking*, appeared in 1921 while he was still in Japan. He later taught in Peking, Wuhan, and Canton. Never quite ceasing to be a self-engrossed Bohemian more interested in individual emotions and experience than in politics or social change, Yü Ta-fu nevertheless took part in most of the principal activities that engaged writers in his time. He was a cofounder, with Kuo Mo-jo and others, of the Creation Society in 1921. He briefly joined them at Canton in 1926 to take part in the revolutionary activities underway there, but he soon dropped out to return to Shanghai to poke satiric fun at the experience. In 1930 he was among the founders of the League of Leftist Writers but shortly left it for the same highly personal and individualistic reasons. In 1938, Yü Ta-fu went into exile to escape the invading Japanese, and had to flee them again when they captured Singapore in 1942. He got as far as Sumatra where he somehow survived the war years only to be killed by Japanese police immediately after the Japanese surrender in 1945, an ironic end, it has been remarked, "for a writer who was neither a Communist nor very patriotic."

"Intoxicating Spring Nights," the story that represents Yü Ta-fu here, was written in 1923. It suggests the qualities for which he won and kept the regard not only of a reading public but of his literary peers quite beyond the bounds of their conflicting attitudes toward literature and their politics. This story appeared, English translation by George A. Kennedy, in the *China Forum*, March 15, 1932.

YEH SHAO-CHÜN (Yeh Sheng-t'ao) (1894– ?)
Yeh Shao-chün's note about himself, supplied in 1934, was as follows:

"I was born in Soochow, Kiangsu. My father was an estate manager for a big landlord. He was simple and honest and my mother added the quality of caution. I am a composite of both of them. I studied for the official examinations but had no success. Later I taught primary school for nine years, middle school for four, and finally became an editor in a book company where I have remained these past ten years. I began writing at twenty, and I can date my interest in literature from my reading of Irving's *Sketch Book* when I was a boy in middle school. I wrote first in the *wen yen* and later in *pai hua*. I have written one novel and more than one hundred short stories."

In subsequent years, Yeh Shao-chün published stories, essays, and children's tales, staying always with the experiences of plain people as he knew them, caught in the turmoil of his time. In 1949 he became an official of the Communist government in Peking, rising to the post of vice-minister of education in 1954. He reportedly died of an illness not long thereafter but no further firm information about him could be found in available sources.

Yeh Shao-chün is represented here by one of his early stories, "Mr. Pan in Distress," written in 1924, and by "Three to Five Bushels More," written in 1933, both of which reflect his characteristic style, his eye for detail, and his intimate knowledge of the people about whom he wrote.

TING LING (Chiang Ping-chih) (1905–   )
Ting Ling was born in Changsha, Hunan. Her father's name was Chiang, but when she went to school in Shanghai, she adopted her mother's surname, an early characteristic gesture of independence. She acquired in these early years something of the vaguely anarchistic frame of mind or outlook that became part of the makeup of so many of those young intellectuals who later joined the Communist Party. For some years, however, her rebellion was directed against the conventional status of women in Chinese society and her energies fixed on finding some meaningful expression of love in her life. In Peking Ting Ling met Hu Yeh-p'in, then already a budding poet and on his way to his brief experience as a Communist activist. It was not until 1930 that Ting

Ling joined the ranks of the radical writers in Shanghai. In November that year, she gave birth to Hu Yeh-p'in's son, just three months before Hu was arrested and executed by the Kuomintang authorities. Ting Ling thereafter became a leading figure herself among the left-wing writers and in the Communist Party. In May 1933, she was kidnapped by Kuomintang agents from her apartment in the Shanghai International Settlement and imprisoned in Nanking.

Freed by the political changes that came with the establishment of the new Kuomintang-Communist united front in 1936, Ting Ling went to Yenan, the Communist capital in the northwest, where she quickly became a figure of power and of controversy. In the long subsequent history of intermittent conflict between the Communist Party bureaucracy and Communist writers, Ting Ling at one time or another played an important role on both sides of this confrontation. now asserting her prickly independence in the spirit of her onetime mentor, Lu Hsün, and being violently attacked for doing so, now joining, as a leading bureaucrat herself, in the attack on literary dissidents. A novel Ting Ling wrote shortly after the Communists came to power was awarded the Stalin Prize for literature in 1951. But Ting Ling found herself unable to keep on satisfying the Party's unremitting demand for undeviating subservience, or to keep herself in a protected position among the long-standing personal and factional conflicts in the Communist literary milieu. In 1957 she was purged, deprived of her posts, expelled from the Party, and sent off to do penance at hard labor in some distant corner of the hinterland. Her name reappeared fleetingly in 1960, in a report that listed her as present at a meeting, but it did not appear again. Through all the subsequent years, including the whole period of the Cultural Revolution, Ting Ling did not come again into view, except as a target

of attack. Her present situation and whereabouts remain unknown.

"Why did I begin to write?" she asked herself in a rumina-
tive personal essay in the early 1930s. "Shall I say it
emerged from a feeling of loneliness? I was dissatisfied with
the world and saw no way out for myself . . . even unable
to find someone to listen to what I had to say, unable to
find my place despite my desperate longing to do
something. . . ."

Ting Ling's "Diary of Miss Sophia" was written in 1927
during her pre-Communist years in Peking. Ill, neurotic, her
heroine is bold and unmincing, scorning the shy timidity of
the conventional Chinese girl, casting about for some new
and more satisfying role that she cannot find for herself. She
bitterly reflects in the end: "Life has been my own toy. I've
wasted enough of it away. . . . I'm going to take the train
southward and waste what's left. . . ."

Ting Ling went south to Shanghai and followed her young
husband into the Communist movement in 1930. The second
story that represents her here is "One Certain Night," written in 1931, published in an English translation by George
A. Kennedy in the *China Forum*, July 9, 1933. Compared to
"The Diary of Miss Sophia," this story shows what effect the
Communist political conversion could have on the gifts of a
creative writer. But such a judgment must somehow include
appreciation of the fact that on one such certain night such
a group was executed by Kuomintang soldiers, that one of
them was Ting Ling's husband, and that there were many
such certain nights in that time of terror: the crude political
art of these activist-writers could not begin to cope with the
crude political reality that surrounded them in Kuomintang
China. Ting Ling, lonely somewhere now in Communist
China, is 68, and there is no way for us to know whether
she is still dissatisfied with the world, still looking for some-

one to listen to what she has to say, still unable to find her place, still desperately longing to do something, or is finally just wasting away what is left.

CHIANG KUANG-TZ'U (1901–1931)

Chiang Kuang-tz'u was born in Anhwei. He took part as a student in the May 4 movement in 1919. In 1921 he was among the first students sent by the newly-founded Chinese Communist Party to Russia to be schooled as fledgling revolutionists. He returned to China in 1924. After a brief period in the Northwest and in Peking, he lived in Shanghai as teacher, writer, and Communist activist. In 1927 he fled the anti-Communist purge from Shanghai to Wuhan and back again to Shanghai. In 1929 he fled again, to Japan this time, but this time it was apparently more a flight from the pressure of the demands made upon him as a Communist activist, his feeling being that he ought to be spending his time writing, not distributing leaflets or demonstrating under constant threat of arrest in the streets of Shanghai. Unhappy in exile, Chiang returned to Shanghai, where, late in 1930, he resigned from the Communist Party. The Party thereupon expelled him as a petty bourgeois dilettante more devoted to luxury and personal comfort than to the revolution. The bad health Chiang had pleaded as a major reason for his flight to Japan—the Party expulsion order called it a "deceitful excuse"—resulted in his death in a Shanghai hospital in June 1931.

Chiang was the author of poetry, short stories, and several novels. None of his work has ever been recognized as having any enduring merit. He seems to be remembered more as a personality, an exemplar of so many of his fellows of the time, romantic, posturing, Byronic, persuaded of his own gifts but unable to write anything that would persuade anyone else, and unable in the end to reconcile the ego demands of his belief in his own genius with the superego demands of the Party and "the revolution."

For reasons that might have had to do with Kuo Mo-jo's nostalgia for the powerfully romantic attitudes which he shared with Chiang in the earlier years and which he had warmly admired, or possibly with a more obscure latter-day reprise of old party strife, Chuang Kuang-tz'u was "rehabilitated" in 1953. His remains were moved from their obscure grave to a place of honor among the Communist dead in Hung Ch'iao Cemetery in Shanghai, and in a curious graveside ceremony, led by Ch'en Yi, mayor of Shanghai, Chiang was celebrated as a memorable fighter for the revolutionary cause.

Chiang Kuang-tz'u is represented here by a little story, "Hassan," written in 1929, which is very much in the accepted genre of that time. In one of his letters about this collection, Lu Hsün, who was on record as having scant regard for this writer and, indeed, the whole type he represented, indicated indifference as to which of his stories might be used, but no objection to including him.

SHIH YI (Lou Chien-nan) (1903– ?)
Lou Chien-nan was born in Shiang Yu, Chekiang, into a small landlord's family. He worked as an apprentice in a money exchange shop and later as a bank clerk. With Ying Hsu-jen (Ting Chiu) and other fellow workers he organized a reading circle in Shanghai. In 1927 he went to Hankow to engage in political activity there, but was forced to flee thereafter, first back to Shanghai and then on to Japan. He returned to Shanghai and became an active member of the League of Leftist Writers. In 1932, when the Japanese attacked the city of Shanghai, he joined the Nineteenth Route Army to take part in its independent stand against the invaders and fought as a common soldier during the five weeks

that battle lasted. In September 1933, he was arrested and sentenced to a life term at the military prison in Nanking.

Up to that time, Lou Shih-yi had published one collection of short stories, *The Third Period*, and many translations from the Japanese. In his 1929 story "Salt," which appears in this collection, he made one of the rare efforts of the time to dissect what had happened in the stunning reversal of revolutionary fortunes that had taken place at the climax of the Kuomintang-Communist alliance in 1927. His story illustrates with unusual sharpness how the imagined "bloc of classes" of that time led the working poor—in this case in the Kiangsu salt fields—momentarily out of their condition of servitude and then pushed them back into it. If this story reads more like reportage than like fiction, it is because it undoubtedly tells the story of an actual episode. The same is even more poignantly true of his 1933 story, "Death," which also appears in this collection.

Shih Yi survived to become an important official of various cultural and publishing organizations in China after 1949. His most recent listing in available sources dates from 1957 and there is no information available about what happened to him thereafter.

HU YEH-P'IN (1905–1931)

Hu Yeh-p'in was born in Foochow, Fukien. He began to study classics as a boy but straitened circumstances forced his family to apprentice him to a goldsmith. In 1919 his first exposure to Shanghai newspapers stirred the desire to see the great world outside, a feeling spurred by the ill-treatment he suffered at the hands of the goldsmith. He stole a small gold bracelet and ran away to Shanghai. Friends of his father located him, and he was sent to a naval school in Tientsin which closed down three years later. He tried to enter Peking National University but failed because of a foreign language deficiency. In Peking he met and married Ting Ling, the girl writer, and in 1925 began writing his own poems and stories. These were in the love-romantic vein until, in Shanghai in mid-1930, he joined the League of Leftist Writers, and shortly thereafter became a member of the Communist Party. Ting Ling gave birth to Hu Yeh-p'in's son on November 8, 1930. On January 17, 1931, Hu was arrested in the International Settlement in Shanghai. He was executed on February 7 at the Lunghua Garrison Headquarters.

His stories of this brief period, and one novel, *Light Ahead of Us*, were written in the revolutionary-romantic vein, illustrated by the example here, "Living Together," about new styles of life in the Soviet districts of Kiangsi, which Hu never visited. This story, written a few months before the end of his life, first appeared in English translation, by George A. Kennedy, in the *China Forum*, January 20, 1932.

JOU SHIH (Chao P'ing-fu) (1901–1931)
Jou Shih was born in Ninghai, Chekiang. His father and grandfather were scholars, although neither one ever passed the civil examinations. His father went into business. Jou Shih was a sickly child and was first tutored by his aunt. He eventually went to school, became a family tutor, and studied for a time in Peking where he attended lectures by Lu Hsün. Back in Ninghai in 1927 during the brief revolutionary phase of the Northern Expedition, he became director of education. When the reaction set in after Chiang Kai-shek's coup in Shanghai, Jou Shih came into conflict with local authorities and in 1928 fled to Shanghai, where he became part of the circle around Lu Hsün and served as editor of various literary magazines, some of them short-lived. He joined the Communist Party in 1930 and was one of the organizers of the League of Leftist Writers. Jou Shih was the oldest of the five writers arrested, along with others, in

Shanghai on the night of January 17, 1931, handed over by the foreign authorities of the International Settlement to the Kuomintang military garrison headquarters at Lunghua, and executed there on February 7.

Jou Shih was the author of some early unpublished poetry, a novel, *February*, and a number of short stories of which "Slave Mother" is perhaps the most memorable. It first appeared in English translation, by George A. Kennedy, in the *China Forum*, April 16–23, 1932.

MAO TUN (Shen Yen-ping) (1896–   )
In 1934, Mao Tun supplied the following biographical note for use in this volume:

"Two years after the Sino-Japanese War of 1894, I was born in a market town in what used to be known as Chia-hsing Prefecture, in Chekiang Province. I was the great-grandson in the principal household in the clan, that is to say, my father was the eldest son, and his father before him the eldest son in each generation.

"We were originally a family of farmers, later becoming merchants and eventually attaining gentry status as a family of government officials. By the time I was born, however, it had already become a gentry family in an advanced stage of decline.

"My grandfather was an optimist. He was not much inclined to concern himself with the daily management of the family's affairs. My grandmother was the daughter of a large landowner and was strongly opposed to the new-style schools, but my father was in sympathy with the reform movement, and it was by his decision that I was sent to the first primary school established in our district. I was only ten when he died. His will called for me to enter an engineering school. He believed that China would soon be entering upon a period of major troubles. By becoming an engineer, I would be able to work abroad if I could not work in China. I failed to respect his wish. Eight years after his death, in 1912, I entered the Humanities Department of Peking University Preparatory School. After finishing the preparatory course, I went to Shanghai and got a job as a minor editor for Commercial Press. Around 1921, when the Press management wanted to reorganize the magazine *Hsiao-shuo yueh-pao* (*Short Story Magazine*), I became its editor. This was my first formal connection with literary work. After two years as editor, I was removed because the Press was unhappy with my attacks on the feudal 'Saturday school' of writers. In 1926 I went to Canton and served for two months as secretary in the Central Kuomintang propaganda department. When the Kuomintang Northern Expedition occupied Wuhan, I went to Hankow to become editor of the *Min-kuo jih-pao* (*Republican Daily*). When the Kuomintang-Communist split came, I escaped to Shanghai and there began to write fiction. The three novelettes *Huan-mieh* (*Disillusion*), *Tung-yao* (*Vacillation*), and *Chui-ch'iu* (*Pursuit*) were written at that time [published as a trilogy in 1930 as *Shih* (*Eclipse*)].

"In the fall of 1928, I went to Japan and remained there for two years. The full-length novel *Hung* (*Rainbow*) was completed there. In the spring of 1930, I returned to Shanghai and joined the League of Leftist Writers. Works after that include the novel *Tzu-yeh* (*Midnight*), and the short stories collected under the title *Ch'un-ts'an* (*Spring Silkworms*)."

Mao Tun's works of this period established him as the most gifted and most promising of the younger writers coming up behind Lu Hsün, who became Mao Tun's friend and mentor in these years. In these short novels and stories, Mao Tun tried to deal with the experience of individuals in the convulsive events of the 1926–1927 period. Even though his concern was more with the political and class implications of his subject, he was able to give his characters a quality of intimate and complex reality not often found in the work of the younger radical writers of this period. A more ironic touch applied to these same events appears more fleetingly in the briefer piece of this genre included in this collection, "Comedy," which was written in 1931 and published, in an English translation by George A. Kennedy, in the *China Forum*, June 18, 1932. His more famous stories of the plight of peasants under the old order, "Spring Silkworms" and "Autumn Harvest," both of which date from 1932, suggest how much more "realism" there was in Mao Tun's expression of the "New Realism" than in the work of most of the younger writers who were trying to write in that style at the time.

Mao Tun went on to become a major figure in the Communist literary environment, first at Yenan and later in the Communist government in Peking, where he became Minister of Culture. His known work as a creative writer apparently ceased after 1945, but he appeared in various roles in the recurring collisions between writers and ideologues and artists and bureaucrats during the 1940s and 1950s. He apparently tried to remain orthodox while also trying in one way or another to defend the integrity of the writer and his art against ideological or factional Party onslaughts. He finally fell from this slippery path, was dismissed as Minister of Culture in 1965, and disappeared from public view during the Cultural Revolution. His name suddenly reappeared early in 1972, on the guest list of the reception given for President Richard Nixon when he visited Peking. There has been no known reappearance of Mao Tun, either by name or in person, and at least as far as presently available sources show, his present situation remains unknown.

TING CHIU (Ying Hsu-jen) (1899–1933)
Ting Chiu was born in the Ningpo district, Chekiang. He left a job in a Shanghai bank in 1925 to join the Commu-

nist Party. In 1927 he worked in the labor department of the short-lived Left Kuomintang government at Wuhan. In 1928 he went to Moscow, returning in 1930 to become head of the agitation and propaganda work of the Communist Party in Kiangsu. On May 14, 1933, Ting Chiu came to visit Ting Ling at her room on Quinsan Road in Shanghai, unaware that Ting Ling and a fellow writer, Pan Chu-nien, had been kidnapped a few hours earlier by Kuomintang agents and that three of the agents were still waiting there to take any friends of Ting Ling who might appear. Ting Chiu fought with the men and was thrown from a third-story window to the street. Next day the newspapers carried reports of the "unidentified youth with Communist documents in his pockets found dead in the street."

A response to this event, written by Ting Chiu's longtime friend, Shih Yi, a writer represented by a story elsewhere in this collection, appeared under the title "Hsu-jen Lives On In My Heart," in the *China Forum*, June 19, 1933. An excerpt will convey something about the lives of these young men caught up in the turmoil of their time and place:

"My friend of nearly nine years, Ying Hsu-jen, lay a corpse in Quinsan Gardens on May 14. He died fighting the brutal hirelings of the Kuomintang. But Hsu-jen lives on in my heart. His tall, thin form, his mild manner of speech, the way he used to sing the songs of spring, his every little word and mannerism, his naive, almost childish simplicity, from the days when I first knew him until he died, hurled from an upper story window by three beasts—all these are enshrined in my heart and will leave me no peace.

"A few years after the stirring days of May 4, a group of young men found life unbearable at their desks within the marble walls of a Shanghai bank. They talked with each other and felt there must be something more to life than ledgers and counting boards. From their discontent emerged the 'Cooperative Reading Society,' with which they established a little library. Hsu-jen was the eldest of our group and was tacitly accepted as our leader. As we began to collect books and extend the scope of our reading, we began to feel we could not just go on keeping it to ourselves, so we collected some money and turned our little venture into a public library. . . .

"Those were days of great change for China. The monumental strike of the Peking-Hankow Railway workers, the February 7 movement [1923], and the dawning of May 30 [1925] opened a new era. . . . Intellectuals came to realize they could not go on quietly reading among themselves. One night I received a note from Hsu-jen. 'Tomorrow I'm off for the battle,' he said. Hsu-jen was leaving us and step by step finding his place in the revolutionary movement. He not only threw up his job with the bank but left his home. 'I'll never forget you, mother,' he wrote before he left, 'but for you and thousands of other mothers, I cannot just remain at your side.' Hsu-jen left Shanghai after that and for a long time we never saw him. . . .

"Two years ago Hsu-jen came back to Shanghai. . . . Sometimes we passed him on the street. He was still thin and delicate and he greeted us in the same mild voice, but in his silences we felt a new strength. . . . A few days after May Day (1933) I met Hsu-jen in the street. We exchanged a silent greeting with our eyes. I passed on but several steps further I turned in hopes of having a talk with him. He had already disappeared in the crowd. Could it have occurred to me then that it was the last time I would exchange a greeting with my friend and comrade?

"When we learned of his death—and knew it was really he—a number of us sat silently around a table. What was there to say to each other? We remembered Hsu-jen. We also knew that the dying regime was shedding blood which would help wash it away. . . . My friend and comrade, Hsu-jen, lives on in my heart!"

Ting Chiu's rather deft propagandist touch appears in the story included in this collection, "Three Pagodas," which appeared in English translation, by George A. Kennedy, in the *China Forum*, May 28, 1932.

WANG T'UNG-CHAO (1898–1957)

The following note from Wang T'ung-chao was written in 1934:

"I was born at Chuchen, Shantung, into an old family. My father loved music and painting, and when he died, a youth of twenty-eight, he left behind two volumes of music and one of short poems. He was a meek personality. My mother was a native of Peking and traveled widely with her father and acquired in the process a solid store of common sense. She read and wrote fairly well and was a wise and resolute person. After the death of my father she struggled successfully to educate her children. Since my seventh year, my education has been entirely due to her efforts and I have felt her influence throughout my life.

"When I was ten, I began to read the old Chinese literature and entered primary school. After entering Tsinan High School at the age of sixteen I began to write and produced a novel written in the old style which was published. Two years after I entered college, the May Fourth movement occurred. Along with the youth of that period I was attracted by the new literature and wrote short stories and poems. With Cheng Chen-to and Shen Yen-ping (Mao Tun) I helped organize the Society for the Study of Literature. I taught for several years after graduation but soon stopped. 'One Leaf,' 'Night of Spring Rain,' and 'Evening' all appeared about 1921. Subsequently I wrote two collections of short stories, *Trace of the Forest* and *Horn*. In 1933 I published a novel, *Mountain Rain*, which describes the collapse of village economy in North China. I have also published two collections of poems, *Child's Heart* and *This Era*."

In the story which represents him here, Wang T'ung-chao describes a bit of the system employed in the "bandit-suppression" efforts of the Kuomintang regime in the early 1930s in central China. The tradition of banditry and banditry-suppression is an old one in rural China. In Chiang Kai-shek's day these were the terms used in connection with his efforts to suppress the Communist-led peasant bands which became the Chinese Red Army. The magazine in which this story was published in 1933 was banned on the grounds that Wang had written a satire of Chiang Kai-shek's "bandit-suppression" campaign.

The only available additional information about Wang T'ung-chao is an indication that he died in 1957.

CHENG NUNG (Hsia Cheng-nung) (1904– ?)
Cheng Nung supplied this note about himself in 1934:

"I was born in Nanchang district, Kiangsi, into the family of a petty landlord. I learned the Four Books and the Thirteen Classics and wrote my *pa ku* (thesis for a degree under the old system). I entered primary school at fifteen and middle school two years later, but was twice expelled. At twenty I entered Ching Ling University at Nanking and in 1925, I joined the revolutionary party. In 1926, I returned to Nanchang to work in the peasant movement there but returned to Shanghai after the breakup. I entered Fu Tan University but was arrested in 1929 before my graduation. I spent one year in prison and have been leading an underground existence ever since. I have also been in the south during this period. I am now twenty-nine.

"My first story, 'Crime and Punishment,' was written while

I was still at Fu Tan and was published in the university magazine. My work later appeared in other publications. Actually I began writing only last year [1933] when 'On the Threshing Field' was published in the *Literature Monthly*. I will shortly issue my stories in a collection and am planning two novels, one on prison life and the other a picture of village life."

No further account of Hsia Cheng-nung's writing or political life appears in available sources, but he was listed in 1964 as director of the Propaganda Department of the East China Bureau of the Communist Party. It was the Propaganda Department of the Communist Party that was the main target of the internal purges that began with the Cultural Revolution in 1966. The entire propaganda bureaucracy was dismantled and all its members dismissed, purged, sent to distant exile, or otherwise put out of the way, and it seems reasonable to assume that this too was the fate of Hsia Cheng-nung.

TUNG P'ING (Ch'iu Tung-p'ing) (? –1941)
In a note attached to the story "Courier," which appears in this collection, Mao Tun in 1934 described Tung P'ing as a Communist who worked in the Soviet district near the Kwangtung border where the scene of the story is laid. It appeared in *Literature Monthly* (*Wen-hsueh yueh-pao*), No. 4, in the spring of 1933. Tung P'ing became a soldier who continued to write short stories—one listing includes a collection by him called *Company Seven*—while taking part in the fighting against the Japanese until he was killed in action in northern Kiangsu in 1941.

HO KU-T'IEN (1907– ?)
To accompany his story, "Land of Snow," the first he had

ever published, Ho Ku-t'ien supplied this note about himself in 1933:

"I was born into a petty landlord family on the western frontier of Szechwan near Sik'ang. My family had gone into trading but failed at it. My father died when I was five, and my other relatives tried to wrest our property from my mother. She opposed them and with great difficulty succeeded in bringing up my younger brother and myself. I had only been two years in middle school when my mother pressed me to marry and sent me off to be a junior officer on the Szechwan frontier, where I remained for four years. I studied in a military school and began to write. Before 'Land of Snow' was published, I had written and destroyed more than 200,000 characters of writing. The death of my younger brother, who was also in the army, influenced my life a great deal. Besides 'Land of Snow,' I have also written 'Hatred,' 'A Hero,' 'Hsüeh Jen-kuei's Eastern Expedition,' and 'Division.' "

Ho Ku-t'ien made his way to Yenan after the beginning of the war with Japan in 1937. There he headed the Yenan branch of the National Writers' Anti-Aggression Association and edited a literary magazine with Ting Ling and others, and published several collections of short stories. He eventually became a cultural bureaucrat under the name of Chou Wen, and died, apparently of natural causes, sometime between 1949 and 1953.

YIN FU (Hsü Pai) (1909–1931)
Yin Fu was born in Chekiang, son of a middle peasant family. He began his career as a revolutionist while still a boy in his early teens, sharing in the turmoil of Shanghai between the May 30 events in 1925 and the Chiang Kai-shek coup in April 1927. He was one of those arrested during

those last bloody days of that month, but thanks to the intervention of an older brother who was an officer in the Kuomintang army, he was released after three months. He entered T'ung Chi University but left in 1929 to devote himself entirely to revolutionary activity. He was arrested again in September that year for being involved in a silk workers' strike. Again, his brother intervened and won his release. Yin Fu had begun to write in 1928, his poems appearing in various underground magazines. In 1930, he joined the newly formed League of Leftist Writers. He must have been one of the very few members of that organization whose party work actually involved him with factory workers, and it was quite possibly in his capacity as a union organizer, rather than as a writer, that he attended the meeting of January 17, 1931, at which he was arrested, going to his death at Lunghua with the others on the night of February 7.

The poem "Words of Blood," by which he is represented here, is an example of a style common among the radical poets of the time. It appeared, translated by George A. Kennedy, in the *China Forum* on May 28, 1932. Yin Fu also wrote under the name of "Pai Mang" and one of his stories under that name, "Little Mother," appeared in English translation, also by George Kennedy, in the *Forum* of June 11, 1932. He would have been better represented, perhaps, as a writer of more substance by his poem "Good-bye Brother," written in 1929. Part of this poem—addressed to the brother who had twice rescued him from prison—appeared in an English rendering in T. A. Hsia's *Gate of Darkness.*[14] It begins:

Good-bye, my dearest brother,
Your letter has made up my mind.

14. Pp. 202–203.

'Tis a pity that I cannot for the last time hold your hand
Before I take, independently, my strides ahead.

Twenty years of brotherly love and fondness,
Twenty years of protection and bringing up,
Please take them back in this last teardrop;
Take them back, as if they were only a nightmare.

The next time he was arrested, Yin Fu, twenty-two years old, paid for his choice with his life. He was the youngest of the victims executed that night at Lunghua.

LU HSÜN

Diary of a Madman

Two brothers were both good friends of mine in middle
school. After a lengthy separation during which we never
even exchanged letters, I was shocked one day to hear that
one of them was seriously ill. On a trip back to my native
village I went out of my way to call on them. I found only
the elder at home. He thanked me for calling and told me
that his brother had long since recovered and was now a
candidate for civil position. With much laughter he pulled
out two notebooks filled with writing and offered them to
me. He said they were his brother's diary, kept during his
illness. They would give me some idea of just how sick he
had been, the older brother told me.

  Upon reading them I realized that my friend must have
been temporarily insane. It was written entirely without order and much of it made no sense at all. There were no
dates. Only the different-colored inks and the change in his
scrawling characters showed where the entries began and
ended. Once in a while there were paragraphs which seemed
to be more intelligible and continuous, and I've copied them
down here for the study of medical men. I have left all his

mistakes unchanged. The names of the locality and the persons involved, although of no consequence, have been altered. The title was affixed by the writer of the diary after his cure.

April 2, 1918

1

The moon is extremely bright tonight.

For nearly thirty years I have not been able to see the moon and I find myself exceedingly pleased with it. I realize now that all these thirty years I have wasted like an addle-pated fool. I must be careful, otherwise why did the dog in Chao's store bark at me? My fears are well founded.

2

I know something must have gone wrong for there is no moon tonight. I went out this morning and went carefully on my way. Chao Kuei-weng looked at me strangely and seemed to be wanting to murder me. Eight others whispered about me behind my back. All the other people on the street were just the same and many grinned at me with wide mouths. I was frozen from head to foot with fear. I knew they were preparing to murder me. But I walked boldly forward. There were children playing up in front of me and they too talked about me with their ghostly dark faces and the expression in their eyes so like Chao Kuei-weng's. What was there between those children and me that they should regard me so cruelly? "Tell me!" I asked them in a loud voice. But they ran away.

What grudge could Chao Kuei-weng and all the other people in the street have against me? Twenty years ago I did provoke Mr. Ku Chiu* by stepping on his ledger and that

*Literally, "Mr. Antiquity."

2

must now be known to Chao Kuei-weng. They surely never knew each other but Chao must now be angry on Ku's behalf and he arranged with the people on the street to stand against me. But what about the children? They were not even born at that time, yet they stare at me with fear and a desire to persecute me. This is dreadful, amazing, and sad.

I understand now. Their parents must have taught them to be so!

3

I never can sleep nights. But there is nothing that cannot be understood if it is subjected to study.

Some of those who had been put into stocks by the magistrate, beaten by the gentry, or whose wives had been abused by the officials in the yamen,* or others whose parents had been done to death by the pressure of their creditors—they had not such fear or such a fiendish expression on their faces as I saw yesterday.

I was most astonished to find a woman beating her child on the street during my walk. "I want to sink my teeth into you, Lao Tze!" Her eyes were directed toward me. I was unable to conceal my shock. All the ghostly blue-faced men with their glittering teeth laughed. Ch'en Lao-wu rushed up and dragged me home. There all the members of my family pretended to be strange to me and their eyes bore the same expression as the others. They locked me in the study like a chicken in his coop. I cannot figure it out.

The tenant on the land at Wolf Village came several days ago to report famine in his district. An evil man is said to have been beaten to death in their village. The people tore out his heart and liver and fried them for food, for they felt they would be emboldened in that way. When I tried to join

*Office of the local district authorities.

in their talk, both the tenant and my brother glanced at me queerly. Only now I realize that the expression in their eyes was the same as all the others.

The thought of it chills me from head to foot. They can eat others. It's not impossible that they should devour me!

The woman's threat to sink her teeth into the child's flesh, the laughter of the blue-faced men, and the tenant's story are all signals of this. There was poison in his talk and knives in their laughter. Their piercingly white teeth are all used to devour men.

Thinking it over, it seems to me that I am not an evil man, though ever since trampling Mr. Ku's ledger I cannot be sure. All those people harbor thoughts I cannot divine. Whenever anyone displeases them, they call him an evil man. When my brother was teaching me to write essays, whenever I criticized those regarded by others as worthy, he would mark that passage with a circle to show approval, and when I found excuses for bad people, he would say, "Good! You show originality." How can I divine their thoughts, especially when they all want to devour me?

But there is nothing that cannot be understood if it is subjected to study. I vaguely remember that men often ate men in ancient times. In an undated history I found on almost every page nothing but the four characters *Jen* (Kindness), *Yi* (Righteousness), *Tao* (Truth), and *Teh* (Virtue). Since it is impossible for me to sleep in any case, I have pored over this volume through half the night and eventually I found other characters between the lines. They were all the characters for "Devour Man!" Words like this are in the book and in the mouth of the tenant. And they all stared at me smiling. I am a man too. Surely they want to devour me!

4

This morning I was sitting quietly by myself when Ch'en Lao-wu brought me my food, a bowl of vegetables and another of steamed fish. The eyes of the fish were white and hard. Its mouth yawned open, just like the men who seek to devour other men. The meat of it was so smooth that I was unable to decide whether it was really the flesh of a fish or of man. I vomited it all out.

"Tell my brother I am bored and want to go out into the garden, Lao-wu." Without answer he left but soon returned to open the door. I did not move. I decided to wait and see what they were going to do with me. I know they won't let me off lightly. As I expected, my brother soon appeared. An old man was with him and they walked slowly. The old man's eyes burned with a fiendish light. Fearing I would see what was going on, he bowed his head and only looked out at me from the corners of his spectacles. "You seem to be all right today," said my brother. "Yes," I replied. "Then let Dr. Ho have a look at you." I said all right.

Didn't I know this old man was just the executioner come in disguise? He was simply checking my pulse as a pretext to see how plump I might be. For his trouble he would partake of the feast when they disposed of me. I was not afraid, however. My courage is greater than theirs, although I do not eat the flesh of man. I held out both my fists and waited to see what he would do. The old man sat there for a long time, closed his eyes, and felt my wrists. Then his devil's eyes at last opened.

"Don't bother thinking about anything," he said. "Just rest and everything will be all right in a few days."

Rest and keep from thinking! Then I should only grow fatter and they would have a better meal! What advantage is that to me? How can I be what they call "good"? These people desire to devour men but they dare not do it openly and forthrightly. This seemed extremely funny to me and I burst into laughter. And I know there was an uprightness and a courage in my laughter which frightened my brother and the old man and put them out of countenance.

Because I have courage, they desire more and more to devour me that they might partake of the courage that is mine. As they were leaving the room, the old man whispered to my brother, "Eat quickly!" My brother nodded. So you, too, my brother, are among them! This was not entirely unexpected although the discovery shocked me.

The Man-eater is my own brother!

I am the brother of a man-eater!

I am to be eaten by the people and I am the brother of a man-eater!

5

At this time I paused to reflect a bit. Even supposing the old man was not an executioner in disguise but a real doctor, still, he eats flesh. In the *Pen Ts'ao* Pharmacop-something-or-other written by Li Shih-chen, the ancestor of all physicians, it is clearly stated: "Human flesh can be cooked for food." Does the old man deny that he eats man-flesh?

As for my brother, I have not suspected him falsely at all. When he used to explain books to me he once used the phrase "exchange the son for food." Another time when he was talking about an evil man, he said that he not only thought he deserved to be beheaded but "his flesh should be eaten and his skin used for bedding!" My heart beat fast for a long time as I was then still very young. The other day when the tenant told him how the people ripped the heart and liver from the man's body, he just nodded. His heart was as cruel as before. Since sons can be exhanged between families for food anything can be exchanged in the same way and anyone can be eaten. In the old days I used to accept his words as forthright reason and truth. But now I see not only the fat of man's flesh drooling on his lips when he speaks but his mind is thick with the desire to devour his fellow men.

6

It is pitch dark and I cannot make out whether it is day or night. Chao's dog is again barking. They have the ferocity of lions, the cowardice of rabbits, and the cunning of the fox. . . .

7

I know how they do it. They won't kill a man directly. The fear of consequences coming upon themselves prevents them from doing so. Therefore they are all working together, weaving a net to throw around me, trying to get me to commit suicide. But the appearance of those people on the street a few days ago and the recent actions of my brother have revealed that sufficiently to me. The best thing for me to do, I suppose, would be to strangle myself with my belt flung over the beam in the ceiling. Wouldn't they chuckle for joy? Their desires would be satisfied without cost to themselves. Then again I might die of shock or sorrow. I would be thinner and offer less flesh for their feast, yet they would doubtless nod their heads in a satisfied way.

They can only eat dead flesh! In that same book I read about a beast called a hyena which is ugly in face and appearance as well as in the customary expression around its eyes. It eats dead flesh always and even gnaws down the largest bones. A horrible animal. But the hyena is related to the wolf which is related to the dog. And day before last, Chao's dog stared at me. He is also in the plot against me. Can that old man deceive me by looking into the ground?

Most pitiful of all is my brother. He too is a man and should fear man-eaters, yet he can conspire with them without being afraid. Is it because he is accustomed to this and therefore no longer considers it to be wrong? Or has he lost his conscience and therefore does it deliberately? In cursing these man-eaters, I'll begin with my own brother, and in reforming them, I'll begin with him.

They ought to have understood by now. . . .

Unexpectedly a youth of about twenty came to see me. I could not make out his features clearly but he smiled a false smile and nodded to me. "Is it right to eat the flesh of man?" I asked. "It's not famine time. Why should anybody eat man flesh?" he replied, smiling again. But I knew he belonged to the same crew of man-eaters, and mustering all my courage I persisted.

"Is it right?"

"Why ask such . . . you really . . . you're joking. Isn't the weather fine today?"

The moon is shining and the weather is fair. I asked again. "Is it right?" He was irritated and replied indistinctly, "No . . . ."

"No? Then why do they do it?"

"They do no such thing!"

"No such thing? They ate flesh at Wolf Village only a few days ago and it is also freshly written in the book!"

His face fell and his eyes goggled. "Maybe it is so. . . . Maybe it's always been so. . . ."

"Does 'always' make it right?"

"Don't ask me such questions. Anyway, you shouldn't talk. It's a great mistake for you to talk."

I jumped up and looked everywhere but the man was no more to be seen. I was in a horrible sweat. This man was so much younger than my brother yet he belongs to the same group. He must have been taught by his parents and he, too, will teach his children. That's why the children stared at me in the street so hatefully.

9

They want to devour people but are themselves afraid of being devoured. They look upon each other with eyes full of hate and suspicion. How much better it would be if instead they could work, walk, eat, and sleep at their ease! It is just beyond the pass, just over the threshold a step. Yet they cling together, fathers and sons, husbands and wives, teachers and students, brothers and sisters, friends and enemies—all sorts of strange people, persuading each other and preventing each other from crossing over. . . .

10

Early in the morning I sought out my brother. He was standing outside the hall gazing up at the sky. I approached him from the rear and, blocking the doorway, I said in an especially calm and friendly voice, "Brother, I have something to tell you."

"Say it then," he turned to me, nodding.

"I've only a few things to say but I hardly know how to begin, my brother. Maybe all the early savages used to eat the flesh of man. Later on their minds developed in different ways. Eventually some became real men and ceased to eat the flesh of their fellows. Some continued to eat other men. Some of the worms grew to be fish, birds, monkeys, and ultimately men, while others remained worms, even until today. How much more shameful are those who eat man next to those who don't, perhaps far more shameful than the worms are next to monkeys! It was in the early times when Yi Ya* cooked his son to

*A famous cook of Chou Dynasty times.

feed Chieh and Chou.* Ever since P'an Ku† opened the
skies men were eaten, down to the son of Yi Ya, from
him to Hsu Hsi-ling¶ and from Hsu Hsi-ling to the man
caught at Wolf Village. Last year when they killed a criminal in town, a man with tuberculosis ate bread soaked in
his blood.

"Of course, you can do nothing alone when they set out to
devour me. But it is scarcely necessary for you to join them!
To what lengths will they not go? If they can eat me, they
can eat you and tear at each other. Only if you reach out
and try to change all this can you hope for peace and quiet.
Although this has been going on since olden times, we can
certainly make a special effort to improve things and cry
out, 'That won't do!' I know you can say it, brother. The
other day you shouted 'That won't do!' when the tenant
asked for a reduction in rent."

At first, he merely laughed coldly. His expression grew increasingly fierce and when I got to the crux of the matter,
he turned blue. A crowd of people were around the gate,
among them Chao Kuei-weng and his dog. They began by
looking in and finally squeezed inside. Some of their faces
were indistinct, as though they were masking them with
cloth. Others, with their same old blue faces and glittering
teeth, tried to hide their amusement. I knew them all to be
man-eaters. Yet their minds varied. Some of them considered
it quite traditional, something which had existed ever since
history began. Others knew they should not go on with it,
but went on with it anyway. They were always in fear that

*Chieh of the Hsia Dynasty and Chou of the Shang Dynasty, both notori-
ous as the worst emperors of their day.
†Mythical first ruler, creator of the world.
¶An early revolutionist who assassinated a Manchu official. When he was
caught, the bodyguards of the murdered official insisted on getting their revenge by cutting out his heart and liver and eating them.

others would expose them. That is why they were so irritated at my words and that is why they hid their faces and laughed so coldly. My brother suddenly turned fiercely upon them:

"Get out, all of you! What is there to see in a madman!"

So, another trick of theirs. They not only go on eating the flesh of man but they have already planned to make a madman out of me! So they will devour me and win thanks for it into the bargain. Just like the tenant who related how they devoured the evil man in their village as if it had been a great deed! An old trick! Ch'en Lao-wu came up angrily but how could he stop me? I insisted upon talking to them.

"You can change all this!" I cried. "You can change from the depths of your hearts! You must know that man-eaters will have no place in the world of the future! You will devour yourselves if you don't change. Even if you can still multiply, you'll be extinguished by the real human beings just like wolves by hunters! Like vermin!"

Ch'en Lao-wu drove the people away. I have no idea where my brother went. He persuaded me to go to a darkened room. The beams and the posts shuddered above me. They trembled awhile and then expanded, piling up on top of me. I was unable to stir under their weight. They wanted me to die there. But I knew the weight was false, so I struggled out. The perspiration ran down me in streams. I kept saying: "Change yourselves from the depth of your hearts! You must know man-eaters will not be tolerated in the future. . . ."

11

A sunless day. The door is sealed shut. Only two meals a day. I think of my brother whenever I pick up the chopsticks. I know he was responsible for the death of my little sister who was then only five, so lovable, so pitiable, I can

Lu Hsün

see her before my eyes now. Mother cried bitterly but brother tried to persuade her not to cry. Perhaps the tears made
him sorry for the little girl he devoured. If only he could feel
sorrow; I wonder if mother knew little sister was devoured
by our brother. She probably was aware, though she said
nothing when she cried over her death. Probably she just
thought that was the way things were meant to be. Once
when I was only four or five and was sitting outside to catch
a cool breeze, my brother said that when a parent is ill, a
good son should slash a piece of his own flesh from his body
for medicine. Only then would the son be regarded as a
good man. Mother raised no objection. But if one piece can
be eaten, then naturally so could the whole child. However,
the way she cried, as I now recall it, really made a person
feel distressed. How strange.

12

I can think no more.

A nation with four thousand years of man-eating history,
and to think I've been living in it for so long and yet only
now do I see what is really going on. My sister died when
my brother was head of the house. It is not unlikely that he
secretly fed us the flesh of my sister. Perhaps I ate some of
my sister's flesh—and now it is my turn.

I, with a background of four thousand years of man-eating
history behind me, unknown to me for so long, and now that
I understand, how can I face real humans!

13

There may still be children who have never eaten man. Save
them. . . . Save the children.

Medicine

1

It was in the early hours of an autumn morning, after the passing of the moon and before the coming of daylight. Only a sheet of blue-black sky remained, under which all lay asleep save the creatures of the night.

Old Hua Shuan sat up suddenly. Striking a match, he lighted a greasy oil lamp, the greenish glow from which filtered through the two rooms of the tea-shop.

"Little Shuan's dad!" came an old woman's voice, "Are you going now?" At the same time there was a spell of coughing in the small inner room.

"Hm!" Old Shuan grunted in reply as he buttoned up his clothing. He stretched out one hand. "Give it to me!"

Mother Hua rummaged about beneath the pillow for a long time, finally bringing to light a parcel of dollars which she handed over to Old Shuan. He took it from her with trembling hands and thrust it into his pocket, giving it a pat to make sure it was there. Then he lit a paper lantern, extinguished the lamp, and walked into the inner room. There

Translated by George A. Kennedy.

was a rustling noise followed by a succession of coughs. Old Shuan waited for it to quiet down, then spoke in a low voice, "Little Shuan! . . . Don't get up. . . . The shop? . . . Your mother will manage all right."

There was no answer from his son, and thinking that he had dropped off quietly to sleep, Old Shuan stepped through the door and out on to the street. The streets were dark and deserted. Nothing was visible but the gray stretch of roadway and his two feet illuminated by the lantern following one behind the other. From time to time he met a few dogs, but not one of them made a sound. The air was much colder than it had been in the house. Old Shuan found it exhilarating. With the coming of this dawn, somehow, he was a youth again, blessed with mystic insight, filled with life-imparting power. His stride lengthened and the road, as he walked, became clearer and the sky brighter.

Old Shuan's whole attention had been riveted on the road, when he started back suddenly as he saw ahead where it ended clearly at a cross street. He retraced a few steps and, finding a little shop still tightly shuttered, took shelter under the eaves and stood leaning up against the door. Some time passed and he realized that he was cold.

"Hey, an old fellow over there!"

"Seems cheerful enough. . . ."

Old Shuan started a second time as, staring ahead, he saw a number of people passing by in front of him. One of them turned his head to look at him. His figure was indistinct, but he had the manner of a long-starved wretch lighting upon food, his eyes glittering with greedy desire.

The lantern had gone out, Old Shuan noticed. He felt the pocket inside his clothing. It was still there, hard and firm. He raised his head and looked about him. Numbers of fantastic creatures were wandering about like devils in groups of twos or threes. He kept staring, but could discover nothing else that seemed strange.

It was not long before he saw several soldiers moving about, the great white circular design on the front and back of their clothing being visible even from a distance. Of those who passed nearer by he could make out in addition the dark red trimming on the uniforms.

There was a rush of trampling feet, and in a twinkling a large crowd had gone jostling by. The scattered groups of twos and threes formed suddenly into a mass, rolling forward like a tide. Reaching the street crossing, the crowd came to an abrupt halt and ranged itself in a semicircle. Old Shuan gazed in their direction but saw only a multitude of human backs. Necks were craned like those of so many ducks being pulled upwards in the clutch of invisible hands. After a period of deep silence, there seemed to come a faint sound and then the crowd became agitated once more. With a deep rumble it streamed back again, past where Old Shuan was standing, sweeping him almost off his feet.

"Hey Old Shuan! Pass over the money with one hand and take your stuff in the other!"

In front of him stood a fellow dressed from head to foot in black and with eyes like two swords that bored into Old Shuan, shriveling him to half his usual size. One of the man's huge hands was stretched out toward him, while the other clutched a bright red roll of steamed bread from which the redness was still dripping drop by drop. Old Shuan fumbled hastily for his money and held it out tremblingly but could not bring himself to take the thing the other held.

"What are you scared of?" the man said impatiently, "Why don't you take it?"

As Old Shuan still held back, the fellow in black snatched up his lantern, ripped off the paper shade, and wrapping it around the bread, thrust the parcel in Old Shuan's hand. Then he snatched up the money, tried the feel of it, turned, and was gone. "The old fool . . ." he muttered.

"Who's the medicine for?" Old Shuan thought he heard someone questioning him but he did not answer. All his thought was concentrated on his package. It seemed as precious as the last of ten generations of only-begotten sons. All other thoughts were subordinate to this. He must now transplant into his home the fresh life that his package held and reap its harvest of happiness.

The sun had risen. In front of him it lit up a broad street stretching straight to his house; behind him it touched the faded gilt characters on the broken signboard at the street-crossing: "Site of the Ancient . . . Pavilion."

2

When Old Shuan arrived home he found the shop cleaned and set in order with its rows of smoothly glistening tea tables. There were no customers, only Little Shuan eating at one of the inner tables. Great drops of sweat rolled down from his forehead and his lined coat clung to his spine where the shoulder blades stuck out like a raised number eight.* Old Shuan's face clouded over at sight of him. His wife came hastily from behind the cooking range and her lips trembled somewhat as she peered at him.

"Did you get it?"

"Yes."

They went together to the back of the cooking range. There was a moment's consultation; then Mother Hua went out, to return shortly with an old lotus leaf which she laid on the table. Old Shuan unfolded the lantern shade and wrapped the scarlet bread roll up again in the lotus leaf.

*The Chinese character for "eight": 八 .

Litte Shuan had finished his rice. His mother called hurriedly to him:

"Little Shuan! Sit still! Don't come over here!"

She was stirring up the fire in the oven. Old Shuan took the deep green parcel and the torn white shade splotched with red and placed them together on the coals. There was a dull red flare, and then the shop filled with a strange fragrance.

"That's a fine smell! What are you cooking?" Hunchback Sao-yeh the Fifth had come in. He invariably spent the whole of every day in the tea shop, being the first to arrive as well as the last to leave. He had just come limping up to the table in the corner next to the street, but no one paid any attention to his question.

"Is it rice porridge?" Still no one answered him although Old Shuan hurried out and poured him some tea.

"Come in here, Little Shuan!"

Mother Hua led him into the inner room in the middle of which she had placed a bench. When he was seated she handed him a plate on which was something round and very black. She said gently, "Eat this up. . . . You're going to get all well again."

Little Shuan picked up the black object and looked at it with inexpressible wonder as though he were holding his own life in his hands. He broke it open carefully. From within the charred shell came a cloud of white steam which drifted away to leave two halves of a bread roll made from white flour.

In a short time he had finished it but he could remember nothing of its taste. The empty plate was before him, and beside him were his father and mother, one on either side, with eyes fixed on him as though they expected to infuse something into his body and to withdraw something at the same time. This made his heart beat quicker. He clutched his chest and burst out in another fit of coughing.

"Sleep a little while. . . . You're going to be all right."

Little Shuan went coughing to bed as his mother directed. Mother Hua waited for his breathing to become quieter before she gently covered him with the collection of patches that made his quilt.

3

There were a great many people sitting in the shop. Old Shuan was very busy carrying his great copper kettle about to fill up the tea-cups of his guests. His eyes were ringed with dark circles.

"Is there something the matter with you, Old Shuan? Are you sick?" asked a gray-bearded man.

"No."

"No? I thought from your smiles that you didn't look. . . ." The gray-bearded man did not finish.

"He works too hard. Now if his son. . . ." The Hunchback's speech was interrupted by a sallow-faced man who burst into the shop wearing a dark gown thrown over his shoulders with the buttons all unfastened and held carelessly around his waist by a loose dark sash. As soon as he was through the door, he shouted out to Old Shuan:

"Has he eaten it? Is he better? Old Shuan, I've brought you luck! It's a good thing that I've a nose for news. . . ."

Old Shuan was all smiles as he listened, one hand holding the teakettle and the other lowered in a respectful gesture. All the people in the room listened respectfully, in fact. And Mother Hua, with darkly ringed eyes, came smiling out to proffer a teacup and tea leaves, adding an olive as an extra delicacy. Old Shuan poured on the boiling water.

"This is a sure thing! This is quite exceptional. Think of it!" The sallow-skinned man kept up boisterously. "Brought home while warm and swallowed down still warm!"

"That's right!" Mother Hua thanked him warmly. "If it hadn't been for your kindly interest, Uncle K'ang, how could we. . . ."

"Guaranteed, guaranteed! Taken hot like this—a roll of bread with human blood—guaranteed to cure any form of consumption!"

At the word "consumption" a change came over Mother Hua's face. She seemed displeased, but immediately put on a smile and walked away mumbling to herself. Uncle K'ang, however, had noted nothing. He continued to shout at the top of his voice until Little Shuan woke to keep him company with his coughing.

"To think," said the gray-bearded customer, "that your Little Shuan should have such a stroke of good fortune! Of course he will recover completely. No wonder you smile all day long, Old Shuan." Having spoken, he stepped over to Uncle K'ang and said in a low voice, "We have heard, Uncle K'ang, that the criminal who met his end this morning was some child in the Hsia household. Whose child was he really and what was it about?"

"Who was he? Why, the son of the widow Hsia. The young scoundrel!" Uncle K'ang noted a general pricking up of ears and grew highly animated. His yellow skin blew itself out and his voice took up a higher pitch. "That little wretch didn't deserve to live. Well, that's all right. But there was nothing in it for me this time. They even stripped his clothes off him and Red-eyed Ah Yi, the jailer, got it all. Uncle Shuan here was the luckiest; the next was Hsia's third son who got twenty-five snow-white ounces of silver to stick in his purse without having to spend a single cash."

Little Shuan had come slowly out from the little room clutching his chest with both hands and coughing continuously. He filled a bowl with cold rice from the range, poured hot water over it, and sat down to eat. Mother Hua followed him. "Do you feel better, Little Shuan?" she asked quietly. "Are you still as hungry as ever?"

Uncle K'ang glanced at Little Shuan. "Guaranteed! Cure absolutely guaranteed!" Then he turned back to his audience. "That third Hsia is a foxy one all right. If he hadn't turned him in first, all his own property would have been confiscated and the whole family implicated. But look at him now! Silver!—That little fellow was absolutely unbelievable. Even in jail he tried to get his keeper to join the revolution!"

"Ai-ya! Imagine that!" A young fellow of twenty or so spoke up angrily from the back row.

"You see, Red-eyed Ah Yi tried to find out from him what the story was, but the kid gave him a political lecture. He said the Great Ch'ing Empire by rights belongs to all of us. Think of that! Does that make any sense? Red-eye knew, of course, that he had only an old mother at home. He hadn't realized, however, that the child was too poor to be squeezed of the tiniest bribe. Red-eye was bursting with anger over that already, so when that kid with his politics scratched the head of a tiger, old Red-eye let him have a few cuffs for his trouble."

"Brother Yi has a good fist!" spoke up the hunchback gleefully from his corner. "I'll bet those two punches did the trick all right!"

"Nah, you couldn't frighten a worthless scoundrel like him. He kept saying 'What a pity, what a pity!' "

"Pity?" said the graybeard. "Who's to have pity for a creature like that?"

Uncle K'ang looked him up and down with infinite scorn. "You misunderstood me. What he meant apparently was that Ah Yi deserved pity."

The listeners suddenly dropped their eyes and a silence fell.

Little Shuan had finished eating his rice. He was perspiring so freely that his head seemed to be steaming.

"Pity for Ah Yi! What rot! He must have been completely mad!" The graybeard blurted out his words in a burst of sudden clarity.

"Absolutely mad!" agreed a man of twenty, also suddenly clear about it.

Thereupon the customers in the shop began to liven up and chat and laugh again. Little Shuan, taking advantage of the commotion, coughed vigorously, but Uncle K'ang stepped over to him and patted him on the shoulder.

"Guaranteed! Don't cough this way, Little Shuan, I guarantee it!"

"He was mad!" said Hunchback Sao-yeh the Fifth nodding his head.

4

Outside the west gate and lying close to the foot of the city wall was a piece of land that had always been government property. Diagonally across it ran a narrow crooked path, which, starting as a shortcut trodden out by the shoes of passers-by, had ended by becoming a natural boundary. On the left of the road were burial mounds of such criminals as had been executed or had died from exposure in jail; on the right was a burying ground for paupers. Both sides were already crowded with rows and files of mounds like the ceremonial cakes at a rich man's birthday party.

It was unusually cold at the spring festival this year. The buds on the poplars and willows were scarcely half the size of a grain of rice. Not long after daybreak Mother Hua stood before a fresh grave on the right hand side of the path. She set out four plates of food and a bowl of rice, wept a while, and burned sacrificial money. Then she sat mutely on the ground, apparently waiting for something, though she could not herself have told what it was she expected. A faint breeze ruffled her thin hair, whiter by far than it had been the year before.

Along the path came another woman, also gray-haired, with ragged coat and skirt. She carried a round broken basket that had once been red lacquer and a string of sacrificial paper money. She had to rest every few steps. Suddenly she saw Mother Hua sitting on the ground watching her. She hesitated and an embarrassed flush spread over her pale thin face. Then, summoning her courage, she made her way over to a grave on the left-hand side and put down her basket.

This grave was in the same row as that of Little Shuan, separated only by the narrow path. Mother Hua watched the woman set out the four dishes of food and the bowl of rice, saw her stand and weep and then ignite the paper money. "It will be a son," she was thinking to herself, "in that grave, too."

The old woman had been moving about to survey things when she gave a sudden start and, staggering backwards, stood staring in terror. Mother Hua feared that the woman was going insane from grief, and she felt constrained to rise, cross the path, and speak to her.

"Lao Nai-nai," she said quietly, "don't take it so hard. Let's go back home."

The woman nodded, but her eyes remained in a fixed stare. "Look!" she stammered, "Look, what's that?"

Mother Hua followed her pointing finger and her eyes fell on the grave in front of them. It was ugly enough, with patches of yellow dirt where the grass had not grown. But a closer look produced a shudder of amazement—for there, clearly encircling the rounded tip of the grave, was a wreath of red and white flowers.

Even to their age-dimmed eyes the flowers were quite distinct. There were not many of them; they were somewhat wilted; but they were arranged very regularly in a perfect circle. Mother Hua took a hasty look at her son's grave and at the others, but she saw nothing beyond a few bluish wildflowers braving the cold here and there. She was possessed by a sudden feeling of emptiness and was reluctant to examine further. The old woman went nearer to the grave and regarded it carefully, muttering to herself.

"They have no roots. They don't seem to have grown of themselves. But who could have come here? . . . Children wouldn't play here. . . . Relatives stopped coming long ago. . . . What can have happened?" Suddenly she broke out in a sobbing cry. "Oh, my child! They all wronged you! And you can't forget it. Are you still grieving? And is this a sign from the spirit world you give me so that I will know?" Looking about her she saw a black crow sitting on a leafless tree. "I know now," she continued. "Oh, my child! They murdered you. They'll get their punishment some day, Heaven knows. Just close your eyes. . . . But if you are really here, if you are listening to me, give me a sign . . . make that crow fly on to your grave."

The breeze had died away. The blades of dry grass stood up stiffly like copper wire. The quivering thread of sound echoed more and more faintly on the air and was gone. All around was the stillness of death. The two stood in the withered grass gazing up at the black crow; and the crow, with head tucked in, sat on his branch as though he were cast in iron.

A long time passed. The visitors to the graves increased in number. Old and young passed in and out amongst the grave mounds.

Mother Hua felt relieved of a great burden and turned to go. "Come," she urged, "we had better go back."

The old woman sighed and listlessly gathered up the dishes of food. She hesitated still a moment, then walked slowly away. "What can it all mean?" she mumbled to herself.

They had gone not more than twenty or thirty steps when a loud caw sounded behind them. With a jerk, they turned their heads to look. The black crow spread his wings, gave a preliminary flap, and took flight like an arrow into the distance.

K'ung I-chi

The wine shops of Luchen are arranged rather differently from those in other places. They all consist of a huge L-shaped bar facing on the street inside of which hot water is kept ready for warming up the wine. At noon and at evening the laborers coming from work would invariably stop to spend four cash for a bowl of wine—that was twenty years ago, and the price has now risen to ten cash—and, standing up against the bar, would imbibe its comforting warmth. If one were willing to spend an extra cash, one might have a dish of salted bamboo shoots or of spiced beans to accompany the wine. If one could afford ten or more cash, one might have a meat dish. But these customers were all of the short-coated class, and were very rarely so extravagant. It was only the long-gowned gentlemen who would step through to the inner adjoining room, order wine and meats, and sit down for a leisurely drink.

From the age of twelve on, I served as an apprentice in the Prosperity Wine Shop. The barkeeper remarked that my manners were too crude for waiting on the long gowns, so I

Translated by George A. Kennedy.

was given work on the outside. It was easy enough to get along with the short-coat customers, and yet among them, even, there were a good many fussy and garrulous ones. These were never satisfied unless they were permitted to see with their own eyes the dipping of the yellow wine from the jar to make sure by   examination that there was no water in the bottom of the pot and to personally supervise the placing of it in the hot bath. Under such rigorous inspection it was, of course, extremely difficult to water the wine, so, after a few days, the barkeeper decided that I was equally inept at this job. Fortunately I had been recommended by an influential person. Since he could not dismiss me, he transferred me to the single uninteresting operation of warming up the wine.

Thereafter I stood the whole day long inside the bar attending to my one responsibility and, although I was kept employed, nevertheless I found the work monotonous and tiresome. The barkeeper was a stern-faced man, and the customers were not very genial, so that I could not be lively. It was only when K'ung I-chi came to the shop that I was able to laugh a little, and for that reason I still remember him.

K'ung I-chi was the only long-gowned customer we had who stood at the bar to drink. He was a very large man with a scraggly, unkempt gray beard and a sallow face whose wrinkles were generally full of scars. He was dressed in a long gown, to be sure, albeit a most dirty and ragged one which seemed not to have been mended for more than ten years—nor washed, either. His speech was heavily interlarded with classical particles which people only half understood. Because his surname was K'ung, he had been given the nickname I-chi, from the meaningless line in the elementary copybooks: "Shang ta jen k'ung i chi."*

*Literally this could mean "Above the great man—" followed by three

K'ung I-chi

As soon as K'ung I-chi arrived in the shop, all the drinkers would look at him and laugh and someone would call out, "K'ung I-chi! You've added a few new scars on your face."

He never answered but would call across the bar, "Warm up two bowls of wine and give me a dish of spiced beans." Meanwhile he laid out nine large cash.

Then they would deliberately set up a shout. "Well, well! You've been stealing again, that's for sure!"

K'ung I-chi would open his eyes wide and say, "How can you thus groundlessly defame the spotless—"

"Spotless, eh? Why, day before yesterday with my own eyes I saw you strung up and beaten for stealing someone's books!"

K'ung I-chi would grow red in the face while the veins stood out on his forehead. "The larceny of books," he protested, "cannot be classed with stealing. . . . The larceny of literature! . . . That is a scholar's business. Can it be considered theft?" He would continue in a string of unintelligible phrases, something about "Sit philosophus indigens," a succession of "wherefores" and "whereases," until the whole crowd would burst into laughter and the shop was filled with merriment.

Gossip had it that K'ung I-chi had studied books all night, but that he hadn't ever been to a proper school and was unable to make a living. He had grown poorer and poorer with time until he was now practically a beggar. Luckily he wrote a good hand and could earn a bowl of rice by copying

---

meaningless syllables, *k'ung-i-chi*. *K'ung* was the surname of Confucius and since many Chinese names are trisyllabic, the people of the place gave these three syllables to the old man as his surname and given name. Actually all calligraphic copybooks began with these characters simply because they included all the basic strokes needed for learning how to write Chinese characters. Since many had begun to study but never gotten far, the words were widely known, even by the unlettered.

out manuscripts for people. But he had one unfortunate trait: he loved drinking and was averse to work. He would have been at his copying only a day or two when books, paper, pen, and inkslab, as well as copyist, would all vanish completely. After a few such incidents, no one could be found to give him further copying work to do, and K'ung I-chi had no recourse but to indulge in a little occasional thievery. When at our shop, however, his behavior was exemplary. That is to say, he never failed to settle his account and, although he was sometimes temporarily without ready cash and had to be posted on the blackboard, still it was never more than a month before he was all clear and the name of K'ung I-chi was erased from the board.

After K'ung I-chi had drunk half a bowl of his wine and his face had gradually lost its fiery expression, one of the bystanders asked him, "Kung I-chi, can you really read characters?"

K'ung I-chi gazed at his questioner with a look of lofty disdain.

"How did it happen," they asked him again, "that you couldn't manage even half a degree for yourself?"

K'ung I-chi appeared immediately to droop uncomfortably, and his face turned ashen gray. He made some remark, but this time it was so entirely literary that no one understood a word. Again the whole crowd burst into laughter and the shop was filled with an air of merriment.

At times like these I could join in the laughing without being rebuked by the barkeeper. The barkeeper himself, in fact, on seeing K'ung I-chi would invariably ask him some question to give the others a laugh. K'ung I-chi realized that he could not converse with any of them but must confine himself to the children. Once he said to me, "Have you studied? Then I shall examine you. How do you write the character spice in the word 'spiced beans'?"

I thought to myself that it was no business of a beggarly fellow like that to examine me, so I turned my face away and paid no further attention to him. K'ung I-chi waited a long time, then spoke pleadingly.

"Can you not write it? Then I will teach you. Now remember! You should commit such characters to memory because when you are a barkeeper later on you will need to write them in the accounts."

I reflected that I was a long way from being barkeeper and that in any case our barkeeper never charged up spiced beans on the bills, so with a mixture of impatience and amusement I replied lazily, "Who wants instruction from you? Isn't it the character '*hui*' meaning return, with the grass radical over it?"

K'ung I-chi appeared highly pleased and, tapping on the bar with two long fingernails, nodded his head. "Right! Right! Now there are four ways of writing the character '*hui*.' Do you know those?"

I grew more impatient, and, pursing up my lips, walked away from him. K'ung I-chi had just dipped a finger in his wine and was preparing to write on the surface of the bar, but noting that I was not in the least interested he heaved a sigh and looked very crestfallen.

On some occasions the children of the neighborhood would be attracted by the sound of laughter and would gather about K'ung I-chi. He would present them with spiced beans, one bean for each child. When they finished eating, their eyes remained fixed on the dish. Once K'ung I-chi grew alarmed and spread out his five fingers over the plate, at the same time bending down to say, "There are not many more. There are not many left for me."

Then he straightened up and inspected the beans, shaking his head sadly, "Not many! Not many! Lo, are there indeed many? Nay, forsooth, there be not many!" Whereupon the crowd of children ran laughing away.

Such a man as this was K'ung I-chi, one to make others merry. And yet without him the world went on just the same.

One day—it must have been two or three days before Mid-Autumn—the barkeeper was slowly casting up his accounts and had taken down the board, when he suddenly exclaimed, "K'ung I-chi has not been here for some time! He still owes nineteen cash!"

I realized it to be a fact that we had not seen him for a long period.

"How can he come?" remarked one of the customers. "He's had his legs broken."

"Oh!" said the barkeeper.

"He would keep on with his stealing. This time it was his own foolhardiness. He got into the home of Mr. Ting, the provincial scholar. You can't steal things in that house, you know."

"Then what happened?"

"Then?—first he had to write a confession. Then they beat him. They beat him more than half the night. And then they broke his legs."

"What happened after the legs were broken?"

"What happened? Who knows? Probably he's dead."

The barkeeper had no further questions but resumed his slow calculation on the accounts.

After Mid-Autumn the wind grew daily colder until the beginning of winter seemed at hand. Though I stuck close to the fire all day long, I still had to put on a quilted coat. One afternoon, when there were no customers, I was sitting with closed eyes when I suddenly heard a voice, "Warm up a bowl of wine!"

The voice was very low, but none the less familiar. There was no one in sight. I stook up and peered outside. K'ung I-chi was sitting on the floor by the door. His face was haggard and dark; he looked awful. He was wearing a thin lined coat wrapped around his legs. A piece of coarse sacking and some grass ropes supported these from around his shoulders.

"Warm a bowl of wine," he repeated at sight of me.

Thereupon the barkeeper put out his head. "Is it K'ung I-chi?" he inquired. "You still owe us nineteen cash!"

K'ung I-chi lifted his face and replied humbly, "That? I'll settle everything next time. This time it's cash and I want good wine."

The barkeeper laughed in his usual way and said, "K'ung I-chi, you've been stealing again!"

This time he offered no vigorous denial, saying merely, "Don't jest."

"Jest? If you weren't stealing, how did you get your legs broken?"

"I fell and broke them." K'ung I-chi replied in a low voice. "I had a fall. . . . I. . . ." His eyes seemed pleading with the barkeeper not to mention the matter again.

By this time a few others had gathered to share the amusement with the barkeeper. I warmed the wine, carried it out, and set it on the doorstep. From his ragged pocket he dug out four large cash and placed them in my hand. I saw that his own hands were covered with dirt. He had, in fact, come pulling himself along with his hands.

A few minutes later he had finished the wine and again, amidst the laughter of the bystanders, he went slowly off, crawling with his hands.

K'ung I-chi was not seen after that for a long time. At the end of the year the barkeeper took down the board and said, "K'ung I-chi still owes us nineteen cash!" The next year at the fifth of the fifth moon, he said again, "K'ung I-chi still owes us nineteen cash!" But at Mid-Autumn he said nothing, nor did we see K'ung I-chi at the end of that year.

I myself have never seen him since. It is most probable that this time K'ung I-chi is really dead.

Gust of Wind

(A record of a country happening at the time of Chang Hsun's attempted restoration of the monarchy in 1917.)

The sun's rays drew slowly away from the little field on the river bank. As the sunlight receded, the leaves of the small dark tallow tree, which stood near the water's edge, fluttered, as though sighing with relief. Under the outstretched lower boughs a cluster of mosquitoes were buzzing, singing loudly in the quiet evening. Smoke thinned lazily from the chimneys over the peasant huts which faced the water. The women emerged, pouring used water from their large basins onto the ground in front of their own doors to keep the dust down. Little square tables and plain low stools were brought out and arranged. It was suppertime. The elders and the men of the family sat down idly gossiping, fanning themselves with large plantain leaves. Children ran about breathlessly playing. Some were absorbed in a game of stones under the tree. Soon the women appeared with steaming bowls of steam-dried vegetables and fresh cooked brown rice and set them down on the tables.

Some distance away a party of literary-minded young men from town floated slowly along the river in a small boat. The apparent beatific idyll of the whole surrounding scene stirred their poetic souls. "How carefree country life is—how idyllic!" But they sighed thus only because they could not hear Grandmother Nine Catty who at that particular moment was scolding furiously in her customary fashion. Whacking her broken plantain leaf fan against the leg of her stool, she cried:

"I've lived long enough! Seventy-nine years now and I don't want to see our family going to ruin! Better to die now! Here we are about to eat supper and there she goes eating beans! This family is going to the dogs!"

The little object of this wrathful outburst was at the moment running toward the old lady with a handful of beans eagerly outstretched. It was her granddaughter, Six Catty. When the tide of words struck her, she swerved from her course with a sure instinct and made directly for the riverbank and hid herself behind the tallow tree. In a moment, however, her implike head with its tiny braids over either ear, like a pair of soft black horns, darted out from behind the trunk. "Old fossil!" she cried. Despite her age the old lady was by no means deaf. But the little girl's disrespectful epithet went quite unheeded, for the old one was shaking her head as she always did, repeating again and again to herself:

"So comes degeneration, one generation after another. . . ."

In this village there was a strange old custom observed by almost every family. When babies were born, they were weighed and the number of catties thus recorded forthwith became their given names. Grandmother Nine Catty had grown increasingly querulous and critical after her fiftieth birthday. When she was young the weather was far milder, far less hot, far more pleasant. The beans were not as hard as they were now. Indeed, nothing was as good now as it used to be. Besides, Six Catty was three catties lighter than her grandfather had been and was even a catty under her own father. Could better proof be asked? "Thus comes degeneration, one generation after another. . . ." This reminder was a regular punctuation to the quiet course of family life.

In the midst of the tirade her daughter-in-law, Mrs. Seven Catty, came up to the table and irritably threw the rice basket down before the old lady. "You're at it again! Was Six Catty not six catties and five ounces when she was born? And didn't you use a special scale with eighteen-ounce catties? If you'd used the regular sixteen-ounce scale our Six Catty would have been over seven. And anyway, I don't believe Grandfather and Father were actually nine and eight catties at all. I bet they used a fourteen-ounce scale!"

"So comes degeneration, one generation after another. . . ." repeated the old lady, shaking her head. Mrs. Seven Catty was about to retort when she saw her husband coming toward the house. She turned her vexed face toward him. "Corpse! Where does a corpse carry himself off to—coming home as late as this!" she shouted. "You don't care how long you make people wait for their supper, do you?"

Although his family had long lived in the village, he had always had ambitions to rise higher in life. Neither Seven Catty, his father, nor his grandfather had ever worked in the fields. Boatmen all, they considered themselves a rung above their neighbors in the social scale. As his father and father's father had done before him, Seven Catty poled his boat down the river to town and back, once each day. In the morning he set out from Luchen and returned by evening. Because of this he was always up on the latest news. Perhaps a Centipede Spirit had been struck dead somewhere by the Thunder God. Or maybe somewhere else a virgin had given birth to an evil Yaksha demon. With such tales to tell,

Lu Hsün

Seven Catty was an important man among his fellow-villagers. Although he did not till the soil, his family still observed the peasant habit of not eating by lamplight during the summer. Now it was growing dark, and Mrs. Seven Catty had cause to scold.

With his long and slender bamboo pipe in his hand—it was almost as long as he was tall, with an ivory mouthpiece and a bowl of bronze—Seven Catty walked slowly to his stool, head down, eyes fixed on the ground. Little Six Catty clambered up beside him but he didn't even answer when she called him—"Papa!"

"Thus comes degeneration, one generation after another. . . ." muttered Grandmother Nine Catty. Seven Catty looked up. He sighed and spoke slowly.

"The Emperor is again on his Throne."

His wife looked at him dumbly for a moment. Then she suddenly understood. "Well, that's good news. Doesn't this mean another royal amnesty?"

Seven Catty sighed again.

"I have no queue," he said.

"Does the Emperor insist on queues?"

"Yes."

"How do you know?" Worry began to edge her tone.

"Everybody in the Prosperity Wine Shop said so."

Intuitively, Mrs. Seven Catty knew that this must be a serious matter because she knew that the Prosperity Wine Shop was a place where information was quick and certain. She looked at her husband's shaved head resentfully. He was all to blame for it. A feeling of despair came over her. She filled his rice bowl and set it heavily down before him.

"Come and eat! Do you expect to grow a queue again by making such a long face?"

The sun gathered up the last threads of vagrant rays, and a

cool breeze came softly across the water. Only the clicking chopsticks busily shoveling rice from bowls into wide mouths was heard. Setting down her third bowl, Mrs. Seven Catty raised her head. She started and her heart began thumping violently, for there approaching from beyond the tallow tree was the stocky figure of Mr. Chao. He was crossing the slender single-plank bridge, and she could see that he was wearing a fine gown of dark blue cloth.

Mr. Chao owned the Mao Yuan Wine Shop in a neighboring village and was the only scholar and man of parts within a radius of thirty *li*. He was a man of learning and a lover of the imperial tradition. He owned the ten volumes of the *Romance of the Three Kingdoms* with commentaries by Chin Sheng-t'an. He had read them so often, word by word, that he was not only able to repeat the names of the Five Great Generals but he even knew that Huang Chung was also called Han Seng and that Ma Ch'ao was known as Meng Ch'i.* After the Revolution he wound his queue on top of his head like a Taoist. If only Chao Tzu-lung (one of the great generals) were living, he used to sigh, the world would not be so evil a place. But Mrs. Seven Catty's sharp eyes had already discovered that Mr. Chao no longer looked like a Taoist priest. The front of his head shone shaven and clear. On the very top she distinguished a round patch of black hair. Enough. She knew now for certain that the Emperor was back on his Throne and that queues were again required. There was more. She knew too that her husband must be in danger indeed, for Mr. Chao didn't wear his fine blue gown just like that. He wore it only to celebrate some particularly happy event in his own life or some calamity in the life of an enemy. He had worn it twice only during the

*This is equivalent to praising an American's erudition because he knows the story of George Washington and the cherry tree.

last three years, once when the pockmarked Ah Szu, who had quarreled with him, fell sick, and the second time, when the eldest Mr. Lu, who had once wrecked his wine shop, died. Now, portentously, he was wearing it for a third time. Either some good had befallen him, or some disaster befallen an enemy. One day two years back Seven Catty had imbibed more than heavily and in his cups had cast serious aspersions on the Seventh Mr. Chao's birth. Mrs. Seven Catty remembered all this in a flash and her fears for her husband rose sharply in her breast. No wonder her heart beat so strangely and so quickly!

All the people at their tables rose as Mr. Chao approached. Pointing with their chopsticks to the rice, they called to him: "Would you be pleased to dine with us, Master Chao?"

"Please, please, go right ahead with your dinner," he said, nodding to them all but going on to the table of Seven Catty. Everyone fluttered excitedly. But Mr. Chao just continued, smiling and murmuring, "Please, please, go right ahead," looking over the food on the table before him as he did so.

"Those vegetables smell good. . . ." he began. He was standing directly behind Seven Catty, facing the latter's wife. He looked up from the food to them, and his tone changed abruptly.

"Have you heard the news?"

"The Emperor is back on the Throne," replied Seven Catty glumly.

With anxious looks at Mr. Chao, Mrs. Seven Catty smiled wanly. "When shall the Imperial amnesty come if the Emperor is again on his Throne?" she asked.

"Amnesty . . . ?" repeated Mr. Chao. "Oh, yes, the amnesty. I suppose that will come bye and bye." He glared at Seven Catty's head.

"But where is your queue, Seven Catty, where is your

queue? That's the important question. In the times of the Long Hairs,* you know, it was 'Lose your head to save your hair; lose your hair to save your head!' "

Neither Seven Catty nor his wife could read, so the historical reference made no impression upon them, but they knew it must be important and true if the learned Seventh Mr. Chao said it. Both began to feel as though they had already been sentenced to death, and their ears began to hum with fear. Both were speechless.

"So comes degeneration, one generation after another. . . ." broke in Grandmother Nine Catty. "The Long Hairs today simply cut off people's queues, making them look neither like Buddhist monks nor like Taoist priests. Were the Long Hairs in the old days like this? I've lived seventy-nine years and I've lived enough now. The Long Hairs in the old days used to wrap their heads in red satin and let it hang on down, down to the heels . . . princes wore yellow satin. . . . I've lived long enough now."

Mrs. Seven Catty rose uneasily. "What can we do now?" she murmured almost to herself. "He's the family's main support. . . ."

Mr. Chao shook his head. "There's nothing to be done," he said, "nothing to be done." He shook his head some more. "What could be worse? To be without a queue! It is written clearly in the book, word for word. No matter how many in the family depend on him."

As soon as Mrs. Seven Catty heard it was written in the book, she gave up all hope. Now thoroughly frightened, she suddenly turned on her husband in wrath, and, shaking her chopsticks under his nose, she shouted: "This wretched corpse! Now you'll get just what you deserve. When the re-

---

*The Taiping rebels, who unsuccessfully challenged the Manchu Dynasty in the mid-nineteenth century.

bellion began I told him to stop poling his boat. I told him not to go into town anymore. But he would go. Soon his queue was gone. His queue had been so shining black before—but now he looks neither like a monk or a Taoist. This convict here, he did it!" she screamed, "and he shall suffer for it. But what will become of us because of a convict-corpse like this?"

When Mr. Chao came, all the other villagers had left their food and crowded around Seven Catty's table to listen. Seven Catty knew that he was the principal character in the scene, and he was equally aware that it was most inglorious to be scolded thus by his wife in front of all his neighbors. He lifted his hand and said slowly:

"Now you're saying 'I told you so'—"

"Living corpse of a jail-bird!" she retorted.

Among all the listeners, most kindly was Mrs. Pa I, who stood behind Mrs. Seven Catty with her little two-year-old son, whose father had died before he was born, in her arms. She felt sorry for Seven Catty and spoke up.

"Let bygones be bygones, Mrs. Seven Catty. We're only humans, not gods. How are we to know the future? And didn't you yourself remark that he wasn't at all bad-looking without his queue? Besides, there is no notice yet from the magistrate . . ."

Mrs. Seven Catty felt her blood rising hot to her very ears. She could not listen to another word, but, swinging her shaking chopsticks around to point at Mrs. Pa I's nose, she shouted: "What do you mean by that? How could I speak such rubbish? Everybody saw me cry for three whole days. Even Little Six Catty cried. . . ." Little Six Catty had just finished her rice and held out her bowl howling for more. Her voice only seemed to heighten her mother's rage. Mrs. Seven Catty brought her chopsticks down on the little girl's head between her two braids. "Who asked you anything, you . . . you husband-stealing widow!"* The bowl clattered to the ground and broke in several pieces as it glanced off a loose stone. Seven Catty jumped from his seat and began picking up the pieces and fitting them together. "Rape of her mother!" he growled and gave little Six Catty a box across her ear. She lay down on the ground and wailed. Grandmother Nine Catty picked her up and holding her hand walked off. "So comes degeneration, one generation after another . . ." she muttered.

Mrs. Pa I was also good and angry by now. "Why take it out on your daughter, Mrs. Seven Catty?"

Mr. Chao watched the scene with a quiet, contented smile. But Mrs. Pa I's remark that no official announcement had yet come irritated him vastly. "What of it?" he said, "The army will come soon and the Emperor's defender is the Great General Chang. Do you know he is a descendant of Chang I-te of Yen? He uses a spear like a serpent eighteen feet long and he can fight ten thousand soldiers singlehanded! Who dares to stand up to him?" He held his two fists up in front of him as though they were eighteen-foot serpents and shook them at Mrs. Pa I. "Can *you* resist him?"

Mrs. Pa I, her child clasped close to her, trembled as Mr. Chao came nearer to her, his face covered with beads of perspiration and his eyes bulging. She was so frightened that she took off through the crowd and Mr. Chao followed her. The villagers thought Mrs. Pa I was only getting what she deserved for meddling. They respectfully opened a path for Mr. Chao to pass through. Not a few hid behind their fellows lest he look too closely at their own heads, but the Seventh Mr. Chao looked neither to left nor right until he reached the tallow tree. "Who can stand up to him?" he

---

*Invective or other disparaging remarks would be frequently addressed to a third person or even to an inanimate object. Here Six Catty becomes the innocent object of Mrs. Seven Catty's wrath against Mrs. Pa-I.

flung over his shoulder, and majestically he stalked off across the plank bridge.

Still standing where he'd left them in a knot around Seven Catty's table, the villagers turned the matter over in their minds. There was no chance, surely, of resisting the Great Chang. Surely all hope was lost for Seven Catty now. Not a few were pleased at his predicament. Seven Catty was often proud and haughty with his long pipe in his mouth when he told them the latest news from town. He would not be so proud of himself now that he faced the threat of the Emperor's displeasure. Everyone wanted to say something but nobody could think of anything to say. Amid a general murmur everyone walked to his own hut, while swarms of mosquitoes moved with them, going back to their nests under the outstretched boughs of the tallow tree. Doors were closed, and before long the village was asleep. Groaning to herself, Mrs. Seven Catty gathered up bowls, utensils, the table, and the stools, and took them inside. She too was soon asleep. Seven Catty, with the broken pieces of Six Catty's bowl in his hands, sat down on the threshold and lighted his long pipe. But he was too upset and too confused to smoke. The flowing tobacco quickly turned to gray ash in the little bronze bowl. He felt that he was in great danger and tried to think of a way out of the mess. But he could not think clearly.

Queues. Where is my queue? Serpent spears eighteen feet long. Degeneration one generation after another. The Emperor is back on his Throne! This broken bowl will have to be mended in town. Who can stand up to him? It is written word for word in the book. Rape his mother!

Next morning Seven Catty poled his boat out of Luchen into town as usual. He came back with his long bamboo pipe and Little Six Catty's bowl. At supper he told Grandmother Nine Catty that it had taken sixteen brass clamps to patch and that each one had cost three cash, making forty-eight cash altogether.

"Degeneration, degeneration . . ." replied the old lady irritably. "I've lived long enough. Even a small clamp costs three cash. Were clamps like this in the olden days? Clamps in old days. . . . I've lived seventy-nine years now. . . ."

Seven Catty went into town every day as usual, but at home and in the village much had changed. His neighbors avoided him and no longer gathered to hear him tell the latest news from town. His wife was barely ever civil to him and always called him "the jailbird." More than ten days thus went by. Finally one evening Seven Catty came home and quickly saw that his wife had recovered her old pleasant look and seemed to be quite satisfied with the world.

"Any news?" she asked.

"I didn't hear any."

"Is the Emperor really back on the Throne?"

"Nobody said anything about it."

"Not in Prosperity Wine Shop either?"

"No one said anything about it."

"Then I'm sure that he's not on the Throne at all!" said Mrs. Seven Catty triumphantly. "I passed Mr. Chao's wine shop today. He sat there reading with his queue rolled up again and he wasn't wearing his blue gown!"

"So . . . ?"

"Do you think he won't sit on the Throne then?"

"Probably not."

Seven Catty once more basked in the respect and esteem of his wife and neighbors. When summer came they again took their meals sitting outside and greeted each other with smiles when they met, and once more Seven Catty related the day's news as he smoked his long bamboo pipe. Grandmother Nine Catty passed her eightieth birthday strong as ever and as volubly critical of the times. Little Six Catty's two tiny braids were now rolled into a single fat queue, and she now helped her mother around the house despite her newly bound feet. Often she could be seen limping around outside the house with her small, uncertain steps, holding a bowl patched with sixteen brass clamps.

Cho Wen-chün

(A Play in Three Acts, Abridged)

The Characters

Cho Wen-chün, twenty-four years old
Hung Shiao, her maidservant, about twenty
Cho Wang-sun, Wen-chün's father, over forty
Chen Cheng, her father-in-law, also over forty
Wang Chi, a younger man, mayor of Ning Chung and a
friend of Hsiang-ju
Szu-ma Hsiang-ju, a young man of thirty
Wen-chün's brother
Wen-chün's sister
Chou Ta, a servant
Chin Erh, a servant

Time: The early years of the reign of Han Wu-ti.*
Place: A suburb of the Lin Chiung district, Szechwan.

*Han Wu-ti ascended the throne in 140 B.C.

Kuo Mo-jo

ACT I

A garden pool in the moonlight, surrounded by trees and artificial hills and rock formations. Above and behind the latter can be seen the decorated eaves of the roof of the house. On the right bank of the pool stands a spacious pavilion called Yang Hsu Loh. It has broad windows and a wide verandah. It opens into the main house through a moon gate on the right. The main house cannot be seen. There are several chairs of bamboo and a table in the main room of the pavilion. On the side facing the pool there are protective railings over which you can lean and look either into the water or up into the sky. Among the trees there are many magnolias richly blooming.

  Cho Wen-chün and her maid, Hung Shiao, enter through the side door.

HUNG SHIAO: Oh, what a beautiful moon! It draws the whole world into its light!

WEN-CHÜN: Maybe we're late. The moon is now directly overhead in the sky.

HUNG SHIAO: But the moon is also in the bottom of the pool.

WEN-CHÜN: Why is the lute still silent?

HUNG-SHIAO: The same moon in two hearts. *(Sighs.)* Yet while you hold him to your heart, does he think the same of you?

WEN-CHÜN: Oh, you're joking again! *(Making as if to strike Hung Shiao)*

(The maid runs up the flight of stairs leading to the pavilion and Wen-chün runs after her. They chase each other around the room until finally Hung Shiao flings herself to her knees to beg her mistress's pardon.)

HUNG SHIAO: Forgive me, mistress, forgive me!

WEN-CHÜN: Ai-yo, you weak worm! The words fell smoothly enough when you spoke. Now that you've said them, you bow before me. I should only blemish my noble hand were I to strike you!

HUNG SHIAO *(gets up angrily and leans over the railing)*: Ai, yo!

you mistresses and ladies are so noble and strong. And since you are, why ask me, a mere maidservant, to do everything for you?

WEN-CHÜN: Oh, now you're angry. You're angry. *(Stroking her shoulder)*

HUNG SHIAO: How dare a slave be angry? We're footstools and beyond all provocation.

WEN-CHÜN: Oh, please do not be angry! Forgive my lack of restraint. . . . How fragrant the magnolias are!

HUNG SHIAO: Ay, fragrant only for the mistresses.

WEN-CHÜN: Strike me! Strike me and release your anger! *(Kneels down before Hung Shiao.)* Miss Hung Shiao, raise your hand and strike me, this bowing, humble maidservant!

HUNG SHIAO *(giggling despite herself):* Hm, you're really strong now!

WEN-CHÜN: My troubles lie in my weaknesses, otherwise I should long ago have escaped this crystal prison.

HUNG SHIAO *(gesturing for attention):* Listen! I seem to hear the lute. . . .

WEN-CHÜN *(seating herself next to Hung Shiao):* Don't deceive me. I heard nothing. Oh, how fragrant the magnolias are! Intoxicating! Their fragrance always makes me feel that I am leading a new life.

HUNG SHIAO: Did you not faint at the fragrance of the magnolias last year?

WEN-CHÜN: That would be entirely forgotten if you did not refer to it. Aye, magnolias truly were painful to me.

HUNG SHIAO: Why painful?

WEN-CHÜN: Have you forgotten, Hung Shiao . . . ?

HUNG SHIAO: What?

WEN-CHÜN: Four years ago when I was married, was it not when the magnolias were blooming? On the night before my marriage did we not both faint from weeping amid this same fragrance in this very pavilion?

HUNG SHIAO: Yes, I remember. It was all my fault. I discovered that Mr. Cheng was unlettered and I should not have let you know at once. You thought of suicide.

WEN-CHÜN *(wistfully):* I've always loved the magnolias. I love the white petals, the emerald leaves, and the pervading fragrance of them. Yet ever since my marriage this same fragrance makes me faint.

HUNG SHIAO: But you are quite all right this year.

WEN-CHÜN: I don't know why. Since you told me that we could hear his lute from here, I have come to this place every night. We wait and listen and we forget everything, even I my faintness. Now when I inhale the scent of the magnolias, I feel that my earlier life of virginal purity is coming back to me. I do not know the reason for it yet.

HUNG SHIAO: Perhaps it is because your Mr. Chen is dead.

WEN-CHÜN: It is almost midnight now. Why is the lute still silent?

HUNG SHIAO: The second watch of the night has not yet sounded.*

(Both remain silent for a brief pause.)

WEN-CHÜN: Listen! Isn't that it?

HUNG SHIAO: It is the wind whistling through the bamboo grove.

WEN-CHÜN: It seems to come from below. . . .

HUNG SHIAO: No, that is only the tinkle of the moon in the ripples of the pool.

WEN-CHÜN: It comes from far away.

HUNG SHIAO: . . . No. I hear nothing at all, not even the hungry cry of the owl nor the bark of the dog at the moon. . . .

WEN-CHÜN: Oh, nothing. It is really nothing. My ears are mocking me.

(Silence. The second watch sounds far off.)

*Midnight is the third watch.

HUNG SHIAO: Harken, mistress, the second watch.

WEN-CHÜN: Indeed, only the second watch. I have been worrying lest he be sick.

HUNG SHIAO: You are worrying about his health, mistress. He is truly ill. It is said that he left the Kingdom of Liang because of his illness.

WEN-CHÜN: And what is it?

HUNG SHIAO: Perhaps the poet's melancholy or perhaps the waning of the moon? Each night he played joyfully on the lute and during the day raced along the highroad on his white charger. Surely he cannot be seriously ill, but just as the moon fills out night after night until it reaches its capacity and wanes without seeming reason, so might his illness be due to loneliness.

WEN-CHÜN: A new diagnosis! You should be recognized as the woman Pien Chiao!*

HUNG SHIAO: You, indeed, should be the doctor.

WEN-CHÜN: Here you are again! When I read his poem on Tzu Hsu I recall that I thought the poet must indeed have been a man of ancient times. I never dreamed that he would be a native of our own West Shu† nor did I remotely imagine that he breathed precisely the same air with us here in Lin Chiung. Oh how fortunate we are! That so great a genius should be born in so secluded a spot as West Shu. The future will render him his place in the history of literature along with Ch'u Yüan and Chia Yi. His achievements will be unlimited! Oh, I hope he will heal rapidly and not die at the height of his life's powers like Ch'u Yüan and Chia Yi.

HUNG SHIAO: As it is, mistress, he will not die. He will live forever. Did you not just say he would win his place in history with Chu and Chia?

*A renowned physician of ancient times.
†Szechwan.

WEN-CHÜN: But Hung Shiao, I don't know why it should be—but there is so much that is unreasonable in the world. Many insignificant persons enjoy wealth, nobility, love life, and a happy death, while men of talent are always troubled with poverty, illness, and sorrow.

HUNG SHIAO: That is decreed by the immutable fates.

WEN-CHÜN: That is what I fail to understand. Why should the world be marred by unchallengeable fates? Take myself, for example. I am too cruelly toyed with by these forces of darkness. . . . I married Cheng under my father's orders. . . . Oh, I'm . . . I'm like a broken vase. . . .
(Bursts into tears.)

HUNG SHIAO: Mistress, mistress. . . .

WEN-CHÜN: You know, Hung Shiao, that I shall return to the Chengs no more. I will never see that old beast of a father-in-law again!

HUNG SHIAO: All the better that you do not go, mistress. Fortunate that you are free now.

WEN-CHÜN: Ai, all children are ruined by their parents!

HUNG SHIAO: Not necessarily.

WEN-CHÜN: Why not?

HUNG SHIAO: I cannot speak.

WEN-CHÜN: Speak! Why do you fear to speak?

HUNG SHIAO: If I speak you will be angry.

WEN-CHÜN: I will not be angry. Speak out!

HUNG SHIAO: Then I'll say–*(Pauses.)*

WEN-CHÜN: Why do you hesitate?

HUNG SHIAO: You won't be angry with me?

WEN-CHÜN: Oh, my silly Hung Shiao! I will not be angry.

HUNG SHIAO: Well, mistress, let us say rather that children ruin their parents. Why don't we develop our own lives instead of waiting for our parents to become persecutors of their children? I am an orphan and it is less difficult for me.

I decide on my own life, now and forever. That I should serve you for so many years is owing to the bond of love between us. Since you do not treat me as a slave I am content to accept the fate of a slave. Otherwise I. . . .

WEN-CHÜN: Speak no more, Hung Shiao. You are quite right, you know. From now on I'm going to listen to you and follow your advice.

HUNG SHIAO: You are always like this, mistress! You are really so modest, it embarrasses me. Everyone *should* develop his own life. Nobody should ever dictate to others what to do nor is anyone really capable of doing so. You are faced now, mistress, with a great trial. Read this—*(Hands Wen-chün a note.)*

(Wen-chün takes it and holds it out in the moonlight the better to read.)

WEN-CHÜN *(reading):*

"High over all four seas have I soared in search of my
     bride;
And I, the phoenix, have returned home to find her.
My heart is tortured with your nearness and your distance,
How can our paths be made to cross, how can the birds be
     mated?
Would that I might forever hold you clasped to me,
I, the phoenix, your bridegroom, shall follow no other,
For through the moonlight, you and I, heart to heart, will
     fly to our end."

Where did you get this, Hung Shiao?

HUNG SHIAO: Chin Erh gave it to me just a moment ago. He told me that when he went into town this morning he met Mr. Szu-ma Chang Chin at the hostel. Mr. Szu-ma asked after the player of the lute he had heard in our house. Chin Erh revealed to him that it was you. Upon hearing this Mr. Szu-ma detained him while he wrote this short note and asked him to deliver it to you. Since Chin Erh did not dare to call, he gave it to me.

WEN-CHÜN: He is indeed bold. Would there not be trouble if this note fell into my father's hands?

HUNG SHIAO: How will you answer him, mistress?

WEN-CHÜN: What answer do you think I can make? I certainly can't reply to a demand like this! Why did he not ask my father about this?

HUNG SHIAO (scornfully): You are still depending upon your father, mistress. What if he refuses?

WEN-CHÜN: Ai! I'm still a weakling. . . . Wait a bit, let me think some more.

HUNG SHIAO: Shh . . . someone's coming!

(They are both silent. Cho Wen-chün's younger sister and brother come in together from the side door carrying a red lantern. The girl is perhaps fifteen. The boy is about ten.)

BROTHER: Somebody is talking in the Yang Hsu Loh.

SISTER: That must be sister and Hung Shiao. Sister! We've searched everywhere for you!

WEN-CHÜN: Don't run. You'll fall into the pool.

(The boy and girl come up the steps into the pavilion and the boy rushes to Wen-chün.)

SISTER: Father is looking for you, sister.

BROTHER: Lie! Lie! She herself wants you to teach her the lute.

SISTER: Stop fibbing, you naughty brother!

BROTHER: You're the one who is fibbing!

WEN-CHÜN: Now don't quarrel, don't quarrel! Behave yourselves. You go on back and I shall come immediately.

BROTHER: No, I will not go. I want to wait for you.

SISTER: I won't go back alone either!

WEN-CHÜN: Then Hung Shiao, please go with sister.

HUNG SHIAO: Come on, Second Miss.

(They go down the steps together.)

SISTER: Listening for the lute again, Hung Shiao?

HUNG SHIAO: We are looking at the moon.

SISTER: I know, you are listening to the lute until the late hours. I know it quite well.

HUNG SHIAO: Don't go gossiping like that, Second Miss. . . .
(Both exit from the side door.)

WEN-CHÜN: Hasn't Father gone to bed yet?

BROTHER: No, not yet.

WEN-CHÜN: How did you know we were here?

BROTHER: We were unable to find you in your room. Second Sister believed you were here for she saw you come here these last two nights.

WEN-CHÜN: Has Father said anything?

BROTHER: He spoke of the feast tomorrow.

WEN-CHÜN: Who are invited?

BROTHER: Uncle Cheng, Mayor Wang, and another man . . . ai, he has a two-character surname.

WEN-CHÜN: A two-character surname?

BROTHER: Yes, they said he just recently arrived. Oh, I can't remember it. . . .

WEN-CHÜN *(brightly):* Oh, how wonderful if he really comes!

BROTHER: Do you know him, sister?

WEN-CHÜN: Silence!

(From left comes the sweet music of a lute. Soon it is accompanied by a tenor voice, singing sadly. Wen-chün and her brother stand as if transfixed by the sound, holding each other's hands tightly.)

THE VOICE:

Thin strands of willow shadows gently sway,
All about is like a dream-world.
Atop the city wall the second watch has sounded.

To the moon I strum my lute in song,
My heart and soul now full aroused.
Will I ever find a moon goddess
To ease my lonely life?

So sad, a life half-wasted,
No place to rest my soul.
Like an autumn leaf that bids its branch farewell,
I'm buffeted, the winds do shift me place to place.

Wearied to my depths of wandering,
My health now failing,
I've come at last to my natal soil—
My old hometown!
But this too, a city of sorrows.

Cities of sorrow, are they not everywhere?
Where does Utopia exist?
So many times have I thought, hefting up my mighty
  three-foot sword,
Send this soul of mine aloft.

(The singing stops . . .)
BROTHER: Why do you shed tears, sister?
(Wen-chün still listens.)
BROTHER: Why are you troubled, sister?
WEN-CHÜN: Oh—*(Recovers herself.)* It is late and growing cold.
Let us go back.
(They go down the stairs and stroll along the veranda.)
BROTHER: Do you know the gentleman with the two-charac-
ter surname?
WEN-CHÜN: Perhaps he is the Mr. Szu-ma who lives nearby
in the hostel.
BROTHER: Yes, yes, it is Szu-ma. Strange name. Dead horse!*
WEN-CHÜN *(smiling.)*: No, not dead horse, but Szu-ma.
BROTHER: Never mind, then, whether it's *sze ma* or *wu ma*,
how do you know him?

---

*A play on words. *Szu-ma* can sound as if it means "dead horse," or "four
horses," as in the sentence, "four or five horses." The actual characters used
carry neither meaning.

WEN-CHÜN: I don't know him. I only know he can play the lute . . .

BROTHER: Same as you can, sister!

WEN-CHÜN: . . . Can write poetry. . . .

BROTHER: Also like you!

WEN-CHÜN: Watch how you walk lest you fall.

BROTHER: Would you like me to sing you a song, sister?

WEN-CHÜN: Surely.

BROTHER (*dances around the edge of the pool and sings*):

Lady moon, in the sky, combing on her tresses
The river is her mirror.
Her reflection on the water
She, herself, on high.
Each to the other gazing,
Until a cloud in passing
    severs their connection.

(*They exit through the side door, but the boy's voice is still heard.*)

Sister moon, bathing in the water,
Many stars are peeking.
Sister moon, so vexed at this,
While they remain and blink at her,
Until a cloud in passing
    covers o'er the river.

End of Act I

ACT II
(Resume)
A bond of love between Chin Erh, the servant boy, and Hung Shiao is suggested in the early scenes of the act. Cho Wang-sun, father of Wen-chün, is seen to be a worshipper of wealth. The father of her late husband, Cheng Cheng, is shown to be a lecherous old man. He is a follower of Confucius and scarcely ever speaks without including one or more allusions to the master's sayings. But secretly he is scheming for the favors of his bereaved daughter-in-law. Both Cho and Cheng insist that in conformity with ancient custom Wen-chün should guard

*her virtue and her dignity by never marrying again. Cho celebrates a
feast in honor of Szu-ma Hsiang-ju, whom he despises as a poor man
but whom he honors because of Szu-ma's close friendship with Mayor
Wang. Szu-ma Hsiang-ju is late in coming. While waiting Mayor
Wang proposes a match between Wen-chün and his friend, Szu-ma.
The suggestion is politely turned aside.*

ACT III

*On the right is the back wall of the house of Cho Wang-sun. It is
whitewashed. A garden and buildings can be seen within. There is a
back door facing left which opens onto a raised platform with a stone
railing around it. From this, one descends to a stone landing and
thence to the road. In the left background, the city wall of Lin Chiung
is dimly visible. Willow trees line the road which runs into the city.
They extend to the door on the right and to the hostel on the left.
There is an open door leading from the hostel which faces the door to
Cho's house, and throughout the action the sound of a lute is heard
coming from there. It is late and the moon is again high. Chou Ta,
the elderly servant, is leaning on the stone railing looking at the moon.
Chin Erh, the younger servant, comes through the back door, evidently
in some haste.*

CHOU *(Seeing Chin Erh):* **Where are you off to?**
CHIN: **Oh, it's you. You surprised me.**
CHOU: **Where are you going so late at night?**
CHIN: **Just for a walk. I haven't any place to go.**
CHOU: **You appeared to be quite happy tonight, Chin Erh.
Are you indeed possessed of some happiness?**
CHIN: **What happiness might I have? What can we servants
hope for? Hai, Chou Ta, for us servants fifty years lived can
be reckoned as only twenty-five in a normal life.**
CHOU: **What do you mean?**
CHIN: **Others may have all the days and all the nights to
themselves. We may have the nights only and even most of**

this free time is robbed by the irresistible demands of sleep.

CHOU: Hm, you sound as if you were talking in a play. The speeches of servants in plays are all poet's illusions. You—may have something of a poet in you!

CHIN: Your tongue is always so sharp, Chou Ta!

CHOU: It is not that I am sharp. I did not like the way you spoke of the "irresistible demands of sleep." During the day we are slaves and all others kings; we are pigs, others are divinities. Only at night are divinities and kings leveled down to slaves and pigs, not a hair nor a horn more. I look forward to the fair equality of sleep each night. You seem to be bored by it. What do you think I am doing here, Chin Erh?

CHIN: Looking at the moon? Listening to the lute?

CHOU: Hmph. I'm not a poet like you. I'm out here wishing for sleep. I cannot sleep these nights. Miss Wen-chün enjoys playing the lute, but she seldom plays at night. But that man living across there *(lowering his voice and pointing to the hostel)* whom they call dead horse or dead ox, he's always tinkling away from evening until the cocks crow. How I hate it! Several times I've had a mind to stop him. But why should these great gentlemen worry about the sufferings of servants?

CHIN: He may refuse to see you should you go to him. If he does not want to stir he will not, even should there be an earthquake! How they tried to get him to the feast today! When he finally came, looking upon our master and Mr. Cheng like so many flies—and they're almost like living gods to me!—he immediately began playing on Miss Wen-chün's green lute. He was so absorbed in it that nobody could call him in nor move him by their applause. Heaving several sighs when he finished, he left the feast untouched and went away. It seems he missed having somebody to appreciate him. Queer fellow, that.

He never dreamed that a female Po Ya* was listening to him all the time. Mistress Wen-chün said, "He seems to be playing on my heart although 'tis the lute that is in his hands. I tremble at his music." Hung Shiao told me this herself.

CHOU: Tremble? Good and well, tremble! Thus the lute is transformed into a bed! Ah, my boy, you are fortunate too, I see. Hung Shiao is indeed good to you.

CHIN: Hai, Chou Ta, how did you know my trouble? I am unable to sleep nights. It is not the lute that disturbs me but thoughts of her.

CHOU: Whom can you blame for this but your own foolish self? Why not ask for her hand?

CHIN: Oh, but didn't I? She always replies that we must wait. She says there is no freedom for slaves. We must either beg leave of the master or else elope. As for asking leave, I dare not and she deigns not. She says we must wait an opportunity to elope. I tell you this, Chou Ta, because you are unlike the others. You know I am helpless before her.

CHOU: Foolish boy! Where and how can you elope? Have the female's charms driven you from your senses? Your wisdom is like the size of a sparrow. The officials have greater strength than you. They will arrive at your destination even sooner than you do! Besides, other than slaving, what means have we to feed wives? Elope! You think of it too lightly, my boy!

CHIN: Impossible to elope?

CHOU: Show me how it can be done!

CHIN: Then I'm done with! I'm done with! I shall go insane! Oh! Oh!

(He runs around the platform, hands to his head.)

*Po Ya, whose surname was Yu, was a famous flute player of the Chou Dynasty whose friend, Chung Chi, was his most appreciative listener. When Chung died, Po Ya played no more.

CHOU: What are you doing, Chin Erh? What's the matter with you? *(Chin weeps.)* Are you crazy?

CHIN: I wish . . . I'd rather . . . rather be insane. . . .

CHOU: Humph, you *are* talking like a madman. Why weep?

CHIN: One thing I will tell you, Chou Ta, but you must not tell others.

CHOU: It is not for me to carry tales. Have I told anyone of the meeting between you and Hung Shiao that night?

CHIN: Thank you! You have never told. Beside Hung Shiao I believe in you alone.

CHOU: Then tell me.

CHIN: Oh, you don't know, Chou Ta. The other day at this very place I met Mr. Szu-ma. He gave me a note. Just now Hung Shiao gave me a note to be delivered to him. She told me it was the reply of our Mistress. Hung Shiao asked me to make preparations for our elopement for we will soon have an opportunity to go. We will meet at the hostel with Mr. Szu-ma and run for Chengtu. And according to you, I am simply dreaming mad dreams! When shall my suffering end if there can be no escape? Oh. . . . *(Weeps.)*

CHOU *(after a pause):* Foolish boy! You will not help matters by weeping. Where is the letter? Have you delivered it?

CHIN: No, it is still in my pocket.

CHOU *(slapping his thigh):* Ha ha! You shut your door to the kindly fates and pull the stars from heaven to use as fire stones. You are foolish indeed! Foolish indeed!

CHIN *(Uncomprehending and angry):* Don't mock me! What good fortune can I have?

CHOU: I, mock you? Rather say I am filled with sympathy for you. Show me the letter.

CHIN *(takes it out):* Can you read it?

CHOU: I? Read? do not be so foolish! But our master will be able to read it.

CHIN: What of that?

CHOU: Show it to him!

CHIN: You suggest that I betray them?

CHOU: Yes, that is where the fates are preparing good fortune for you.

CHIN: But Chin Erh is no villain. How could I answer to my Hung Shiao for such a deed? What will benefit me should I break the bonds of love between others? How could I do so vile a thing?

CHOU: You are still befuddled. What kind of a man do you think Mr. Szu-ma is? Nothing but a frivolous ne'er-do-well. He can write poetry, but can he boast the prosperity of Mr. Cheng? Mr. Cheng has money and leisure. He can command the riches of a nation without the least effort by selling a single vase or an old book. See how prosperous he is! Moreover do you know that Mr. Szu-ma is ill and that his illness is due to promiscuity? He will be the ruin of our mistress and of us if we run to him! You will save her if you reveal this plan to the master!

CHIN: What else?

CHOU: In the second place it is not at all improbable that he would seduce your Hung Shiao with his frivolous and sensuous ways . . .

CHIN: Oh, how could he do that!

CHOU: . . . So you'll save Hung Shiao too if you tell the master now.

CHIN: How will that benefit me if still I do not marry her?

CHOU: Listen calmly. You will gain yours in the end. You know our master despises these literary men. It is only because Mr. Szu-ma is a friend of Mayor Wang that he pays him any respect at all. Our master places great store on the laws of the family and the maintenance of its virtue and its position. Should Wen-chün elope that will provoke him to death. So you will save the master too if you tell him.

CHIN: That's all the same to me.

CHOU: All the same! Your share would come afterward, you fool! Your purpose in helping Szu-ma is to get Hung Shiao for yourself. If he seduces her before you succeed, what will remain for you? When you are arrested—and you will be— all the torture and punishment will fall upon you and Hung Shiao. You two low slaves! You will be whipped, mark you! But, on the other hand, you will surely win the master's pleasure if you tell him. You will win his consent for one hundred like Hung Shiao! That is where the benefit will come to you!

CHIN: You really think so? *(He is impressed but still doubtful.)*

CHOU: Ah, foolish lad! *(Tapping him on the shoulder)* You are a dull bird! What are you dreaming? Wake up! How could it be otherwise? How can you suffer any disadvantage? Are you prepared to sacrifice everything for a vagrant poet? Or will you benefit yourself by blocking his evil designs?

CHIN: You're right. I was dreaming. I'm awake now. Thank you! Thank you, I'm going at once! *(He starts off.)*

CHOU: Where are you off to?

CHIN: Off to tell the master.

CHOU: And your evidence?

CHIN: Oh—I'd forgotten. Yes, the letter. Give it to me and I will go. It is almost the third watch now.

CHOU: Go ahead. I'll stop them if they come out. I will benefit likewise since you can tell the master that I planned this with you.

CHIN: Yes, I know. *(Exit)*

CHOU: Ah! How good I feel! *(He strolls across the platform, stops, yawns.)* Getting sleepy now. But I'll have to stay here and see what happens. *(The third watch sounds from the city wall.)* The third watch! And they're not here yet.
(The flutter of steps approaching the door is heard.)

VOICE *(from inside):* Chin Erh must be waiting impatiently. Do you hear him sighing, mistress?

(Chou Ta walks upstage to the back of the platform. Wen-chün and Hung Shiao enter.)

HUNG SHIAO: Chin Erh, how long have you been waiting?

CHOU: I am not Chin Erh. I'm Chou Ta.

HUNG SHIAO *(surprised):* But where has Chin Erh gone?

CHOU: To deliver the letter.

HUNG SHIAO: To whom? For whom?

CHOU: For the mistress to the old master.

HUNG SHIAO *(She is shocked and angry. Wen-chün blanches.)* Chin Erh, villain! . . . I never thought that he. . . .

CHOU: Villain! Villain, indeed! He showed me the letter our mistress wrote for Mr. Szu-ma and discussed it with me. He said he wanted to tell the old master about it. I said, 'How can you answer for that to the mistress?' He replied that he had thought it over and over but his conscience would not permit him to keep the matter secret. He declared that Mr. Szu-ma was evil, frivolous, and wanton. He could not let our mistress marry him. He wanted to save her, therefore he had to disclose the letter. Again, he said that if our mistress should marry Mr. Szu-ma, our old master would certainly die of anger and distress. Thus to save our master he was forced to tell. He said he had to be loyal to our master and to the mistress. He did not want to listen to the evil instigations of Hung Shiao and ruin the house of Cho and he did not want to break the law but wanted to save himself from crime. He regretted bitterly that he had accepted bribes from Mr. Szu-ma and plotted with him against our mistress. To make up for his evil deed he even wanted to set fire to the hostel but I stopped him. I told him the hostel was an official building and if it burned it would be indeed a serious matter and even so Mr. Szu-ma would be quite safe for he could run away. So he did not set fire to it but insisted he would bring the letter to the old master. I could not hinder him. I see, Mistress, you. . . .

(Uproar inside the house. The patter of hurried steps and indistinguishable voices. Cho, Cheng, and Chin Erh enter.)

CHO: Heaven and earth are shattered and destroyed! Heaven and earth are shattered and destroyed! Where are you going, Hung Shiao? *(Sees Wen-chün.)* And you, Wen-chün! So learned as you are I never believed that you would defame the name of our family so shamelessly! What is this wild nonsense in this letter? *(Thrusts the letter at Wen-chün. It falls to the ground. Cheng picks it up.)*

CHENG *(goes up to Wen-chün):* Do not be too angered, honorable relative. The ancient sage has well said: 'Only women and people of the lower classes are difficult to keep.' I see that we cannot blame Wen-chün for good or for evil. Read you from the letter that it was Hung Shiao who persuaded her to listen to the lute. The poem "Phoenix Looking for a Bride" was received through Chin Erh from Hung Shiao and it was she who delivered it. It was Hung Shiao who handed the reply to Chin Erh and arranged for Wen-chün to escape. To me it is clear that Hung Shiao is guilty of everything. "What goes on in the inner apartment may not be told." But I see that their crime is still only in their intentions. Let us see how it can be smoothed over. . . . Ah, Wen-chün! *(Turns to her.)* You spoke in your letter of the decay of the family and the restraints of our traditions. But is it truly worth your "body of gold and precious stones" to follow that wanton man of letters? You have indeed slandered me in some of your remarks, but I shall not hold this against you. It is common for young people to misunderstand. We should "conceal the evil and spread the good" of people. Yet I seek to break through your stubbornness so I shall venture to tell you what kind of a man Szu-ma Chang Ching is. Do you truly believe him the noblest and kindest of poets? Then you are a victim of your own illusions. When he was in the Kingdom of Liang he submerged himself in wine and women. He was finally obliged to return home poverty-stricken and diseased. Moreover, he is now penniless and depends entirely upon our mayor, His Excellency Wang. Is it worth your life to deliver yourself up to such a man as this? His knowledge is "flowery but not fruitful." He is "shallow and useless" in his deportment. He is boastful and frivolous and vain of his talents. He has nothing but the four walls around him. Is he worth your love? "Ah, Heaven has no pity and delivers upon me, a poor single man, a catastrophe!" Unfortunately, my son died too soon. Yet my property is surely enough to offer you the joys of every pleasure. But if you do not desire to go, then you would do well to retain your purity. How can you insult your own body of gold and jade and commit such crimes against tradition and custom? You are. . . .

CHO: Now is no time to reason with her! I desire nothing further, lest more be added to my burden of ill fortune in owning so disobedient a daughter. I desire only her speedy death. *(Addresses Wen-chün.)* You coquette, you slayer of our family name! Die if you have any sense of shame! *(Thrusts a sword toward Wen-chün.)*

WEN-CHÜN *(breaks her silence, speaks resolutely):* Just a moment. Spare your anger.

CHO: What are you saying? To whom do you speak?

WEN-CHÜN: I have always behaved before you as a dutiful daughter. Now I shall act like a human being.

CHO *(waving his arms):* Worse and worse! Rebellious! *(Rushes toward Wen-chün as if to strike her. Cheng grasps his arm and stops him.)*

WEN-CHÜN *(calmly):* One of you accuses me of breaking ancient customs and traditions. The other asks me to die. You are the ones who should die!

CHO: You—*(Attempts to tear loose from Cheng.)*

WEN-CHÜN: You say I shatter the old. I say I'm starting the

new! You old men and your old traditions have no claim on women and on our youth!

CHO *(still struggling to break loose):* Why are you holding on to me? You old turtle! You wanted to seduce my daughter.

WEN-CHÜN *(points at Cheng):* Cheng, answer me truly. You with your long train of wives, you still seek after flesh like an unsatiated bloodsucker. How dare you speak before people about others? Have you not yourself ruined all the traditions you talk about? Has the family not putrefied for your sake? Where is your sincerity and your usefulness while you charge others with frivolity? I shall state myself quite plainly. You always sought after me, to keep me in your house. Why then should you come to my door at midnight?

CHENG: No such thing! You lie, you slander me!

CHO: Shame! Shame a thousandfold! This whore will enrage me till I burst in death!

WEN-CHÜN I do not believe that women may not marry again when men are free to do so. Mine is the command of my conscience. *(Turns to Cho.)* Father!

CHO: Who is your father? I shall die of rage and shame!

WEN-CHÜN: You have no right to command me to die. You helped bring me into the world but even that is the trickery of nature! No. I have my own life now and shall not take it at your behest. Despite your curse I shall live it fully. *(Turns to Hung Shiao.)* Sister Hung Shiao, let us travel together and trample down the thorns. Give me that sword, the better to clear them from our path. *(Grasps it and takes Hung Shiao by the hand. Hung Shiao refuses to move.)*

CHO *(spluttering with rage):* I'll die of it! I'll die of it! Chin Erh! Chou Ta! Bind that shrew! Oh—*(Collapses in Cheng's arms.)*

WEN-CHÜN: Come near us if you dare!

(Chin Erh trembles. Chou Ta makes as if to move toward Wen-chün. She gestures threateningly with the sword.)

CHENG: You are going too far, Wen-chün. You can make yourself clear without using weapons. You should set a good example to your brother and sister.

WEN-CHÜN: I am an excellent model for them!

CHENG: Will you leave them like this? They will cry for you and miss you!

WEN-CHÜN: When they awaken tell them to come to the hostel. I have a new brother for them there.

CHENG: And your duties as a daughter?

WEN-CHÜN: My duties are those of a human being. To follow you blindly is not filial piety.

CHENG: Are you not afraid of being mocked?

WEN-CHÜN: I believe the future will applaud me.

CHENG: There is wealth and ease. . . .

WEN-CHÜN: Don't speak of these humiliating things before me. Come, Hung Shiao, come!

(Hung Shiao has been standing all through these interchanges with downcast face and hanging head. When Wen-chün calls her, she lifts her head slowly.)

HUNG SHIAO: Chin Erh, Chin Erh, come! *(Chin moves up to her slowly, shamedly.)* Give me your sword, mistress. *(With a swift movement she takes the sword from Wen-chün's hand.)* Chin Erh, you slave, you pitiful slave. I loved you, yet you are pitiful, a pitiful slave. Let me free you now! *(Plunges the sword into Chin's breast.)*

CHIN *(falls with a gasping cry):* Oh Hung Shiao . . . it was Chou Ta . . . Chou . . . *(Collapses, dies.)*

CHOU TA *(runs toward the door):* How horrible, how horrible!

CHENG: They have gone mad! It is dangerous! They are mad! *(Pulls Cho behind him through the door. Slams it shut.)*

HUNG SHIAO *(dragging Chin's body down from the landing into the road):* Ha Ha! Are you truly dead? You slave whom I loved? You have escaped with me at last! *(Looks up at Wen-chün who has followed her, dazed.)* We shall live forever, mistress. I shall follow you always! We shall live forever—*(Chin's body is stretched out on the ground clear in the moonlight.)* Oh, you beloved slave, why you? Your face defies the moon for fairness and your hair is like the shadowed clouds for darkness. You have the meek soul of a sheep and your eyes are transparent like the stars. Now the stars have fallen into the darkness and the shackles on your neck have been broken. You have escaped with me at last, my beloved! The hostel is before us, mistress. My soul shall follow you there. . . . *(Thrusts the sword into her own breast, falls across the body of Chin Erh.)*

WEN-CHÜN *(falling to the ground and lifting Hung Shiao's head into her lap, weeping):* Hung Shiao! Hung Shiao! Hung Shiao, oh Hung Shiao! Have you gone? Is my life worthy of your sacrifice? Hung Shiao! Hung Shiao! Have you gone? Shall our wedding feast be your funeral? *(Holds up Hung Shiao's head and cries to the moon.)* Go quickly, pale moon! I am thirsty for sunlight. Sunlight, my light and my life, why do you not shine? Oh my Hung Shiao, my Hung Shiao! Shall I and my beloved be united only to bury you together? Hung Shiao, must you die? *(Buries her head in Hung Shiao's breast, weeping, sobbing bitterly.)*

(The sound of the lute stops. The silence is oppressive. The sound of the music has been scarcely noticeable during the scene but one misses it as soon as it stops.)

HUNG SHIAO *(opening her eyes . . . in a failing voice):* Mistress, he . . . the man is not dying. He comes. . . . *(Faints, dies.)*

(Szu-ma Hsiang-ju comes out of the hostel in a long gown that trails the ground. Wen-chün raises her head and looks at him. He stops and they look at each other for a long time. The curtain comes slowly down.

End

YÜ TA-FU

Intoxicating Spring Nights

1

During the half year that I spent in Shanghai idle as the result of being out of a job, I was forced to change my lodging three times. At the start I went into a sort of voluntary
imprisonment south of Bubbling Well Road in a cell the size
of a birdcage into which the sun never shone. Apart from a
few ferocious tailors who were more like robbers or petty
thieves, the inhabitants of this prison-like dwelling were all
wretched and obscure writers. For that reason I nicknamed
the place "Yellow Grub Street." After living a month in
Grub Street a sudden increase in the rent forced me to cart
my few battered books off and move near the Racecourse
into a tiny hotel whose owner I knew. Later on, life became
full of annoyances here also, and I was obliged to move
again. I found a tiny room in the slums facing Jihsin Alley
on Dent Road in the quarter north of Garden Bridge and
transferred myself there.

These rows of houses on Dent Road measured only about
fifteen feet from the ground to the top of the roof. The room

Translated by George A. Kennedy.

which I occupied on the second floor was, of course, frightfully low, so low that if a man stood on the floor and stretched himself, his hands would go straight through the grimy roof. From the narrow alley in front one step through the door of the house brought you into the room occupied by the owner. Edging your way a few feet among piles of rags, tin cans, bottles, and bits of machinery, you found leaning against the wall a ladder with a number of broken rungs. By poking the top of the ladder up through a hole two feet square, you could get into the upstairs. A dark, gloomy attic, no larger than a cat's forehead to begin with, had been partitioned off by the owner to form two tiny cubicles. The one in front was occupied by a girl who worked in a cigarette factory; mine was the diminutive room at the head of the ladder. Inasmuch as the front lodger was obliged to pass in and out through this room, the monthly rent on it was slightly less than that on the outer room.

My landlord was a bent old man of about fifty, with a sallow face lit by a dark oily gleam. One eye was larger than the other, his cheekbones were very prominent, and the wrinkles in his forehead and cheeks were stuffed with coal dust which his morning wash seemed unable to remove. He rose each day at eight or nine o'clock, indulged in a spell of coughing, swung a couple of bamboo baskets over his shoulder, and went out. Around three or four in the afternoon he returned, generally with the same empty baskets. Whenever he did have a load, it consisted merely of rags, bottles, broken machinery, and the like. On such evenings he would buy himself a little wine, and, sitting on the edge of his bed, would pour forth a torrent of confused and unintelligible speech.

My first meeting with my fellow lodger next door took place in the afternoon of the day I moved in. It was after five o'clock on a day near the end of a swiftly passing

spring. I lighted a candle and began putting out the worn
volumes that I had just brought over from the hotel. I first
arranged them in two square piles, one somewhat larger
than the other. On the top of the larger pile I placed two
picture frames, each about two feet long. All the rest of my
possessions had been sold and this pile of books and the two
frames had therefore to serve me as a writing-desk by day
and as a bed at night. After laying the boards of the picture
frames on the larger pile, I sat down on the smaller pile,
facing my table built of books, and smoked with my back toward the opening for the ladder.

I was smoking and gazing idly at the candle flame, when I
heard a sudden movement of the ladder. Turning my head I
saw nothing but an enlarged projection of my own shadow,
but, although I could distinguish nothing, my sense of hearing told me plainly that someone was ascending. After I had
stared fixedly into the darkness for several seconds, a pale
round face and half of a slender female form finally came
into view. I realized at once that this must be my next-door
neighbor. When I had come looking for a room, the old
landlord had told me that besides himself the only other
person in the house was a factory girl in an upstairs room. I
had settled on the room immediately because of the low rent
in the first place, and, in the second place, because of the
fact that there would be no other women and children in
the house.

I waited now until the person coming up had stepped off
the ladder, then stood up and nodded to her.

"Pardon me. I just moved in today. I hope we'll get on all
right."

She listened to me, but made no reply. After giving me a
long serious look from her lacquer-black eyes, she walked
over to her door, unlocked it, and entered her room. From
this brief meeting with her, I felt—I could not say why—

that she was a girl very much to be pitied. The high-bridged nose, the pale oval face, the short slender body—all seemed to call in a special way for sympathy. I was then, however, too much concerned over the problems of my own existence to be able to spare time to pity a factory girl who, in any event, had a job. After a moment or two I was sitting again in a motionless position on my pile of books staring stupidly at the candle. I had lived in this slum for better than a week and during this time every morning she would go out to work at seven and return a little after six in the evening, always seeing me perched on top of a pile of books staring stupidly at the candle flame or the oil lamp. Doubtless her curiosity was aroused by my half-insane manner. One day as she came up from work and I had stood up, as on the first day, in order to let her pass by, she suddenly stopped, gave me a look, and stammered out timidly as though afraid of something.

"What books are these that you read here every day?" (She spoke in the soft Soochow dialect but as the impression made by her voice could not possibly be set down in writing, I can only translate her words into ordinary speech.)

Her question made me blush. In reality, although I had a few foreign books spread out before me as I sat idly day after day here, my mind was so confused that I could not grasp the meaning of a single sentence or phrase. Sometimes I allowed my imagination to fill in the white spaces between the lines with fanciful figures. Sometimes I merely turned over the pictures in the books and let them mingle themselves in grotesque phantasms. Through lack of sleep or proper food I was really already physically sick. Besides, my single treasure, a long quilted gown, was so unmercifully ragged that I could not go out for a walk in the daytime. In my room it was necessary to have either a candle or a lamp the whole time since no ray of light ever penetrated here.

Because of this not only was my physical condition quite abnormal but my eyes and leg muscles were to some extent atrophied.

These being the facts, I could not help blushing at her question and replied stammering.

"I'm not really reading. I merely put the books out because it would not look well for me to sit doing absolutely nothing."

At my reply she gave me another earnest look, made a gesture of incomprehension, and passed into her room as usual.

It would not be correct to say that I made no attempt whatever during these days to find a job, or that I did no work. At times, when my brain seemed slightly clearer, I had translated a few short poems from English and French as well as one or two short stories from German averaging less than four thousand characters each. At night when people were fast asleep, I had stolen noiselessly out to mail these to some newly established publishers. My hopes for securing a position anywhere had long since been completely blasted, so that this was the only remaining resource for my withered brain. If, by any chance, I should strike the fancy of the editors and have my translations published, I should be able to count on receiving a few dollars. Since moving to Dent Road, therefore, and up to the time of my first conversation with my neighbor, I had sent out manuscripts on three or four occasions.

2

Living amidst the bustle of the International Settlement of Shanghai, one is not readily conscious of the change in the seasons or of the passing of days. The only intimation I had after moving to the slums on Dent Road was the fact that the quilted gown I wore grew daily heavier and warmer. I said to myself, "Spring must be about over."

But in my penniless condition a pleasure trip was out of the question, and so I remained sitting idly in the eternal lamplight of that gloomy room. One day—I supposed it was afternoon—I was sitting thus when my fellow lodger came up with two paper packages in her hands. As I stood to let her pass, she placed one of the packages on my book-built table and said, "Those are some currant buns. Please take them. You can eat them tomorrow. I have some bananas here, besides. Won't you come into my room and eat them with me?"

I held the package for her while she opened her door and invited me to come in. After two weeks of this common life, she seemed to have come to the conclusion that I was an honest sort of fellow. I saw that the suspicion which had shown in her face at our first meeting had completely disappeared. On entering her room I had my first intimation that it was still light outside for she had a window that faced south. Rays of sunshine came through the window lighting up the tiny room, a bed constructed of two boards, a narrow table painted black, a rough wooden box, and a round stool. The bed had no mosquito net, but there were two clean blue quilts on it. On the table was a small tin box in which, I assumed, she kept her toilet articles as there were grease spots on the lid. She moved the few articles of old clothing—a wadded cotton coat, coarse cotton trousers, and the like—from the stool onto the bed and invited me to sit down. Her careful hospitality began to embarrass me somewhat, so I said, "We are just fellow lodgers. Why should you be so polite?"

"I'm not being polite, but you always stand up to let me by when I come home and I feel I put you to a lot of trouble."

With this she unwrapped the bananas and offered them to me. Taking one herself, she sat down on the bed and began questioning me as she ate.

"Why is it that you just stay at home? Why don't you go out to look for work?"

"That's a good question, but I've looked everywhere and can't find anything to do."

"Have you any friends?"

"I have friends all right, but at a time like this they don't have anything to do with me."

"Have you ever been to school?"

"I've studied abroad a few years."

"Where's your home? Why don't you go home?"

Her question awakened me suddenly to a realization of my predicament. Since the previous year I had been growing more lifeless day by day until I had almost completely lost track of such thoughts as "Who am I?" "What are my present circumstances?" "Do I feel happiness or sorrow?" Her question brought vividly to mind the various stages in my half year of misery and left me staring stupidly at her without a word to offer. From my manner she inferred that I was a homeless wanderer, and a lonely expression came swiftly into her face. She gave a little sigh.

"So you are the same as I am, are you?"

After this remark she became silent. I could see her eyes filling, so to change the subject I asked, "What sort of work do you do in the factory?"

"Packing cigarettes."

"How many hours a day?"

"We start at seven in the morning and stop at six at night with an hour's rest at noon. Ten hours a day. If you work an hour less, you get docked."

"Docked how much?"

"The pay is nine dollars a month. That's three dollars for ten days, three cents per hour."

"What does your food cost you?"

"Four dollars a month."

"In that case, if you don't miss a single hour in the month, you can save five dollars over and above your food. Is that enough for your room and clothes?"

"Of course not! Besides—besides, that foreman is always wanting. . . . Oh . . . I . . . that's why I hate the factory so. Do you smoke?"

"Yes."

"I wish you wouldn't. If you must smoke, don't smoke the cigarettes that we put out. I couldn't stand them here."

Seeing her embittered mood, I did not feel like continuing the conversation. I took a few bites of the half of a banana that I was holding and gazed about me. Her room was rather grimy, too. I stood up, thanked her, and returned to mine. I suppose it was because of the fatigue from work that she generally went immediately to bed on coming home. Tonight she seemed not to get to sleep till past midnight. From that time on she chatted a little with me every day when she came home. I learned from her that her family name was Chen, her given name Erh-mei, and that she came from the countryside east of Soochow. From childhood she had lived near Shanghai. Her father had also been a cigarette factory worker, but he had died during the previous autumn. Before that they had lived together in the room, and gone together to their daily work. Now she was completely alone. For over a month after his death she had cried all the way to work and all the way home. She was seventeen this year, without any brothers or sisters or any near relatives. Before his death, her father had turned over fifteen dollars to the old man downstairs and the latter had looked after all the arrangements for the funeral.

"The old man downstairs," she said, "is really quite a good man and has never attempted to harm me. So I stay on here and keep going to work just as when my father was alive.

But there's a foreman, Li, at the factory who is a thorough scoundrel. He knows that my father is dead and is always trying to flirt with me."

I learned practically her whole life history and that of her father, but as to what sort of a person her mother was, whether she was dead or alive, and, if alive, where she was staying—to these things she never once referred.

3

The weather seemed to be changing. For the past few days the fetid air in my only world, my gloomy little room, had been like the steam of a cooker making me faint and dizzy. The neurasthenia that afflicted me every year during the change from spring to summer, combined with this sort of an atmosphere, was making me half crazy. So during these recent evenings, after the streets quieted down, I had been going out for walks. Strolling alone on the street, looking up at the stars in the narrow strip of deep blue sky, going along slowly indulging in boundless and unrestrained fancy—all this was like a tonic to me.

On such aimless, spring-intoxicated nights, I would wander purposelessly about, not returning until almost daybreak. These walks tired me out, so much so that I would sleep until the middle of the next day; several times it was not until the time for Erh-mei to come home from work that I got up. Through having a sufficiency of sleep I began gradually to recover my health, and my stomach, which had been refusing to take more than half a loaf of bread, improved from the start of these nightly walks until it could digest almost a pound.

Although this naturally cost more, yet the added nourishment made my brain more capable of concentration than before. In intervals between my return from walking and my going to sleep, I had written several short stories in the style of Edgar Allan Poe. They did not seem so bad to me when I read them over, so, after polishing them up and copying them out several times, I mailed them. I was slightly hopeful about them at first, but when I realized that I had never had any word from my earlier translations, I soon forgot all about them.

When Erh-mei went to work in the mornings I was always sound asleep. It was only when she came back in the afternoons that there was any opportunity of speaking with her. I was conscious that for some reason her attitude toward me had reverted to her original one of suspicious apprehension. Sometimes she looked at me long and earnestly, her black crystal liquid eyes full of reproof and entreaty.

It was about twenty days after my arrival in the slums. One afternoon I had just lighted my candle and was looking at a novel that I had bought in a second-hand bookstore when Erh-mei came clattering up the ladder.

"There's a letter carrier downstairs. He wants you to take your seal down and get a letter."

Her suspicious dread of me seemed to be increased. She appeared to be saying, "Aha! They've found out about you!" Her manner annoyed me so that I answered rather impatiently.

"I have no mail. It's not mine."

The irritation in my voice seemed to her only another proof that she was right, and a cynical smile showed on her face.

"Go look after it yourself. Nobody knows your business but yourself."

At the same time I became aware that there was actually someone, probably a postman, calling out from below. "Registered letter!"

When I saw the letter, my heart began to beat violently. One of the translations from the German which I had mailed a short while ago had already appeared in a magazine and the letter contained a postal order for five dollars. My purse was almost empty. With these five dollars I could not only rest easy as to the next month's rent, which had to be paid in advance, but after paying the rent I should still have enough for food for several days. You can imagine the degree of usefulness which these five dollars represented to me.

The next afternoon I went to the post office to cash the order. After walking a short while in the sunshine of the open street, I found myself suddenly bathed in perspiration. I looked at the pedestrians all around me, then back at myself, and hid my head in shame while the perspiration poured like a heavy rain from my head and neck. There had been no sun in my nocturnal wanderings, only the chilliness of spring and the pale dawn from the east sweeping through the lonely streets, so that I had never felt that my torn quilted gown was so very inappropriate to the season. Here I was striding along the road under a warm spring midday sun, all unconscious of the fact that I had donned that wretched night costume as usual. As I compared myself with the fellow humans to right and left of me who had kept up with the season, I felt very much abashed.

Immediately I forgot all about the rent that must be paid in a few days, forgot the exhausted condition of my purse, and walked slowly toward the second-hand clothing shops on Fukien Road. It was so long since I had walked about in the daytime that the motorcars and rickshas passing by, the well-dressed young men and women sitting in them, the beautiful window displays in the silk and jewelry stores lining the street, the confused hum around me of voices, footsteps, carriage bells—all this seemed to transport me into a seventh heaven of delight. I forgot about my personal existence and longed to mingle in the merrymaking of my fellows. Quite involuntarily I began to sing an operatic air that I thought I had long since forgotten. But as I was about to cross the street to turn into Fukien Road, this ecstatic paradise was rudely shattered by the clanging of a bell. Lifting my head I saw that a tram car was bearing down in front of me. The fat motorman standing in front leaned halfway out of the car and shouted at me in an irate voice.

"Pig! Ain't yer got no eyes? If you get run over, it's another yellow dog dead!"

I stopped and stared stupidly after the cloud of dust behind the train rolling northward. I don't know where the impulse came from, but I broke into a loud laugh. Then, seeing that the people about me were staring, I blushed and went slowly into Fukien Road.

I went into several clothing shops and asked the price of a light lined gown, mentioning what I could afford to pay, but the clerks, as though all coached by the same tutor, replied with a sneer.

"What's your game? If you can't afford it, you don't have to buy, you know!"

After inquiring all the way along to Canton Road, I decided that a lined gown was out of the question, so in a little shop I bought a thin cotton gown and changed into it immediately. With the discarded gown done up into a bundle I started quietly homewards.

"I haven't enough money anyway," I thought to myself, "I might just as well have a good time spending it." I recollected the bread and bananas that Erh-mei had given me that day. Without a moment's hesitation I sought out a candy shop, went in, and bought a dollar's worth of chocolates, bananas, sweets, cakes, and such. As I stood in the shop waiting for the clerk to make up my package, I suddenly remembered that I had not had a bath in more than a month and decided that it would not be a bad idea to have one right away.

When I returned to Dent Road after bathing, carrying a bundle of clothing and a package of candy, the shops on both sides of the street had already turned on their electric lights and pedestrians were rather scarce. The cool twilight breeze from the Whangpoo River made me shiver. I returned to my room and lit my candle, but a glance at Erh-mei's door told me that she was not yet home. Although I was very hungry, I refused on any condition to open up the package of sweets that I had bought as I wished to wait and share them with Erh-mei. I took up a book to read and contented myself with swallowing hard. I waited a long time but Erh-mei did not appear. Weariness overpowered me—I did not know when—and I fell asleep leaning on my pile of books.

4

When the sound of Erh-mei's return awakened me, I saw that two inches of my candle—out of a twelve-ounce package—were gone. I asked her what the time was.

"The ten o'clock whistle has just blown."

"Why are you so late today?"

"Business is booming and they want us to do night work. They pay us extra, of course, but it's awfully tiresome."

"Well, then, don't go."

"There aren't enough workers. We have to do it."

At this, two tears rolled down from her eyes. I suppose she felt bad because she was so tired, and, while I was sorry for her, I found her childishness somewhat amusing. I opened up the package of sweets, offered her some, and said consolingly, "When you first do night work you are not accustomed to it, so you feel fatigued. But after you get used to it, it isn't bad."

She did not answer, but sat on my low table of books and

ate a few chocolates, throwing occasional glances at me as though she had something she wanted to say but couldn't.

"What were you going to say?" I urged her.

She remained still for a moment, then said very hesitantly, "I . . . I . . . wanted to ask you before. You've been going out every night recently. Are you associating with bad people?"

I was astounded at her question, which seemed to imply that I was spending my nights in the company of thieves or crooks. When I did not answer immediately, she assumed that she had ferreted out the truth and continued very tenderly.

"Why must you have such fine things to eat or such fine clothes to wear? You know that that sort of business is risky. If you should get caught, how could you have the face to go on living? Never mind about the past, but you'll make a fresh start, won't you? . . ."

I was staring at her wide-eyed and open-mouthed. Her ideas were so extraordinary that I could not think of any defense. After a silence she went on.

"Take just your smoking alone. If you would give that up, you could save quite a few coppers a day, couldn't you? I advised you long ago not to smoke and particularly not to smoke the cigarettes of our factory that I hate so much. But you won't listen to me."

There were tears again as she said this. I knew that they were tears of vexation over the factory, but in my heart I tried to believe that they were shed over me. I thought for a moment or two, while she recovered herself, and then told her all about the registered letter that had come the day before and about getting the money and making the purchases that day. Finally I explained about my nervousness, which made it necessary for me to take walks at night. She accepted my explanation and, when I was finished, she blushed suddenly and dropped her eyes to the table in an embarrassed way.

"Oh, I was all wrong about you—all wrong. Please don't take it to heart. I didn't mean anything bad. But you acted so queerly that I thought right away of some crookedness. If you can keep working steadily, that will be fine, won't it? The thing you just mentioned—what did you call it?—that you could get five dollars for. If you could make one of those every day, wouldn't that be splendid?"

Her delightful simplicity suddenly aroused in me a curious emotion. I wanted to put my arms out and take her to me, but my reason told me, "Don't make a slip again. Don't you realize the position you are in? Are you set on poisoning this innocent young virgin? Beast! You have no right to love anyone now."

I had closed my eyes under the stress of my emotion. When, sobered by reason, I reopened them, I found everything about me suddenly brighter than before. I smiled at her.

"It's late," I urged. "You ought to sleep. You have to go to work again tomorrow. Beginning from today, I'll give up smoking."

She listened to me happily, rose, and went to her room.

After she had gone, I lit a fresh candle and sat plunged in meditation.

Five dollars, the first result of my labor, and three of them spent already. With the dollar or so that I possessed before I shall have, after paying the rent, just two or three dimes. What am I to do about it?

Pawn my ragged gown? Probably the pawn shops would not take it.

I am sorry for this girl, but I am in worse condition than she. Work that she doesn't want comes demanding her while I, who want to work, cannot find a thing to do.

How about physical work? I fear these weak wrists of mine could never stand the weight of a ricksha.

Suicide? If I had had the courage, I would have done it long ago. Yet the fact that I can even think of it is proof that my will is not completely gone.

Ho, ho, ho! That motorman on the tram. How was it that he cursed me? "Yellow dog!" Not a bad name, yellow dog. . . .

All manner of disconnected thoughts streamed through my mind, but from none of them could I derive a plan for escaping from my immediate poverty. A mill whistle blew announcing twelve o'clock. I got up and put on my ragged quilted gown, blew out the candle, and went out to walk.

The slum dwellers were all asleep. In Jihsin Alley opposite in the row of foreign-style houses bordering on Dent Road a few people still had their colored lamps lit and were playing the balalaika. One or two sweet voices tinged with melancholy were borne on the cold still midnight air. There were Russian girl refugees there, probably singing for money. The sky was overcast with thin cadaverous gray clouds. One or two stars showed through the patches in the cloud sheet but the darkness around them seemed to hold nothing but an infinite grief.

Mr. Pan in Distress

1

The station was filled with people, each one busy with his own concerns. Clearly something out of the ordinary was happening. The porters stood around sleepily with their hands in the pockets of their uniforms. They knew it was not yet time for them to make extra money, so it was useless to look alert. The air was so oppressive it made breathing a little difficult, a portent of coming rain. The electric lights had been turned on for awhile, yet they seemed dimmer and yellower than usual, casting a dreamy mist over everyone and everything. A notice on the blackboard announced that the express from the west would arrive four hours late. This was already known to everybody for hours, so the notice was now like a weathered signboard outside a theater unnoticed by passersby. It had been the same for almost every train every day for the past week. What was unusual came to be accepted by everyone as a matter of course.

Finally the train the whole world seemed to be waiting for pulled into the station. The quiet and gloomy station was turned into a bustling place. Arriving passengers were relieved, departing guests were glad, and the porters made a small fortune. But let us pass over all these and talk about a Mr. Pan who was coming from Jang-li.

Before the train reached the station Mr. Pan had methodically made his preparations to alight. He stood at the head of the line with a black bag in his right hand. With his left hand he held on to a child of seven who in turn held behind him the hand of his elder brother of nine who in his turn held on to Mrs. Pan, their mother. It was Mr. Pan's theory that the difficulty of taking care of so many persons could be overcome by thus forming a sinuous line like a snake, enabling them to penetrate into any crowd without getting separated. He bid them again and again to hold each other tightly and not to let go. Lest his warning be insufficient, he repeatedly pumped his left hand up and down and the tremors passed down the line like a telegram from station to station.

Mr. Pan's theory was an excellent one, but it was not without defect. When the train came into the station all the passengers crowded with their baggage out toward the door and the Pan family snake found itself unable to proceed forward. Mr. Pan used his black bag as a wedge and pushed his body forward with all his might. In this way he succeeded in advancing to within two windows of the door. But his seven-year-old was unable to move, lodged in a spot four windows behind the door between passengers and seats. His two arms were stretched out in either direction as far as they would go, and equal pressure seemed to be pulling him both ways as if his arms were about to be pulled off. He cried out anxiously, "My arms! My arms!" His half-weeping voice apprised the people around him that a child was being squeezed somewhere below their waistlines. A careful look revealed four members of the Pan family in a row, hand still holding hand.

"Let him loose at once!" exclaimed one of the passengers, "Else you'll have the child pulled in two parts!"

"Why isn't that child being carried?" said another in a withering tone, although he himself lost no chance, however slim, of shoving himself forward.

"No!" Mr. Pan felt that they were all wrong. His reasons for stretching out in a line were ample and justified. But on second thought he did not proceed with the argument because he knew that few could appreciate sound reasoning like him, and it would be a futile expenditure of energy to launch into a debate. But he could move neither forward nor backward and his seven-year-old was still crying, "My arms! My arms!" Mr. Pan was finally obliged to violate his own orders, and he loosened his grip on the child's hand, anxiously shouting his command, "Watch me! Watch me!"

With a jerk the train came to a full stop. The crowd leaped forward as though shot from a cannon. The press grew easier up in front as some alighted but the sudden increase of pressure from behind drove Mr. Pan inexorably forward. He could not turn back to take care of his charges. He could only shout into someone else's back, "Just follow me! Just follow me!" In a moment Mr. Pan was propelled out of the door. He turned around to see if his wife and children were in sight. He was certain they were still in the train, and he determined to hold his ground there at the door until they appeared. More than a hundred people emerged before he finally caught a glimpse of his seven-year-old's head and torso. Under the electric light he looked as if he was about to cry. He edged forward several times but he was repeatedly pushed back by passengers coming down the train. Mr. Pan finally managed to grasp the child in his left arm and deposit him safely down on the landing. In a few minutes Mrs. Pan and the nine-year-old boy got down too. "Ah-yo! Ah-yo!" panted Mrs. Pan. Her suffering eyes beseeched Mr. Pan's face, like those of a child waiting to be comforted.

More composed, Mr. Pan again ordered his troop to form ranks. "Let's line up again hand in hand or else we'll lose each other," he said. "There are so many people on the platform and there's a terrible squeeze at the ticket gate!"

The seven-year-old whimpered. He grabbed his father's knee. "Carry me, papa. . . ."

"Useless little thing!" fumed Mr. Pan. But he checked himself, bent down, and took the boy in his arms. The older boy was instructed to hold on to the back of his father's gown with one hand and hold on to his mother with the other. Mr. Pan's hands were now fully occupied. Mrs. Pan had never faced such difficulties before. There had been so much trouble getting off the train and now there was another siege before them. "If I'd known it was going to be like this," she complained, "I'd have rather died at home than take refuge here!"

"What are you lamenting about?" asked Mr. Pan, half-angry, half-ready to sympathize with his wife. "No use complaining now that we're here. Besides, life is safe now. Go ahead, watch your step."

The line of Pans moved forward again. It plunged into the crowd and through the ticket collector's gate as in a dream. Like a drop of water in a rushing torrent, Mr. Pan could not change course. He could only follow the force of the crowd, his feet scarcely touching the ground. In a moment he was beyond the iron railing which surrounded the station and had crossed the tramway line to the cement sidewalk. When he hurriedly turned and looked behind him, he saw only a mass of blurry faces, pale under the lamplight. Loaded with countless bundles and packages they swarmed toward him. Suddenly he realized that the hand was no longer clutching his gown. When he had lost it, he did not know.

He was troubled beyond words. Wildly, he turned this way and that, seeing nothing. The fear of losing part of his family suddenly engulfed him. Involuntarily two drops of tears rolled down, blurring his vision of lamplights and human figures.

Fortunately the child in his arms had sharp eyesight and recognized his mother as soon as he saw her coarse hair. Pointing his finger he cried, "Look, mama's there!" Mr. Pan was almost unable to believe his ears for joy. He rubbed his eyes on the child's shirt and looked again. After a moment's search he saw his wife butting against people like a blind mouse, shielding the older child in front of her. They had not yet crossed the tram tracks. Calling his older son he went forward to lead them back to the sidewalk. When they were finally all together again, Mr. Pan set the younger child down and sighing wiped the perspiration from his face. "We're all right now!" he said.

And so they were. Everything was safe now, no soldiers, no fires or looting or threatened attacks. They were now beyond the railing. Moreover, good fortune was surely with them if wife and son, lost, were so quickly found again. Did that not prove that these four lives and the black bag were quite safe from injury? Certainly it was sufficient to warrant Mr. Pan's reassuring "We're all right now."

"Wang-pau-tz'oh!" Mr. Pan called for a ricksha in the local dialect and several of them rapidly collected around the Pan family demanding to know where they were going and how much they were ready to pay. Mr. Pan held his head up in arrogant fashion and extending two fingers, "Two only, only two!" he said. "Ten coppers to Fourth Road," he added after a pause. "Come along if you want to!" This was to show that he knew Shanghai ways. A long argument followed, and they finally agreed upon twelve coppers. Mrs. Pan and the elder child mounted one and Mr. Pan took the younger boy and the black bag and stepped into the other. They were about to start when the Sikh traffic policeman with his rifle over his shoulder stretched out an arm and made them stop short. The younger child was frightened by the policeman's face and turned around to hide his own in his father's chest.

"Don't be be afraid. That's just a Sikh policeman," Mr. Pan understood the boy's fear and hastened to explain. "If we had such good policemen in our town, we wouldn't have had to run to Shanghai. Look at his red turban. He'll protect us with his gun. And what a funny beard he has, like a *lohan*!* Look at it!"

But the child was frightened and not even the *lohan's* beard interested him. Soon the ding-dong of the bell aroused his curiosity and he slowly turned until he could look out onto the street out of the corner of his eye. He saw brightly lit houses flash by and, caught by the colors, he forgot the man with the black beard and raised himself so that he could see the sights.

When they arrived at the street they sought, they found eight or nine hotels with signs out, "Rooms Full." Nor could they argue about it because all of these places even had beds out in the halls. They finally came to one which also had the sign out but, as they passed, somebody called out lackadaisically, "Looking for a room?"

"Yes, do you still have one?" A feeling of relief flooded over Mr. Pan, as though he had reached home.

"We have just one. A guest just moved away to a place of his own. If you'd come a moment later it would probably have been gone."

"Then let's take it." said Mr. Pan. He set the younger child down and turned to help his wife and older one.

*A Buddhist temple figure.

"Luck is with us!" he exclaimed. Expanding with their good fortune, he added a copper to the price agreed upon with the ricksha pullers. For he believed fortune would favor him further if he improved the fortunes of others. The pullers were not satisfied, however, and demanded five coppers more for their extra trouble in hauling them up and down the street. The hotel man intervened and Mr. Pan spent four extra coppers.

The room was on the ground floor. Under the electric light they saw a bed, a table, and two chairs. The air was thick and smoky. Strong odors of rancid oil and of wine greeted their noses when they followed the servant in. "What a stink!" muttered Mr. Pan, displeased. When they heard food sizzling in the oiled pot, they realized that their room used to be part of the kitchen, which was just next door. But Mr. Pan quickly agreed to himself that evil odors were more tolerable than sleeping in open air with bullets around them, so he relaxed and sat down with a sigh of comfort in one of the chairs.

"Want supper?" asked the servant setting down the bag.

"I want ham soup and rice," cried the younger child sucking on his finger. Mrs. Pan turned upon him.

"Ham soup and rice!" she repeated. "We're taking refuge here now. You ought to be glad you have anything to eat and yet you think you can put on such a show!"

The elder boy showed no greater appreciation of their situation. Appealing to Mr. Pan, he said, "We're in Shanghai now, papa. You can get me foreign food!"

"Why you heartless brats!" stammered Mrs. Pan, angry now, "you deserve to starve and get nothing!"

"The children don't understand," said the embarrassed Mr. Pan as if nothing was going on. "Children don't understand." He turned to the servant. "We ate on our way here," he said. "Bring two bowls of fried rice with eggs."

Mr. Pan in Distress

The servant half-nodded and left the room. But he was only a few steps beyond the door when Mr. Pan called him back. "Bring me a catty of wine and ten cents worth of smoked fish," he said. When the servant had gone again Mr. Pan turned to his wife with a cheerful smile, "We can afford to loosen up with a bit of wine now. Just think! We got out of the war area and escaped safely to a safe place like this. That's only point number one. A few moments ago I was terribly afraid of having lost you. And if it weren't for the cleverness of little Ah Erh here . . ." he pulled the boy closer and gently patted him. "He spotted you so easily. Only then could I come over to get you. That's point number two. So let's have a happy cupful now!" He raised an empty hand as if to drink, his face beaming.

Mrs. Pan remained silent. She was thinking of her home. They had brought what they could in the bag and packed some off to store in the church, but much had still been left behind in the house. Mrs. Pan wondered whether Wang Ma was dependable, and whether that family next door, which was rather poor, knew they had gone, leaving only Wang Ma to watch over the house. And would she forget a single door or window at nighttime? Mrs. Pan thought of the hens in the yard, Ah Erh's unfinished trousers, and even of the bowl of cooked duck which had been left in the kitchen. . . . These and many other things flashed through her mind in an instant, like the throbs of an electric current. This made her ill at ease. "I wish I knew what was going on there," she sighed. The children were disappointed, vaguely feeling that Shanghai was not as much fun as their parents had made it out to be.

Drops of rain swept into the room through the open window. "It's raining! Lucky it waited till now!" said Mr. Pan, closing the window, and as he did so his eye fell upon a piece of hitherto hidden paper tacked to the wall. "Notice to travelers." This brought his attention to something important, so he fixed his eyes on that notice. "No discounts. Two dollars!" He read this aloud in astonishment. His jaw dropped as he turned to his wife.

2

The next morning the servants were still asleep stretched out on benches in the corridor. A small patch of sunlight shone on the tiny sliver of a courtyard. Dull yellow lights lingered on in some rooms. Mr. and Mrs. Pan were already talking to each other, and the two boys, hoping the new day would prove Shanghai to be a better place, were tickling each other and chortling in bed, for their parents had ordered them to rest a little longer.

"You must not go home," Mrs. Pan was saying in anxious tones. "The newspaper can't be relied upon and since we came out of there despite all the difficulties why should you go back so quickly?"

"I've thought of it," replied Mr. Pan. "Bureau Head Ku is really very strict. Look—'Since there is no fighting in the town, the schools will open.'—Those are surely his words. I know the correspondent too, he's an official in the bureau of education. Wouldn't he know what was going on? I'll have to go."

"But it's dangerous, you know that!" said Mrs. Pan wretchedly. "The fighting will probably spread to our town in two or three days, and what students will come even if you do open the school? Suppose nothing does happen there, you still have an answer for the bureau head if he taxes you with not opening the school. Just ask him which is more important, life or the school! Since he's got a life of his own to protect, he won't be too strict with you!"

"What do you know about it?" said Mr. Pan condescendingly. "Words like these could only come from a female, whispered in the privacy of the home. Do you think men like us could say anything like that without being shamed? Now, don't stop me." His voice became a little more conciliatory. "I have to go back and I tell you there won't be any danger. I know how to take care of myself. Anyway," and he smiled at his cleverness, "aren't you worrying about the things we left at home? I'll take care of them when I get back and you can stay here without worrying. When peace is restored I'll come down immediately to get you and take you home."

Mrs. Pan knew there was no use trying to dissuade him. It would be good to have all the things looked after, but since the rumors were so threatening it might be like throwing a pearl into the sea. Who could guarantee its recovery? She feared in her heart that she would never see him again and she scarce dared look at him. Tears were already filling her eyes. But she thought that tears for no apparent reason would be unlucky. How could she weep from grief? So she restrained herself, and, for her own comfort, she said:

"All right, go and have a look. If the news about the bureau head's order for reopening the school is not correct then you can come back either on the train this afternoon or first thing tomorrow morning. Don't forget." She could not help shedding a tear on her hand. She quickly wiped it on her shirt. "I'll be worrying about you."

Mr. Pan was distracted by his dilemma. He could not possibly find anything wrong with the bureau head's decision to open the school. He obviously had to go, but how could he bear to leave his family here? He was touched by his wife's concern. It seemed unkind just to go. And besides he was not in a position to promise that nothing would happen to them, a woman and two children, weak and helpless in a strange city. He felt a deep resentment against the men who were causing all the trouble, the generals who were shifting their armies around preparing for battle and the head of the bureau of education, who insisted upon opening the school. He was also conscious of regret over not having a grown son to help him with his troubles. But naturally he was not like women. He thought everything out from all possible angles and decided that the proper thing to do was to return. So he forthwith set aside all doubts and regrets. "If the report proves wrong, I'll be back on the afternoon train, just as you suggest." He picked up his wife's thought without betraying his own.

The children caught the drift of their parents' talk about going home and coming back again. The little one leaned over the edge of the bed and announced like a spoilt child, "I want to go back too!"

"No, *I'm* going with papa and mama, and we'll leave you alone here," said the older boy making a face. The younger one let out a wail. He rubbed his eyes with his hand but no tears came.

"Both of you will stay here with mama," Mr. Pan raised his voice and said. "Stop being naughty and get up for breakfast." He gave a few more words of instruction to Mrs. Pan and directly went out to get a ricksha to take him to the station. On the way he heard rumors that the railway line had been cut and no trains were leaving. He found the news half comforting, half disappointing. "If trains really don't leave, I might as well stop worrying," he said to himself. "Even if they discharge me, there's nothing I can do about it!" But, he thought, if luck stayed with him, he would probably not meet such disappointments. In that case, the rumor in the street might not turn out to be true. To still these doubts, he wished the ricksha would hurry up.

Luck was indeed with him, and there was no announcement that the line was cut. The night train would be four hours late and had not arrived yet. That was all that the notice board said. The ticket window was not crowded. One or two people went up from time to time to buy tickets. But there was a considerable crowd milling around, some of them here to meet the train and some just to look around. Some even brought their cameras, waiting for the arrival of the night train to record the scene of crowding, as if preparing to add a page to some future book of great events. The baggage room was filled with trunks and boxes of all sorts, piled nearly up to the ceiling.

Mr. Pan was both comforted and anxious, and after a moment's hesitation went up and bought a third class ticket. He boarded the train and found himself a seat. The car was bright with the morning sunlight and it was warm without being hot. There was more than enough room, and Mr. Pan could almost stretch out on one of the benches. "This is quite unusual," thought Mr. Pan. "It would be a pleasant trip if there were nothing to worry about."

The train was delayed all along the way. They had to wait for military orders and repeatedly had to wait for military trains to pass. It was already three o'clock that afternoon when it arrived finally at Jang-li. Mr. Pan went directly home from the station and sighed with relief when he saw the gate tightly shut. They had warned Wang Ma about this one thing more than anything else—to keep the gate closed. Now Mr. Pan had to knock many times before Wang Ma opened the gate. She was astonished when she saw Mr. Pan. "Why has the master come back? No need for running any more?"

Mr. Pan muttered something, ran into the house, and looked all around. He then opened the lock of the bedroom and carefully examined everything. He was relieved to find that nothing had changed, everything was just as they had left it yesterday. Yet he was still somewhat worried, so he locked the bedroom door and went out. "You must still lock the front door," he admonished Wang Ma. Fastening the gate behind him, Wang Ma shook her head over Mr. Pan's behavior. She thought that the master and his family must be staying right here in town. He must have feared that she would want to go with them, so he had lied to her about going to Shanghai. "Else how could master turn around and come home?" Wang Ma wondered. "And mistress and the two children, where are they hiding if they didn't come home? But why didn't they let me go with them? Must be afraid there would be too many people. They must be staying in that foreigners' red house. It's been arranged with the soldiers not to attack that house during the fighting. To tell the truth I wouldn't go even if they asked me to. I'm not afraid. My burial gown is ready if the fighting should come here." Wang Ma thought of a pair of embroidered slippers presented to her by a niece. They were very beautiful. It would be good to go to her rest wearing them. Yen Wang* would look upon her differently. She felt somewhat comforted and thought no more of where the master's family had gone.

Mr. Pan made his way to the office of the education official who he knew was a correspondent, and asked him if the bureau head was really planning to open the school. The official replied: "Of course he is! He even said that some teachers thought only of escape and not of their duty. This proved them to be unfit for educational work. It would not be a bad idea to dismiss them." Mr. Pan shivered as he listened, but he also congratulated himself for his own decision to return. He hurried back to the school and began writing announcements to be sent out to all the parents of students. Although war was threatening, he wrote, education remained an urgent need for all children, just as urgent as

*King of the Underworld.

clothes and food. During the Great War the Europeans continued to conduct their schools in air raid shelters. We cannot permit such a spirit to characterize other nations and not our own, and therefore, he concluded with a flourish, school would open as usual at the end of the prescribed recess. He hoped the elders of the family would consider the matter in this light and send their children as if nothing were amiss, not only for their own benefit and for the good of the school, but for the glory of the nation.

Mr. Pan read his composition over three times and felt entirely satisfied with it. He would surely win the bureau head's praise for the forethought. The letter was transferred onto the stencil and one hundred copies were made, enclosed in envelopes and duly sent off with the servant for delivery. When he had done his public duty, Mr. Pan thought again of his family affairs. If school opened, he could not return to Shanghai, and there was nothing he could do to help the woman and children he left behind in the hotel. He resolved to write a letter telling them to remain there and not to worry, but to be careful about everything. He wrote a letter to his wife and shortly afterward posted it.

Next day his heart sank, however, when he heard from the teahouse that the railway line had indeed been cut. His dearly beloved wife and two children seemed to have blown away with the wind, far, far away, almost disappearing. He returned to school with downcast face. There he found the servant who told him that twenty of the families he had gone to were locked behind their gates and refused to open them. He had to slip the letters in through door cracks. At thirty other homes there were only servants. The parents had fled with their children to Shanghai and nobody could say when they would come back to school. Of the rest, some replied, "We'll see." Others said, "Let books come second. We've got to worry about our lives first."

"So be it," said Mr. Pan absently, his mind on his own concerns. He smoked a cigarette and decided on a course of action. He made his way to the office of the Red Cross. He paid in the membership fee and announced that his school was large enough to be used as a refuge for women in case of need. This was an act of benevolence and of course was warmly acclaimed. Besides, Mr. Pan was already a well-known personage in town. He was given a flag with a big red cross on it to hoist over his school and a badge showing that he was a member of the society.

The sight of the flag and the badge gave him a mystic sense of joy and security, as if they were life-saving charms. "Everything is safe now! But. . . ." His thought broke off and he turned smiling to the official. "Give me another flag and a few more badges, will you?" He explained that he also wanted to put a flag on the side door of the school. And about the badges, why, he might lose one, it was so small, and therefore he wanted several to keep in reserve. The official demurred and pointed out jokingly that one couldn't eat them or play with them and that a person could only be one member no matter how many badges he had, but in the end he yielded to Mr. Pan's request.

Both flags now flew in the early autumn breeze. But there was none at the side door of the school. The extra banner now fluttered over Mr. Pan's own house. One of the red badges appeared on the front of Mr. Pan's gown, glistening and giving him a sense of new dignity and courage. The extra badges he wrapped up and carefully hid in the pocket of his innermost garment. "One is for her, one for Ah Ta, and one for Ah Erh," he said to himself. They were refugees far away in Shanghai, but now it was as if he had bought them extra insurance, and he felt it would somehow afford them new courage too.

3

Fighting was going on at Pi-chuang.

Rarely did houses open their doors at Jang-li. Shops, naturally, were closed. The streets were filled with a constant stream of soldiers going up to the front. On their passage they seemed to have become omnipotent. They could smash anything they pleased, and now too began the seizure of coolies for forced labor with the army. Those who feared this would happen to them fled. The impressed men were strung together on a single line to which they were all bound and they marched along one following another. Everybody in town was afraid to go out into the streets. If it was absolutely necessary, they traveled through narrow lanes and paths rather than on the main streets. Even men like Mr. Pan dared not walk out into the open despite Red Cross badges and other evidences of dignity. The streets of Jang-li were quiet and somehow looked wider.

There had not been any Shanghai papers for some days. The local militia frequently posted news from the front, usually news of victories for their side and defeats for the enemy. Whenever these reports were posted many came to read them, although they afforded little comfort. It was as if other news was hiding behind the notice board. Many went away frowning with uncertainty.

During this time Mr. Pan was in utter despair. Hardest to bear was the separation from his wife and children, and the fact that he had had no news of them. He felt as if his difficulties would go on forever. Then there was his own safety. They were only a hundred *li* from Pi-chuang. The badge was useful, but there was no guarantee on it. And suppose it proved useless, to whom could he appeal? Bullets, artillery, looting, and fire were all real and near, they were not idle jests. He would have to ask around and find other solutions.

So Mr. Pan set out in search of news from the front. If the news was no different from rumors he had already heard, he would tend to believe it. But every time he saw somebody rushing down the street, he was consumed with fear and curiosity because he felt certain that some true and dreadful information must be the cause of the man's haste. Only because he knew none of them was he able to check his impulse to ask them—"What is it?"

The most dependable news came from the Red Cross Society because there were often rescue workers coming back from the front on the military train. But Mr. Pan hesitated to go there too often, even though he was a member. He feared that his anxiety would disclose his fears. But he went every evening to visit a Red Cross official named Wu. He would be relieved every time he was told that nothing startling had occurred or that the fighting had now moved to such and such a place. That evening as usual he went to Mr. Wu and had a long wait before he finally appeared.

"Nothing bad, I hope?" asked Mr. Pan anxiously. "The official announcement said that a general offensive was started yesterday against the enemy."

"Not good," said Mr. Wu sadly. He choked back his words, twisting his short whiskers on the sides of his lips.

"What is it?" Mr. Pan's heart jumped a beat, his body felt as though something were restraining it. Mr. Wu leaned over and whispered, as if afraid of eavesdroppers.

"The truth is that Cheng-an, eight *li* from Pi-chuang, was lost this morning!"

"Ai!" shouted Mr. Pan like a madman. And after a pause he said, "I'm going home." He turned around and left.

The street lights seemed especially dim. Mournfully, with sidewise steps, Mr. Pan hurried home, as if pursued by someone.

"You can bolt the door and go to sleep," he said to Wang

Mr. Pan in Distress

Ma when he got home. "I'll be leaving again and will not return tonight. It's urgent business." In an old chest he found a cotton-padded crepe gown which they had forgotten to pack. It was far from new but was worth keeping. There were several lined jackets belonging to the children. They were also old, but upon examining them closely, Mr. Pan decided they could still be used. Then there was Mrs. Pan's old silk skirt which he was not sure she would care to lose. Mr. Pan made a hasty package of them all and carried them with him.

"Ricksha! Ricksha! The red house on Fu-hsing Street. Ten cents."

"Ten cents?" said the ricksha man lazily. "How many rickshas do you think you see around anyway? We'd have run off long ago if we didn't have to risk our lives for food. Thirty cents—it's up to you."

"All right, thirty cents," replied Mr. Pan, stepping in and getting settled. "But you'll have to run faster."

"Where are you going, Mr. Pan?" A colleague by the name of Huang met him along the way and stopped to ask him.

"Oh, Mr. . . . I'm going. . . ." Mr. Pan answered helplessly, not knowing whose voice it was. It suddenly occurred to him that there was too much to say. The wheels were going too fast, and the man would not pursue him with further questions. Mr. Pan held back.

The red house was already full of people, most of them moved in ten days back. With children running around crying and the adults moving about and talking and lights glimmering in the rooms, it presented a lively appearance. "There's really no space left," said the host. "But we can't refuse you since your things are already stored here. Some people just arrived and we put them in the side room used for a kitchen. We couldn't refuse them either. We might ask them if they mind having you come in with them."

"I'm sure they'd agree after talking it over," replied Mr. Pan, who felt as comforted as if he were home. "Anyway, I wouldn't try to sleep at a time like this. Just a place to sit down will be enough."

When he stepped into the side room with his bag, he scarcely believed his eyes. He thought perhaps the excitement had been too much for him, and his eyes had become blurry. That was why he was making a mistake. He closed his eyes and opened them again, but there was the same man over at the window talking to someone. And was it not the head of the bureau of education, with that thick mustache on his upper lip? Mr. Pan hesitated and, while he felt like fleeing, he also knew that it would not look good if he turned and left. The bureau head also saw him and greeted him with an awkward smile. "So you've come too, Mr. Pan, come on in and rest yourself," he said. When the host saw that they were acquainted, he left.

"Mr. Bureau Head is already here," replied Mr. Pan. "Will it be convenient to have one more?"

"We're only three. You're perfectly welcome. It's not cold and we have a mat there on which we can take turns lying down."

Mr. Pan thought that the bureau head was especially friendly. None of his usual dignity nor his majestic air now! Mr. Pan stepped forward with no more misgivings. "Then excuse my impertinence," he said. "I'll spend the night here with you three."

The room was rather narrow. On the mat in the center sat a middle-aged man who looked rather tired but who showed no intention of going to sleep. On one side were the rows of pans and the stove, and on the other under the window were three stools. The bureau head sat on one of them. A young man of about twenty with shining hair, a cousin of the bureau head, sat on the second. The third stool was empty. In the corner next to the stove were three bundles and a woven willow suitcase. These things no doubt belonged to the three men. There was little space to spare. The dust-covered electric bulb shed a misty light, illuminating men and objects but indistinctly. Mr. Pan laid his bundle with the others and modestly sat down on the empty stool. After introducing him to the others, the bureau head asked, "Have you heard the news about Cheng-an?"

"Yes," replied Mr. Pan, "It will be hard to keep Pi-chuang with Cheng-an gone."

"They must have been careless over there. The loss of Cheng-an proved it. Pi-chuang is easiest to take through Cheng-an. Maybe they're there already! Horrible to think of it!"

"We'll be ruined here if that's true."

"But our General Tu is not stupid. They say he's famous for the way he employs his troops. He must have thought of this and will prepare for it. Maybe he'll be able to reverse the situation, turn the defensive into an offensive and attack the enemy in their own nest like splitting a bamboo. . . ."

"If that happens everything will be all right. The war would finish and then we in the teaching business could open school and run it as usual."

Mention of the school made the bureau head conscious of his position. He stroked his beard and sighed. "Don't talk about it. This war is certainly terrible for all the students!" The uneasy feeling of hiding away in this cramped side room gave way to a remote sense of the majesty of sitting behind a desk in the office of the bureau of education. The middle-aged man sitting on the mat lifted his head and spoke with anger:

"That General Chu on the other side is hateful—why should he resist when attacked? There's no chance for him to win. If he would wisely retreat, there wouldn't be any war!"

"He's a fool," chimed in the bureau head's cousin. "He won't give in until the end. Only we've got to suffer for all of them sitting in a dark narrow room like this." He finished half in jest.

Mr. Pan was thinking of his wife and children in Shanghai. Were they safe? Would they have any difficulties? Would they all be asleep at this moment? He could not picture them very distinctly. In reality he was in the worse position. He looked out of the window into the small yard. He was silent and sorrowful.

"We just don't know what is happening!" he broke out involuntarily after a pause. He was thinking of the horrible news and anticipated danger.

"Hard to say," mused the bureau head, assuming an air of long experience with military matters. "The trick of fighting rests entirely in matters of chance which are constantly changing. Maybe unexpectedly . . . maybe. . . ." He smiled at the middle-aged man.

The middle-aged man, the cousin of the bureau head, and Mr. Pan all understood the meaning of that smile. Everyone thought nothing much would happen to them sitting here, so everyone felt at ease and smiled.

The small yard was full of overgrown weeds. It had become the safe domain of mosquitoes and all kinds of insects. They were flocking toward the light in the side room. The four startled gentlemen had enough of them. These small creatures flew all around their heads, and if a mosquito suddenly stung one of them, he would slap it in pain. From time to time, they would stop talking to listen fearfully for the thunder of guns and the voices of men. No one slept in peace, but as the bureau head had suggested, everyone took turns lying down on the mat for a rest.

Early next morning, Mr. Pan, his eyes bloodshot, felt chilly when the breezes of dawn filtered in. An urgent desire to know what was going on outside took possession of him, and he slipped out of the red house. The street presented its usual aspect. Stray dogs looked animatedly this way and that. Occasionally one or two sleepy-eyed people passed by. Mr. Pan turned down another street. Everything was as usual. He laughed aloud at the hasty and ridiculous way in which he had fled the night before from his own home. But Mr. Pan immediately reflected that sufficient caution was better than needless risk, so he had really conducted himself quite correctly.

Having consumed a total of twenty days, the war came to an end. Everybody in the town felt relieved. "All is well now," they sighed, "and will be well if war doesn't break out again." Mr. Pan was far from satisfied, for there were still no trains from Shanghai. There was no way of bringing his family back at once. He had received two letters but they were so brief as not to be very reassuring. More than anything else he regretted his own lack of foresight. If he had only known what would happen, he would have saved the cost of running away and spared himself the loneliness suffered during their separation. He went to the bureau of education, certain that the question of reopening school would now be discussed. In the reception room he found a number of officials of the department cutting paper and preparing large quantities of ink, as if preparing for some celebration.

"Here's Mr. Pan, just on time!" they cried. "You write so well in the *yen* style. Here, you do it."

"Only Mr. Pan can write such big characters!" chimed in others.

"What do you want me to write? What's it all about?"

"We're preparing to welcome back the triumphant General

Tu. Two sets of colored arches will be set up at both ends of the station for the General's carriage to pass under. Now we need appropriate characters to adorn the arches.''

"Don't be so polite, Mr. Pan, we all desire it!" they declared in a single voice, and the brush was thrust into Mr. Pan's hand. Mr. Pan was enjoying this moment. He dipped the brush into the ink. After thinking for a moment he scrawled four characters across the shining paper: *Kung Kao Yo Mu.** On the second piece he wrote: *Wei Chen Tung Nan.*† On the third he wrote: *Teh Lung En P'u.*¶

As he wrote the last characters he thought of the men being dragged in bonds to toil for the army, he heard the firing of cannon and saw the burning of houses, he imagined the screams of women, and he saw pictures of starving people and decaying corpses. In an instant the pictures flashed before him and passed away. A man by his side looked judicially at his handiwork.

"That last phrase is still more to the point and the characters are best written of all. . . ."

"Now what will he say to go with it?" asked another.

---

*"Greater in Service than Yo and Mu," referring to a famous statesman and a general in the mythical days of the Emperors Yao and Shu.
†"Power Threatening East and South."
¶"Eminent Virtue and Broad Benevolence."

LU HSÜN

Remorse

Handwritten Notes by Chuan-sheng

If I can possibly do it, I want to write down the story of my remorse and my sorrow; I want to do it for Tzu-chun's sake and for my own.

This deserted little room in a forgotten corner of the guild is so desolate and empty. Time has gone by so fast. A whole year has passed since I began to love Tzu-chun and with her at my side escaped from this solitude and emptiness. When I returned, as my bad luck would have it, this same empty room was the one available, the same broken window, the same fading old locust tree and the same old wistaria creeping around the sill. Here is my old square table at the window, the same soiled walls, the boards I use for my bed. When I lie upon them sometimes in the night it seems as though I had never loved and lived with Tzu-chun. All that happened this past year seems erased from memory, as if it never really took place at all. I never really moved out of this shabby room. I never went with high hope to establish that little home in Chi Chao Hutung.

This room used to be vibrant with anticipation of the coming of Tzu-chun. After I had fretted for a long time with impatience, how my heart would jump when I would hear the click of her heels on the brick walk outside. Her pale round face with its laughing dimples and her thin white arms; her striped cotton blouse and her black skirt. She would bring in some fresh leaves from the withering locust tree and call my attention to the clusters of light purple blossoms on the iron-heavy old wistaria vine. But now the solitude and the emptiness is back. Tzu-chun will never come again, never, never again.

When Tzu-chun was not in my shabby room, I could not see anything. If I picked up a book, I was aware neither of its title nor of anything else. My whole being waited and listened. Among the footsteps passing outside, I waited eagerly for the tic-toc of her heels. I hated the servant's son, whose cloth shoes made no sound like Tzu-chun's, and I hated the neighbor who wore shoes too much like hers. Had she been run over by a tram? I wanted to grab my hat and go look for her, but then I remembered the time her uncle scolded me rudely to my face. Then suddenly came her tapping steps steadily nearer, and I ran out to meet her. But she was already past the wistaria arbor and almost to the door. There was a dimpled smile on her face. She was living in her uncle's house then, and evidently there had not been any more unpleasantness. I felt relaxed.

We gazed at each other for a moment, but soon the shabby room buzzed with my talk. I would talk about our tyrannical family system, about breaking away from the old ways, about sex equality, about Ibsen, Tagore, and Shelley. Her eyes would fill with wonder and she kept nodding. A picture of Shelley hung on the wall, cut from a magazine, a beautiful picture. When I pointed this out to her, she glanced at it briefly and turned her face away, as if in embarrassment. Tzu-chun was not entirely free of the old ways in things like this. Later I thought of replacing it with something else, like Ibsen's picture, but I never did. Now even this is gone.

"I belong to myself! None of them has any right to interfere!" Tzu-chun spoke quietly but with clarity and determination. It was six months after our friendship began and we were talking about her uncle who lived here and her father at home. She spoke after a long pause. I had already unburdened to her my life and my dreams and my ideas and my faults. I concealed virtually nothing. Therefore she understood me perfectly. Her words shook my soul, and, sounding in my ears for days afterward, left me in ecstasy. I felt a bright light dawning for the women of China. Surely they were not as hopeless as the pessimists insisted.

When I saw her out, we usually left about ten paces between us. Whenever we did, the old man with whiskers like a catfish would look at us, his face pressed against the dirty window pane, his nose flattened. In the outer yard, that little person with the cream-smeared face would watch us pass. But Tzu-chun fixed her eyes proudly before her and did not notice them. I returned with a heart filled with pride. "I belong to myself! None of them has any right to interfere!" This thought was firmly in her mind, more firmly than in mine. To her the flattened nose and the smeared face meant nothing.

I have already forgotten how I expressed my true and passionate love to her. Even at the time it became a blur to me almost immediately afterward. When I tried to reconstruct it for myself that same night, I could only recall fragments. Two months after we had come to live together even those fragments had vanished like a dream. I could only remember one thing clearly. For more than ten days beforehand I had carefully rehearsed my speech. I prepared myself for my protestation of love and steeled myself in advance for a possible refusal. But all these preparations proved useless when the moment came. In utter confusion and despite myself, I imitated the scene I had seen so often on the screen. Whenever I thought of it afterward I burned with shame, but it always remained clear in my memory, and it does now. In a dark room, with the single lamp lighting up the tears in my eyes, I took her hand in mine and knelt on one knee before her. . . . I have forgotten my own words and what she said and did, only that she promised herself to me. I also remembered that she first turned pale, then blushed, a blush I had never seen before and will never see again. In her childlike eyes there was sorrow and joy, wide with both wonder and confusion. But I only glimpsed them, for they tried to escape me, timid and tremulous, as if seeking to dart away through the window. I know she promised to be mine, but how she said it or whether she did say it, I cannot recall.

But Tzu-chun remembered everything. She could repeat my words like a lesson committed to memory. She could narrate in every particular how I had acted and what I had done, so graphically and in such detail that it seemed to pass before us like a moving picture, and of course it included that awkward movie-like scene which I would rather have erased from my mind. In the quiet of midnight she would often make me go over it, like an examiner, and order me to repeat my words over again. But often she would have to supply most of them and correct me like a teacher correcting a dim-witted pupil. This happened less often after a while. But sometimes she would seem to take flight from herself and the expression on her face became surpassingly, smilingly sweet and her dimples deepened. I always knew that she was going over it again in her own mind. I only feared that she would again see that preposterous flash of moving picture heroics. I knew she would see it, she insisted upon seeing it. But Tzu-chun saw nothing ridiculous in it at all, not even the things I found laughable or despicable. I understood this perfectly well, for she loved me with passion and sincerity.

Late last spring was our happiest and busiest time. My heart was settled and at the same time very unsettled. It was only then that we started to walk openly side by side. We used to take walks in the park, but most of our time we spent looking for a place to live. On our way, I often felt the inquiring, mocking looks of passersby and thought I heard murmured jibes and insults. It would make me tremble in every limb and I would summon up all my pride and defiance to keep a grip on myself. But Tzu-chun was utterly fearless and paid no attention to any of this. She walked with measured steps and unflurried composure, as if she lived in a land without any other inhabitants.

It was not easy to find lodgings. Most often we were refused on some pretext. Other times we found the places unsuitable for us. In the beginning we expected much, not really so much, but still the places we saw did not seem to be suitable for us. In the end, we searched hopefully for any place which a landlord would let us have. Finally, after much weary tramping and more than twenty failures, we found two small rooms facing north in a small house on Chi Chao Hutung. Our landlord, who was a petty official but yet a man of understanding, lived in the master's rooms and a side room with his wife, their baby girl, and a servant girl from the country. The household was very quiet and calm except when the baby cried.

Most of my money went for furniture, although our purchases were simple indeed. To help, Tzu-chun sold her gold rings and earrings. She did so over my protest. I had to give in because I knew that she would not be able to live there unless she were a shareholder in our joint enterprise. Tzu-

chun had quarreled with her uncle and he got angry enough
to disown her as his niece. I too had to break with several of
our friends who advised us against this step, either because
they feared the consequences I might suffer, or because
they were envious. We were left to enjoy ourselves in
solitude.

Every afternoon after work was done and the long slow
ride home finally ended, we found time to sit together, sometimes gazing at each other in silence, or talking openly and
intimately, and then falling again into silence. Sometimes we
lowered our heads in thought but really thought of nothing.
Gradually I learned to read her like a book, body and soul.
In three short weeks, I felt I understood her far better than I
had before, removing barriers between us that I had not
even been aware were there.

Tzu-chun grew livelier day by day. She did not seem to
like flowers. Once I brought two plants from the market, but
after four days without being watered, they curled up and
died. But Tzu-chun did develop a liking for animals. Perhaps she picked it up from our landlord's wife. Our family
suddenly increased in less than a month; four tiny chicks
pattered around the courtyard together with the dozen
which belonged to the landlady. They seemed to be able to
recognize which ones belonged to whom. Not long after that,
we acquired a spotted puppy, also bought at the market. As
I remember, it already had a name, but Tzu-chun gave it a
new one. She called it Ah Sui.

It is true that love must be constantly renewed; it must
grow and be creative and always fresh. I talked to Tzu-chun
of this and she nodded understandingly. Oh, how happy and
peaceful those nights were!

When peace and happiness come into life, its rough edges
are leveled off. While I lived at the guild we still had misun-

derstandings and conflicts of views. From the time that we moved to Chi Chao Hutung these vanished. All we had to do was sit under the lamp and talk of our former experiences. We would retaste the joy of our reconciliations after those old disputes.

Tzu-chun grew fat and her cheeks red. She became exceedingly busy. Even the time we used to spend in talking became absorbed into household affairs, to say nothing of the time once spent in reading and walking. We always used to say that we should have a servant. Sometimes I would be upset on my return to find her sulking over some unpleasantness. To make it worse, she would try to assume sweet smiles for me. I would discover that it was only over some quarrel with the landlord's wife about nothing but the four little chickens. But why conceal the fact from me? Every one should have his own home and live independently, I thought. A place like this was insufferable.

The course of my life was molded to a fixed routine. Six days out of every week I went back and forth between home and the Bureau. My work there was copying, endlessly copying letters and documents of various kinds. At home it was my job to help with the stove, to cook rice and steam the man-t'ou.* I learned how to cook for the first time in my life. My food was much better now than I had ever had in the guild. Tzu-chun was no cooking expert but she put her whole mind to it. She exhausted herself and her energies at it day and night. I could not but join her in this, if only to have a sense of sharing her hardships. She perspired and her short bangs stuck to her forehead and her white hands began to grow coarse. Besides, she had to feed Ah Sui and the chickens. I assured her it was not so important to eat, that she must not keep so busy and be forever tired. She made no answer but only looked at me sadly. There was nothing to do

*A steamed bread commonly eaten in North China.

but shrug and say no more, and Tzu-chun went on working.

The blow which I had long expected at last fell. One night I was sitting idly watching as Tzu-chun washed up the dinner dishes when a knock came at the door. A messenger from the Bureau handed me a slip of paper. I guessed its contents, and my guess was confirmed when I held it under the lamp: "The Bureau Head has ordered that Shih Chuansheng need no longer report for work in the Bureau.—The Secretary."

I had felt this coming even before I left the guild. The neighbor with the smeared face was a gambling companion of the son of the Bureau Head, and I felt certain that through him the story would get back with embellishments. Indeed, it had come later than I had expected. Actually it was not so much of a blow. Anticipating it, I had figured I could copy for someone else, or teach, or, with some effort, even translate. The editor of the magazine *Friends of Liberty* was an acquaintance with whom I had been in correspondence two months before. Nonetheless, my heart beat hard as I stared at the notice. The pain was made no easier when I saw even the fearless Tzu-chun turn pale. She had begun recently to be a little scared.

"What of it?" she said weakly. "We'll begin something new. . . . We'll. . . ." She did not finish. It seemed to me that her voice was very uncertain. Even the lamplight seemed dimmer than ever before. The human being is preposterously ready to be affected deeply by trivial things. At first we only looked at each other in silence. After a while we discussed our situation, and finally we came to a decision. We would thriftily conserve the money we had and would put an advertisement in the papers seeking some copying or teaching work. I would also write to my editor friend, tell him of my circumstances, and urge him to accept my translations to help me out of this difficulty.

"Let's get to work on it, then, now that we've decided! Let's open up a new road for ourselves!" I turned and went to the table. I pushed away the bottle of oil and the dish of vinegar and Tzu-chun brought me the dim lamp. I would first write out my advertisement and then select the books for translation. They were dusty, never touched since we had moved there. I finally began my letter. I hesitated for a long while, pondering my words and the form of my phrases. When I lifted my brush for a pause I glanced at Tzu-chun and found her face very sad under the yellow light. It had never occurred to me that such a trivial occurrence could cause so great a change in the resolute, fearless Tzu-chun. She had been growing more timid, I knew. It had not begun only this night. I felt more upset and confused. Suddenly I had a vision of tranquility—it was my own previous life in the shabby room at the guild!—but before I could fix my eyes on it, there was again only the dim light of the lamp. After a long time the letter was finished. It was long and I felt fatigued, as if I too had grown timid. We would insert the advertisement and mail the letter off at the same time tomorrow. We stretched out on our backs, both of us, and in that perfect silence it seemed to me that we must feel somehow the persistently strong spirit of each other. Both of us surely must have felt hopes for a new life germinating.

Blows from the outside could only arouse new spirit in us. Life at the Bureau, after all, was like the bird in the shop of the bird dealer. It could continue to exist on a few seeds but could never grow fat. As time passed it would no longer be able to fly, even if you released it from its cage, for its wings would have lost their powers. I was free of my cage now. While I could still remember how to do it, I would fan my wings and soar high into the broad new sky from this very evening!

I could not hope for immediate results from the advertisement, and translating was not such an easy task as it seemed. Sections which had seemed easy on first reading now presented all sorts of difficulties and ambiguities when I actually began to work upon them. My progress was therefore extremely slow, but I was determined to work hard at it, and before a fortnight had passed my dictionary was black with thumbing. The editor of the *Friends of Liberty* had promised that no writings of quality would be refused by his magazine. But it was a pity I had no quiet room in which to work. Tzu-chun was not as quiet and considerate as before. Dishes and utensils were scattered around the room and smoke swirled from the stove. It was not easy to work, and for this I suppose I had myself to blame, because I could not afford to have a study to myself, but then there was Ah Sui and the chickens, who were growing and causing endless quarrels between the two families. And the meals! They came as regularly as the flowing current of a stream. Tzu-chun seemed to feel that her whole merit in life was concentrated in these meals. The merits she used to recognize seemed forgotten. It never occurred to her that I might be annoyed and my train of thought and work broken by these summonses to eat—to eat. She only worried about the money for each meal, and that over, she would worry about the next. Then she would feed Ah Sui and the chickens. Even if I looked angrily at her when we sat down, she never seemed to notice and would go on eating unconcernedly, like a dolt.

It took five weeks to make her understand that my work could not be governed by her meal schedules. Perhaps she was not pleased when I upbraided her. But she gave no indication of it. After that my work went more quickly and before long I had completed fifty thousand words of translation. A little more work and the whole manuscript, together with two short essays already finished, could be sent off to the *Friends of Liberty*.

Eating was again a source of difficulty. Cold vegetables were all right but not enough. Sometimes even rice ran short, although I did not eat as much as I used to since I began sitting home using nothing but my brains. This was because she fed Ah Sui before she fed me. Recently she had been buying mutton—which we could not afford—for the dog. She said that the landlady laughed at her because Ah Sui was so pitifully thin. Such mockery was hard for her to bear. Only the chickens had to wait for me to finish before they could have their meal. I did not realize this until long afterward. I thought of Huxley's description of the position of man in the universe and I defined my own position as coming between a little dog and chickens.

During the course of a long process of protests and persuasion, the chickens were gradually converted into meals. Ah Sui, Tzu-chun, and myself made them last more than ten days. Actually they offered up little, for they were all quite thin, having been fed for a long time on only a few grains of millet a day. With the chickens gone it was much quieter. But Tzu-chun grew languid and melancholy and seemed barely willing even to open her mouth. How quickly people can change!

Soon Ah Sui had to go too. We had given up hope of getting replies from any promising source, and for many days Tzu-chun had no food with which to lure him to a begging position. Winter was rapidly approaching, and we would soon have the problem of keeping a fire going in our room. Ah Sui's appetite had long been more of a burden than we could support. We might perhaps have made a few coppers if we had taken him to the temple market and offered him for sale. But neither of us could have done this even if we wanted to, so we covered him with a piece of cloth and I took him out to the western suburbs and let him go. He tried to follow me back, and I pushed him down into a shallow pit. I felt relieved when I got home, but Tzu-chun's tragic air shocked me. I had never seen an expression like that on her face before. Of course, it was because of Ah Sui, I understood, but how could it affect her so much? I did not tell her that I had pushed the dog into a pit.

Coldness was added to her melancholy in the night.

"Why . . . what is it? What's come over you today, Tzu-chun?" I could no longer hold my peace.

"Oh, nothing, nothing at all."

I sensed that Tzu-chun thought me hardhearted. Actually I was suffering the pains and burdens of living mostly on her account, even in things like getting rid of Ah Sui. For myself, I could live quite easily. As a matter of pride I never had anything to do with my father's friends. My own friends were estranged from me after I moved from the guild. Despite all this, my life still opened broadly before me if only I could break free of this suffocating whirl out to where I could breathe fresh air again. Tzu-chun seemed unable to conceive our situation in these terms. Her sense of judgment, her perceptions, and her feelings seemed to me to grow more shallow each day. Once I took the time to explain to her exactly how I felt. She nodded her head as if she understood, but before long her actions showed me that she had either not understood me at all or had not believed what I said.

Coldness in the air and in the heart of Tzu-chun drove me from our home. But where to? In the street and in the park I did not have to encounter frozen, bitter looks, but the biting wind lashed at my flesh. I finally found my haven in the public library. There was no fee, and there were two iron stoves in the reading room. They were kept less than half-filled with the lowest-grade coal, yet the mere sight of them brought a new feeling of revival and warmth. There was nothing worth reading, only old books worn through their bindings. But reading was not my purpose in coming anyway. Nor did it seem to be the driving motive behind the presence of my companions in the reading room, usually more than ten in number and all of them shivering in light gowns. Like me, they came for warmth and used reading as an excuse. This suited me precisely because in the streets I ran the chance of encountering some old friends and of shying away from their glances. But I was absolutely safe from them here, for they were sure to have other stoves to sit around in their own homes and elsewhere.

There were no books for me to read, but there was time and silence in which to think. As I sat there by myself I contemplated my past half-year of life and reflected that I had given up all other important things in life for love, blind love. The first rule of life was to make a living. A man had to make a living before his love could have something to hang on to. There was no lack of ways to make a living for a man who sought it. I felt myself failing more than ever before. Yet I still remembered and desired to spread my wings and fly. . . .

The reading room vanished, and I saw the fisherman fighting angry breakers, soldiers in the trenches, the mighty in the motorcars, the speculators in the stock exchange, the heroes of the people in the mountains and the forests, the professors in their classrooms, athletes in the late afternoon, thieves on their midnight prowl. . . . Tzu-chun was not at my side. She had lost her courage and herself in her cooking and her grief for Ah Sui. Was it not strange she grew no thinner?

The last few coals burnt themselves out, finally, and it grew cold. It was closing time. I had to return now to Chi Chao Hutung to face the cold there. Once or twice recently there had been a brief respite of warmth, but these had only deepened my pain. One night the childlike light gone for so long reappeared in Tzu-chun's eyes, and she talked to me once

more of the times when we were in the guild, but she spoke
with fear in her voice. I knew she felt the growing gap, and
I made an effort to comfort her by smiling and talking in
the old way. But when I smiled and talked and the words
left my mouth they turned into drafty mockeries that echoed
and reechoed in my brain and buried me beneath an insufferable and malicious scorn.

Tzu-chun also seemed to be aware of this. She shook herself from her numb immobility and gave signs of interest
and anxiety despite her attempts to cover it. She was far
sweeter to me now. I wanted to speak to her frankly but I
dared not. My determination always thinned into a forced
smile when that childish look of enquiry returned to her
face. It mocked me.

She would once more rehearse our old talks, and I was
obliged to make many softly tender answers to her questions
while in my heart I would write down the script of my false-
hoods. My heart became overweighted with them, and I
could not longer breathe. Twisted with pain I tried to think
straight and clearly. It required great courage to speak the
truth. If I permitted myself to remain entangled in false-
hoods and could not acquire such courage, then I was not
the person to blaze a new road to life. More, I would simply
never have lived as a man!

In the cold of the morning Tzu-chun's face bore an expression of bitterness that I had never seen before. Perhaps I
only read it into her. I was vexed with her, but coldly and
from a distance. I laughed silently at her. All her polished
thoughts, her fearlessness and her intelligence had disappeared in the vacuum which she herself had created, although unaware of doing so. She had long since stopped
reading. She did not know that the first task of our life was
to reach out for survival. Men and women must struggle for
survival hand in hand, otherwise must go alone. If one of

the two travelers sought only to hang to the hem or the other's gown, then both would perish together. Even a soldier could not continue to fight in such circumstances.

I felt that only in our separation was there hope. She should leave. The thought of her death also came to me, but I drew back from it and repented. Luckily, it was still early morning. There was time for me to speak out my heart and my thoughts. This was our chance to hew open a new way. Everything depended on this. I began to talk with her. I deliberately spoke of our past, of literature, of foreign writers and their works, of Nora and *The Women of The Sea*—I praised Nora for her courage and her decision. These were precisely the talks we had in that broken-down room in the guild less than a year before, yet how hollow they sounded issuing from my own mouth and passing into my ears. It seemed to me that some naughty child was mimicking me behind my back.

In the beginning Tzu-chun nodded and indicated agreement. After a bit she was silent. My voice trailed off and passed away into empty space.

"Yes," she said after a long pause. "But . . . Chuan-sheng, you've seemed different recently. Am I right? Tell me . . . you . . . tell me frankly."

This was like a shattering blow struck on my temples but I pulled myself back to composure and patience. I told her what I had been thinking, of my dreams of hewing a new way in life that we might escape from perishing together. In the end I paused, then went on resolutely:

". . . You want me to speak frankly. You are right. People should not be false. So let me tell you frankly—I no longer love you. This is all the better for you . . . you can go on without worrying about anything. . . ."

I expected some great calamity, I don't know what. But instead there was just silence. The color drained from her face after a shocked pause and left it deathly yellow. It flowed back in a second and that childlike look again filled her eyes, and like a hungry infant seeking everywhere for its mother she only looked into space, avoiding my eyes in horror. I was unable to look at her any more. Luckily it was morning. I ran out into the cold air and up the street against the biting wind toward the library.

I found a copy of *Friends of Liberty* there, and to my surprise, as if some new life were actually dawning for me, I found both of my short essays published in it. There were many ways out, I reflected, but none of them was possible under present circumstances.

I began to visit some of my long-estranged friends once or twice. Their rooms were warm, and I was shiveringly cold down to the marrow of my bones. In the night I could only curl up in the icy room in Chi Chao Hutung. There were needles of ice driven into my soul, and I suffered a constant numbed pain. There were many ways open to me to make a living. I still remembered to flap my wings. I would think— again the idea of her death flashed before me, but instantly I reproached myself and repented the thought. Often in the library I saw light, and the way to the new life was clearer before me. Tzu-chun courageously and resolutely left our icy home. Moreover, she left without showing resentment. Then I would feel light as the cloud buffeted in the void, above me the blue sky and below the mountains and oceans, battlefields, gigantic buildings, automobiles and markets, the mansions of the rich, bustling streets under the bright sunlight or quiet in the darkness of black nights. . . .

What is more, truly I felt this new life coming.

Somehow, we managed to live through Peking's insufferable winter. During winter man was like a dragonfly in the hands of a mischievous boy, held by the thinnest of threads and dangled and manipulated and persecuted although not quite killed. He stayed alive but could only shrivel up on the ground and struggle to live a few minutes longer.

The editor of *Friends of Liberty* replied at last to my third letter. He sent me two book coupons, one for thirty cents, another for twenty. And I had spent nine cents postage asking for them! More hunger and emptiness after the labor that had profited me nothing! But meanwhile what I had expected at home finally happened. It was during those days which were neither winter nor spring. The wind was no longer so bitingly cold and I spent more of my time wandering outside, often returning home only after dark. On one such evening I turned slowly down our street, and the sight of our gate filled me with the greatest reluctance and I approached it most unwillingly. I finally entered the room. There was no light. Groping for matches I lit the lamp. The room was oddly quiet and empty. As I stood rooted to the floor the wife of the landlord called to me. She came to the window and called me out.

"Tzu-chun's father came today and took her back with him," she said plainly. I had the sensation of someone striking a stinging blow across the back of my head. I stood speechless.

"She's gone?" I managed to say after a moment.

"Yes, gone."

"She . . . did she say anything?"

"Nothing. Just asked me to tell you when you got back that she was gone."

I still did not believe it although the room was unmistakably empty. I looked around still seeking Tzu-chun but saw only the few broken and discolored pieces of furniture which seemed far too bare and scanty to hide anybody. I thought perhaps she might have scribbled a few words on a piece of paper but there was nothing. Only the remains of salt, some

dried peppers, flour, and part of a head of cabbage. Beside
them stood a small heap of coppers. I looked at the collection, all our life's store of belongings. Now she had left them
to me alone and was earnestly asking me in silence to go on
with my dream of living myself into the future.

The room seemed to bend its walls to enclose me, and I
ran out into the darkness of the courtyard. But behind the
paper window of the north room a lamp gleamed, and I
heard the people there teasing their baby. My quickly-
beating heart began to calm, and I saw through my heavy
burden a way of escape, gradually, indistinctly beginning to
take form. Wild mountains and giant swamps, foreign markets and a gay feast under electric lights, trenches and the
black nights, the blow of a sharp spear and deadly, silent
steps coming near. . . .

My heart grew lighter and my body relaxed and I
breathed longer breaths. I lay there and watched the dream
road of my fantasy unfold before my closed eyes. It passed in
review as the hours broke toward midnight. It led to an un-
beautiful heap of food which was replaced in the darkness
by Tzu-chun's pale yellow face, its childlike eyes widely
looking at me, pleading with me. When I concentrated my
gaze upon her the whole vision vanished.

Weights bore down upon me. Why should I have spoken to
her so impatiently and not waited a while longer? I could
see clearly what stretched before her—her father's despotism,
as harsh as the burning sun, and the frosty disdain and contemptuous, pitying looks of others. Nothing else in life for
Tzu-chun. Emptiness. How horrible to go on living with the
weight of a vacuum on one's back, burdened with harshness,
despotism, and contempt! That road led to a grave without
even a piece of stone to mark it. I should not have spoken of
realities to Tzu-chun. I should forever have solaced her with
my lies, for we loved each other. If truth had value it should

not mean a burdened void for Tzu-chun. Lying too was empty, yet it could not possess the stonelike weight that truth was now for Tzu-chun. I fancied that when I spoke to her truthfully she would march forward resolutely and without care, as she had before we came to live together. Perhaps I was wrong. *Surely* I was wrong! Her intrepid courage of those days was born of our love. I loaded upon her the burdens of truth because I lacked the courage to bear the weight of falsehood. For her love of me she was now traveling the road back through harshness, despotism, contempt, and death. I thought of her death. . . . I saw myself a coward, unacceptable to the strong, be they false or true. While from beginning to end she had hoped I would be able to extend my life. . . .

It was so empty and strangely lonely in that room. I wanted to leave Chi Chao Hutung. If I could leave it would still seem to me that Tzu-chun was by my side, I thought. At least I might hope for an unexpected visit, like she used to make when I lived in the guild. Letters and pleadings brought no replies. In the end I was forced to visit an old friend of my father's whom I had long neglected. He had been a schoolmate of my uncle and had been promoted into the official ranks for his scholarship. He had lived in Peking for many years and had a wide circle of friends. Perhaps it was the raggedness of my clothes which earned me the spiteful look of the gateman. I was not easily admitted, and when I was the atmosphere was cool although I was still recognized. He knew the whole story of my past.

"Of course you cannot stay here any longer," he said in a frozen tone when I asked him to find me a job elsewhere. "But where will you go? Hm, quite difficult. . . . Your— what was she—your friend?—Tzu-chun, you know, she's dead."

"Are you certain?" I stammered.

"Of course, of course, it's true. My friend Wang Shun lives in the same village as they do."

"But . . . do you know in what manner she died?"

"Who knows?" he shrugged. "Anyway, she's dead and that's all there is to it."

I returned home. I do not know how I took my leave of him. I knew he never lied. Tzu-chun would never come again as she had last year. Even if she desired to travel the road to life with her burdens, amid harshness, despotism, and coldness, it had already become impossible for her to do so. Her fate had been decided. Extermination in the truth I had exposed to her! There is no love in the world! Of course I could not stay in that room anymore. But where would I go? The vast emptiness of unfilled space surrounded me. I distinctly saw how dark death was for those people who cherished no love. I heard all the last whispers of distress and hopeless struggle.

I was still looking for something new, something unexpected out of the void, although day after day passed in unbroken, deadly solitude. I seldom went out. I sat or slept in that emptiness, and I let my loneliness etch its own pattern on my soul. Sometimes it would retire trembling, and my vague hopes for something—I knew not what, whence it might come, or why—would reappear and temporarily take possession of me. One gloomy morning when even the sun was unable to break through the clouds that stifled it and the air seemed heavy with fatigue, I heard the patter of light, broken steps, and the faintness of light, unsteady breathing. I opened my eyes. The room was still empty but when I looked to the floor I saw there a small animal, wasted to its skin and bones, dragging itself with difficulty, covered with filth and sores. My heart stopped beating. It was Ah Sui come back.

It was rather because of Ah Sui than on account of the cold pity of the landlord, his wife, and their amah that finally I moved from Chi Chao Hutung. I knew somehow that many paths were open before me. I could even see them vaguely and feel them. But I was still ignorant of how and when to take the first step along any of them. In the end I decided that only the guild was suitable for me. There again I would find my deserted room, my wooden board bed, the dying locust tree, and the wistaria vine. But the thing that had given my life hope and joy and love was no more. In its place I had a vast emptiness which I had won in exchange for truth.

New ways were surely many. Since I still lived I had to enter upon one of them, but still I did not know where to take my first step. Sometimes I felt that the road itself was rushing upon me like a gray snake while I stood pertrified and waited for its attack. Then when it seemed almost upon me, it vanished in the darkness. Spring nights were still long. During my long silences I recalled the funeral I had seen on the street one morning. Before the bier came persons made of paper, and horses and chariots too, while the wailing of the mourners rose sadly into the wind. I realized now how clever they were. How easy and simple was life thus measured! But now I thought of the funeral of Tzu-chun. She was all alone walking along the pale, long road with a tremendous burden on her back. But the vision wilted under the contempt and the coldness that surrounded her. I wish there were really ghosts, a real hell. Then even in the roar of the winds and the whining of the breezes I could look for Tzu-chun and pour out before her my regrets and my sorrows and beg her forgiveness. Or if I could not find her there then hell's fumes of poison and smoke could seize upon me and in fierce rage devour my repentance and my sorrows. In the winds and amid the fumes I would embrace

Tzu-chun and ask her pardon. Perhaps it would make her happy. . . .

But this was more empty than any new road to life. I have now only the early spring night which is still very long. I am living so I must step forward toward the new way. To write down my regrets and my sorrows and my repentance for Tzu-chun has been the first step. I have only to bury Tzu-chun in forgetfulness. I want to forget. I do not want to think of the fact that I buried Tzu-chun with forgetfulness. I want to take the first step toward a new life, and I shall go on silently burying truth deeply in the wounds of my heart and let forgetfulness and lies be my guides along the way. . . .

TING LING

The Diary of Miss Sophia

Dec. 24—It blows again today! The wind awoke me before daybreak. And now the servant comes in to make the fire. I know I'm not going to be able to sleep anymore. I also know if I don't get up I'll soon be dizzy. I'm too fond of mulling over many strange things when I lie under my quilt. The doctor told me the best thing is to sleep a lot, eat a lot, and not to read or think, but this is precisely what I can't manage to do. I can't ever get to sleep before two or three in the morning, and I'm always awake before it's light. It's impossible not to think of the many irritating things that come to one's head during weather like this. You can't go out to amuse yourself in all this wind, and shut up indoors you find nothing to read. What else are you going to do? Can one sit there like an idiot waiting for time to go by? Day by day I wait, dragging on, wishing this winter would end soon. With the warm weather my cough is bound to improve; then I can go back south if I like, return to school if I like. This winter is too long!

I'm heating milk for the third time as the sunlight hits the

Translated by A. L. Chin.

129

paper window-panes. Yesterday I heated milk four times, not always because I wanted to drink it but to ease my vexation on a windy day. Of course this kind of thing can while away an hour or so, but sometimes it actually adds to my annoyance. I stopped doing it all last week. But yesterday, out of desperation I had to rely on it again, patiently, like an old man, to pass away some time.

The newspaper comes. I begin and systematically read first the big-character headings in domestic news, then the important foreign news, and finally the local miscellaneous news. I finish reading about education, political information, economic conditions, and the price of bonds. . . . After all this I go back and review the all too familiar advertisements of positions for men and women, calls for registration of men and women students, lawsuits over family division of property, and even items like ads for 606 and *po-ling-chi*,* cosmetic remedies, the latest shows at the K'ai-ming Theater, and movies at the Chen-kuang. After I know all this backward and forward I finally put aside the newspaper. Occasionally, I do find a new ad or two, nothing more than an announcement of an anniversary sale in some fabric shop or some obituaries.

Emptiness after the paper. I sit sullenly in front of the stove. What annoys me is nothing new. Everyday, I listen to the other tenants shout for the servant in the corridor outside my window and I get a headache. The voices are loud, coarse, and monotonous: "Waiter, bring boiling water! Washing water, waiter!" As everyone knows, this kind of voice can grate on your nerves. Then all day there are people speaking into the telephone downstairs. But if there's no sound at all the silence is fearfully gloomy. Especially the four whitewashed walls. Wherever you sit, they seem to stop your eyes. If you escape into bed the white ceiling weighs

*A specific for veneral disease and a widely advertised aphrodisiac.

down on you. I can't find anything which doesn't disgust me: there is the pockmarked servant with the food that smells just like the dishcloth, the window frame which is impossible to keep clean, and the mirror over the wash-basin. . . .

That mirror can make your face look a foot long, and if you turn just a little slantwise it will flatten enough to scare you. I'm annoyed again and again by all these things. Maybe I'm the only one feeling this way, but in that case I would rather find something new to be displeased or dissatisfied with, although anything new, good or bad, seems miles away from me here.

Brother Wei arrives after my midday meal. His characteristically quick steps reach me from the other end of the corridor and comfort me, as if releasing me from a suffocating room. But I don't know how to express it. When Brother Wei comes in I receive him in silence. He thinks I'm annoyed again, so holding my hands tightly in his he says over and over again, "Sister, sister!" And I, I smile, of course. I know what I'm smiling about. I know what's hidden behind those eyes, those lively eyes. How long is it, now, Brother Wei, that you've been in love with me? But am I captivated by him? Naturally, I cannot take any responsibility for this. This is how a woman should behave. Actually I'm faithful enough. I don't think there can be another woman who would refrain from playing with him the way I do. Furthermore, I truly feel sorry for him. I can hardly keep from pointing out to him: "Brother Wei, is it possible for you to change your ways? You only displease me this way!" If Brother Wei were a little cleverer, I could get to like him more. But he only knows how to express his sincerity in this honest way!

He is satisfied when he sees me smile and skips over to the bed and takes off his coat and his big fur cap. If he turned to look at me now, he'd surely feel a little unhappy from what he could see in my eyes. Why is it he is unable to understand me better? I always wish for someone who can understand me thoroughly. Without understanding, what use have I for love and sympathy? My father and my sisters and my friends all love me with such a blind love. I really don't see what is it that they love in me: my pride, my temper, or my consumption? Sometimes I feel both angry and sad at this, yet they all give way before me, love me all the more, murmuring words of comfort that are so wrong I want to strike them. At such times I truly wish for someone who can understand me. Even a scolding from such a person would bring me happiness and pride.

When people don't come to visit me, pay attention to me, I long for them or feel angry at them. When they do come, I can unintentionally embarrass them. I can't help this. Recently, just to see if I could discipline myself, I've tried to hold my tongue, to suppress remarks which leap to my lips and lacerate the feelings of my friends, though I say these things in jest. Because of this, one can imagine in what mood I sit with Brother Wei. But if he should get up and talk about leaving, out of my loneliness and depression I would hate him. Brother Wei has known this for a long time, so he sits here right on through the afternoon and evening. It's ten o'clock before he leaves. I'm not deceiving anyone except myself. I know that Brother Wei's remaining here doesn't profit him any. It only makes me take him for granted and even pity him more for his deficiency in the art of love.

Dec. 28—Today I invite Yu-fang and Yun-lin to come to the movies with me. Yu-fang brings Chien-ju along. I feel almost like crying with rage. Instead I let out a laugh. Chien-ju! She is so capable of destroying my self respect. Because her face and bearing are so much like that of my childhood best friend, I found myself pursuing her. And she, she deliberately encouraged me to be close to her. But I met with unbearable treatment from her. Whenever I think about this, I hate my past and my irretrievably shameful behavior. I wrote her eight long letters in a single week and never had a reply. What on earth was Yu-fang thinking, deliberately inviting her to come when she knows perfectly well I'm unwilling to dig up my past, as if purposely to provoke my hatred? I am so peeved! As to my laughter, neither Yu-fang or Yun-lin would notice that there's anything strange in it, but Chien-ju would. She could assume an air of innocence and chat with me as though there were nothing between us. I am about to say something sharp to her but I curb my words, remembering my own resolution. Besides, if I were so much in earnest, this would only give her satisfaction. I bear with this and go out with them.

It is early when we get to the Chen-kuang cinema and we meet a number of girls who come from my native place. I pay them no courtesy at all, for I detest these automatically smiling faces and the sight of all these people going into the theater. While Yu-fang is busily chatting, I slip away, abandoning my guests, and quietly return home. Nobody will forgive me but myself. Everybody is criticizing me but none of them knows what people arouse in me and what I have to endure. People say I'm eccentric, but none of them sees how I accommodate them and try to please them. But people are entirely too unwilling to encourage me to say what goes against the grain. They often give me opportunities to reflect upon my behavior, leaving me to drift farther and farther away from people.

The hostel is utterly quiet this midnight. I've stretched out in bed for many hours straightening my mind of a lot of things. What have I really to be sad about?

Dec. 29—Yu-fang telephoned me early this morning. She's honest and wouldn't tell any lies. She says Chien-ju is sick, and probably this is so. Yu-fang also says I'm the cause of it and wants me to go so that Chien-ju can explain. But both Yu-fang and Chien-ju are wrong. Sophia doesn't like to listen to explanations. I don't believe there is anything in the universe which needs any explanation. If friends get along together, that's well and good. If not, and one of them causes the other suffering, that too is natural and aboveboard. I think I'm bighearted enough never to revenge myself on others. Still, now that Chien-ju is sick on my account, I feel oddly happy. The news that anyone is sick because of me will never be unwelcome to me. Moreover, Chien-ju's illness can even lessen a little of my own feeling of self-condemnation.

I am at a loss to know how to analyze my feelings. Sometimes I can feel a vague and indefinable sorrow for a patch of white cloud being dissolved by the wind. But when a man over twenty—(Brother Wei is four years older than I)—sheds tears, drop after drop, onto my hand, I laugh with satisfaction like a savage. Brother Wei comes to see me with a gift of stationery he has just brought from East City. And because he smiles and looks happy, I perversely provoke him, not to be satisfied till he cries. "Spare your tears," I then tell him. "Don't think I'm like other people's women who are so fragile they can't bear to see a teardrop. . . . Go home if you have to keep on crying. I detest tears. . . ." He naturally doesn't leave, neither does he defend himself or get angry. He merely sits there, crouched in a corner of the chair, shedding those silent, simple, endless tears which come from nowhere. And I, naturally I am satisfied now, and actually begin to feel remorseful. So I stroke his hair and use a sisterly voice to tell him to wash his face. He is smiling before his

eyes are dry. I've made a good man miserable purely to satisfy my heartless nature. Yet after he's gone I truly wish I
could call him back. I want to tell him one thing: "I know
my own weakness. Please stop loving the kind of woman
who doesn't deserve to receive such pure love!"

Jan. 1—I don't know how the New Year merrymakers are
celebrating this day. I only add an egg to my milk. The egg
was brought to me by Brother Wei yesterday. I received
twenty eggs from him, and after cooking seven of them with
tea leaves and sauce I still have thirteen, which will probably last me two weeks. If Brother Wei comes in at noontime
I can look for at least two cans of delicacies. I hope so much
he will come. Because of this I went to Tan P'ai Lou and
bought four boxes of candy, two packages of pastries, and a
basket of oranges and apples. All this is for him to eat when
he comes. I'm certain that today he alone will come.

But the noon meal is past and he isn't here. I've written
five letters, all with the fine paper and pen he brought me
the other day. I wish I could receive some beautiful cards,
but I know I won't. Even some of my sisters, who like to do
this sort of thing, have forgotten to give me my due. It is
nothing not to have the cards, but it vexes me to think that
they've forgotten me. But I've never sent anyone a New
Year's greeting, so I suppose this is only what I deserve.

Supper too I eat alone. I'm filled with ennui.

In the evening Yu-fang and Yun-lin come in, bringing with
them a tall young man. They're lucky, those two. Yu-fang
has Yun-lin to love her. She is satisfied and so is he. Happiness is not in having someone to love, but in two people
avoiding stronger desires, sharing thoughts with each other
and passing the days contentedly. Of course there are some
who think this life too commonplace to be worthwhile. That

might be true of somebody else but not of my Yu-fang. She is a good person. She has her Yun-lin, so she wants to see "all lovers united." Last year she tried to make a love match for Ma Li, and hopes that I will grow to love Brother Wei. That's why she asks about him every time she comes. She and Yun-lin and the tall one are eating up all the good things I bought for Brother Wei.

That tall one is handsome! This is the first time I've ever been struck by any man's good looks. In the past I've never paid any attention to such things, but always thought it a man's job to talk, to show good judgment, and to be cautious. But not so when I look at this tall friend of theirs. I'm beginning to see that man can be cast into a nobler mold. Next to him Yun-lin looks so insignificant and clumsy that I pity him. If he were conscious of this misfortune, of how he appears next to this big man, he would be so grief-stricken over his own vulgar bearing and manners. I wonder even more how Yu-fang would feel if she were aware of the contrast between the two men, the one so tall and the other so puny!

How shall I describe him, this stranger? Obvious to anyone is his stature, his fair face, thin lips, and soft hair. All this is pleasing enough to the eye. But there is something else, a certain elusive, indefinable grace in his carriage which sways your heart. When I ask his name, he has a way of handing over his name card with an unexpectedly smooth and unhurried gesture. I raise my eyes and ah, I see those bright red, finely drawn lips. How could I tell anyone that I'm looking at those tempting lips like a child longing for candy? Even though what I want won't injure anyone else, I know that in this world I will not be permitted to take what I want to satisfy my stirrings, my desires. So I bend my head and patiently, silently read the words on the card:

"Ling Chi-shih, Singapore. . . ."

The Diary of Miss Sophia

He is talking freely and without restraint, as though he were among old friends. Can it be that he is deliberately mocking my shyness? It is because I must force myself to resist temptation that I dare not raise my eyes to look at that disturbingly exciting figure. Even my poor, shabby slippers, of which I was never ashamed before, keep me from going into the lamplight in front of the desk. Furthermore, I'm angry with myself. Why am I so restrained and artless in my speech? I've always despised the way people make acquaintances, but I'm discovering now how dull, foolish, and stupid I must appear to other people. Ai-ya! He must think me a silly country girl newly come to the city!

Yun-lin and Yu-fang sense that I'm acting unnaturally, and they think I'm displeased about their friend. They keep interrupting him, and soon they take him away. Am I supposed to be grateful for a kindness like this? I watch the three figures, one tall and two short, disappear in the courtyard below, and while I watch I know I hate to return to this room with the imprint of that man's foot on the floor, the sound of his voice, and the crumbs of the cake he was eating only a few moments ago.

Jan 3—I've coughed without stopping for two nights now. I would never have any confidence in medicine. How can there be any relationship between medicine and my illness? I'm clearly tired of that bitter liquid but I still take it as prescribed. If I cut it out altogether what would I have to rest my hopes upon? Threat of suffering before death is evidently God's way of imposing patience on people, keeping people from embracing death. As for me, it's because my life is so short and limited that I crave more living. I'm not afraid of death but I feel I haven't enjoyed all there is to life. I want to make myself happy. Night and day I dream of a way to experience no regret at the time of my death. I imagine myself lying on a bed in a beautiful room with my sisters kneeling on the bear rug next to my bed praying for me and my father turning toward the window softly sighing. And I would be reading many long letters from people who love me, from friends who would shed honest tears in remembrance of me. I desperately need this kind of love, and I crave all these things in impossible dreams. But what have people given me? For two more days now I've been imprisoned in this hostel and not a single friend has been to visit me. Nor have I received a single letter. I cough in bed. I cough when I sit next to the stove or at the table. I still think of these hateful people. . . . Yes, I have one letter, but it only adds to my annoyance, and nothing more than mere annoyance. This is from a coarse and vulgar man from Anhuei who used to irritate me. The pages are filled to overflowing with declarations of love, "this love" and "that love." This only disgusts me. I tear them into tiny pieces without finishing it.

Jan. 4—Things go wrong more and more. Why should I think of moving, and why in my confusion should I have lied to Yun-lin? Lied so effortlessly, as though lying were part of my nature. How sad Yun-lin would be if he knew Sophia can lie to him too. She's always been such a loving little sister to both of them. Of course I feel uneasy and I'm sorry for it now. Still, can I make up my mind? Shall I move or not?

I can't help telling myself—"You're thinking of the shadow of that tall man!" Yes, and for days and nights I've been falling into that temptation. Why hasn't he come alone to see me these last few days? He ought to know that he has no right to make me think of him so much. He should come up here and tell me how he has thought of me too. If he comes, I wouldn't refuse to listen to his words of affection for me.

Moreover, I'd tell him about the desire in my heart. But he hasn't come and I guess all my fantasies can only dissolve into thin air. Do you mean to say that I should go see him? No good would come from a woman with such lack of restraint. But I do so want to win his admiration. I can't think of a good way out, so I leave here after the noon meal in all this wind to search out Yun-lin over in East City.

Yun-lin studies at the Ching Tu University and lives in Ch'ing-nien Hutung, which runs between the first and second colleges. I'm lucky to find him in, even Yu-fang isn't there. He is surprised that I've come on so rough a day but I tell him I've dropped in on my way back from the German Hospital. He believes this to be the truth. When he asks me how I feel I easily turn the conversation back to the other night and before long I learn that my tall man is living in the fourth dormitory next to the second college. Soon I'm sighing and saying in many different words how lonely and dull my life is over in the West City. I lie again and tell Yun-lin that my one wish is to be near Yu-fang, knowing that she will soon move into his place. I ask Yun-lin to look for a room nearby, and he is of course pleased and agrees with alacrity to help me.

While we're hunting a room we run into Ling Chi-shih and he goes around with us. I feel happy, so happy that my timidity flees and I fix my eyes directly upon him several times, but he doesn't notice it. He asks after my health and when I tell him I'm fully recovered he smiles unbelievingly.

I've selected a small, mouldy room with a low ceiling in the Ta Yuan Hostel next to Yun-lin's. Both my companions disapprove of it, saying it is too damp, but I insist that I want to move tomorrow. Why so quickly? I'm bored with the old place, and besides I'm impatient now to be near Yu-fang. Yun-lin can't do anything but yield and promises to come to me tomorrow morning with Yu-fang to help me.

How can I tell anyone? The only reason I've selected this room is that it's just about midway between the fourth dormitory and Yun-lin's place.

He has not said goodbye to me, so I go back with them to Yun-lin's. I'm laughing and talking freely now, and I've scrutinized every bit of him. I feel there isn't any of him that does not need the imprint of my lips. Does he know I'm looking at him and thinking about him? Later I deliberately say I'm thinking of asking him to teach me English. Yun-lin laughs, but he seems to be embarrassed and mumbles his reply. I say to myself that he is not a bad sort if, tall and big as he is, he can still blush. This makes my fires blaze all the more warmly. Yet I don't want people to see through me, to figure me out too easily. So I force myself to return early.

As I think it over, I can't imagine my willfulness driving me into any worse position. Let me stay in this room with its stove. Is it possible to say that I've fallen in love with that man from Nanyang* when I don't know him at all? What nonsense is all this, about his brow, his lips, the corners of his eyes and his fingertips . . . ! I must be bewitched. This isn't anything anyone should want, should think about. I'm not going to move; I'm going to stay here and concentrate on resting. I'm determined now. I'm sorry, sorry for all I've done wrong today. No decent woman would ever have done it.

Jan. 6—Everybody is surprised to find that I've moved. Chin-ying from the South City, Chiang and Chou from the West City have all come to this low and damp room. I laugh and roll over in my bed, and they think I've grown more childish. This makes me laugh all the more and makes me want to tell them what is really in my heart. Brother

*South Seas, applied to Southeast Asia and the islands of Oceania.

Wei comes in the afternoon. He is most displeased of all because I didn't discuss the matter with him, and I'm now farther away from him. When Yun-lin comes in he won't even talk to him, and his face is dark with anger as Yun-lin looks at him amazed and puzzled. I think it is all so funny. "He's got the wrong end of it," I say to myself, "what a pity!" Yu-fang stops talking about Chien-ju. Since I have seemed so anxious to live next to her, she's decided to move in with Yun-lin in about three days, for she doesn't want me to be lonely here. Both she and Yun-lin are even kinder to me than before.

Jan. 10—I see Ling Chi-shih almost every day now, but I never say much to him and am determined not to be the first to mention English lessons. It amuses me to find him going to Yun-lin's one or twice each day now for I'm sure they weren't so intimate before. Although he's asked me how things are after moving, I've replied only with a smile, as if I didn't understand what he's driving at. I have not once asked him to visit me because I'm still unwilling to take for myself the thing I desire. I must seek every conceivable means of having it offered to me voluntarily. I'm using all my ingenuity on this now, as though I'm engaged in a fierce struggle. Yes, I'm perfectly aware I'm a woman with all the woman's ways. A woman likes nothing better than concentrating on the man she is to conquer. I want to possess him so that he offers up his heart unconditionally and kneels before me pleading for a kiss. I'm insane, mad. I'm scheming and turning over and over in my mind every step I'm to take. I'm utterly insane.

My excitement is going completely over the heads of Yun-lin and Yu-fang who think I'm getting better. I don't want them to know anything, and I look pleased every time they tell me how much improved I seem to be.

Jan. 12—Yu-fang moves in but immediately Yun-lin moves out. Is there such a pair as this in all the world—afraid to live together for fear of having children! I think they themselves cannot be certain that embracing each other in bed will have other consequences, so they're avoiding the chance by not letting their bodies even come into contact with each other! As to kissing and embracing otherwise, this is guaranteed against danger. All it needs is privacy and there's no risk at all! So they do this from time to time, gently, because it is not forbidden. I can't help laughing at them. These puritans! How is it that they don't feel the urge to embrace each other's naked bodies? Why suppress this expression of love? How can two people plague themselves with things not worth worrying about even before they get under a single quilt together? I don't believe love can be rational and scientific! Instead of being annoyed at my mocking them, they're proud of their purity and accuse me of childishness. I can understand the feelings of their hearts but I can't explain all the strange things in this world.

We're telling ghost stories at Yun-lin's—or Yu-fang's it now is—and not leaving until late. When I was still a child I always used to sit on my aunt's lap and listen to ghost stories from the *Liao Chai* told by my uncle. I loved to hear them, especially at night. My fear I kept secretly to myself for otherwise Uncle would have gone away to his study and the children wouldn't have been allowed to come down from bed, and that would have meant no more ghost stories. Then in school I learned some of the common sense of science, and the confidence with which my teacher Mr. Freckle-Faced Chou inspired me soon led me to disdain fear of ghosts. Now that I'm grown up I always deny that any ghosts exist. Yet the mere mention of the word never fails to give me goose pimples and make my pores open. People never know that I try to divert the conversation into other channels when ghosts are mentioned because I know such talk will lead me to sad thoughts of my dead aunt and uncle once I'm alone under my covers.

The black little lane is filled with shivery shadows. I won't be entirely surprised if some monstrous yellow face or a hairy hand should rise from some frozen corner. Yet with my tall bodyguard by my side I've really no need to fear. Therefore to Yu-fang's anxiety I reply, "Never mind, I'm not afraid." Yun-lin leaves with us and turns away southward to his new room. His rubber-padded steps fade away into the night. My companion passes his arm around my waist.

"You must be afraid, Sophia!"

I try in vain to free myself. My head is under his arm. How ridiculous I must look here encircled in the arm of a man a whole head taller than I! Crouching, I slip from under, and he also releases me and stands there while I knock at my door. Although the lane is pitch dark, I can feel his eyes, and my heart beats more quickly while waiting for the door to open.

"You are afraid, Sophia!"

The wooden latch rasps back of the door and the servant is asking "Who's there?" I turn—

"Good—" He grasps my hand in his, and I stop speaking. The servant is obviously surprised to see me followed in by such a giant of a man. My boldness is of no use, now that we're alone in this room. I can't bring a single polite phrase to my lips. Bidding him sit down, I turn to wash my face. Ghosts are entirely forgotten.

"Do you still want to learn English, Sophia?" he asks suddenly.

He is the one to bring up the matter of English! Of course he doesn't want to waste his time teaching. Does he think he can fool a woman over twenty with talk like this? I'm amused.

"Too dull," I reply. "I'm afraid I am unequal to it. I might disgrace myself."

He doesn't answer but fingers a picture of a baby standing on my desk. It is my sister's one-year-old daughter. I have finished washing my face now and I'm sitting now across the desk from him. He looks from me to the picture and back to me. Yes, the baby girl is much like me.

"Doesn't it look like me?" I ask.

"Who is it?" earnestly.

"Isn't it lovable?"

He persists in his question. I realize what's in his mind. Once again it's my impulse to lie.

"Mine!" and I grasp the picture from him and kiss it.

He believes me, I see, and I'm pleased with the deception. His charm and attractiveness seem reduced now. Otherwise how can I remain so indifferent to his eyes and the purse of his lips, showing surprise at my answer? But now this triumph has cooled my fervor. After he's gone I'm sorry. Didn't I throw away every possible opportunity? It only needed some kind of response to the pressure of his hand to let him know he wouldn't be refused. He would surely then have grown bolder. I'm sure that if I don't find such a person repulsive, such boldness between the sexes could produce ineffable happiness, a feeling as though the flesh were melting away. Why should I have treated him with such sharp aloofness? For what, anyway, did I move to this broken-down little room?

Jan. 15—I'm not at all lonely now, passing the days at my friends' homes and the evenings talking with my new friend.

Yet I am more ill than ever and still more disheartened.
What can I desire, seeing that nothing helps me? Could it
be that I'm in love? I laugh at almost everything, yet the
thought of death makes me sad. I understand the expression
on Dr. K's face. I know, say it. Is it hopeless now? Who can
guess, among all who see me laugh, how much I cry in the
middle of the night?

Ling Chi-shih has been coming to me for several evenings
running now, announcing to others that he is teaching me
English. He really begins to do so in earnest, but I take the
book away from him. "Don't tell people you're teaching me
English," I say. "Nobody will believe you. I'm sick."

"Will I be able to teach you when you're well, Sophia? If
only you'll let me—" he replies quickly.

My new friend is so attractive, yet I hardly pay any attention to this. Still, I'm sorry to see him go away unsatisfied
every evening. So, as he's putting on his coat, I tell him:

"Please excuse me for my illness." He thinks I'm standing
on ceremony with him.

"Never mind," he replies, "I'm not afraid of infection."

After he's gone I think there might be some other construction to be placed on his answer. I can't be sure people are as
simple and straightforward as I think.

Jan. 16—I have a letter from Sister Wen in Shanghai
which is horribly depressing. "There's no use either in life or
in love for me any more," she writes. Neither the comfort I
give her nor my tears help any. I can guess what her married life is like although she doesn't speak of it explicitly in
her letter. Why does God play tricks on those who love? Sister Wen was always of a nervous and sentimental temperament. She could not bear the obvious cooling off and the
false front of affection in her life. I want her to come to Peking. But can she?

I show it to Brother Wei, and he is deeply concerned, for the man who is the cause of my sister's mood is his own brother. I tell him what my philosophy of life has grown to be, and as usual all he can do is weep. I watch frozen while his eyes turn red and he lifts the back of his hand to wipe the tears away. I make things worse by making cruel comments on everything he does. It doesn't occur to me that he is one of the most honest people on earth. Then leaving him there without a word I slip out the door. Not until nearly midnight do I return from the deserted park where I've fled to avoid all friends. All I can think is that life is meaningless. Better to die quickly and get done with it.

Jan. 17—I may have been mad. If I am really insane I won't mind it so much. I won't be conscious of life's problems and complexities then. I'm drinking a lot of wine today out of a jug put away six months ago because of my illness. It cannot stain my sputum more red than it is. I feel as though my heart is under the control of something else. And this wine, it seems that it could poison me tonight. I'm tired of thinking about all those complicated things now. . . .

Jan. 18—I'm still lying on this bed here, but soon I'll leave this place, maybe forever. Can I say that I'll ever enjoy things again—this pillow, this quilt? Yu-fang, Yun-lin, Brother Wei, Chin, and Hsia are all sitting around me dejectedly waiting for daybreak to get me to the hospital. Their whispering has awakened me and I lie silently thinking about yesterday morning, not interested in talk. Only the lingering odor of blood and wine in my room brings me back to reality and makes my heart ache and tears stream from my eyes. They are so silent, so sorrowful and gloomy. They make me feel as though death were coming close. Suppose I should just sleep on without ever awaking, would they sit around my stiffening corpse in just this same way?

The Diary of Miss Sophia

They see that I'm awake and come over to speak to me. Now I really fear the parting of death. I grasp their hands and look closely into each of their faces, as if this could fix them indelibly in my memory. Their tear drops fall on my hand, as if I were leaving them for a long journey to the kingdom of death. Brother Wei especially cries till his face is swollen and ugly. Ai! I say to myself, "Dear friends, please give me a little happiness." And I'm smiling now. I ask them to help me pack a few things, so they drag out the big wicker chest under the bed and bring me some small packages tied up in flowered handkerchiefs. "I want them," I say. "I want to have them with me when I go to the Hsieh Ho Hospital." I show them that these packages are full of letters, and I add, laughing, "including yours." This seems to lighten their mood a little. Brother Wei quickly takes out a book of photographs from the drawer, as if wanting me to take it. I smile, because in it are seven or eight pictures of him alone. I also let him kiss my hand and rub it against his face. Now this room no longer looks as if it really contains a corpse. Day is breaking and the sky is now milky white. They are busy looking for rickshas and getting my things together. I'm going to the hospital.

Mar. 4—Twenty days have passed since the telegram announcing the death of Sister Wen arrived. I myself have been improving steadily and I've been brought back to this same room by the same friends who took me to the hospital. The room has been swept clean, and a small foreign-style stove has been put in to keep me warm. I don't know how to express my gratitude to them, especially Brother Wei and Yu-fang. Chin and Chou have remained two nights to look after me and, lying in bed the whole day long, I feel as comfortable here as if I were not in a hostel but at home. Yu-fang is going to stay with me a little longer, and when the days get warmer she's going to look for a place in the Western Hills where I can go for a long rest. I'm anxious to leave Peking and the hateful cold weather, even though it is March! Yu-fang insists on staying here. I cannot absolutely refuse her, so the small bed put in only a few days ago now remains for her use.

My days in the hospital have changed my outlook too. This is truly due to the care of my friends, which has warmed my heart. The world seems to be full of love. I was especially proud when Ling Chi-shih came to see me at the hospital. It seems to me that only a man with his grace should go and visit a sick girlfriend in the hospital. I was keenly aware that the nurses envied me. One day pretty Miss Yang asked about him.

"Who is that tall man?"

"A friend," said I, ignoring the impolite implications in her query.

"Someone from your home district?"

"No, from the South Seas."

"Schoolmate, then?"

"No."

Then she smiled knowingly. "Only a friend?"

I had no cause to blush. But I was too shy and embarrassed to disabuse her and the way I lay there distressed, with eyes tightly shut, made her walk off, still smiling. After that I continued to be annoyed at her. And to avoid trouble, I lied to those who asked me about Brother Wei, saying he was my own brother. A good friend of Chou's I either said was a relative or someone from my home district.

When Yu-fang is at class and I'm alone in my room, I look over the letters I've received in the past month. This makes me happy and contented, thinking of all the people who remember me. I need people's good wishes and remembrance, the more the better. As for father, needless to say he sends me another picture of himself, his hair whiter than before. My sisters are well, but too busy taking care of their children to write me often.

Before I finish reading my letters Ling Chi-shih comes. I'm about to stand up, but he stops me. He holds my hand, and I'm so happy I could cry. I say to him:

"Did you think that I would come back to this house?"

He gazes through the window at a shop on the other side, looking displeased. So I tell him the other two guests have left, the bed is for Yu-fang. When he hears this he tells me he wouldn't come here tonight for fear Yu-fang might be annoyed at him. I'm secretly satisfied: "So you're not afraid I might be annoyed?"

He sits on the bed and slowly tells me what's happened to him this month, how he crossed words with Yun-lin. He was in favor of my leaving the hospital early, but Yun-lin insisted I shouldn't. Yu-fang was on Yun-lin's side. Ling Chi-shih realized that he'd known me only recently and his opinion didn't carry weight, so he washed his hands of the whole matter, and when he met Yun-lin in the hospital he simply left first.

I know what bothers him but I deliberately say: "Why do you talk about Yun-lin like this? Without him I would still be in the hospital—it's so comfortable there." He silently turns his head without answering me.

He leaves just before he thinks Yu-fang will arrive, softly saying that he will come back tomorrow. Soon Yu-fang does return, but she doesn't ask and I tell her nothing. Out of concern for my illness, she doesn't want to tire me out by too much talking, and I'm glad enough to turn my thoughts to other idle topics.

Mar. 6—Yu-fang has gone off to her classes, and I'm alone here thinking about the strange relations between man and woman. I'm not boasting, but I think I've had more experience along this line than most of my friends put together. Still, I don't understand these relationships, especially now. My heart jumps whenever that tall man is with me, and I feel shy and afraid while he sits there at his ease, telling me of his past life, sometimes with my hand in his, always calm and simple and natural. But soon my hand cannot remain placidly in his; it grows more and more feverish. When he gets up to leave, I feel unaccountably anxious, a sense of disquiet taking command of me. As I fix my gaze on him, I'm not sure whether I'm looking for his pity and sympathy or whether I hate him. But whatever my eyes do say, he does not make it out. Even if he does understand, all he says is: "Yu-fang is coming." He's afraid of Yu-fang. What should I say to that?

There was a time when I would much rather keep my chaotic and unreasonable thoughts to myself. But now I begin to feel the need of somebody to understand what is going on inside of me. I've sometimes tried to talk in a vague way with Yu-fang, but she just carefully tucks my quilt around me and busies herself with my medicine. I'm a little overtaken with sadness.

Mar. 8—Yu-fang has gone back, but Brother Wei wants to take over the nursing duty. I know if Brother Wei comes he would be better than Yu-fang. If I want some tea at night, I wouldn't have to listen to that deep snoring or see the unwilling head duck under the covers. Of course I couldn't accept his offer, and when he insists I tell him: "Your presence would be inconvenient for me. Besides, I'm feeling better now." He still wants to show me the empty room next to mine which he can occupy. Just as I wonder what to do with him Ling Chi-shih comes. I thought they didn't know each other, but Ling Chi-shih is already shaking Brother

Wei's hand, saying they had seen each other twice at the hospital. Brother Wei is cool to him so I smile and say to Ling Chi-shih:

"This is my younger brother. He's young and inexperienced in company. Come and see him often."

Brother Wei, acting like a child, dejectedly gets up and leaves. I hide my unhappiness in front of these two and feel a little apologetic toward Ling Chi-shih. But he doesn't mind and asks:

"Isn't his family name Pai? How can he be your brother?"

I say laughing: "Then do you only allow Lings to call you their brother?" And he laughs too.

When young men get together they always want to talk about "love." Although I seem to understand some of it, I can't express it. I know the little things that take place between man and woman—perhaps I see them too clearly. This may even be the reason why I feel confused about "love" itself and lack the courage to nourish love. For the same reason, I sometimes doubt if I am a girl simple and innocent enough to be loved. I therefore suspect the "love" I hear on people's tongues and the "love" I receive. I have always been troubled by this ever since I began to have a glimmer of understanding. When I was in school people slandered me and humiliated me so that even my friends deserted me. Later, out of fear of the oppression of this love, I finally left school. As I was growing up, I've always felt this kind of entanglement to be meaningless and rather disdained the intimacy it inferred. Brother Wei has always proclaimed his love for me. Then why does he bring me sorrow instead of joy? Take tonight, for example.

He comes in and the sight of me seems to start him weeping and sobbing without restraint. I ask him again and again, "What is it, Brother Wei? Tell me what troubles you. I beg of you, say something!" But he just weeps on without reply. This had never happened quite this way before. I can't imagine what his trouble is, so how can I begin to figure it out? When he's finally exhausted with weeping, he bursts out: "I hate him! I hate him! I don't like that tall man who's now your friend!" Oh! So now he's venting his anger on me. I can't help laughing. Is this love, this meaningless jealousy and selfish desire to possess? I laugh, and it is not very comforting to my poor ambitious Brother Wei. Indeed, my disregard rouses his great anger, and his glistening eyes glare as though he could bite into human flesh. "Come, now!" I say. But he hangs his head, shakes with sobbing, and walks out, his hands rubbing his eyes.

This may be a true expression of so-called violent love. Yet to express it spontaneously leads naturally to failure. I don't want falsehood or artificiality in love. But neither does childish behavior like this move me. Maybe I was born with a hard heart. If so, I deserve the sorrows and vexations which my disagreeable nature brings down upon me.

But this has roused my own feelings and makes me think of the kind of tenderness that is open, straightforward, and yet sensitive. This attitude is so intoxicatingly enjoyable that it stirs feelings of melting intimacy. I scribble on a card and call a servant to take it at once to the fourth dormitory.

Mar. 9—The sight of Ling Chi-shih casually sitting here in my room makes me pity Brother Wei. I hope no one else like me ignores or despises the priceless sincerity which ends up by plunging him into such bottomless despair. I hope some pure-hearted girl retrieves his love and fills the great emptiness he must feel.

Mar. 13—I haven't written anything for several days. Whether it's due to my bad mood or the lack of so-called emotion, I don't know. Since yesterday I've wanted to cry.

The Diary of Miss Sophia

People imagine I am dreaming of my home and lamenting my continued illness. If they find me gay, they think me happy and congratulate me on these signs of returning health. They're all the same. To whom can I open my foolish heart, which disdains tears yet cannot summon up laughter? Since I understand perfectly my own lingering desires in this world and the distress that results from every effort to attain them, I can no longer feel sorry for myself for the pain which comes on so inexplicably. How can I then express all my regrets and self-hatred with my pen?

Yes, I'm complaining again. But since all this is revolving in my own mind, there's no harm in it. I've never had the ability to display before others my worries and miseries, although many indiscriminately call me lonesome, proud, and queer. I don't want to complain. I want to cry. I want somebody to hold me close, to weep on. I want to say "I'm wasting myself again." But who will understand me and caress away my tears? I can only swallow my tears in laughter.

It's hard to say why I feel this way. I haven't fully agreed with myself that I'm in love with that tall man. Yet what a special place he occupies in my scheme of things! His stature, his good looks and soft eyes and sensitive mouth can of course attract girls who like this sort of thing, and his proud manners will win the affection of some. Yet am I to be attracted by this Nanyang Apollo just because of his senseless beauty? I'm fully aware from what he's told me of his outlook and pathetic desires. What does he want? Money. A young wife who'll receive his business friends in the drawing room. A few fat sons dressed in fine linens. What is love to him? Something he can buy with his money in brothels where he can enjoy the pleasures of the flesh on a soft sofa with a slender, perfumed body on his lap and smoke cigarettes like a young gallant and, crossing his knees, talk boastfully about it to his friends. And if he happens not to enjoy it, he can return to his wife. He would be an enthusiastic speechmaker, a tennis player. He would go to Harvard and become a diplomat, an ambassador. Or perhaps he would go into his father's business, be a rubber merchant in Singapore, a capitalist! These are his dreams and the boundaries of his existence. Except for concern over the unsatisfactorily small dimensions of amounts of money he has been getting from his father, he has nothing to lose sleep over. Or perhaps the scarcity of beautiful women in Peking, a defect which makes the parks and theaters less attractive. What can I say now? When I realize that in that noble figure of a man resides so cheap and mean a soul, and that I've accepted from him intimacies that measure up to less than half of what he squanders away at the brothels! When I think of the time he brushed my hair with his lips, I could cry for shame. Don't I offer myself to him for his amusement like the girls who sell their smiles? But the blame can only be on me, and this adds to my suffering. If I were harder, I'd check his boldness and then I'd think his timidity was because he has never experienced passion. Ai! How I should damn myself!

Mar. 14—Is this love? Perhaps only love has the power to work such rapid changes in one's thoughts. I detested that handsome man when I lay down to sleep, but upon waking from my dreams it is the image of that cheap trader which first comes to my mind! Is he coming today? This morning? Afternoon? Then I pick up the large volume of Wilson's speeches Ling left here last night and fondle the bound edge of it with my fingers.

Mar. 14, evening—I can act out such beautiful dreams with Ling playing the principal role, the hero and the villain at the same time. With thoughts of him I can spend my morning in the ambience of love drinking the sweet wine of youth. And with thoughts of him too I realize what this business of life really is, and, disheartened, I begin to think of death again. I even hate my willing downfall. Actually what I'm getting is the lightest of punishments! Truly, sometimes for the sake of my beloved I ask myself "Do I have the strength to kill somebody?" To better preserve my beautiful dreams and avoid diminishing my life I had better leave immediately for the Western Hills. But Yu-fang tells me she hasn't heard from her friend who's looking for a place for me. How can I rush her? Nevertheless, I've decided to let the tall fellow have a taste of arrogance, insult, and unreasonableness.

Mar. 17—Brother Wei went home displeased the other night. Today he comes back carefully and voluntarily to make peace. He makes me laugh, but at the same time appears lovable to me. If a woman only wants a loyal man to be her lifelong companion, she would find no one more dependable than Brother Wei. I asked him laughing: "Does Brother Wei still hate his sister?" He shyly replied: "I don't dare. But please understand me, sister, I only ask that you don't abandon me. I have no other designs. I'll do anything for you to make you happy!" Isn't this sincere and moving? How does he compare with that fair face and red lips? But later I said: "Brother Wei, you are a good man, the future will surely bring you many satisfactions." He replied with a sad smile: "Not in this world! But I wish for what you said. . . ." What is this, to add to my suffering? If I only could kneel down in front of him and beg him to give me only the love of a brother or a friend. For selfish reasons only, I could wish for fewer complications and more happiness. Brother Wei loves me and knows how to say nice things. But he neglects something: first, he should scale down his hopes, secondly, he must hide his love. To feel so sorry for such an honest man is not easy to bear.

Mar. 18—I'm again asking Hsia to look for a place for me in the Western Hills.

Mar. 19—Ling Chi-shih has not been here for several days. Of course I can't deck myself out prettily, nor receive guests properly, nor manage household affairs. I suffer from consumption and I have no money. Why should he come to me? I don't have to have him come. Yet that he should have stopped coming pains me and proves his frivolity. But is it possible that he is honest, like Brother Wei, and that when I wrote, "I'm sick. Please don't come to trouble me," he took me seriously and hesitates to disobey? This makes me want to see him again, if only to make sure just how this monster thinks of me in his heart.

Mar. 20—I've been to Yun-lin's three times today without meeting the one I want to see. Yun-lin seems to suspect my purpose for he asks me whether I've been seeing Ling Chi-shih lately. I'm back here disheartened. I'm impatient with myself and with everything, for can I deny that I've been thinking of him almost constantly?

At seven o'clock Yu-fang and Yun-lin come to ask me to join them at the English debate in the Third College. Ling Chi-shih is captain of the B team. My heart jumps at this last news but I refuse to go, pleading my illness. I was hoping to avoid him. I'm a useless weakling, and I can't stand excitement. But as they rise to leave, I ask them to convey my greetings to Ling Chi-shih. Ai—How stupid and meaningless!

Mar. 21—I've just had my milk and eggs and there's a familiar knock on the door and a familiar tall shadow against the paper windowpane. I want to jump to the door but something keeps me silent in my chair.

"Are you up, Sophia?" The voice is so soft and tender it makes me want to cry. Can he know that I'm already sitting in a chair? Can he know that I'm refusing him because I have no way to vent my anger? He gently opens the door and comes in but I don't dare raise my eyes for him to see the tears in them.

"Are you better, Sophia? Have you just gotten out of bed?"

I can't speak.

"You are really angry with me, then, Sophia. All I can do now is leave."

Of course it should suit me to have him go, but I suddenly raise my head and with my eyes keep his hand from the door. He understands, the rascal, and boldly grasps both my hands.

"You've been playing with me, Sophia. Every day I've passed here without daring to come in. If Yun-lin hadn't told me you couldn't possibly be angry with me I wouldn't have dared come today. Tell me, Sophia, are you annoyed with me?"

Anyone can see that if he takes me in his arms and showers kisses on me now I'll cling to him weeping and say, "I love you! I love you!" But he is cool. So cool that I hate him. Yet I'm thinking, "Come, embrace me, I want to kiss your face!" Of course, his hands still hold mine, and his eyes are fixed upon me. I study his face looking vainly for signs that he will grant what I am waiting for. Why is it that he only knows that I'm useless and contemptuous, that he cannot understand the special place he occupies in my heart? I wish I could just kick him out. But I am held by other emotions, so I only shake my head and indicate I'm not irritated about his coming. I yield again to his shallow emotions and sit and listen to more of his self-satisfied talk about his vile enjoyments and the philosophy of "making money and spending money." I even let him give me many hints as to how to be a woman. These things now make me despise him, silently curse him and mock him, and inwardly hit my heart with my fist. Yet when he haughtily walks out of my room I can't help but want to cry. And because I'm suppressing my hot desires, I have not pleaded with him to stay a while. Ai! he's gone!

Mar. 21, evening—What was my life a year ago? Under the unwavering love of Sister Wen I pretended to be sick and lay in bed reluctant to get up. Because I wanted to bask in her unfailing concern for me, and because of those tears of desperation she shed over her inability to comfort me, I would bury my face in my arms and cry over trivialities. Sometimes I end up with a sweet sadness from a day of solitary contemplation, but even that kind of loneliness is a sentiment I'm reluctant to let go, as if within it I can taste a hint of sweetness. At night I would stretch out on the grass in the French Park and listen to Sister Wen sing a song about the peony pavilion. This is something I would rather not think about, because had she not fallen in love with the palefaced man, as if tricked into it by some god, she would surely still be living and I wouldn't have drifted to Peking alone, to struggle with my illness without anyone to care for me. I have some friends here, and they are quite concerned about me, but can I weigh in the balance what I can sense about our relationship against Sister Wen's love? When I think about her I ought to cry hard as I used to do like a spoilt child. In the past year, because I've grown up a little, I often suppress my crying for fear people will be annoyed at me. Recently, I can't understand why I feel so anxious. I can't even find the time to weigh the good and the bad in what I've done, what I've been thinking, my health, my rep-

utation, and my future. The whole day long my confused
mind revolves around something I don't want to think
about, because this is what I want to escape from. And that
makes me suffer from an unbearable irritability. But aside
from saying "death is what I deserve," I have no other hope.
Dare I ask for sympathy and comfort? Yet it seems that I'm
begging for it now.

Yu-fang and Yun-lin come to my place as soon as supper is
over. It is already nine and I still don't want them to go. I
know Yu-fang stays on account of face, but Yun-lin insists
on going on the pretext of preparing for tomorrow's lesson.
So I carefully reveal to Yu-fang some of my recent distress. I
only hope she can understand me and accomplish for me
what I have failed to do: force me to change my way of living. But, putting the wrong interpretation on my words, she
gives me this friendly advice: "Sophia, you are not honest
enough. You are too careless with your eyes, though you
don't do it intentionally. You should know that people like
Ling Chi-shih, unlike those fellows who went around with us
in Shanghai, don't have many opportunities to be with
women, and are not used to getting their attention. Take
care that he doesn't suffer from disappointments later. It's
clear to me. How can you end up loving him?" Doesn't it
seem that the blame is now on me? If instead of asking for
help I were complaining, would I have avoided hearing
these words which make me even angrier, sadder than before? Restraining my anger, I laugh and said: "Sister Fang,
don't make me out to be that bad!" Yu-fang is willing to
stay the night but I insist that she go.

There are talented girls who on the provocation of the
slightest suffering can write poetry, in the new style or the
old—"Oh, I am sensitive and so full of sorrow. . . ." or "Oh
how sad my heart"—but I am unpromising and untalented.
I am oppressed by a poetic situation yet even in tears I fail

to express the conflict of my emotions. For this inferiority of mine, I should have compensated by behaving satisfactorily, even taking a thousand steps backward to win glory in praise in the mouths of the shallow and the eyes of the backward. I should never hold either pen or gun. Shall I actually bury myself in this pain, far more insufferable than death, all for the soft hair and red lips—of a man?

I'm dreaming about the medieval knights of Europe—not a bad comparison if you have seen Ling Chi-shih. He can even preserve that special Eastern quality of gentleness. God has given him all the advantages, but why did he not add a little intelligence? Ling doesn't even understand real love, truly not, though he already has a wife (Yu-fang said so tonight), though once in Singapore he rode a bicycle in pursuit of a lady in a car, and was in love with her for a while, and though he used to visit houses of pleasure. Still, has he really been loved by a woman? Has he loved a woman? I can't be sure.

A strange idea flickers in my mind. I've decided to teach that university student a lesson. Things are not as simple as he thinks in this world!

Mar. 22—I have written these daily records in a state of confusion. They were begun at the persistent request of Sister Wen. Although she's been dead for a long time, it still goes on as a sort of tribute to her memory and all her loving guidance. No matter how little I desire to take up the pen, even if I'm already in bed, the sight of her picture on the wall is sufficient to pull me up to write a page or two if only to avoid the accusation of my memories. Of course I'm unwilling to show it to anybody but her. First, because it was written specially for her and, second, I fear the pain of being shown up by people of intelligence, as if I might really feel guilty of some crime because other people worship their mo-

The Diary of Miss Sophia

ral conventions. So this black-covered book has always been hidden beneath my pillow. But today I acted against my better judgment though out of need. Brother Wei has for so long misunderstood me and in doing so has caused himself much unhappiness and me much discomfort. I believe that in my behavior I have always made my attitude perfectly clear. Why doesn't he understand? How can I be blunt and forbid him to love me? I've often thought that if it weren't Brother Wei but another man I'd know how to handle him better. But he is almost unbearably good. I can only show him my diary to let him know just how hopeless his love is and how shallow and inconsistent a woman I am. If he had ever understood me truly, I would have regarded him as the only friend to whom I could have ever opened up my heart and I would have hugged him close. I would have wished for him the love of the most beautiful woman in the world.

Now he's read the diary through several times and he's shed tears over it, although he is remarkably composed. I hadn't expected it.

"Do you understand me now?"

He nods.

"Do you believe in me now?"

"In what way do you mean?" he replies.

So I understand his nod. Who could understand me? Even if he understood this diary, it would express only one part in ten thousand of my thoughts. This too pains me—the inadequacy of this diary. That I should show anyone this attempt at an explanation of myself in words is itself painful enough. And now Brother Wei, fearing lest I do not get his point, adds at last,

"You love him! You love him! I'm not worthy of you!"

I want to take this diary and rip it into shreds. Have I not wasted it? But to him, I can only say,

"I want to sleep. Please come tomorrow."

Don't ever ask anything of this world. Can anything be worse than that? If Sister Wen had lived to read these pages, I'm sure she would have clasped me to her and shed tears. But Sister Wen is gone now. How can I weep over this diary of mine?

Mar. 23—Ling Chi-shih says to me: "Sophia, you're a strange girl." I know he doesn't mean to praise me out of any real understanding of me. What surprises him are the things he finds unfamiliar. The torn gloves. The dresser drawer over there without perfume in it. The new, but strangely torn, cotton gown, and the little old toys that have been saved for so long. What more? Queer laughter. He sees nothing beyond these and I've told him nothing about myself. When he exclaims, "Hereafter, I've got to devote all my efforts to making money!" I only laugh. When he talks of how some friends chased after girl students, and he concludes—"interesting indeed, Sophia"—I only laugh the more. Of course, I'm sorry I've been unable to make myself clearly understood and respected by him. Now I want nothing but to go off to the Western Hills. I'm laughing at all these past fantasies of mine!

Mar. 24—When he is alone with me, the sight of his face and the sound of his voice make my feelings rise. Why shouldn't I rush over to kiss his lips, his shoulder, all of him? Sometimes words like these are on my lips! "My Ling, let me caress you!" Yet reason—no, I've never been reasonable—say, self-respect—has always checked me. Ai! No matter how cheap or small his ideas, he has unquestionably turned my heart inside out. Why then do I refuse to acknowledge my love for him? And I'm sure, should he hold me firmly in his arms, should he surrender his body to my kisses and then throw me into the ocean or the fire, I'd wait for death contentedly—for it would forever preserve my love. Ai! I *do* love him! Only death at his hands would satisfy me!

Mar. 24, midnight—I have made up my mind. To save myself from temptation of the flesh and a fall into decadence, I'm going to Hsia's tomorrow in order to avoid Ling Chi-shih. This pain has had me in its grip long enough!

Mar. 26—In order to avoid one involvement, I run into another which makes me rush back to my own place. On the second day of my visit to Hsia, Meng-ju also comes. Although she comes to see someone else, I feel very displeased. At night, she begins to hold forth on some recently acquired theory on emotions, directing its hidden sarcasm toward me. I remain silent, but unwilling to grant her any satisfaction, I lie awake on Hsia's bed and wait till daybreak before returning with anger in my heart.

Yu-fang tells me a room has been found far out in the Western Hills. She even found a companion for me, a very good friend of Yu-fang's who's also recuperating from illness. I should be glad at this news, but barely does a hint of gladness cross my face when a shadow of sadness creeps across it. Although I left home quite young, drifting around, I've been close to relatives and friends. The Western Hills are only a score or so *li* away, yet for someone like me who's already twenty, this is the first time that I'm going to a strange place alone. If I should quietly die in these hills, who's going to be the first to discover my corpse? Can I be sure I won't die there? Maybe others would laugh at me for worrying over these little things, but they've actually made me weep. I ask Yu-fang if she could bear the thought but she only laughs, saying it's a childish question. What is there to think about in moving such a short distance? I wipe away my tears sheepishly only when Yu-fang promises to come up to the Hills to see me once a week.

Ting Ling

In the afternoon I go to see Brother Wei. He too says he
will come up to see me every week, on a day Yu-fang can't
go.

I'm back here this evening alone to arrange my things. I
weep over leaving all my friends in Peking. But the thought
that none of them is shedding tears drives away mine. I'm
going to leave this old city alone, quite alone. And in my
loneliness I think again of Ling Chi-shih. No, actually,
thoughts of him can't be said to be here, or coming again.
They're in my mind all the time. I can only say: "Let me
talk of my Ling Chi-shih again." The gap between us these
days is of my own making, but to me it is an incalculable
loss. Yet while I mean to loosen his hold on me, I've only
helped tighten it. Since I can't pluck him from my heart by
the roots, why should I not see him? This annoys me greatly.
I can't leave him like this. I can't go to the Western Hills
all alone. . . .

Mar. 27—Yu-fang went to the Western Hills early this
morning to arrange my rooms for my arrival. I'm going out
tomorrow. I can't be grateful enough to her. I want to stay
over another day here—but I can't very well say so. And
just now comes Ling Chi-shih! I grasp both his hands.

"I've not seen you for days, Sophia!

I want to cry, to hold him and cry. Instead I laugh and
can't help shedding tears at the same time. He is surprised
that I am moving to the Hills. Then he sighs. He turns to
comfort me, and I smile. He squeezes my hands so tightly
they hurt. As if resenting something, he says:

"You're smiling! You're smiling!"

The pain in my fingers fills me with a glowing sense of
comfort and well-being, as if my heart were at the same
time being struck by something. I want to fall into his arms.

There is a knock at the door and Brother Wei comes in. He is perfectly aware I don't want him here, so he stays. "Don't you have a class now?" I nod meaningfully to Ling Chi-shih, and we walk out together. He asks when I'm due to leave. I tell him and ask him if he'll return. He promises to do so quickly. And I look upon him now joyfully. All his smallness is forgotten. To me now he is a fairy-tale lover of romance. Yes, Sophia now has a lover!

Mar. 27, evening—It's five hours since I drove Brother Wei out. How can I describe this lapse of time? Like an ant on a burning pot, I'm sitting, standing, and walking to the door to peek through the crack. He's not coming! I'm sure he's not coming. I want to cry because I'm going to leave here in lonely sorrow after all. Isn't there a single person in all Peking who will feel with me when I go? Yes, I'm leaving tomorrow. Nobody in Peking will have to be bored any more by the ill Sophia. If only for her friends' comfort, it's good for Sophia to go out to the hills to die. Yet that they should all be content to see her leave alone without getting any affection! It probably won't harm anyone or move anyone even if she doesn't die. Stop it! Stop it! Stop thinking! What is there to think about? If Sophia hadn't been so greedy for affection, wouldn't she be satisfied with the apparent sympathy of her friends? I'll stop talking about friends. I'm sure Sophia will never be content with human friendship. But what will satisfy me? Ling Chi-shih promised to come and it's already nine o'clock. And would I be happy if he came? Would he give me what I desire?

He hasn't come and I hate myself unto death. A long, long time ago I knew at least how to conduct myself toward certain types of men. Now I'm just a silly fool. When I asked if he was coming, how could I reveal my begging eyes? One should not be too honest to a handsome man, he will only despise you. Yet I love him. Why should I employ indirection and coquettish tricks? Shouldn't I express love openly and directly? And if it injures no one, why shouldn't one kiss a hundred times over?

He promised, but he isn't keeping his promise. It is obvious he is just playing with me. It wouldn't have been a loss to you, my friend, to preserve some show of kindness before Sophia leaves!

I'm mad, without sense or coherence tonight. How useless words are at a time like this! Tiny mice seem to be gnawing at my heart. Or is a fire smoldering there? I want to break something or run out into the night air. I cannot control the stirring of my emotions. My passion is like a bed of needles, piercing me whether I lie this way or that, or like a caldron of boiling oil, and I'm listening to the gasp of the flames inside me and feeling the great heat on my body. Why don't I run out? I'm waiting here for the birth of some vague and meaningless hope. It is red lips I'm mad about! If it were still possible to hope—I can't keep myself from laughing as I put the question to myself—"Love *him*?" Ha! Ha! Ha! Sophia wouldn't be such a damned fool as to love that South Seas Islander! Is it possible that I can't do something which leaves everyone else unhurt—simply because I won't acknowledge my love for him? If he really doesn't come tonight, how can I willingly and indifferently go up to the hills?

Twenty minutes to ten!

Mar. 28—Three o'clock in the morning. In this world Sophia yearns too deeply and too earnestly after sympathy and understanding. That's why she's forever drowning in the distress of disappointment. Only she knows how many tears she sheds. Let's call this record a collection of Sophia's tears, drop by drop upon her heart, rather than a diary of her life. That would be truer. Yet now this diary is approaching its end. Sophia no longer needs it. Tears comfort her or release her anger because she is aware of the senselessness of life. Tears only express that absence of meaning. On its last page Sophia should celebrate happily. From the infinite depths of disappointment she suddenly emerges to feel a satisfaction that should mean final happiness. But from that satisfaction I only find victory, and from that victory, loneliness, and a deeper understanding of my pitiful, ludicrous self. Before this, the little patch of "beauty" which has haunted me vanishes. This beauty was the elegance of that tall fellow.

How to explain the psychology of a woman driven to the brink of insanity by the figure of a man? Obviously I cannot love him, for locked within his noble proportions is a lowly, ugly soul. None the less I admire him and think of him. I even feel all life would lose significance without him. How often have I thought that if only my lips could meet his one day I'd be glad to see my body dissolve in the laughter of my heart. More—for a gentle caress by this knightly person, for the lightest touch of his fingers upon any part of my body, I have been prepared for any sacrifice.

I should go mad. All the traces in my fantasy have at last become real, effortlessly and like a dream. But from it, did I experience what I imagined would be a soul-intoxicating happiness?

No.

When Ling Chi-shih came himself toward ten o'clock last night and began telling me haltingly how he'd been thinking of me, my heart leaped, but I soon became afraid when I caught his burning eyes, feverish with desire. And when I heard those hideous vows coming out of his vile mind, my self-respect was rekindled. The stream of trite and creepy love-talk would have swayed other women and won him someone's heart, but when it was turned upon me, the power of those words drove me ineffable distances from him. Poor fool! You were endowed with a beautiful body but God has his joke by cheapening your spirit! Do you think my hope is a family, my joy, money, my pride, social position? What a pitiful man you are before me!

I almost want to cry over the tragedy of him. But with his eyes still riveted on me, full of passion, how fearsome he becomes! More, if all he wants is satisfaction of the flesh, he could have destroyed my heart with his lust. But half-weeping, he says:

"Sophia, believe me. I will not fail you!"

Poor simple fool. He doesn't know yet that all he arouses with his blubber is my contemptuous pity. I even laugh and say how funny it is when he says he understands love and loves me. Don't those hot eyes which hold his desires tell me he knows only his shallow, despicable desires, and nothing more?

"Be smarter, my friend, and go away. Off to a house of pleasure. That's the place for the joys you're looking for!"

That is what I ought to be saying. It's what I'm thinking since I now clearly see his measurements. I ought to tell this beast of creatures to get out. I mock him. Yet when he boldly wraps me in his arms, all my pride and my self-respect flee and I am completely possessed by all he has: his elegant appearance. In my heart I'm saying, "Tighter! Hold me close and don't let me go, for I'm leaving tomorrow!" If I had any self-control left, I would have thought of something besides his good looks and thrown him from the room like a stone. Now with what words can I give form to the lash on my brain, on my heart? He, Ling Chi-shih, a despicable creature, has kissed me, and I received it in silence. What did I feel in my heart with his soft warm lips on my face? I can't swoon into the arms of a lover like other women are supposed to do. I looked at him with wide eyes. "I've won! I've won!" I thought. The power he had to haunt me was revealed to me in his kiss. I now know the taste of it. And with it I despised myself. I thrust him from me and wept.

He ignored my tears, perhaps thinking how tender and smooth his lips were on mine, satisfied in the certainty that my heart must have dissolved in the intoxication of his love. He sat close to me and poured forth a new stream of protestations, all in language I abhorred.

"Stop this babbling," I said. "Maybe tomorrow I die."

I don't know what he thought when I said this. He tried to kiss me again. My face avoided his and his kiss fell on my hand. I made up my mind. I was in full possession of my faculties and I wanted him to go, to get out. He lingered with a wondering, complaining expression on his face. "Why are you so stubborn and stupid?" I said to myself. It was 12:30 when, finally, he left.

After he was gone, I went over what had happened. I would like to tear my heart out from me and beat it with all my strength. Why could I stand the kisses of a man I despise? I do not love him. I mock him, yet I let him embrace me. Has this shell of a knight the power to pull me down so low? I've defiled myself. Man is his own fiercest enemy. My heaven, how shall I begin to revenge and retrieve all I've lost? Life has been my own toy. I've wasted enough of it away, so it is of no material importance that this new experience has plunged me into a new abyss. I don't want to stay in Peking and I don't want to go to the Western Hills. I'm going to take the train southward where no one knows me and waste away what's left of my life. Out of the pain, my heart revives. And now I look on myself with pity and I laugh.

"Live and die your own way, unnoticed. Oh, how I pity you, Sophia!"

CHIANG KUANG-TZ'U

Hassan

When Hassan went down to the cell block like any other prisoner, his collar in the grasp of a White Russian policeman and under the supervision of a British inspector, he began to see a glimmer of light about many things he had never quite understood before.

It had all happened only a few days earlier when Hassan caught a student distributing handbills on the street and a worker shouting slogans. He had no idea why these people insisted on coming out into the streets in groups and creating disturbances. He had only just come from his own country far away.* The Chinese language was strange to him, and he understood nothing of what they said or the meaning of the characters on the little green and red papers that fluttered to the sidewalk. Hassan was a policeman, and it was his duty to keep the peace on the streets. This kind of thing was entirely out of order, and it was his business to stop it.

*Sikhs were brought from India in considerable numbers to serve, along with Englishmen, White Russians, and Chinese, in the police force of the British-dominated International Settlement of Shanghai.

The first time he collared two of them and brought them down to the Central Police Station, just as he had been brought there today. They were "Bolsheviks," these trouble-makers, more to be hated, he was told, than thieves or kid-nappers. Hassan did not know what a "Bolshevik" was, and it never occurred to him to ask. He simply followed the in-structions issued by the British officers. They said these Bol-sheviks were evil criminals, and it was wholly natural and in the order of things, therefore, for Hassan to arrest them.

"*Ts'ao niang ko pi!** Pigs!" he said as he walked down the street with his prisoners. He swore at them but in fact he was turning this "Bolshevik" business over in his mind and he became conscious of a desire to ask his prisoners just what they were doing and why. But his knowledge of Chi-nese was still restricted to these two Shanghai epithets which all newly arrived Sikhs learn, almost as the first article of the police regulations. Hassan looked speculatively at his two prisoners. A number of questions slowly took form in his brain, but he did not know how to express them.

"*Ts'ao niang ko pi!*" he repeated in a mildly querying tone, as if he thought these words might somehow express his per-plexity. There was nothing in his voice to suggest that he even suspected their meaning. But these were his prisoners. Hassan gripped his service revolver and brandished it at them every few minutes. But in his brown face, half-hidden beneath a thick beard, there was no hatred.

"*Tsou-kou! Wang kuo nu!*"† The student's lip curled.

"*Ts'ao niang ko pi!*" replied Hassan, shaking his head.

He brought his prisoners into the station and turned them over to the sergeant, quite pleased with the look of approval which was bestowed upon him.

*An obscenity for which "Rape your mother!" is a mild equivalent.
†*Tsou-kou* means "running dog," equivalent to lackey or slavish follower. *Wang kuo nu* means "slave without a country."

Today was again some kind of memorial day, it seemed. Students and workmen were again causing trouble, and before he left on his beat Hassan was instructed to keep a sharp lookout for them. Sure enough, when he got over to his post there were red and green papers fluttering about again and groups were gathered on the corners. Damn these Bolsheviks! Couldn't they keep quiet? Hassan sailed in and grabbed a student who was distributing leaflets in the crowd.

"*Ts'ao niang ko pi!*" he shouted. Pigs! Hassan had not added to his Chinese vocabulary. But to his surprise this time the student turned to him with a bitter smile and spoke in English. Hassan had heard this language in his own country, and the officers down at the station also spoke it.

"We're all oppressed people, my friend," said the student. "All we want is to see our people free. Why do you stand against us? Have you forgotten your own country? We ought to get together. . . ."

These ideas filtered slowly into Hassan's brain. His own country. Freedom. He'd heard about this before. The light in the student's eyes affected him so much and the sudden impact of a new revelation struck him so sharply that he loosened his grip on the boy's collar. He cursed softly in Hindustani and turned away. Something was stirring in his own mind. Free our people. India. Englishmen. The face of the British inspector was before him, his mouth moving convulsively.

"You——son of a bitch! Why did you let that student go?" A White Russian policeman grabbed Hassan's arm.

"But he wasn't doing anything," said Hassan bewildered.

"You fifthy dog! Not doing anything? Are you a damned Bolshevik too?" Hassan stood dumbfounded. "I saw you talking to him and then you released him," went on the inspector. "What did you talk about? What the hell do you think you're here for anyway?"

"He . . . he said he wanted to free his people," said Hassan. "There's nothing wrong in that, is there?"

"So! Here you, take this bastard!" The British officer spoke to the Russian and thumbed at Hassan.

And now Hassan, who had never heard of Bolsheviks before—who had certainly never imagined that he could be called one—was thrown into jail like any other prisoner. "Take this bastard!" The order still sounded dully in his brain. He thought about things for a long time, and soon he began to think that maybe he did know what a Bolshevik was, after all.

SHIH YI

Salt

1

Vagrant stars gleamed faintly through breaks in the dark
winter clouds. The long dike was only vaguely visible, while
behind it the roaring breakers and on it the northwest wind
blowing through the dry trees sang a bitter, lowing tune in
the darkness. Except for glowing pinpoints in the distance,
lamps in the village, all mankind seemed dead, or at least
submerged in an unbroken black silence.

On top of the dike, strewn in careless heaps, were wooden
buckets, used for drawing the water from the sea, and the
flat boards used for drying the salt in the sun. The general
disorder and the fact that they were dry and cracking indicated long disuse. Among them the dark shadow of a man
was making his way unsteadily. Sometimes he stopped to
look back before stumbling forward again. The dike, stretching east and west for thirty *li*, was not only a protection
against the tides that came in from the sea and not only a
convenient place for baking the salt, but was also used as a
road. The scattered starlight dimly helped light the path,
and when that failed there was the faint but luminous reflection from the surface of the water. As a matter of fact,
Lao Ting was on his way home from the wine shop of the

Widow Fong, and he was so saturated with alcohol that his normal acquaintance with his surroundings no longer governed any conscious actions on his part. The world was limited to the path under his feet. It was an easy world when the path was clear, a damnable one when he barked his shins against boards or buckets. Only a faint instinct remained to guide his steps in the general direction of his home.

Home. Back there among his noisy friends, downing cup after cup of warm wine, he had thought of his home, a low shedlike pen, filled principally with damp salt barrels which kept everything eternally wet. Here lived his people. Were they really people or were they ghosts? His old wife, with her gray hair and her face forever darkened by an unrelieved cloud of sorrow, his seventeen-year-old daughter, dumb and vacant, with her hair hanging untidily about her shoulders, the snivelling boy, forever crying with hunger. He beat on the table.

"Four more ounces, hostess!" He held out four fingers to make sure he was understood.

"Damn, still drinking?" asked the Widow Fong with the long face. Actually she was never shocked at the amount of wine consumed by the men who came to her shop. The place belonged to Mr. Yuan, boss of the salt warehouse. "Sell to them on credit," he had said to her, "so long as you're sure they still have ten salt boards." But she felt that too many were drinking on credit now and less and less money came into the till. That was something no shopkeeper liked. So although she poured out the four ounces, she could not forbear cursing. Lao Ting sipped his drink slowly. He could not order any more but did not want to leave. Others were going, however, some upstairs to gamble, some shuffling across the street to Hsia Tsai-hua's place for opium.

"Come on, I want to close up now." Thus every night the

Widow Fong shooed off her remaining customers, mainly because she was anxious to go upstairs and help Liu Chu-to at the gambling table.

"Liang-ti! I don't want to go home!" said Lao Ting petulantly.

"Come on, come on, go on home and come back tomorrow," urged the widow. "You're not gambling and you're not smoking. You're so damned old any way you'd better watch your step. Come on, get up."

She pulled his arm. He nodded and docilely rose, supporting himself against the table with one hand.

"Excuse me again today, excuse me . . ." he mumbled.

"Yes, I know. Go ahead," said the Widow Fong. With her arms akimbo she watched him stagger from the shop. She threw back her head and laughed as she marked down his night's spending on the board.

The wind lashed him like the curling thongs of a whip, and he tried to shrink inside his ragged cotton clothes like a turtle into its shell. But he continued to tremble with the cold. His nose was burning hot and running. To sniff it back caused him extreme discomfort. His checks too prickled with pain. The lights of Lu Chao came more closely into his view now, and with unsteady steps he clambered down the side of the dike onto the small path which led to his home. The door was never barred. There were many thieves in the neighborhood, but it would never occur to anyone to steal the barrels of salt which were all over the place. He pushed in the door and passed between the rows of barrels to the bed where his wife and children already lay under the torn cotton quilt. His fumbling steps and the audible rasp of his hard-drawn breath sounded loudly. His wife, still awake, looked at him from the bed.

"Don't shut the door. Chen-ho isn't back yet," she said.

Chen-ho was their eldest son, twenty-three years old. Ever since the warehouse people announced they would take no more salt he had had no work on the dike. But even though the warehouse wanted no more salt, their stomachs were not equally content to go without food. So Chen-ho soon joined a gang of salt smugglers who transported the salt in small lots to a city fifty *li* away where they sold it. The warehouse had announced to the salt workers that they had a surfeit of salt in stock. But in the city the people faced a salt shortage. The merchants held back their stocks waiting for higher prices. In these circumstances smuggling became profitable, although dangerous. The armed customs police were on duty all along the road to the city. The smugglers used to take three-hundred-catty loads on their shoulders and go off up the mountain paths, taking a circuitous route around the guarded road. They had to travel forty more *li* that way. If they were challenged they often used their bamboo carrying poles as weapons, but they were no match for the guns and bayonets of the police. Only their own tenacity, desperation, and numbers kept them at it. Chen-ho's smuggling kept the family alive but only increased his mother's burden of sorrow. Whenever Chen-ho went off on one of his trips to the city she had constant visions of guns and bayonets. But she never tried to stop him, for the money that tinkled in the pocket of his denim jacket when he returned was all they had to live on.

Credit could still be had at the brothels, the opium dens, gambling houses, and wine shops, all of them owned by the salt field capitalists. But the rice shops, which used to give rice (half mixed with husks!) on credit and deduct the price from the money paid out for salt at the warehouse every day, had turned their rice baskets upside down and stopped the grinding machines as soon as the warehouse closed. The rice boats had stopped coming, they said. It was possible to get rice only with cash, unless you were lucky enough to have some money still left on deposit with the salt field owner for lease of the salt boards. None of the salt workers had any other source of income, and most of them had exhausted the board money. Many of them dug up wild roots by the seashore or cooked the weeds washed in by the waves. Soon there would be no roots, for with approaching winter they ceased to grow. The warehouse had been closed for two months, but the owners still considered the price of salt too low to reopen.

"Gone down to the city again?" said Lao Ting. The significance of it penetrated even his foggy brain. At the wine shop he had heard how enraged the bosses were over the discovery of the wide sale of smuggled salt in the town. The head of the Salt Bureau was furious, and Mr. Yuan himself had offered three thousand dollars to help maintain a corps of soldiers to guard the fields and prevent salt from being carried out. "I've heard it's more and more dangerous these days," muttered Lao Ting.

"Yes, they're watching more closely," replied his wife. "Chen-ho stayed home several days on account of it. A while ago Ah-chun, the son of Ma Lao-pao, called him out, and he hasn't come back yet. I don't know what it was for."

"Much better not to meddle with them," said Lao Ting sleepily. "No good will come of it." He crawled into bed and was fast asleep in an instant.

His wife turned irritably away from the stench of his breath. While the rest of them went hungry he drank every day. Before long he would finish off the money left on their salt boards. Chen-ho risked his life to get food for them, and here the old man complained about him behind his back. But her annoyance with him soon faded into impatient waiting for the sound of her son at the door. Listening, she heard only the sound of the wind on the roof and an occasional snatch of a baby's wail from a neighboring hut. That Chen-ho should be getting mixed up with Ma Lao-pao worried her more than she would have been if he had made another trip to the city.

All the salt people within a radius of forty *li* knew Ma Lao-pao. He had once been a sailor and had several junks of his own. But with passing years he lost them one by one to Yuan and Kao, the salt field bosses, who incorporated them into their own fleet for shipping salt and rice. Subsequently Ma became an officer in the anti-smuggling police, but before long he gathered around him many salt workers who could no longer make their living and organized systematic smuggling. When business was brisk they worked for Ma Lao-pao. When it was slow, he supported them. They all respectfully called him Shiata Lao-yeh—"our master!" —and were ready to sacrifice their lives at a word from him. Ma Lao-pao had as many guns as Yuan and Kao, but nobody knew where they were. The salt people in the fields called him Ma Lao-pao behind his back, but to his face it was always "Mr. Ma."

They all liked him and especially liked his son, Ah-chun, who used to strike his chest and say: "Shiata Lao-yeh wants to rob the rich and give to the poor!" Yuan and Kao, the salt field owners, hated and feared him. They had stolen his land and his boats, and his presence was a constant reminder of that fact. Moreover, he maintained his band of followers and his strength was such that even the head of the Customs Bureau, who was actually an employee of Yuan and Kao, had to do him honor and invite him to dinner now and again.

"What are they doing?" The old woman did not know, nor did most of the people in the salt fields, who could not bake any more salt. Around them was the same sea and the same sunshine. But the warehouses were shut against the salt barrels piled up in their homes. The salt was there for them to produce, yet they could not make use of it to feed themselves. Boss Kao, they heard, was buying up another five hundred *mow* of sea frontage, and Boss Yuan was just supervising the completion of his new house. Bits of information like this scattered from town to the villages. No one understood why heaven forbade the salt people to share in the good fortune of Yuan and Kao.

"Why do they refuse salt?" This was another question that haunted everybody. The older folks remembered that the same thing had happened several times before. They remembered once when nearly twenty thousand people formed a long procession with petitions and incense and marched to the boss's house, only to be driven away. In the same manner they knelt before the gate of the yamen and were turned away again. Then they appointed a delegation of several score to go down to the provincial capital, where they met with the same treatment. When after five months the warehouses reopened, hundreds of workers had starved to death. They were forced to conclude that the warehouses could be opened and closed only upon the express desire of the owners. Yet despite all their earnest pleas they would not open up. Why? Salt would never decay and could be sold sooner or later. The owners had more money than they could use, yet the people were dying of starvation. Everybody looked at the barred gates, expecting that with a nod of the owner's head they would spring open, and the people could again bring their salt and get the money which would keep their wives and children from starving. Yet the owners, like the mountains beyond the sea plain, never nodded, and the gates remained shut.

"Something will surely happen." She did not know why she

expected something to happen—or what exactly. But with people like Chen-ho—and there were many others—so busy, she was sure something was in the wind. As the hours went by and drew near midnight, her fears replaced her speculations and she began to feel with Lao Ting—"No good will come of it!"

2

What profit to them if the gates did open? Now that the warehouse was closed, anxiety to have it reopen drove into the far background of everyone's memory the treatment to which they were subjected when it was open. The sea and the sunshine and their own exhausting labor produced day after day picul after picul of salt. Satisfied with the day's output, they would lift it to tired shoulders and carry it home to weigh. Two hundred and fifty catties. Next day the load would be carefully carried to the warehouse. There the gates were forever crowded with people and their sacks of salt, awaiting turns to enter. When the worker finally reached the scales inside, the weigher, without even looking, turned and shouted:

"Two hundred and ten! One hundred and eighty catties without the sack!"

"Please, sir . . . it was two hundred and fifty when I weighed it just before——" The flat of the man's hand swiped him across the ear.

"Well, then, get the hell out of here! Who wants to squeeze your salt anyway?" The load was kicked out of the way. "Next!"

"Please, sir . . . please. . . ." If the warehouse refused his salt, he had no other place to take it to, so he tugged at the man's hand and whimpered. The man pulled himself free and shouted at him.

"Get the devil out of here! We don't want your salt, not a

grain of it. Go and sell it, call it two hundred and fifty catties!"

Not until he had made repeated excuses and apologies and others had interceded for him would the weigher hand over a receipt—for one hundred and eighty catties. Money was paid out at the counter down at the other end where the accounts were first checked for credits at the wine shop and the rice store. Rarely was there ever any money left over. Usually they went out again with their empty sacks and stopped in to buy more rice on new credits. But supposing there was money coming to them, there were other tricks. The price of salt was fifteen cents a catty. The workers got three.

"At three cents. A hundred times three is three dollars . . . hm . . . three times eight is twenty-four . . . that makes five dollars and forty cents . . . here's five dollars. What? Get out! You're lucky at that!"

The warehouse cashed every dollar ten cents of credit for one dollar. "You're making ten cents, you beggar! Get out!"

So he left finally, clutching the five shining dollars in his hand. He wrapped them in his blue cloth and set out to buy rice and fuel. But on the way he had to pass the Widow Fong's, and the smell of rice wine is strong in the sunlight. There were men in there and lively voices. Damn, why shouldn't he get some pleasure out of it? So he let himself be drawn by the fragrance of the wine and the smell of the chickens and ducks hanging up in front. On such days Widow Fong's face was always redder than ever, and with a fluent tongue and a cajoling air she reeled off the new dishes that could be had for cash. The men drank and laughed, and even before sundown gambling began upstairs and lasted well into the night. Ten percent went to the police, who in any case had instructions from their bosses—again the owners of the warehouses—not to molest the shops on salt collection days. And thicker than ever was the smoke which came through the front curtain of the opium den across the street and louder than ever the laughter and the voices of the girls in the brothels.

"Hopeless swine!" laughed the owners. Boss Yuan laughed too, but in the back of his mind he thought uneasily of an article somebody had sent him, published by the students in a local magazine. "Improve the conditions of the salt workers!" it was headed. And now and again servants heard stories of strangers who came and went and secret meetings of the younger people. These things were not meant to help him, he was sure. But he laughed away his thoughts. "For these swine some alcohol, some opium, a gambling table, and some women are quite sufficient!" and he laughed again so hard that the fat flesh quivered like jelly on his neck.

And it often did seem that the salt workers were as hopeless as he thought. When the last silver dollar was gone, they went to the rice shop seeking credit again. Those who had lost their money gambling were usually certain they could recoup. If they still had any board money on deposit there were several moneylending shops down the street where they could take out loans at one cent per dollar per day for gambling capital so long as the board money held out. When that was gone and the boards forfeited, the worker could no longer have a place in the field to make salt. He could then either leave the salt field or starve. Some became day laborers in the salt kiln. Others, if they were able, joined Ma Lao-pao.

Most of the salt people were like Lao Ting. They drudged all day long, pickling their hands in the brine, and soaked themselves in alcohol at night. Between the two they inured themselves to their poverty and the scoldings of their families. Lao Ting had been on this salt field for sixty years. His father had been a worker there before him and had finally killed himself by drinking brine because the moneylenders in the lane pressed him too hard. As a youth Lao Ting worked hard, procured a good number of salt boards, a wife, and a house, and set himself up in the salt field with the desire to become a model salt worker, to let his head be baked by the sun, his hands pickled by the brine, and his ears boxed by the warehouse men and to remain forever an obedient servant of his employers. If weight was deducted from his loads one day he looked philosophically forward to the next and added extra catties to his load. Unlike many others he never mixed sand into salt because he thought it would be poisonous to whomever ate it. But the warehouse people made up for his scruples. They mixed sand and gravel into the salt and sent it into town labeled "best white official salt." There the people paid top prices and cracked their teeth on it.

They looked for the better-quality smuggled salt but it was not easy to find. The preventive police were on the watch everywhere, armed day and night. It was not uncommon to see a captured smuggler, covered with the blood of his own wounds, being led down the street by guards. Many a boat caught with smuggled salt was either confiscated or hacked to pieces. If anybody was observed in unusual circumstances during the night, his house was certain to be searched the next day.

"A crime to use salt"—what more? The government pledged the salt tax revenue for arms to fight its rivals. The capitalists have monopolized the sea and the sun for their own profit and the salt workers crawl in the salt fields, their voices unheard.

"Sunbaked salt is impossible!" cried those who cracked their teeth. And when the cry for oven-baked salt became imperative some of the salt workers on the broad seashore crept into the hot hell of the salt kiln. The great dike was dotted with kilns. The workers in them were paid a daily wage. Some of them carried buckets up from the sea and poured the water into the pan. Others worked at the furnace. Winter or summer the fire blazed there and shone red on their naked bodies before it. The so-called oven was made of reeds caked with mud. The reeds were constantly kept wet, and the mud cracked over the fire, causing the water to leak through. The worker's job at the furnace was hazardous and nerve-wracking. He had to keep his eyes fixed on the mud bottom, and whenever he saw a leak start he had to grab a handful of ready wet mud and thrust through the flames to plug the threatening break. The whole operation could consume but a few seconds and required the utmost speed and skill on the part of the workers, who stood to their job stark naked but for a wet cloth wrapped around their heads. Often they burned themselves badly around the head or even lost their lives in the fire. For this work they received a "special" wage of fifty cents a day. If they died at work, their families received ten dollars.

That was how Bald Ah Yuan lost the skin off his head. The wet cloth fell off as he dashed in, and his hair caught fire. Fortunately he had held on outside with his left hand, and he was able to pull himself out in time and fall screaming to the ground. He saved his life, but his family lost ten dollars. For five months his scalp was a mass of festering sores, and when he went to the kiln to beg for money he was discharged. He finally went to work in the police station, running errands for the police officers. He was content to have his bald, scarred head patted when people were pleased and his stomach filled with the cold rice they left.

The salt workers were content. At least they were not actively discontented. Like the sages of old they "paused a moment for reflection." Those who worked under the sun thought of the men in the kilns. The ordinary workers at the kilns thought of the firemen. The firemen thought of those who had their heads burned and these latter thought of the dead. Since the dead could not think, they were fortunate.

But such could not be the case forever. The gnawing hunger in their stomachs was fed by the invisible germs that seemed to come through the air from the south. The workers of the salt fields were not to remain perpetually content with their lot.

3

Chen-ho returned home just as the winter night was breaking into dawn. His old mother was still awake, and when she heard the door open she rose on her elbow.

"Is that you, Chen-ho?"

"Yes." His voice vibrated in the silent darkness.

"Why so late? It's almost daybreak." She did not expect any reply. She was happy enough to have him home safely. Nor did he reply. He lay stretched out on his bed exhausted, although his mind still buzzed with the excited spirit of the long night's talk. Too many ideas raced through his head for sleep.

"What are you so busy about, anyway?" persisted the old lady after a while. Chen-ho still said nothing. "Why keep on asking?" he thought. "You'll know soon enough." But he was too weary to speak aloud.

A few days later a rumor sped swiftly from mouth to mouth. "The northern army has been defeated again! The northern army has been defeated again!" Few newspapers ever came to the salt field. Few there, indeed, could read. But everybody knew that all around the countryside soldiers were dragging people off to act as burden-bearers for the army. They also knew that most of the soldiers in the Preventive Service had left the neighborhood. And most of them somewhere had got the idea that the new soldiers now to be expected meant well toward the poor. In two places at opposite ends of the salt fields tense excitement reigned. At the house of Boss Yuan, the magistrate, the head of the local guards, and the managers of the warehouses were gathered together. They knew that the military situation deeply concerned them. Boss Yuan announced that he would go to the city himself, find out exactly what was happening, and make provision for the future on the basis of what he learned. Everybody fervently agreed.

Charged with a different current was the atmosphere around Ma Lao-pao's house, where his followers were mounting double guard. A youth who looked like a student had arrived from the city a few days before and spent all his time inside the house. There was much writing of documents and letters, and meetings were held every night. Couriers arrived regularly from the city with all the latest news. That evening a telegram arrived for Mr. Ma. It contained the formula previously agreed upon and for which they had been feverishly waiting. "Act quickly!" it said. "The time is over-ripe!" Two hours later a small boat appeared coming up the river, and a young man stepped ashore and made for the house of Ma Lao-pao. At midnight all was quiet and dark, as it had ever been in the salt fields. Out of the shadows under the dike a compact, moving mass appeared, climbed up on the road and made swiftly, with neither light nor sound, for the headquarters of the Preventive Service.

A single shot rang out in the night, and before its echoes had died down the headquarters were surrounded by workers armed with broad flat swords which gave off a dull, silver sheen in the darkness.

"Surrender your arms!"

The remaining soldiers inside scrambled from their beds in fright and consternation. The front door was flung open and like madmen they fled into the night. In the van of the at-

tackers they saw Ma Lao-pao, mounted and holding a revolver in his hand. In a few minutes the building was empty, and the compact mass of black shadows moved quickly
off toward town.

"Ma Lao-pao has disarmed the Preventive Service troops
and arrested the magistrate! The whole world has fallen into
the hands of the *tangpu*!* The news rolled off from the salt
fields traveling swiftly through the night, even, it seemed,
from tree to tree and rock to rock. The tide struck Boss
Yuan returning in dismal despair in a small boat coming
upriver from the city. His mission had not been a striking
success. He went first to see the district magistrate and found
him a prisoner. He adapted himself quickly to the changed
circumstances and went next door where the new government had been set up under the direction of Lu Shih-yao, a
former teacher in the district primary school. He knew Lu
well and felt secure.

"I was a member of the Lao Tung Meng,"† he said with
an air of camaraderie when ushered into Lu's office. The
newly appointed head of the province, he pointed out, was
one of the principal shareholders in his, Yuan's warehouses.
The new governor had not yet taken office but at least he,
Boss Yuan, should be made the responsible leader of the
movement in the salt fields.

Lu Shih-yao shook the head which perched so angularly on
his tall, thin form. "The man in charge of the Salt People's
Association was sent up by Provincial Headquarters, not by
us," he said. "Otherwise I'm sure it would have been the
best thing to have somebody like Mr. Yuan!" He blinked at
his visitor and smiled.

*Local Kuomintang organization.
†Tung Meng Hui, the predecessor of the Kuomintang, organized by Sun
Yat-sen.

"Sent by Provincial Headquarters," repeated Mr. Yuan, crestfallen. "Why wasn't I informed? Everybody knows I'm the head of the salt people. At least nothing should be done without giving me a share in it!"

"Ho, ho! Mr. Yuan," laughed Mr. Lu. "Under the new regulations the 'salt people' can only include those who work with their hands!"

"Then I can't even qualify as a member of the association! Is this freedom and equality?" stormed the indignant Mr. Yuan. But he was clever enough to know that for the moment, anyway, he had thrown his dice and lost. He rose to take his leave and as he did so the tall figure of Ma Lao-pao stepped through the door.

"How unexpected to find Mr. Yuan here!" said Ma smoothly.

"Ask him about the Salt People's Association," said Lu, thumbing in the direction of the newcomer. "He's in command of the pickets of the party headquarters."

Boss Yuan was glad to see Ma was in town. The younger ones, well, he could handle them. He made hurriedly off.

As his boat approached his fields he saw the new flag of the Salt People's Association already waving over the police station. At the door were two men in ragged cotton jackets standing guard, guns in hand. A steady stream of people was moving in and out. He bit his lip hard and went off directly to his home. When he got inside the gate and leaned against the fastened bolts he panted with relief, as though he had just escaped mortal danger.

The situation changed so radically that even Lao Ting stopped going to the wine shop. The speech of a student newly come from the provincial capital made such an impression on him that he rushed off home, lost in wonder.

"What's the matter?" asked his wife in amazement.

"What can you women know, mother of Chen-ho? There was a young man from the city and he knows our troubles better than we do!" His wife looked at him, too surprised at his sobriety to pay much attention to what he was saying. Lao Ting struck a pose and declaimed: "It's not merely the kindness of the fates which made the bosses rich! They fattened themselves on our sweat and blood!"

Words like these were driving home, and everywhere in the salt field people were for the first time understanding something more than the immutability of the fates. Everybody agreed with alacrity to sign the book of the Salt People's Association and conditions were drawn up to be presented to the owners. They were read out, one by one, by Ah-chun, the son of Ma Lao-pao, who faced a huge crowd from a raised platform.

"The first article—the owners must acknowledge that the Anteng Branch of the Provincial Salt People's Association represents the seventy thousand salt workers of Anteng. Do you agree?"

"With all our hearts!" roared the crowd.

"It passes then. The second article—the warehouses must be opened immediately! This—" An uproar of joy and approval cut him short. "Go on! Go on!"

"Well, the third article—salt weight shall not be discounted!"

"Good!" came the same roar.

"Fourth article—the price paid for salt here must go up in accordance with the retail price!"

"Good!" in a thousand voices.

"Fifth—increase the wages of the kiln workers!"

"Good!"

"Sixth—the stocks shall be immediately opened to sale at a

low price." Another jubilant shout greeted this and the seventh and eighth and so on until the twenty-three demands had all been read.

"Let's go to the house of Boss Yuan! To the house of Boss Yuan!" The thick mass of people began to move in a tide, like the waves of the sea beyond the dike. With Ah-chun, Chen-ho, and others in the lead, the workers formed into a crude line of march that stretched far off across the field in front of the headquarters. Even Bald Ah Yuan was in the foremost ranks. The tide rolled up and into the wide open space in front of Boss Yuan's gate.

"Tell Yuan Kung-ting we want him to come out here for a talk!" Gone was the cringing respect of the past. No longer Mr. Yuan—just plain Yuan Kung-ting. "Tell him to come out for a talk!" Ah-chun thundered on the gate with a stick. It finally opened, and a frightened servant put his head out.

"Your pardon, your pardon. The master has gone to the capital."

"The hell he has, the bastard, he's hiding! Come on in!"

The young man from the capital wanted things to go more calmly. He held up his hand and talked swiftly with Ah Chun and Chen-ho. They nodded and he jumped up on a rock.

"Wait! Don't break order. Let's send in a delegation."

"All right, Mr. Chu" (that was his name). "Ah-chun! Chen-ho!" Twelve were thus named and they went inside. The others waited. "He's run away, the turtle! Let's tear his house down! He won't listen to them!" Excited knots of arguing workers formed in the crowd. The delegation reappeared at the gate.

"He's really gone," called out Ah-chun. "Let's go to Kao Ah-tai!" They all moved swiftly toward Boss Kao's house. The news of their coming sped before them. Kao was there, but helpless. The police and the soldiers were all gone. His own guards, he knew, were useless. He received the delegation on his doorstep and meekly listened to their conditions.

"I, Ah-tai, I entirely agree with your ideas," he said after they had done. "But as long as Mr. Yuan is absent I can decide nothing. I beg you to wait patiently until these matters can be arranged."

"Nonsense, we're starving!"

"Open the warehouse at once and start taking salt. We can't wait any longer!"

"If you want us to wait, give us rice."

"Suppose Yuan Kung-ting turns into a ghost. Does that mean you'll never open the warehouse?"

These voices came from the multitude of workers at the gate. Their delegates could not have checked them had they desired to do so. Kao turned pale with the conviction of defeat. At that moment his wife, famous throughout the fields as a shrew, dashed out from behind the door, where she had evidently been listening, and gave more honest expression to her husband's feelings.

"You damned animals! Watch your manners! You're no better than a gang of robbers with all these demands and yet you talk of your dog of a revolutionary party!" With which she dashed into the crowd in a rage and seized a banner which several of the workers were carrying.

"Sock her one!" And before Mr. Chu could step in, several of the workers closed around her. Ah-chun acted more swiftly. He hopped up the step and grabbed Kao Ah-tai by the collar.

"Don't bother with her, let's take Kao Ah-tai first!" he shouted.

"He's right! Down with Kao Ah-tai!" they shouted, and many could not help laughing at the novelty of the situation. Even Lao Ting, way in the back, laughed, overcome with the daring of the youngsters. He felt times had changed indeed, but it never occurred to him that they might change again and some evil come of it. "Shoot the damned bastard!" But Chu shielded him and took him off to the Salt People's Association headquarters where he was placed under guard. The workers turned to Chen-ho and Ah-chun, whose ideas of direct action were far more closely attuned to the general mood. Under their leadership they returned to Boss Yuan's house and as a gesture of hatred smashed down the gate.

Mr. Chu faced his fellow committeemen with a worried air that night at a meeting. He lectured them like a professor and used words nobody understood. He charged them with "left infantilism." Finally after much urging by Chu, they agreed to turn Kao Ah-tai over to the district office.

4

Mr. Lu Shih-yao was now the most important person in the whole district. Even the magistrate was under his orders. He still wore the black cotton gown he used to wear as a teacher in the primary school, but a felt coat and a walking stick had now been added to his array, especially when he went to dinner with the officials and businessmen of the town. He was deeply dissatisfied with the work of his associates in charge of the workers' and peasants' movement and they were equally dissatisfied with him. A few days before he had received a letter from an old friend, a onetime classmate at Normal School, who was now a member of the provincial *tangpu*. His friend wrote anxiously of the overreaching actions of party workers everywhere. The gravest errors had been committed in overdoing the mass movement. This was to be a united bloc of all classes, he wrote, and no one class should be provoked at the expense of another. Lu was very much impressed by this letter, and he accordingly suggested at the meeting that night that a dinner be given for all the gentry of the town. This was arranged for, the committee viewing the matter in the light of instructions from the capital. Throughout the days of the turnover of power all these people had hidden fearfully behind their doors, wondering what was going to happen to the "rotten gentry" and "evil landlords" who were now the targets of their own former employees and tenants. When the invitations to dinner arrived, bland smiles returned to their blanched faces and they appeared again on the streets.

"Shih-yao is a good fellow. He's all right. All the trouble was caused by loafers from outside!" they nodded reassuringly at each other and attended Lu's dinner in state.

Late one night not long afterward the gateman of the district *tangpu* headquarters came in with the card of the chairman of the local Chamber of Commerce, who was calling on Mr. Lu. They were closeted in Lu's office for some time and it was after midnight when both emerged and went to the chairman's private rooms, where they found Boss Yuan waiting for them. Yuan Kung-ting had just returned from the capital and greeted the newcomers with expansive smiles. They talked about the situation in the capital, the progress of the revolutionary army, the imminent arrival there of the commander-in-chief, and the forthcoming installation of the new provincial chairman. Their voices lowered when they got around to discussing the local situation. Lu felt pangs of shame and hesitated. He thought of the angry eyes of his comrades, and he recalled the heroism of his own early days, when he joined the party while the old militarists still controlled the province. His first impulse was to jump up with rage and denounce the two men who faced him. But their cool confidence frightened him. Boss Yuan was just back from the capital. Perhaps it was better not to antagonize him. In the end he spoke up:

"You know, all this was due to misunderstandings on the part of the people working below. We wanted peaceful methods and we didn't approve of such radicalism. Now we——"

Next day when the question of Kao Ah-tai came up at the meeting of the committee, Chairman Lu cleared his throat nervously and faced his associates.

"I don't think we have to bother with empty talk about this matter. It seems to me the best way is to let one man be responsible for it."

"I second, I second!" said a fat member of the committee who stood up hurriedly and with difficulty.

"How about the others?" Lu looked around at the faces before him. Nobody said anything.

"Then nobody disagrees," put in the fat man. I propose that Chairman Lu take care of it."

Most of the members were impressed with Lu's authority. They had other things to talk about too. So without further discussion, the motion was passed.

Kao Ah-tai was released. Chairman Lu issued a statement criticising the salt workers for not appealing to the law against Kao. His detention was illegal, he said, so no charges could be brought against him. He had committed no crime. "Our aim is to organize the salt workers," he concluded. "One, just one, of the rotten gentry can't do us any harm."

Lu was growing weary of his position. At least, it was easy for a certain girl in a nearby school to distract his attention. He became almost consciously more desirous of evading his responsibilities than of discharging them. He shouldered a rifle, said he was going hunting, and made for the girl's school. After all, she thought he had become the greatest man in all the country. Why shouldn't he?

A few days later a group of thugs came to the gate of the Salt People's Association headquarters and began to force their way in. "Wait a minute!" said the guard.

"Get out of here! We want to see the chairman," they replied. A second guard came up to help and a scuffle started. One of the visitors whistled, and a large band of men with arms in hand came up the street on the run.

"Surrender your arms!" One of the guards at the gate was disarmed but the other defended himself with a bayonet and slashed his way through the gate. He spread the alarm. The salt workers had been organized into a self-defense corps, but few of them had arms. There were some swords, a few spears, and fewer guns. Most of the arms had been brought down to the district *tangpu* and deposited there. The workers gathered, however, and a pitched battle began in the street in front of the police station. But the headquarters were quickly taken. There had been no preparation and the surprise was complete. The fight lasted an hour. Most of the defenders were disarmed and made prisoners. A few officials of the organization escaped. The flags of the association and the party flags as well were torn down. Even the picture of the party leader* hung on the central wall in the meeting room was thrown down and trampled on. The attackers went through all the rooms systematically destroying documents and records. It was almost all over when three men rode up on horses and dismounted in front of the gate. They were Kao Ah-tai, Yuan Kung-ting, and Huang Chuen-shiao, a notorious local pirate whom Ma Lao-pao had once fought and defeated. They surveyed the scene with a satisfied air.

Three hours later a group of fugitives from Anteng led by Ma Ah-chun arrived at *tangpu* headquarters. "We heard several days ago that Kao Ah-tai and Yuan Kung-ting had re-

*Sun Yat-sen.

turned," said young Ma to Lu. "Kao was of course furious over the treatment he'd received and we heard that he told Yuan he was ready to spend five thousand dollars to get his revenge. Yuan, of course, felt the same way. Later we heard that Yuan had gone down the coast and found Huang Chuen-shiao and offered him the money. We didn't believe it because we didn't think the rotten gentry would have that much courage. . . ."

"Well, you must be hungry," said Lu. "Come on in, sit down, and we'll talk it over after you've eaten." He was shocked and frightened by the news and immediately called a meeting of his committee. They discussed the situation for five hours. Someone wanted to know why Kao had been re-leased in the first place. But the fat member said that the immediate problem was the urgent one. In the end he was selected to go down to the capital for soldiers to attack the gentry and restore the salt association. The fugitives remained in the *tangpu* courtyard while Lu exchanged visits with the leading businessmen of the town and the Chamber of Commerce people and spent his spare time at the girls' school.

During the next few days handbills appeared on the streets of the town. "Down with the *tangpu*!" they read. Signed by a New Salt People's Association, the leaflets declared that the people had risen up against the old organization, which abused their rights and abused public opinion by declaring that the salt workers had a share in all property and in all the women of the town. The old association existed only for the purpose of persecuting the people. The younger officials at the *tangpu* scurried around like ants on a hot pan.

"Ma Lao-pao's house has been burned down. All the members of the association have been arrested and are being tortured by Huang Chuen-shiao." The man who brought this piece of news described how one of the old men had been suspended in mid-air, his hands and feet bound to stakes and a huge stone placed in the small of his back and how one of the young women had been raped repeatedly until she had died.

The fat member returned from the capital, breathless and excited. "The capital is in terrific disorder," he reported. "There's a slogan out to refuse office to the new chairman and the workers are fighting with the police on the streets every day. There's not a single soldier to be had for us. They need them all down there. Mr. Tan of the provincial committee said we should solve our problem by peaceful means."

That was it, nodded Lu Shih-yao, peaceful means. Peaceful means. That meant making peace with Yuan and his people. Let the Association continue to exist but remove its more radical members. When he put forth this suggestion everybody agreed. They all felt now that the situation had gotten far beyond them. Warm with a spirit of self-sacrifice, Lu took a sedan chair and five guards and started out for the salt fields. He was sure Yuan Kung-ting would listen to him. He was sure nobody would benefit from a fight. Midnight that same day one of the guards returned.

"Chairman Lu has been made a prisoner by Huang Chuen-shiao!" Ma Lao-pao jumped up, fuming with impatience.

"Let me go to Yuan. I have sixty guns. Why should I fear Huang Chuen-shiao?"

"Good! Fight! Fight!" echoed the younger men.

"Wait!" It was the fat member. "I'm in agreement with Mr. Ma but I feel that should be the last possible measure. If a thing can be solved peacefully, we're not in favor of using force. Now I"—he looked around the room, as though he were trying to measure the atmosphere—"propose that we ask Mr. Yang, president of the Chamber of Commerce, to go to Mr. Yuan. He's a friend of his. If he can convince him, everything will be easily settled."

This was agreed upon and Mr. Yang accepted the mission. With an air of heroism about him he set out in a small boat with two oarsmen. Meanwhile, Ma Lao-pao called a military meeting of his own. His followers were convinced that everything was lost unless they fought and fought hard. Member Pai of the Peasant Department offered to get the help of the peasant self-defense corps of the neighboring district. Outside, Ma's followers were half-deciding their own course. "What use are we if we let our people suffer?"

It was just about that time that Mr. Yang was peacefully passing through the guards at the salt field. He was received cheerfully by Boss Yuan. Mr. Yang shook his head.

"I think the world belongs to them now, Mr. Yuan. I'm afraid you've gone too far."

Mr. Yuan laughed loudly. He laid his hand on Yang's shoulder. "You're mistaken, my friend. The world is about to come into our hands, more strongly than ever!" He sketched rapidly for him the latest news from the capital. "No fear," he concluded. They talked about local matters, and when they got around to the question of Mr. Lu, the chairman of the Chamber of Commerce remonstrated with Boss Yuan.

"Lu has a clearer mind than those other mad dogs," he said. "You should try to save Lu's face. He's been useful. . . ."

"Ho, ho! I'm quite civil to him. I only asked him to stop in my house for a rest. He's grown quite thin from overwork. Have you forgotten what happened the other night?"

"What are you going to do then?" asked Yang, a smile of understanding gradually dawning on his face.

"I know what you've come for and I won't let your labor be in vain, my friend. I don't intend to feed him for nothing all his life. Wei, wei," he called to the servant. "Open the door of that wing and ask Mr. Lu to come here. . . ."

5

Changes had come swiftly and drastically to the salt fields. The world had left its normal course only ten days before. The workers had greeted the first days with shouts of joy at mass meetings. These had now been transformed into shrieks of pain under the torture of Huang Chuen-shiao and his men. Tears of happiness under the promise of a new, undreamed-of freedom changed into tears of anguish on the rack and facing the executioners. Houses in all the villages were being searched day and night. The earth heaped steadily higher on the hill back of the headquarters where the headless bodies of the salt workers were thrown. Huang Chuen-shiao was in charge, his yellow teeth parted in a perpetual grin as he asked each prisoner whether he still wanted "freedom and equality."

Lao Ting sat gloomily in his hut together with his family. Chen-ho was rumored to be in the fields somewhere, and Huang's men had come several times looking for him. But aside from three chickens which Lao Ting's wife had been saving ever since New Year's Day, they got nothing out of them. On one bloody night thirty-eight workers were beaten to death. The next ten were beheaded. Then the old officials of the warehouses returned and came around with their account books. Everybody's name was registered for the New Salt People's Association with a fee of twenty cents. Anybody who demurred was taken to the police station. Lao Ting felt that the dynasty must have changed again and the bosses were again bosses. He resumed going to the Widow Fong's and soon fell into his old ways. His wife worried mostly about Chen-ho. She knew that many people had fled to town but not Chen-ho, for one night late he had come to the door with blood flowing from a head wound. She had bound it for him and urged him to go away. He left and had never again returned.

One night at the temple of Erh Fong To shadows gathered like ghosts come for a conclave. Several remained fixed outside. The rest flitted into the hall and seated themselves on the cold ground. When somebody closed the door behind the last of them even their shadows were no longer visible, not even to each other.

Everything is ready now," whispered a strong voice. "Pickets from the city and the peasant self-defense corps from the neighboring district will come together. We'll collect at the back of the hill behind. We'll have swords. We're short of guns. But when the others start firing out in front the enemy will rush forward and we'll come down the hill and seize the building and attack them from the rear. All clear?"

The voice was held low but everyone knew that Chen-ho spoke. That he had had the courage to plan an attack at a time like this gave them all courage.

"How many will they send? The bastards got a new boatload of guns today."

"Don't worry, at least three hundred, all well armed and able to fight. What the goddamned hell is Huang Chuenshiao? We've nothing to worry about if we carry out our part."

There was a soft knock on the door. It opened and a shadow came through. "Two of those sons of bitches are coming this way."

"Let's get out!" whispered somebody.

"No. They're on the way now and we've no time to disperse. Only two? We can manage. Not bad to stage a little demonstration first!"

Chen-ho was no longer the simple village boy. He clipped his syllables, and in the darkness he drew out of his belt a short knife. "After me!" he hissed and went slowly out into the night. After him filed six young men.

Next day the police station was thrown into a commotion by news that the bodies of two of Huang Chuen-shiao's men had been found in the old well in front of the temple. Almost at the same time came news of the approach of the workers' militia and the peasant army from the next district. There was no time to give to the affair at the temple. Within an area of twenty *li* south from the seashore there were six dikes all facing north, forming a natural fortress. When Huang's men arrived at San T'ong To, the advancing attackers had already occupied the first three, and the battle began within four *li* of the sea. The assault was powerful, and the pirates fell back to Sze Tang. At this moment the salt workers descended the hill with a roar and attacked Huang from the rear. Pressed on both sides, he made off westward and escaped up into the hills, where he rallied his men at a deserted temple.

The salt workers gathered jubilantly. The houses of both Yuan and Kao were razed. A new mass meeting was called and new hope surged back among the workers. "Everything will surely be all right now!" they exulted. And so they felt, because they had won back their gains with their own bodies and blood.

But two days later the face of the world changed again. The workers' pickets and the peasant force were ordered back within one night. A coup in the capital had put all the party officials into prison, and the unwanted governor had taken office under the protection of the army. Soldiers were sent to all points in the province. They flew the same banner with which they had come up from the south, but they bore no more hopes for the poor. The workers and peasants' militia were disbanded and for a while even the *tangpu* almost entirely disappeared from sight. Huang Chuen-shiao, Yuan, and Kao were in full touch with these developments, and even before the soldiers came they swooped down on the salt fields and soon beat down the few swords and guns of the defenders. The world passed once more into the hands of the old masters. Salt workers' heads fell from their bodies. The fields were placed under the strictest guard. Hopes were buried with the mutilated corpses of young and old.

From beginning to end this history has consumed only four months in time. Winter passed and the spring brought its warmth again to the ocean shore. The sea dashed as ever before in foaming white breakers on the dike, and the dike as ever stood firmly under its attacks. Fighting came to an end, and the price of salt rose to the highest levels ever known in the province. The salt barrels in Lao Ting's house were carried picul after picul to the warehouse. The people of the salt fields resumed their toil, and Lao among them, steaming under the sun, poured picul after picul of seawater on the salt boards to bake. The great fires in the kilns blazed again, and the naked bodies of the workers stood by them, their eyes fixed on the mud wall inside. But the men worked in silence. Nobody talked. Hardly anyone looked at his fellow workers. They had learned the price. Besides, there was no use talking about something everybody already knew. The same banner they had raised over the police station still flew there, and under it was the insignia of the Salt People's Association. But over the door was printed on a large white sign: "President, Huang Chuen-shiao. Membership fee, twenty cents."

The ruins of the house of Ma Lao-pao remained. Its onetime owner, it was whispered, had become a bandit on

South Mountain. Nobody knew for sure. All of Ma's men were gone now. Down in town the old people of former days, dressed in jackets and gowns, held official positions where young men had worked only a few months before. They often came to the salt field and joined in feasts and smoked opium at the newly built houses of Kao and Yuan and Huang. They delivered no speeches, called no mass meetings on the field in front of the headquarters. Nobody knew what had happened to the young men who had come to the town and set up their government with so many hopes and promises.

"If we ever get hold of them, we'll kill them sure's Heaven has eyes," muttered the older men. "They've made our lives more bitter still."

The youths who remained on the field said nothing. "They were right about so many things," they thought. "We'll have a chance again someday."

Nobody knew what had become of the young Mr. Chu. Some said he'd been beaten to death in a neighboring district. Others said he'd been arrested by the authorities and shot with a foreign gun. Anyway, he was no more. Sometimes bandits descended on the town. Somebody whispered they were led by Ah-chun. But who really knew?

Time slipped away from the workers in the fields. It all seemed to have happened as in a flash of lightning and a single clap of thunder that had echoed and retreated into the skies.

6

The story seems to be at an end, but for the time being there is one more chapter to add. In the great city six hundred *li* from the salt field* three million people used the salt

*Shanghai.

that came from the coast. Nobody knew or cared that out there where the sea beat in against the shore ragged and dirty people were toiling their days out so that those in the city might eat food tastily seasoned. If they ever thought of the poor at all, certainly their minds would leap first of all to the coolies working on the streets and in the sewers, for in their eyes few could sink lower in life than these men. Half the street was torn up in one place, and only one of the tram lines could operate. The company had fixed up a temporary track where the northbound cars waited for the southbound to pass.

In one waiting car one summer morning the passengers fumed with impatience. Finally a well-dressed young man stepped out of the first-class entrance and helped a young lady down the steps onto the unpaved road. A worker who was splitting stones with a pick by the side of the road watched them.

"Oh, Mr. Lu!" he called. The young man swung around. "Have you forgotten me?" continued the voice that issued from his begrimed face. "I know you, even if you are wearing foreign clothes. . . ." The worker grinned and his white teeth shone out of the black. Mr. Lu bridled. What would the lady think?

"Who are you? I don't know you!" he said gruffly.

"Have you forgotten the Salt People's Association? I'm Chen-ho."

"Eh?" The past rolled back on the smooth and now slightly stouter Lu Shih-yao. He grimaced and started to turn away. No use recalling all that now. But Chen-ho, who still thought Lu had always been their friend back in those days, persisted:

"Is there any news? When do we go home together?"

"Go home?" Mr. Lu was not thinking of going home. He was soon to leave for the provincial capital to take over a good job in the department of education. Through the intercession of an influential friend his party membership had been restored and his early days had been blotted from his record. The apparition of Chen-ho pricked his peace of mind. He looked over at the girl who stood watching the scene with raised eyebrows.

"It's not convenient to talk here. Where do you live? I'll come to visit you."

Chen-ho started to tell him the address, but before he had finished Lu started off. "All right, all right, I'll be there," he said. He took the girl's arm and walked away. "Damn him!" he said and told her the whole story of his early activities. But the way he remembered it, he had been quite a hero.

Chen-ho looked contemptuously after them.

"Who was that?" asked a worker by his side who knew his history.

"A member of our standing committee."

"Still willing to talk to those sons of bitches? Time to do the job ourselves!"

And together they raised their picks high and drove them with all their might into the hard pavement stone.

Living Together

Ours is a small country town. Out of the whole population only the few landowners ever had meat to eat. The rest of them—the farmers—lived on salt cabbage the whole year round. Their life was hard and monotonous, like that of the oxen sweating in the fields.

Nevertheless, conditions now are vastly changed. Men who were once harassed and poverty-stricken have become lively and merry. Even more striking is the gaiety and vivacity of the women. They used to live shut up in homes of poverty, going through the futile round of cooking, washing, caring for the children, feeding the pigs—shut up like prisoners in a jail without a ray of hope for the future. Now they are like birds soaring in the sky. Their life has become free. They are no longer persecuted or oppressed. Nor do they fear their husbands any more. They can make contacts with men as they choose. More than that, they are free to go with comrades to register at the district soviet, and so embark formally on a common life together. Even for the children to

Translated by George A. Kennedy.

whom they give birth there is the provision of public care, so
that the women are relieved of personal worry.

Among these women is the former wife of Wang Ta-pao,
who ought now to be called by her own individual name.
She is Miss Wu, and is twenty-five this year. At the age of
fourteen her parents married her to Wang Ta-pao. Strong as
a man in body, she can carry two full buckets of water on
her shoulders. Her face, tanned black by the sun, shows her
capable and frank. She curls her hair on a bamboo hairpin
to which is always attached a red flower. She is one of those
who used to be bound in the iron chains of domestic economy. Now she is emancipated and does her share in the work
of society. She is a member of the farmers' committee and at
the same time a promising pupil in the Lenin Upper Primary School. She can read newspapers and public notices,
correspondence and pamphlets, and, more than this, she can
draw little pencil cartoons of the fighting of the Red Army.

Her husband has made equal progress. Once Wang Ta-pao
knew absolutely nothing. His comprehension extended only
to the question of the proper time for sowing seed and the
proper time for reaping the grain. Now he can give a disser-
tation on "Imperialism" or the "Counterrevolutionary Administration" and can explain what "Revolution" means. He
is a member of the Land Committee. His work is excellent,
and he has developed unusual ability at his task. He is an
honest man, like most of the agricultural people here, and
not a schemer.

Wang never treated his wife badly, and she was very good
to him. Still they were always conscious of the fact that
there was something not quite right. Miss Wu saw so many
points on which Wang did not agree with her. She liked to
raise sheep, for example, while he hated it. What pleased
him was a litter of little pigs, which she on her part did not

like to feed. Over such small matters as these they were always quarreling. Although Wang Ta-pao had been giving in to her recently and no longer argued with her over the raising of pigs, nevertheless she continued to be conscious of the fact that their interests were mutually incompatible, and she saw clearly that it was not actually a problem about sheep or pigs but a question of natures.

One day as she returned from a meeting of the Farmers' Committee she said to Wang Ta-pao, "I have something I want to tell you."

Wang supposed that it was some committee business or else fresh news of the victories of the Red Army and he replied in good spirits, "Please go ahead and tell me."

"What I have to say is very simple," she began. "During the last ten years you have not treated me badly. And of course, as you yourself know, my behavior toward you has been correct. You have looked after me and I have done a lot of work for you. In the first place, I have managed your home, and in the second place, I have borne you two sons. But now I want to leave you, and I am preparing to go tomorrow with Comrade Chen to register."

Wang Ta-pao listened in stupefaction, his heart beating furiously. The veins stood out on his reddening face.

"You can't do that!" he stammered out miserably.

"Why can't I? Do you think we are still living in the times of the landed gentry? Don't forget that this is the Soviet age. You must be more careful what you say."

She was right. Wang Ta-pao could not oppose her. He hesitated a while and then bethought himself to say, "Why do you want to leave me?"

"For no very important reason," she replied reddening, "Only—well—I feel that living with Comrade Chen would be better than with you. The soviet allows this. You mustn't be cross with me about it. If you feel bad about losing me, remember we can still see each other always at work . . . dear Comrade Wang."

She left him rather cheerfully and busied herself in packing up her things.

Wang Ta-pao sat there in a reverie, meditating. From time to time he stole a glance at her back, and the thought that she was about to leave him made him very melancholy. It struck him that he would soon be a lone bachelor. He reflected also that to get another wife he would need to have a great deal of money to spend, a thing which was out of the question for him. He sat buried in the single thought:

"I shall be lonely as a discarded carrying pole."

That night he did not sleep although the woman who was still his wife lay beside him and urged him continually, "Go to sleep. At dawn you must get up to work."

Still he could not sleep.

The next day, after he had finished a part of his work, he asked for two hours' leave and took his perplexity to the people's committee. The president sat with a cap on, writing in the office. Wang went familiarly up to him.

"Comrade Cheng," he said, "I have come today especially to ask your advice." He stretched out his hand.

The president was a young man of about twenty-five. He had been an apprentice in a dyeing establishment in Wu-han, but during the great revolution of 1925–1927 he became a member of the Red Militia. Afterward, although he had seen military service and had taken part in engagements against the counterrevolutionary forces, he joined the civil administration. Recently he had been unanimously elected to the presidency of the People's Committee of this soviet.

"Welcome!" he said rising. "We're going to talk. That's fine!" He shook hands with a pleasant smile.

"I have a little problem," Wang continued. "Are you not

busy, Comrade Cheng? Probably you know me. I am on the Land Committee. My name is Wang Ta-pao. I have spoken with you twice before. It was in connection with my work."

The president shook his hand again vigorously, giving him a warm fraternal smile.

"Yes, Comrade Wang, we have met before. What is your business now?"

"It's a little thing, just a personal matter. And yet it concerns the People's Committee. That is, I think it concerns it. To put it simply in a word, my wife wants to leave me."

"Ah! There has been a good deal of that lately." The president said laughing, "It is a good sign."

"Yes, you're right! The sign is very good—but—I feel very bad."

"Why?"

"I and my wife, we've been married ten years now. We've got two boys. One's eight and the other's four. We're both very decent. The only trouble is that I have a little bit of a temper. But, after all, aren't most of the men hereabouts just as bad? I think it's just because of this that she can't get along with me and wants to leave me."

The president listened smiling.

"Of course," Wang continued, "as a revolutionist, I approve of this sort of thing. But from my own point of view, I don't like it."

"Whatever is good for the revolution ought to be done."

"Yes, yes! That's right! But, I tell you, getting a wife isn't an easy matter. At the beginning, when I got this one, I spent over a hundred dollars and used up almost everything I had. This business of getting married always ruins the family fortunes and eats up the property. And now I haven't that much money. On the other hand, it isn't pleasant to be a lone bachelor. All the men would say. . . ."

"Then what do you propose be done about it?" asked the president with a smile.

"I have two conditions to submit. The first and best is that she shouldn't leave me because I haven't really treated her badly. The second is that if she insists on leaving me, she ought to pay me back what I spent to get her."

The president laughed. Rising, he laid a hand on Wang's shoulder and said to him earnestly, "Comrade Wang, I can give you this answer: that neither of your proposals can be considered in our soviet."

Wang Ta-pao thought it over.

"Our women here are truly emancipated," the president continued. "Registration is their freedom. They cannot be held in any way responsible to make economic compensation. I am sure you know this already. Free marriage and divorce do not exist in a counterrevolutionary system. They are good things."

"I know that," Wang replied in a disappointed tone. "From what you say it was no use for me to come to you for advice. I wanted you to give me a plan for dealing with the problem."

The president continued to speak earnestly and smilingly. Clapping him on the shoulder in a brotherly way, he said, "Good! Don't worry! I will tell you what to do. I will guarantee on my reputation as president of the People's Committee that in a month at the most you will have found yourself a lover—"

At the word "lover" they both laughed.

"To lose a 'wife' and to gain a lover—that has happened many times already in our soviet. I could cite you a hundred cases in a week. I am sure you have seen cases of it yourself. At any rate, you have heard of it. Doesn't it occur all the time among us here?"

Wang Ta-pao nodded as he listened.

"Good. As far as your case is concerned I think the matter settles itself thus: Your wife wants to leave you. That is not a question for discussion. In a revolutionary soviet, no one can prevent her. But I assure you that if she does not decide to return and if in a month you have found no one to love you or if you still desire to buy a wife with money, then I will compensate you myself for your financial loss, on my honor as committee president. Have you any objections, Comrade Wang?"

"I have no objections," Wang answered in great relief. "Comrade Cheng, all that you have said is true. Our marriage system here is a revolutionary one, and the new system is excellent. Only—well—I tell you. I'm not very handsome. I've got a few pockmarks on my face and I don't think I would have an easy time being attractive to women."

"That has nothing to do with it," the president replied definitely. "It is one of the old ideas to be pleased with a pretty face. People of the soviet cannot have such notions. That idea belongs to the bourgeois and landowning classes, and the people of the soviet must use their revolutionary power to destroy it. As a matter of fact, I think the idea is already eradicated from among our people. The question now is only this: Comrade Wang, how is your work on the Land Committee?"

"Are you asking me whether I work well or not?"

"Yes. That is the important thing."

"Comrade Cheng, I will tell you quite frankly. The revolution can have Wang Ta-pao's life if it wants it. Although I'm not an educated man still I have done quite well on the work which has been given me. Besides that, I am taking target practice and am preparing to join in the fighting of the Red Army."

The president gave a pleased smile.

"Comrade Wang, that is all that is necessary. I guarantee

that in less than a month you will have a sweetheart among our women comrades."

Wang Ta-pao suddenly smiled.

"Have you anything further to say?" asked the president, laying a hand again on his shoulder.

"No, let it be that way."

"Fine! Now, Comrade Wang, you wait and see whether I shall need to compensate you."

The two men laughed and shook hands. The president removed his cap and in a brotherly manner gave him the revolutionary salute. Wang Ta-pao left the office contented and saying to himself, "The marriage system is certainly already revolutionized."

Three weeks later he dispatched a short note to the president.

Comrade President Cheng,

The first thing I have to tell you is that it will not be necessary for you to give me the money. The second thing is that all that you said was true. The third thing is that I have just come back from registering with a girl comrade. It seems to me that this one is nicer than the other. Naturally a sweetheart is better than a wife. We are starting a sweet and happy life. In conclusion, thank you very much, and you don't need to pay me anything.

Greetings of the revolution!

Wang Ta-pao

JOU SHIH

Slave Mother

1

Her husband dealt in skins: that is to say, he collected cow-
hides and the skins of wild animals from hunters all over the
countryside, and took them to the larger towns to sell. Sometimes he supplemented this occupation with a little farm labor. During the busy planting season he used to assist the
farmers in transplanting the young sprouts. He knew just
how to set out each row perfectly straight, and for that reason if there were five working together in a paddy field, he
was always put in the head position to act as marker. Circumstances were against him, nevertheless, and his debts
mounted year after year. Probably it was the hard times
that made him take to smoking, drinking, and gambling.
Soon he had become a surly, hot-tempered fellow, continuing to grow poorer and poorer until people were afraid to
make him even the smallest loans. Illness followed in the
wake of poverty, and his body turned a withered yellow col-
or. His face grew as yellow as a small brass drum. Even the
whites of his eyes changed color. People said that he had the
Translated by George A. Kennedy.

215

jaundice, and children began calling him "Yellow-Bag."
One day he said to his wife, "There's nothing more I can
do. If we go on like this, we'll soon have to part with the
kettle. I think it would be better to let you save us with your
body. If you stay and go hungry with me, what can I do for
you?"

"With my body?" His wife sat behind the cooking stove,
holding her three-year-old son on her lap nursing him at her
breast. She spoke in a subdued tone, haltingly.

"Yes, yours!" replied her husband, his voice weak from illness. "I've already leased you. . . ."

"What's that?" she asked, feeling suddenly faint.

The room was silent for a moment, and then he spoke,
breathing hard:

"Three days ago Wolf Wang sat here for hours demanding
his money. When he left, I went out too. When I got to
Nine-Acre Pool, I felt as if I didn't want to live any longer.
I sat down under a tree. All I needed was to climb it and let
myself drop off into the pool. I kept thinking about it, but I
hadn't the courage to jump. All the time there was an owl
screeching in my ear. It turned my heart cold, and I came
away. But on the road I met the Shen woman. She asked
me what I was doing out so late and I told her. I asked her
to try and raise me a loan, or to borrow some girl's clothes
or jewelry that I could pawn, so that I wouldn't have to see
Wolf Wang's green eyes glittering in my house every day.
But the Shen woman laughed at me and said:

" 'Why do you keep on, then, supporting that wife of yours
at home, and you as yellow as you are?'

"I hung my head and said nothing. 'Of course, you can't
spare the son,' she said, 'having only one. But the wife—'

"I said to myself, 'Surely she isn't telling me to sell my
wife!' 'But the wife,' she went on, 'even though she is your

proper wife, you're poor, and can't help it. What's the use in keeping her at home?'

"Then she came straight to the point and said: 'There's a *hsiu-tsai*, a man with a literary degree, who has no son although he's already fifty. He has had it in mind to buy himself a second wife, but his first wife won't let him. She'll allow him only to lease one for three or five years, and he has asked me to look out for a woman who might suit him, one somewhere around thirty, who has had two or three sons already, who is quiet and honest and willing to work, and who will be submissive to his first wife. Recently the *hsiu-tsai*'s wife spoke to me about it herself, and said that if conditions were satisfied, they would be willing to pay eighty or a hundred dollars purchase price. I've been searching for a suitable woman a good many days but haven't located one.'

"Then she said that as soon as she met me she thought of you, and that you were just the right one. So she asked me straight away what I thought, and after I had cried a little I let myself be persuaded."

At this point his head dropped, while his voice trailed off until it stopped completely. His wife said not a word. She seemed wholly stupefied. After a moment's silence he went on.

"Yesterday the Shen woman went to the *hsiu-tsai*'s house, and she says he is quite keen, and that his wife is pleased too. The price is a hundred dollars and the lease is for three years if there is a son in that time; if not, for five years. The Shen woman has set the date too. It's the eighteenth—five days yet. Today she's having the lease agreement written up."

The wife was quivering in every limb. "Why didn't you tell me earlier?" she stammered out.

"I walked a circle in front of you at three different times

yesterday, but I couldn't get it out. Really and truly, apart from using you as a means there is absolutely nothing we can do."

"You've decided on it?" she asked with trembling lips.

"Just waiting for the agreement to be written out."

"Oh, what a shameful thing! Isn't there any other way at all, my own Spring Treasure's father?" That was the name of the boy in her arms.

"Shameful?—yes, I've thought about it. But we're poor and we don't want to die. What else can we do? I'm afraid I'm not going to be able to do any transplanting this year."

"Have you thought about Spring Treasure? He's only three. What will he do without a mother?"

"I can look after him, can't I? He's already been weaned anyway."

Little by little he seemed to have grown angry. He now strode out through the door. And she—she began to sob, brokenly.

Out of her memories of the past emerged the thing that had happened just a year ago. She had borne a daughter then, and she lay on the bed like one who had died. No— the dead die whole, but her body was shattered into fragments. On a heap of dry grass on the floor, the newborn baby was crying loudly "Caa, caa!" and jerking its arms and legs. The navel string was twisted about it, and by its side the afterbirth had dropped. She made a supreme effort to rise and wash the child, but only her head would lift; her body remained inert on the bed. It was then she had seen that brutal husband of hers, with flaming red face, put a pail of boiling water beside the infant. She had put forth a final effort to shout at him, "Wait! Wait!" But the brute had not allowed a moment's discussion, nor had he returned any answer. Like a butcher holding the lamb he was about to slaughter, he had taken in his hard, rough hands the newborn life, the little daughter with the cries of "Caa, caa!" and plop!—dropped her into the water. She had heard nothing but a splash and the hiss of steaming water. The little girl made no sound. She wondered now why it had not uttered one loud cry. Had it been content to go silently to this undeserved death? Ah, yes! she remembered why she had heard nothing!—She had fainted away then, fainted as she would have done if her heart had been cut out.

When she thought of this, it seemed as though all tears were drained away. "Ah," she sighed softly, "fate is bitter!" Spring Treasure dropped the nipple and looked up at her.

"Mama! Mama!"

2

On the evening before her departure she chose the darkest corner of the house to sit in. An oil lamp was burning in front of the stove, giving out a firefly-like illumination. She held Spring Treasure in her arms and let her head rest on his hair. Her thoughts seemed to have floated very far away, to what far place she could not tell. Slowly they traveled back, back to the immediate present, back to the child. She called to him in a low voice:

"Spring Treasure, my precious!"

"Mama!" he answered, pulling on her nipple.

"Mama is going away tomorrow. . . ."

"Hm," he replied, half comprehending but instinctively rubbing his head against her breast.

"Mama's not coming back. She can't come back, not for three years!" She wiped her eyes.

"Where's mama going?" asked the child, feeling his mouth. "To the temple?"

"No, she's going ten miles away to a family named Li."

"I'm going too!"

"Precious can't go along."

"Ng!" he grunted rebelliously, returning to the slim supply of milk.

"You stay at home with daddy. Daddy will look after my Precious. He'll sleep with Precious, and take Precious out to play. You do what daddy tells you, that's all. And after three years. . . ."

"Daddy will beat me!" the child interrupted in a tearful voice.

"Daddy won't beat you anymore," she said, at the same time stroking his right cheek, running her fingers over a scar from a blow with a hoe handle which his father had given him on the third day after murdering his little sister. She seemed to have had something more to say to the child, but just then her husband came stalking in through the door. He walked over to her, and, reaching in his pocket with one hand, said:

"I've got seventy dollars of the money already. The other thirty will be paid ten days after you arrive there."

There was a pause. "And they've agreed to send a sedan chair for you."

Another pause. "And they've agreed that the chair-bearers will come directly after breakfast."

With that he left her and went out through the door again. That evening neither she nor her husband ate any supper.

The next day there was a drizzle of spring rain.

The sedan chair arrived early. She had not slept the whole night. First she had mended all of Spring Treasure's ragged store of clothing. Spring was almost over, and it would soon be summer. Yet she brought out even the torn quilted coat he used in winter and turned all his things over to the father, who lay already asleep in bed. Then she sat down by his side and tried to talk with him. But the long night dragged slowly by without her having said a word. Once or twice she worked up the courage to call out to him, but she said nothing intelligible, nor was it loud enough for him to hear. Finally she had lain down in silence.

Just as her mind was drifting off into unconsciousness, Spring Treasure awoke. He tugged at his mother and wanted to get up. As she put on his clothes she said to him:

"Precious must be a good boy at home here and not cry so that daddy won't beat you. And mama will buy Precious lots of candy to eat. Precious mustn't cry."

The child, without a trace of sadness, opened his mouth and began to sing. "Don't sing," she said, kissing him beside his lips. "You'll wake up daddy!"

On a bench near the door sat the chair bearers smoking long pipes and telling each other stories. Shortly after, the Shen woman arrived from the neighboring village. She was an old woman, a matchmaker with a wealth of worldly experience. On entering she brushed the raindrops from her and said to them:

"It's raining, it's raining! That's a sign that after this there'll be growth in your home."

She took a turn or two about the room in a businesslike manner and made a few remarks to the child's father, to the general effect that she would appreciate a commission. It was due to her efforts, after all, that the lease agreement had been arranged so smoothly and profitably. "To speak quite frankly, Spring Treasure's father, for another fifty dollars the old fellow could have bought himself a concubine," she said. Then she set about hurrying the woman along, but the latter sat motionless with Spring Treasure in her arms. The old woman shouted at her in a high-pitched voice.

"The chair bearers want to get back to their own place for lunch. You had better get ready to leave."

The woman looked at her as though saying, "Really, I don't want to go! Let me stay here and starve!"

The matchmaker understood what was on her mind. She went over to her with her most engaging smile.

"You are a simple wench, right enough. What more has Yellow-Bag got to give you? Over there is a family that has enough to eat and to spare, two hundred acres of fields, enough money, their own house, hired men, and cattle. The wife is extremely good-natured and extremely polite to others. Every time she meets people she makes them presents of food. As to the old fellow—he isn't really old. He has a white face and no beard at all. From so much studying he has grown round-shouldered in an elegant way. But there's no need for me to tell you. As soon as you step down from the sedan chair you will realize that I never tell lies in my matchmaking."

The woman brushed away the tears.

"Spring Treasure," she said softly. "How can I give him up this way?"

"Don't worry about him," said the old woman, placing a hand on her shoulder and putting her face close to the two of them. "He's three. The ancients said: 'Three or four years and he leaves his mother.' He's ready to leave you. If you'll just put forth an effort with your belly and bear a child or two while you're there, everything will be fine!"

The chair bearers at the door were urging departure. "She isn't a young bride," they grumbled, "to be doing so much crying!"

The old woman took Spring Treasure out of her arms. "Won't you let me take him with me," she pleaded. The child cried and struggled but was finally bundled out through a side door. Just as his mother was getting into the chair she called out to them.

"Take him back into the house. It's raining."

Her husband sat resting his head on his hand and never moved nor spoke.

3

It was ten miles from one village to the other, but the second time the chair was set down they were there. The fine spring rain had blown in through the cloth curtain of the sedan chair and soaked her coat. She was welcomed by a plump-faced lady of fifty-four or five with crafty eyes. "That must be the wife," she said to herself and looked at her in silence, full of embarrassment. The other conducted her in a friendly way to the steps while a tall thin man with a delicate round face came out from the house. After carefully scrutinizing the new arrival he smiled broadly.

"You arrived very early, didn't you? Have you wet your clothes?" he said. The old woman paid no attention to his presence.

"Do you have any things in the chair?" she asked.

"No, I have nothing."

A number of women from the neighborhood had gathered outside the door and were peeking in as they went into the house. She did not understand why she should keep thinking of her old home and why she could not forget Spring Treasure. Certainly it was obvious that she ought to be congratulating herself on the three years of life that were commencing. Both this house and the husband to whom she had been leased were better than the ones she had left. The *hsiu-tsai* was unquestionably a kind and good man with a quiet way of speaking, while even the wife was unexpectedly pleasant with her attentiveness and her unceasing flow of chatter. She told the whole story of her life with her husband from the time of her beautiful and happy marriage down to the present—a period of thirty years. She had borne one child, she said, fifteen or sixteen years previously, but it had died of smallpox before it was ten months old. She had never had a second child. Apparently she had wanted her husband to take a concubine, but whether he had not done so through love of her or through not having met a suitable person, she did not explain. Thus they had continued up to the present. As she listened to her, the simple-natured young woman felt alternately cheered and pained, elated and depressed. Finally the old lady referred to their expectations. This brought a blush to her face, but the old lady said:

"You have already given birth to more than one child. Of course you know all about it. I am sure you know more than I do." And with this she left her.

That evening the *hsiu-tsai* also talked in great detail about family affairs, partly in a boastful way to be sure, and partly to be attractive to her. She was sitting beside a chest of drawers, a red wooden one such as she had never possessed in her own home. She was looking at it wide-eyed when the *hsiu-tsai* came and sat down in front of it.

"What is your name?" he asked.

She did not return an answer or a smile, but rising, went toward the bed. The *hsiu-tsai* followed and laughingly asked her:

"Are you shy? Ha! You're thinking about your husband, aren't you? Ha! Ha! Well I'm your husband now!" His voice was gentle. He put out a hand and pulled at her sleeve. "Don't be sad. I suppose you're thinking about your child too. But—"

He did not finish what he was going to say. With another laugh he began to remove his outer gown. She could hear the wife's voice outside roundly cursing someone. She could not make out who it was. It might be the cook or it might be herself. Somehow she appeared to be the cause of it.

"Come to sleep," called the *hsiu-tsai* from the bed. "She is always carrying on like that. She used to be very fond of the hired man, so she always scolds Mrs. Huang, the cook, because the hired man liked her."

The days passed quickly. Gradually the thoughts of her old

home grew distant while her immediate surroundings became closer and more familiar to her. Sometimes she would hear Spring Treasure crying and on several occasions she had dreamed about him. But the dreams grew vague while the duties with which she was surrounded increased daily. She discovered that the old lady was extremely suspicious. On the surface she appeared gracious, but actually her jealousy turned her into a sleuth, forever spying on every action of her husband in regard to the new woman. If the *hsiu-tsai* came in from outside and spoke with the other first, she immediately suspected that he had bought something special for her, and that night she would call him into her room and deliver an angry lecture. "Are you bewitched by a fox? Do you know how much your old bones weigh?" Such expressions were commonly heard. From then on if the younger woman happened to be alone when the *hsiu-tsai* came in, she hastened to avoid him. Even if the old lady was nearby, it was wise to retire some distance, although she attempted to be as natural and unobtrusive about it as possible. Otherwise the lady would flare up and accuse her of trying to make her appear harsh in the eyes of the bystanders. As time went on, all the responsibilities of the house were heaped on to her shoulders, as though she were a servant. She acted wisely and often washed the old lady's clothes although she was told:

"There is no reason for you to wash my clothes. Even your own clothes can be given to Mrs. Huang to wash." Directly afterwards, however, the old lady would generally say: "Sister, go down to the pigsty and have a look around, will you please? I don't know why those two pigs should be making such a fuss. Probably they haven't enough food. Mrs. Huang never gives them enough."

During the winter eight months later her appetite underwent a change. She did not care to eat rice, only fresh noo-

dles or sweet potatoes. After a few meals she was tired of
these too and wanted *wonton*. If she ate much it would not
stay down. She had a desire for squash and plums, but these
grew in the summer months. Where could one get them
now? The *hsiu-tsai* appreciated the message which these signs
conveyed and smiled the whole day long. Whatever it was
possible to buy he procured for her. He went personally on
the street to get her oranges and to order other fruits to be
bought for her. He would walk up and down the porch muttering things to himself that no one understood. Once he saw
her helping Mrs. Huang to grind flour for the New Year
cakes and called to her before she had finished three *sheng*.
"Take a rest. The hired man can do the grinding. They all
share in the cakes anyhow."

Sometimes in the evenings, while the others were chatting,
he would bring a lamp and sit by himself reading lyrics
from the *Book of the Odes* in its flickering light. Then the
hired man would say to him:

"Why do you study those things, sir? You are not sitting for
an examination now."

Then he would stroke his smooth cheeks and answer merrily.

"Aha, do you know about the joys of life too?

'The night that wedding candles are placed in the
  nuptial chamber,
The day when names are listed on the gilded plaque.'*

Do you understand those two phrases? Those are the two
happiest events in a man's life. Both of them belong to my
past, and yet now I have a joy greater than either of them."

When he said this everyone but his two wives would burst
into laughter. These things were very annoying to the old

*Announcing those who have passed the government examination for offi-
cial position.

lady. At first she had been pleased over the woman's preg-
nancy, but when she noted how the *hsiu-tsai* humored her,
she was angry that her own belly had not been able to pay
the debt. On one occasion—it was in the third month of the
following year—the young woman remained in bed for three
days because of a slight illness and a headache. The *hsiu-tsai*
was quite willing for her to rest—not only so, but he was
continually asking her whether she needed anything. This
sent the old lady into a violent temper. She said the woman
was putting on a delicate air and muttered about it for three
days, heaping malicious ridicule upon her. As soon as the
woman had arrived, she said, she had taken on a high opinion of herself, what with her pains in the side and her pains
in the head—strutting about like a first-class concubine. She
was quite sure that she had never been so pampered while
she had been in her own home. There she had probably
been obliged to do as the bitch in the street does—go hunting her own food with a bellyful of puppies inside her. Now
just because that old codger—this was what she called her
husband—was humoring her, she was pretending to be delicate. "A son!" she once said to Mrs. Huang. "We have all
had children. I carried one myself for nearly ten months. I'll
never believe it is as bad as all this. In any case, this son of
hers is still on the rollbook of the underworld. Who can
guarantee that it won't be an ugly toad when it's born? After the little beast has crawled out of its hole, it will be time
enough for her to strut haughtily in front of me. But it is a
little early for her to be puffing out now while it is still a
lump of flesh!"

The young woman had not eaten that night. She listened
in bed to all these indirect and abusive sneers and cried quietly to herself. The *hsiu-tsai*, sitting half-undressed on the
bed, broke into a cold sweat and trembled as he heard it.
He had the impulse to rise, dress himself, and administer a

beating, pull out her hair, give her a sound thrashing, to give vent to his wrath. But he seemed not to have the strength. His fingers were trembling and his arms felt weak. "Alas!" he sighed. "I have been too kind to her. During thirty years of married life I have never slapped her, never even flicked her with my fingernail. And now she is as hard to satisfy as a crusty dowager!" He moved closer to the young woman and whispered in her ear: "Don't cry, don't cry. Let her bark! She's only a barren hen who can't stand to see others hatching out eggs. If you really bear a son this time I have two jewels for you. I have a green jade ring and a white jade—"

The continued jeering of his wife outside interrupted him. He threw off his clothes and pulled the blankets over his head. Laying his face on her breast he whispered,

"I have a white jade. . . ."

4

Day by day her belly grew more distended until it was the size of a bushel measure, and the old lady finally made arrangements for a midwife. She even went to the length, when others were looking, of getting out brightly colored cloth and sewing clothes for the baby. The cruel hot summer had come to an end, and the whole family had passed the sixth moon in an attitude of expectancy. At the start of autumn cooler breezes began to caress the village. Then, one day, the hopes of the household rose to a high-water mark. The atmosphere in the home was one of thrills, and the *hsiu-tsai*, especially, was in a tense state. He walked back and forth in the courtyard carrying an astrological almanac out of which he appeared to be memorizing something. "Epsilon Leo, Alpha Aquarius, the tiger influence is dominant," he muttered again and again to himself. Sometimes his anxious eyes turned toward the closed window of a room in which could be heard the low moaning of the young woman. Sometimes he stared up at the cloud-covered sun.

"How is it now?" he asked Mrs. Huang, who stood inside the door of the room. She nodded silently at him several times, adding after a moment:

"It will be here soon! It will be here soon!"

Then he took his almanac and began walking up and down the hallway again.

This went on until the twilight haze had commenced to rise from the ground and the lamps blossomed out here and there like flowers in the spring. Then the child—a boy—was born. One could hear his voice crying lustily from the room, and the *hsiu-tsai* sat in a corner ready to cry with happiness. No one in the house had any desire to eat, but they gathered about the plain supper table. There the *hsiu-tsai*'s wife said to the servants:

"Keep the matter hidden for a while, so that the little baby may escape noxious influences. If anyone asks, say that it is a girl that has been born."

They all nodded and smiled knowingly.

After a month the baby's soft white face appeared in the autumn sunshine. He was being nursed by the young woman, surrounded by curious women from the neighborhood. Some of these praised the child's nose, some his mouth, and some his ears. Others remarked that the mother was looking well—better than before. She had grown fairer and put on flesh. But the old lady was about, giving commands and dispensing care in the manner of an old grandmother, and now she said:

"That's enough! Don't start the child crying!"

Regarding a name for the baby the *hsiu-tsai* indulged in long and painful meditation but was not successful in finding appropriate characters. The old lady's notion was to select a name from the phrase "Long Life, Riches, and Honor," or "Happiness, Prosperity, Joy, and Old Age." Best of all, she thought, would be the "Longevity" character or one of its synonyms, like "Ripe Old Age." The *hsiu-tsai*, however, did not agree, considering these names too common and trite. But though he pored over the *Book of Changes* and the *Book of History*, hunting for something out of these volumes, a half month, a whole month passed without his having discovered a name that struck him as suitable. He wished the name on the one hand to pronounce a blessing on the child and on the other hand to express by implication that he had secured the son at an advanced age. It was not easy to do this. One day he was sitting with the three-months-old baby on his knee, holding his book under the lamplight and peering through a pair of spectacles still in search of a name. The mother was sitting idle at one side of the room staring vacantly, her thoughts far away. Suddenly she spoke up:

"I think it would be nice to call him Autumn Treasure." All who were in the room turned eyes toward her and listened. "He was born in the autumn, wasn't he? A precious gift from the autumn! Call him Autumn Treasure."

"Excellent!" The *hsiu-tsai* took her up immediately. "What a lot of fine effort I wasted! Yes, I have reached the autumn of life. I'm over fifty. Then, the child was born in autumn and autumn is the ripening season for all nature. 'Autumn Treasure' is a perfect name! Besides, it can be found in the *Book of History*. 'Still there will be autumn harvest,' it says, and indeed I am having my harvest!"

Then he praised the child's mother, saying that mere study was worthless after all and that intelligence was a gift from Heaven. These remarks made the woman feel very uncomfortable. She dropped her eyes and mused bitterly and tearfully:

"It was only that I was thinking of Spring Treasure!"

Autumn Treasure grew daily sweeter and more attached to his mother. He had amazingly large eyes with which he stared long and inquisitively at strangers, although he recognized his own mother at a glance, even from a distance. All day long he clung to her. In spite of the *hsiu-tsai*'s greater affection for him, the child did not care for his father. The wife of the *hsiu-tsai* appeared to be fond of him and gave the impression that she loved him as much as a child of her own, but in the baby's large eyes she remained a stranger. He followed her movements with a curious stare. The tighter the hold that he took on his mother, the nearer approached the day of her departure. Spring came biting on the tail of winter, while summer's feet followed close behind. So the approaching end of the mother's three years' stay began to loom large in the minds of all.

The *hsiu-tsai*, because of his love for the son, took up the matter first with his wife. He said he wished to pay another hundred dollars and purchase the woman in perpetuity.

"If you want to buy her, just give me poison first!" was his wife's answer.

When the *hsiu-tsai* heard this, he was furious but he said nothing for a long time. Later, forcing a smile, he said:

"Don't you think a child without its mother . . . ?"

"So you don't consider me a suitable mother for him?" replied the old woman sarcastically.

In the mind of the child's mother a struggle was going on between two conflicting feelings. In the first place she had long had echoing in her brain the words "three years." Three years, she had thought, would pass quickly, and so she had accepted the life of a servant in the *hsiu-tsai* household. She found the Spring Treasure of memory as lively and appealing as the Autumn Treasure of reality. If she could not bear to give up the latter, how much harder would it be to relinquish the former? She had an earnest desire, on the other hand, to spend the rest of her life in this new home. She felt that Spring Treasure's father had not long to live, that his sickness would very likely carry him off within three or four years. She planned to ask her second husband to adopt Spring Treasure so that he could be with her also.

Daydreams came most easily in the early summer sunshine on the porch outside the house. Sometimes as she sat there nursing Autumn Treasure, she seemed to see Spring Treasure too standing beside her. She would put out a hand to draw him closer and begin to talk to the two brothers—but the other was not there. In the doorway not far off stood the old woman with the kindly face and cruel eyes watching her attentively. Then she came to a startled realization. "Better to get away as soon as possible! She watches me like a spy!" When, however, the child in her arms gave a cry, she knew that nothing else mattered but this—and this controlled her.

Later on the *hsiu-tsai* modified his plan somewhat. He decided to send for the Shen woman and have her go to Autumn Treasure's mother's first husband to ask whether for thirty dollars—or at the most fifty—he would be willing to renew the lease on his wife for another three years. "When Autumn Treasure is five," he said to his wife, "then he can leave his mother."

The old lady was saying her prayers with a Buddhist rosary in her hand. She continued to mutter "Namu Amithaba." "She has a child of her own at home," she replied finally. "You ought to give her the opportunity of associating with her lawful husband again."

The *hsiu-tsai* hung his head and said hesitatingly: "But think of Autumn Treasure being deprived of his mother at the age of two!"

"I can raise him," said the old woman putting down her

rosary. "I can look after him. Are you afraid I'd assassinate him?"

At her last words the *hsiu-tsai* rose and strode away, his wife calling after him: "It was to help *me* that we had this son. Autumn Treasure is mine. And though it is your family, not mine, which would be in danger of extinction, nevertheless I have to eat your family's food. You have gone daft, childish with age. You have lost all your senses. How many more years do you have to live, that you hang on to this woman with might and main? I don't intend to have my memorial tablet set next to a rival's." The *hsiu-tsai* had moved too far away to hear the rest of the vicious and cutting things that the old lady had to say.

During the summer a boil came out on the baby's head, and sometimes he suffered from a slight fever. The old lady busied herself consulting the gods and procuring Buddhist remedies to rub on the boil or to pour into the baby's stomach. The mother did not consider the matter serious, and she objected to having the child kept in a perspiration from crying so much. She often threw the medicine out secretly after it had been barely tasted.

"You see," complained the old lady to the *hsiu-tsai* loudly, "she isn't at all concerned over the baby's illness and won't admit that he is getting thinner. Love in the heart is deep but love on the surface is false." The young woman wept in secret while the *hsiu-tsai* had nothing to say.

On the occasion of Autumn Treasure's first birthday some thirty or forty guests came to a celebration which lasted all day long. Some brought gifts of clothing, some brought noodles, some brought silver lions to be hung about the baby's neck, others brought gilded images of the God of Long Life to be sewn on the baby's cap. Presents of every kind emerged from the sleeves of the guests. They wished the child an illustrious career and immortal life, while the host's face glowed as though his cheeks reflected the glories of a sunset.

Toward evening of that day, just as the feast was beginning, a guest came into the courtyard, walking through the twilight mist. Staring at him, the people saw a frightfully haggard country yokel, with patched clothes and long hair, carrying a paper package under his arm. The host went over in surprise to receive him and asked him where he came from. The tongue-tied response conveyed nothing to the host, until of a sudden he understood. This must be that trader in skins!

"Why have you brought a present?" he asked in a low tone. "You really didn't need to do that!"

The guest looked timidly about him before answering. "I want—I wanted to—I came to wish the baby long life and a thousand. . . ." He broke off to pull out the paper package and with trembling fingers removed the several layers of paper. Then he produced four characters, each about an inch square, made of brass and coated with silver. The characters read "Longevity Rivaling Southern Mountain." The *hsiu-tsai*'s wife approached and inspected the visitor, appearing not too pleased. The *hsiu-tsai*, however, conducted him to the festal board where the guests were already whispering to one another.

Two hours of meat and wine put the company into a state of maudlin boisterousness. They played at guessing fingers in loud voices, filled large bowls with wine and challenged each other to drink, and made so much noise that the house shook. The skin trader alone, although he drank two cups of wine, remained still and silent. Nor did any of the guests pay the least attention to him. When the influence of the wine was wearing off, each guest hastily gulped down a bowl of rice and repeated his congratulations. The company departed by twos and threes, carrying lanterns. The skin trader ate till the last, and only when the servants came to clear away the dishes did he finally leave the table. He sought out a dark corner of the porch, and there he met his leased wife.

"Why did you have to come?" she asked in a melancholy tone.

"You don't think I wanted to come. I couldn't help it."

"Then why did you come so late?"

"How do you think I got the money to buy a gift? I tramped about the whole morning, begged and pleaded the whole morning. Then I had to go to the city for the birthday present. The walking made me tired and hungry—it made me late."

"And Spring Treasure?" asked the woman quickly.

The man heaved a sigh. "It's about Spring Treasure that I came."

"About Spring Treasure?" she echoed in alarm.

"All summer," he said slowly, "Spring Treasure grew terribly thin, and with the autumn he has fallen ill. I hadn't the money, of course, to get a doctor or medicines for him, so now he's worse. If we don't do something for him, it looks as if he will die." He paused a moment. "And so—I came to borrow some money from you. . . ."

It seemed to the woman that cats were clawing and biting her heart and gnawing at her vitals. She wanted to weep, but on a day like this when all had been voicing happy wishes for Autumn Treasure, how could she follow after with sobs? Restraining her tears she said:

"I have no money either. Here they allow me only two dimes a month for spending money. As a matter of fact I have no use for it so it all goes for the baby. What can we do?"

They were both silent for a while.

"Who is looking after Spring Treasure now?" the woman asked.

"I left him with a neighbor. I expected to be back again by this evening. I had better start now." He wiped the tears from his eyes.

"Wait a moment," said the woman, a lump rising in her throat. "I'll see if I can borrow from him." And she went.

Three days later the *hsiu-tsai* suddenly asked her: "Where is that green jade ring I gave you?"

"I let him have it that night. He took it to pawn."

"Didn't I lend you five dollars?" he asked angrily.

"Five dollars wasn't enough."

"Ah yes," sighed the *hsiu-tsai*. "It's always the first husband and the first son of whom you think, no matter how I treat you. Well, I had been thinking of keeping you another two years, but you had better leave next spring."

The woman was too shocked to cry. A few days later he referred to the matter again.

"That ring was a treasure. I gave it to you so that you could hand it on to Autumn Treasure. I never dreamed that you would pawn it at the first opportunity. It's lucky that she doesn't know about it. Otherwise there would be a good three months of wrangling."

5

The woman grew paler and thinner day by day and a dull look crept into her eyes, while her ears rang with the mockery and abuse that was thrown at her. She thought constantly of Spring Treasure and his sickness and kept on the watch for friends from her village or travelers who might be going to it. She waited anxiously for news that the boy had recovered completely but no news came. She also sought to borrow a dollar or two to buy delicacies to send him, but there was no one to take such things. Much of the time she sat holding Autumn Treasure at the side of the main road that ran past the door, watching those who came and went.

This situation was very annoying to the old lady, and she constantly said to the *hsiu-tsai:*

"Don't you see that she doesn't like being here at all? She wants nothing better than to fly home as soon as possible."

On several nights, dreaming with Autumn Treasure in her arms, she cried out suddenly, wakening the baby and making him cry. The *hsiu-tsai* plied her with questions. "What's the matter? What's the matter?"

There was no reply from the woman, who was patting and crooning to Autumn Treasure.

"Did you dream that your other son was dead? How you yelled! You have even awakened me!"

"No, no!" she said hastily. "I thought I saw a tomb in front of me."

The *hsiu-tsai* asked nothing further and the mournful vision continued to unfold before the woman. She wished she could have entered that tomb.

Winter drew to an end and the little birds that would herald her departure had begun to sing uninterruptedly beneath her window. First the child was weaned, Taoist priests being called in to assist the baby over this crisis in his life. Then the separation—the separation forever of the child from its natural mother—was decided upon.

On that day Mrs. Huang asked the *hsiu-tsai*'s wife quietly: "Shall I call a sedan chair for her?"

"Let her walk," replied the old lady, still counting the beads of her rosary. "The fare would have to be paid at that end, and what money does she have? I understand her husband hasn't even food to eat, so what's the point of her putting on airs by riding home? It isn't so far anyway. I have walked ten to fifteen miles myself in my time and her feet are larger than mine. She can do it in half a day."

As she dressed Autumn Treasure that morning the mother's tears flowed in a torrent. The child kept saying, "Auntie!

Auntie!" This was the name the *hsiu-tsai*'s wife had ordered should be used, as she wished the baby to call herself "mama." The mother answered the baby with sobs. She would have liked to say something to him, something like, "We are leaving each other, my darling boy. 'Mama' will be good to you. Be kind to her in return and never think of me again." The words would not come out. In any case a baby only a year and a half old would understand nothing.

The *hsiu-tsai* came sadly up to her and slipped his arm through hers. In his hand were ten twenty-cent coins. "Take them," he said gently, "these two dollars." She had finished buttoning the child's clothes and dropped the coins into her own inner pocket. The old lady came in and watched the retreating back of the *hsiu-tsai*.

"Let me have Autumn Treasure, so that he won't cry when you leave," she said. The woman said nothing, but the baby refused and slapped the old lady repeatedly in the face, making her very angry.

"Well, take him and have breakfast with him but turn him over to me afterwards."

Mrs. Huang urged her to eat heartily. "You have been acting like this for two weeks, and you are much thinner than you were. Have you looked in the mirror? Take a whole bowl of rice today. You have ten miles to walk yet."

"You have been good to me," answered the woman lifelessly.

The sun had risen high and the weather was splendid. Autumn Treasure still would not leave his mother until the old woman dragged him violently from her arms. He kicked her in the stomach with his little feet and pulled her hair with his tiny hands, yelling loudly. The mother watched them. "Let me stay until after the noon meal," she said.

The old lady turned on her savagely. "You make up your

bundle in a hurry and get out. You have to leave sometime."

The baby's crying sounded more distant to her. As she was
tying up her bundle she heard him cry again. Mrs. Huang
stood beside her trying to cheer her up and at the same time
keep track of what she was putting in. Finally the woman
set out, an old bundle under her arm. As she went through
the front door she heard Autumn Treasure crying again,
and even afer a mile of slow, weary walking, the cries
seemed still there. The road stretched away before her under
the burning sun, endless as the sky. When she reached a
creek, she thought of ending her wearisome tramp by leap-
ing down into the clear water that shone like a mirror. But
after sitting a while beside the stream she again moved her
shadow forward in the same direction.

It was past noon. An old peasant in one of the hamlets told
her that five miles of the journey remained. "Uncle," she
said to him, "would you be good enough to get me a sedan
chair in the neighborhood? I can't walk home."

"Are you sick?"

"Yes." She was sitting in the pavilion at the entrance to
the village.

"Where did you come from?"

She hesitated before replying.

"I'm just going in that direction. I thought this morning
that I could walk it."

The old man said a few kind words to her and found her
two bearers and a chair—one without a canopy because it
was the planting season.

About four o'clock that afternoon a chair with no canopy
was borne down the dirty narrow street of the village. In the
chair lay a middle-aged woman with a face withered and

faded as a dry leaf of yellow cabbage. Her eyes were closed, and her breath came feebly. The people on the street stared at her in surprise and pity while a group of children ran noisily after the chair as though some wonder had descended on the village.

Spring Treasure was among the children who followed the chair. He hooted behind it as though he were driving a herd of pigs, but when the chair turned a corner down the street which led to his home he broke off his game and stood in amazement. He watched it stop at his own door and stood stupefied, leaning against a post, while the other children gathered timidly around. The woman got out, but she was too dazed to see Spring Treasure there, dressed in rags with hair unkempt and hardly larger or taller than he'd been three years before. Suddenly she called out with a sob:

"Spring Treasure!"

The other children were startled. As for Spring Treasure, he fled in terror to his father in the house.

In the dirty, gloomy room the woman sat a long time, but not a word passed between her and her husband. When twilight fell on them he lifted his bowed head and said to her:

"You'd better get supper ready."

She forced herself to rise and went to a corner of the room. After a moment she said weakly, "The rice bin is empty."

"You have been living in the houses of the great," said the man with a sardonic smile. "Rice? It's in the cigarette box."

That night the man said to his son, "Spring Treasure, you sleep with your mother."

The boy, who was standing near the stove, began to cry. His mother went near to him murmuring, "Spring Treasure, my Precious!" but as she reached out to fondle him he darted away.

"Acting strange already?" said the man to the boy. "A beating is what you'll get!"

She lay with wide open eyes on the dirty narrow bench. Spring Treasure lay beside her, strange and unfamiliar. Into her dulled brain came the impression that it was Autumn Treasure, fat and lovable at her side. She put out her arms to take him without recognizing who he was. In his sleep he had turned over, and as she clasped him tight, the boy, snoring gently, buried his face between those breasts that his hands instinctively clutched.

Quiet and cold as death, the interminable sleepless night dragged on . . . dragged on. . . .

MAO TUN

Comedy

1

"One, two, three, four, . . . one, two, three, four."

Young Hua's hand was in his pocket counting over his entire store of worldly treasure. Four copper coins! He was so hungry that everything before him flickered, but he could not make a mistake in the count. One, two, three, four, . . . one, two, three, four! Unquestionably, there were no more than four.

He extended his shrunken brown palm and offered the four coppers respectfully to the big Shantung fellow at the wheat cake stand.

"Hey now, that won't do! Two cakes, eight coppers. You're short four coppers," bellowed the big Shantung man, rubbing a grimy hand on his thigh and glaring ferociously at Hua.

Young Hua shuddered at the sound of the Shantung accent and at the sight of the coarse face and two round eyes glittering red. Before his eyes floated the fierce countenance of

Translated by George A. Kennedy.

the soldier who had arrested him five years previously for distributing leaflets on ——— Road and who had beat him with the butt of his gun. Five years in prison had gradually wiped out the memories of his old friends, but the blow from the rifle butt had driven the image of this giant soldier of Marshal Sun deeper and deeper into his brain. He had served his sentence, and this was his first day of "freedom." Here at his first encounter with another human being, he was met with the same coarse skin, the same pair of cruel eyes, the same Shantung dialect. Could it be that the world, in five years, had not changed in the slightest degree? To his addled mind it seemed as though his arrest had happened only yesterday.

His extended hand began to tremble. He looked at the two cakes in his other hand and stammered out, "Eight coppers? Don't try to cheat me! Why, I buy wheat cakes all the time. Why, only yesterday they were two coppers apiece. . . ."

"Huh? I'll be damned! Two coppers apiece. And you bought them yesterday? You're dreaming. In times like these? Two coppers apiece? This is the era of 'the blue sky and white sun,'* isn't it? Everything has gone up. Maybe you paid two coppers for the wheat cakes your grandmother used to make."

The few laborers gathered about the stand burst out laughing and eyed young Hua up and down. They had sallow faces, all of them, and wore ragged blue clothes, exactly as did the wretches that Hua had grown so familiar with five years ago.

Finding young Hua thoroughly dazed, the Shantung vendor did not trouble to say anything further but took possession of the four coppers, at the same time taking back one of

*Referring to the Kuomintang flag, which featured a white sun on a blue field.

the wheat cakes. Then he turned away to drum up trade elsewhere. Young Hua squatted down mechanically and commenced to eat.

"Revolution, revolution! They've raised the prices of everything we eat or wear! To hell with the revolution!"

Hua raised his head quickly and saw the speaker, a laborer in a short blue coat, who was fishing out coppers in order to purchase cakes.

Revolution? Was it possible that there had been a revolution? Hua looked incredulously about him. On a nearby street corner waved a flag with the white sun in a blue sky over a scarlet field. It was ragged, to be sure, and faded, but the slanting rays of sunlight fell on it gently moving in the breeze. It was unmistakably the "white sun in a blue sky over a scarlet field," and five years ago that would have been good and sufficient cause for head-chopping. The white sun in a blue sky over a scarlet field! Young Hua grew suddenly wide awake. Swallowing the last mouthful of wheat cake, he asked quickly, "Has there been a revolution? When did it happen?"

The big Shantung cake vendor and the other laborers turned to stare at him with a mixture of astonishment and disdain. Hua realized that some explanation was called for.

"You see, I have just come out of West Prison. I was five years in there and I didn't know anything of what went on outside."

"A Communist, I suppose?" said one of the laborers, making a sign to his fellows. His mouth was full of wheat cake.

"Oh no, I'm a member of the Kuomintang."

Thereupon young Hua arose and prepared to recount his adventures and to accept the applause of his audience. But the cake vendor merely made an ugly face and spat vigorously as he set about baking more cakes. The blue short coats gave Hua a suspicious glance and moved rapidly away.

2

After walking ten minutes or so Hua came to a stop on a bridge. The large building on the other end, as he knew, was the Chamber of Commerce. There was a white sun in a blue sky over a scarlet field drooping lazily at the flagstaff. Hua hesitated, not knowing where to turn his steps.

Suddenly he remembered that his district association was not far off, and that he had a slight acquaintance with a man, Chao, who was a clerk there. Since he had nowhere else to go, he might as well try his luck there.

The face of the doorkeeper at the association wore the wrong expression. After staring at young Hua a long time, he remarked reluctantly,

"Mr. Chao is no longer here."

"Any secretary will do. It's important. I must see someone."

The doorkeeper's expression became more unpleasant, and he looked young Hua up and down again out of the corner of his eye. Finally, with an air of great condescension, he jerked his mouth in the direction of a round clock on the wall, and said loudly, "Don't you see what time it is? The office closes at three. The executive secretary has gone home long ago."

What was this? The executive secretary? Hua was amazed and excited by this. Had even the association adopted a new system? He saw for the first time that the world had really taken on a different complexion.

"Then I'll wait here," he said with an air of authority and determination. "I'll wait till tomorrow. I've no other place to go tonight."

"You can't do that. It's not done."

"Whether it's done or not, I have to spend the night somehow."

The doorkeeper gave a superior smile, then abruptly withdrew it to shout fiercely.

"Get out of here! You'd better watch yourself. If you don't go, I'll call the police."

Hua sat down without replying and the doorkeeper went out after swearing angrily at him.

Had he gone for the police? It really didn't matter. In any case there would be a place to sleep. Young Hua thought this over and felt quite peaceful.

Contrary to expectations, it was not a policeman that the doorkeeper brought with him but a weazened gentleman of about forty dressed in a Sun Yat-sen uniform. Something in Hua must have aroused respect, for the weazened one was surprisingly polite.

"I understand, my dear sir, that you are looking for Mr. Chao. What is the honorable business . . . ?"

"Eh . . . eh . . . this . . . a small matter. . . ."

"Is this your first visit to Shanghai?"

"No, I have just been released from West Prison."

"What! West Prison. . . ."

"West Prison. Five years ago, it was revolutionary work, arrested while giving out pamphlets on the street, just out today."

"Five years ago?"

"Yes, five years ago. Shanghai was still in control of Sun Ch'uan-fang. That was before the Kuomintang Revolutionary Army started out on the Northern Expedition." Young Hua's voice gained confidence, and his chest straightened out unconsciously in the conviction that his qualifications entitled him to sleep or eat when and where he chose. Unfortunately, the little gent of forty years appeared unimpressed by Hua's qualifications and worthiness. With a grunt and a faint smile that was not a smile at all, he turned to rebuke the doorkeeper.

"You're getting more and more inefficient in your work. You don't use any intelligence in sizing up people. You have to bring everything to me. Come—"

Drawing out the last word, the weazened gentleman had started to retire, but quicker than the word, Hua had grasped his arm.

"Wait a moment. We haven't settled on a place for me for the night."

"The thin gentleman stood motionless and dumb, rolling his small eyes. A servant had entered, and the doorkeeper, wiping the perspiration from his temples, had stepped forward. The thin one made signs to them to stay still. His glance was fixed fearfully on the pocket in which Hua's right hand rested.

Glances convey meaning, and Hua realized immediately the reason for the gentleman's concern. Throwing back his head, he laughed loudly, but before he had finished he felt the thin arm wriggle out like a snake from his clutch, while at the same time he felt himself seized by powerful hands and dragged several feet away.

When he was brought to a stop he heard the weazened gentleman say, "Search him!"

The search was carried out with entirely negative results. This appeared extremely disconcerting. The thin gentleman hesitated, reached in his pocket, and brought out a cigarette, which he lit.

After emitting several puffs of white smoke, he said bravely, "Hm! Take him to the police station. He's an escaping Communist."

"I don't mind going to the station. But why Communist?" inquired Hua. He received no answer. The thin gentleman had disappeared.

A short fat man with an alcoholic nose, who looked like a police watchman, stepped over to young Hua and clapped him on the shoulder.

"Come on, young fellow. If you've got anything to say, keep it for the station. You can't get out of it. Giving out leaflets during Sun Ch'uan-fang's time! If that isn't Communism, I don't know what is! You'll find out. All the big fellows in the Kuomintang were quite well behaved when Sun Ch'uan-fang was here. I saw it myself."

3

Twenty-four hours later young Hua was again wandering up and down the busy streets. The police sergeant had merely cursed at him, but had been unwilling to lock him up and so solve the pressing problem of food and lodging.

He was different from the person of this same time yesterday. His pockets contained no four coppers, although his brain contained a great many questions.

In his starved condition he was conscious of long strings of ear-shaped question marks drifting in front of him—question marks of all sizes. He paid no attention to where he was going.

The world had certainly changed. The girls had cut their hair and developed protruding pairs of breasts. Their faces were smeared with red or white while their arms and legs were quite bare. Motion picture theaters had increased in number. They displayed wordy advertisements: "New drama of mystery and heroism."

What lay beyond all this he did not know. One thing was certain. There had been a revolution. But the revolution had already proceeded beyond the wildest reaches of his imagination.

He stood stupidly at a tram station on the street corner. All around him were perfumed women with gleaming arms and legs, the rumble of vehicles, the noise of people, the arresting green and red electric signs. An indescribable disgust arose in him.

Suddenly he heard cries:

"Who wants the political news of the day!"

"Political news of the day!"

"Cantonese launch attack on Hunan!"

"Wang Ching-wei in league with Feng and Yen!"

"Read all the news! Communists attack Fukien!"

Hua turned around as a newspaper flashed before him. Apparently it was the *People's Livelihood Daily*. "Generalissimo returned to Nanking yesterday," announced its headlines.

Immediately a political map unrolled in his mind—the old map of five years before when the northbound army had just captured Wuhan and while the occupant at Nanking was Sun, the Marshal. When he put the picture of today alongside that of yesterday and added in that of the day before yesterday—the picture of the period of his arrest—he found himself completely bewildered.

His stomach was making noises. That was the most pressing concern. How to settle this question? Hua made a gesture of dismissing all the political news and pushed back into the crowd, wondering where to find food and shelter. He recalled that Sun Yat-sen's teachings were primarily occupied with problems of food, clothing, shelter, and transportation. Though he was a devoted and reverent follower of these doctrines, he found himself no better off than a homeless dog. He felt very angry and injured.

Anger seemed to offset the hunger, but at the same time

there was a sort of windmill whirling around in his brain making him see double. At a street corner he bumped head-first into someone. The two of them fell.

"Son of a bitch! Are you blind?" swore the first to pick himself up, concurrently administering a kick to the one who lay on the ground, which happened to be Hua. His extreme hunger seemed to have rendered the latter incapable of moving or speaking. As he rolled his eyes up to look at the other, he gave a sudden cry.

"Is that you, Chin? I'm Hua!"

He leaped up. The hunger in the stomach and the irritation in the mind had both vanished.

4

Young Hua was now replete with food, and a Garrick cigarette stuck out from the corner of his mouth. He lounged luxuriously in Chin's living room.

Through a cloud of smoke he addressed his host. "I would never have dreamed that five years would bring about so many changes. Now it is all clear to me. You were so staid and conservative when we were students together. You never took a single false step. Now I can understand and admire you for the man of vision that you were."

"Oh, that! That! I was merely following the ancient philosophy of patient submission. Of course, I had to put up with being called counterrevolutionary by the rest of you. But you can see now that I am one of the true disciples of the revolution."

Chin blew a puff of smoke toward the ceiling. The electric light fell on his fat round face, which glowed like a miniature sun.

Hua smiled and nodded. He puffed furiously at his cigarette and regarded the portrait of Dr. Sun hanging on the wall. "Great Father of the Revolution," he meditated, "thy doctrines have not turned out to be bad checks! Those who adore thy teachings find means of cashing in on them to secure food and clothing and lodging and transportation—to secure them very comfortably, as Chin here has so excellently demonstrated!"

Chin had suddenly elevated a thumb and was describing a circle in the air. Turning to Hua, he said with vehemence, "It's too bad that society contains such a lot of scum who keep up a clamor about taxes and the difficulty of making a living. Bah! They don't seem to realize that a revolution demands some sacrifices. These stupid asses don't deserve to live under a revolutionary government if they aren't willing to make sacrifices!"

"Are the taxes heavy?" inquired Hua automatically. He still remembered some of the stock expressions of five years before and the impression he had received at the biscuit stand was bothering him. Fortunately, Chin was not attending very closely to him. He replied with a faint smile on his lips.

"Well, I can't say they're exactly light. But, Hua, old fellow, it's the businessmen who are the support of the revolution. They have brains enough to cooperate with the government. Those stupid peasants and laborers are the ones who are always bawling about their troubles. Hua, old man, have you any idea how much the revolutionary government has raised in bonds? Nine hundred million! Nine hundred million in four years! That's several times as much as the Peking militarists raised in fifteen years! That's how the businessmen support the government—"

Snatching a puff on his cigarette, he added in a lower tone, "Of course the businessmen make their little profits. The average market value of the bonds is only about fifty percent."

The conversation moved on to other matters—girl friends,

dance halls, motion picture stars, bathing beauty contests. Young Hua had never heard of these before. How the world had changed! And how much more pleasant it was!

But, like one of the characters in the tales of the Arabian Nights, after being filled with stories of the marvels of the world, Hua awoke to the realization that he had not half a cash in his belt nor a place to sleep for the night. He knitted his brows and began to ask his solicitous host for the loan of eight or ten dollars, but he could not work up the courage. He said merely that he was anxious to find work, to do his bit for the revolution.

Chin's forehead wrinkled up. Lighting a fresh cigarette, he puffed vigorously on it as he studied the oil paintings of nudes on the walls.

Hua, seeing that no answer was forthcoming, attempted to carry on his monologue.

"I know it's rather difficult. I've just got out and I'm not yet very well up on the situation in the party—"

He felt very resentful toward Dr. Sun's principles.

"Aha, I have it!" shouted Chin jumping up and terminating at one and the same time Hua's soliloquy and his resentment. Elevating a thumb, Chin advanced toward Hua and spoke with special gravity.

"Didn't you tell me that someone accused you yesterday of being a Communist?"

"Uh-huh."

"That's fine. Now you say that you are a Communist who wants to go over to the government. Then there'll be no difficulty about a job."

"But really, I'm not a Communist."

"Ho, ho, it doesn't hurt to be taken for what you aren't. Besides, you have all the earmarks of one."

Hua opened his mouth wide in astonishment.

"You have nothing to worry about, just go ahead with this plan. Do you think an old friend would give you risky advice the very first time? Well, it's getting late. Let's go to a cabaret."

With a final heave Chin tossed the unfinished cigarette into the ashtray and began to hum "Rio Rita."

When he emerged on the street again, Hua had experienced another transformation in the few hours that had passed. His pockets were still empty and his brain was also now emptied of all his old questions. Instead, it was crammed with notions of gold and beautiful women.

TING LING

One Certain Night

Slish–slosh–slish, slish–slosh, slosh. . . .

From out of the greenish lamplight of the hall an indistinguishable mass of human shadows was moving in the direction of the open field on the outside. Boots and shoes
stamped heavily through the deep snow that covered the
ground. The furious blasts of a winter night met them full in
the face, assaulting them with the fine sleet and heavy snowflakes that had been falling for half a month. The sudden
attack of the icy wind drew involuntary shivers, but the
shadows proceeded—slish–slosh, slish–slosh.

A second gust, roaring mightily, swept pitilessly over them,
cruelly lashing their faces and their bodies. In the middle of
the group, surrounded, helped, driven forward by the mo-
mentum of the others, a delicate youth, handsome in spite of
his haggard look, seemed to awake with a sudden start. The
past—all that had happened—seemed to appear somewhat
distantly, yet clearly, before him. He saw a crafty face, filled
with malice and greed, a full round face, embellished with

Translated by George A. Kennedy.

254

the hated, foreign-style moustaches. There was repressed glee in the evil, arrogant voice as the man had spoken, looking impudently at them from his high platform. "Have you anything further to say? Sentence has been passed upon you and the sentence will be carried out immediately."

Remembering all this the youth felt consumed by fires that blazed up in his soul. He wanted to tear that face to pieces! He would extinguish that voice! For one mad moment he thought of forcing his way out of the crowd and he quickened his step. A short while ago, when he had been condemned to death without a trial, he had been unable to preserve his composure as the rest of his comrades had done, but had lost consciousness in a powerful wave of rage and anguish.

He was a poet, ardent, sincere, energetic.

Bang! A rifle butt crashed heavily on his chest. Thinchested to begin with, he had grown more emaciated from twenty days of malnourishment in the dark and sunless prison. His thoughts were interrupted by the curses of the soldier who struck viciously at him.

"Rape of your mother, what's your hurry! The King of Hell can't wait to get you!"

Clank, clank. The rattle of iron shackles rattled on his hands and feet, and on the hands and feet of the others. There was a confusion of sounds all around him—hobnailed boots crunching more heavily in the thick snow. Slish, slosh! Slish, slish!

Something else became clear. He realized that he was walking somewhere. A strange thought came into his head. He seemed to see another pair of eyes above his own, a pair of lovely, unforgettable eyes that gazed eternally into his soul. He was distinctly conscious of something in the recesses of his heart that was stabbing him there and painfully tearing away his flesh and blood, inch by inch.

Ting Ling

The sky was black—illimitable blackness! Out of the blackness the sleet and the snow sifted down and out of it hissed
the roaring north wind. The world was all gray and foggy,
and the snow threw a dead ashen hue on the night. The
black shadows of the men—the escort and the victims—
moved silently over the snow. There was the clanking of
chains, the rattling of bayonets, but no word spoken. No one
moaned. No one sighed or wept. Steadily they moved toward
the hidden corner of the field which was being used temporarily as a place of execution.

"Damnation!" some were saying to themselves. "How far
do they have to take us to slice off our heads. . . ."

In the second line a girl comrade threw back her head
from time to time with an impatient gesture. The wind kept
blowing her bobbed hair over her forehead and eyes.

The youth made a great effort to suppress the screams that
seemed to be driving him mad with their insistence. He bit
hard on his lips and shuddered with the rage he could not
express. With staring eyes that were scorched with anger he
looked about him devouringly as though in search of something, peering first at this one, then at that.

The faintly reflected light from the snow illuminated the
faces of those near him. A soldier—beetling brows, fierce
eyes! A soldier—the face of an idiot, spreading nostrils, thick
lips! Another. . . . Suddenly his glance lighted on a dear
and familiar face. The face turned on him with a look of
tenderness and quiet, a look that transcended all the power
of words, a look such as only one comrade can give to another in the time of a martyr's death, to comfort and heart-
en. Then a great part of his anger and anxiety slipped form-
lessly away. Love and something else which could only be
described as *life* took possession of his tortured breast. He
yearned to enfold that face and to shower kisses upon it. He

returned the look with a nod full of courage and determination. . . .

Slish, slosh. . . . The sound of their feet in the night was like the disordered beating of victorious drums on every side as the twenty-five marched forward. Above their heads the whistling of the wind was like a giant red banner flapping over them.

"Halt! This is the place!" shouted the uniformed executioner fiercely, tightly clutching his Mauser pistol. "Where are you walking to, you sons of bitches?"

"This is it!" came the dull echo in all hearts.

"Line up the condemned! Tie them up!" The officer spat out the order. The soldiers in their quilted overcoats began to push them recklessly and roughly about, clubbing them with rifle butts and putting ropes around their chests to bind them securely to the stakes behind them. Boots and shoes clumped around in increased confusion over the snow-covered ground.

Not a word was said. An angry silence reigned. It was impossible now to find anything that would express the hatred they felt for their enemies. Hands and feet were shackled already and in addition they were being tightly bound to stakes which had been set up a few days previously. They were not far now from the border of death.

Darkness stretched away before their eyes. The wind and the rain and the snow came down incessantly. The marrow-penetrating cold relentlessly lashed the bodies of the twenty-five, whose overcoats and gowns had been taken from them in the hall. But they had already lost all consciousness of cold.

They stood close together in a row.

"Over here, get over a bit! Dress up that line!"

In the gloom of the night a group of human forms could be

dimly perceived, tugging and pushing at some heavy instrument.

"All right! Put it here! Count the criminals!"

"One . . . two . . . three. . . ." A soldier walked past and counted.

The officer in charge of the execution, coarse of face, passed in front of the line following the soldier and pointed at each one. In that brutal face there seemed to be concentrated all the ferocity of the rulers toward the oppressed. Angry passions flamed up once more in their breasts and burned their eyes and bodies with a fever of pain. They would have lunged out and beaten this devil to death, but their hands were bound fast behind them. They gnashed their teeth in anger and shivered in the icy wind, not from cold but from rage.

"Comrade, be brave," said the one on his right.

He turned his head to look. It was the dear friend with whom he had talked so much at supper time.

"Don't worry, I'm all right."

". . . Twenty-three . . . twenty-four . . . twenty-five! Correct! Good!" The man who had been counting bellowed out the last figure as he stalked heavily across the snow to the heavy black object set there on the ground.

Illimitable emptiness! Incessant wind and snow! Grayness without end, darkness without end. . . !

Gigantic shadows were reflected in that deathlike grayness.

"Good, get ready! Wait for the whistle!" bellowed the officer again.

All hearts grew tenser, like drawn bowstrings. The heavy object before their eyes was death. Several soldiers were busily working over it. The sky was crushing down upon them—darkness would crush down upon them—on the bodies of the twenty-five.

"Comrades!" shouted someone in a ringing voice. "Don't forget! They tell us we are to die, but somewhere else today there is a great convention of our representatives. Our government takes form today. Let us wish our government well. Long live our government . . . !"

At this they all commenced to shout wildly. All the things that had been stored up in their hearts and that they had forgotten to express came back with sudden clarity, so that each one shouted his own feelings.

Darkness disappeared and a light glowed before their eyes—the birth of a new nation.

The shrill whistle blew. Twenty-five strong heroic voices took up the song:

"Arise, ye prisoners of starvation. . . ."

Pit! Pat! Pit! Pat!

The heavy object swept the line horizontally, spitting out a score of bullets.

The singing grew a little weaker although a few voices seemed to swell in volume.

" 'Tis the last fight we face. . . ."

Again the wail of the whistle.

Pit! Pat! Pit! Pat!

A second sweeping across and another score of bullets struck.

The singing began to die more rapidly. Only a few voices remained.

"The Interna. . . ."

A third whistle. A third sweeping patter. The song was silenced.

"Rape of their mothers! The bastards! Now go ahead and sing!" The execution officer swore and turned back in the direction from which he had come.

"Take up the gun," he ordered. "Return to your posts immediately. We'll bury the bodies tomorrow. You don't suppose the corpses will walk off?"

He went back to the hall and the soldiers stamped back homeward over the same snow. Slish, slosh!

The night was ugly and forbidding. The huge snowflakes and the fine sleet drifted through. The wild wind of winter roared by only to come roaring back again. The snow piled up on the hanging heads, to be blown off again by the gale. They were all dumb and motionless, fastened there. In some spots—in one, in two, in three spots—the blood trickled down and mottled the snow in the darkness.

Will the sky ever grow light?

TING CHIU

The Three Pagodas

1

Gold and silver pagodas have sprung up in Tingchow city!
This news has been spreading far and wide.

It spread to a little village in the mountains twenty miles
away from the city. First it was brought by some of the
peasants on their return from town, and this was the story
they had heard:

"One night the Soviet Workers' and Peasants' Bank was illuminated by a red glow which floated down from the sky.
As the red light shone on the earth, there sprang up out of
it a gold pagoda and two silver pagodas, each one as big
around as four dining tables! The people in the bank were
amazed at the sight and went that very evening to report it
to the provincial soviet. The chairman of the provincial soviet could make nothing of the pagodas when he saw them, so
he hurriedly telegraphed to Mao Tse-tung. Back came the
reply by telegraph that these were live pagodas and that if
you should pat one of them, it would lay an egg.

"As soon as this answer had been received, the provincial

Translated by George A. Kennedy.

261

chairman went up to one of the silver pagodas and gave it a gentle pat. Yes, out from the base of the pagoda came rolling a snow-white silver egg! Then he patted the gold pagoda, and a gleaming yellow egg of gold came rolling out from it. Then they set the three pagodas up in the Workers' and Peasants' Bank and now everyone may go to see them."

Some time later a peasant from the south happened to come to the mountain village. He lived farther away from the city—thirty miles and more—but he had also heard the story. His version, however, was different in many respects.

"One day," he said, "Chu Teh won a great battle in which he killed a general of the White Army. That night he had a dream. He saw the Pagoda Spirit standing in front of him with a red flag in one hand and three pagodas in the other. 'I have been commissioned,' the spirit said, 'by the great Jade Emperor to present these three pagodas to the Red Army to be kept in the strongroom of the Tingchow Workers' and Peasants' Bank. The overthrow of the landlords by the Red Army, the protection the Red Army has given to the workers, the peasants, and the poor, their equitable division of the land, their dispossession of the landlords—all this has moved Heaven deeply. Heaven has determined that the Red Army is to bring peace to all beneath the sky and that the soviet is to unite the Middle Kingdom. You and the Red Army carry on the good work!' The red flag waved and Chu Teh awoke. The next day he sent a telegram from Kiangsi to the Workers' and Peasants' Bank of Tingchow. When the bank managers opened up the strongroom and looked in, there they were!—three neatly arranged pagodas, one of gold and two of silver. It took a hundred and twenty men to carry each pagoda—three hundred and sixty in all—and they moved the pagodas out of the strongroom and put them behind the counter in the main hall. Each pagoda is as big around as four large tables, and many, many people have seen them with their own eyes."

The southerner went on to say that this report was absolutely accurate. He said that in his village there was an old teacher who was well versed in the ancient classics. This man declared that during the reign of the first Ming emperor, Chu Feng-wu, there had also been an appearance of silver pagodas—only one, however. According to him, of the three pagodas at Tingchow, the gold one belonged to Ma K'e-szu,* one of the silver ones to a man named Lieh Ning† of the Lieh family, and the last to Chu Teh of the Chu clan. This Chu Teh, he claimed, was the twenty-first descendant of the Ming emperor. When pagodas appeared, he said, it was a sure sign that peace was coming.

Two days later a member of the Red Guards, who had spent the previous night in the city, happened along. When the peasants learned that he came from the city, they crowded about him and begged him to tell them about the gold and silver pagodas. He began by bewailing his fate.

"I was not lucky enough to see them," he said, "because I came through the city at night. If it had been day, no business, however urgent, would have kept me from going to see them. One look was all I wanted. Where but in our soviet could you ever find pagodas made of silver and gold? But it is true! It is not a lie! There are twelve square tables placed together in the Workers' and Peasants' Bank. At night they close up the place, but during the day they allow all to see. Everyone in the city has been to look at them.

"Last night in a restaurant a young apprentice made fun of me. 'Comrade,' he said, 'you are a silver pagoda.'

" 'Heavenly conscience,' I said, 'Comrade, I don't hope to

*Marx
†Lenin

be a silver pagoda. There are four of us in my family and the soviet has allotted to us ground producing eighteen piculs. If only the White Army and the opposition can be destroyed quickly, I should be able to pile up a bronze pagoda. Heavenly conscience! I am quite contented.'

"The young apprentice said, 'Don't you know? The Communist Party has imported three large pagodas from Soviet Russia and has put them in the Workers' and Peasants' Bank. I have seen them myself, yellow and white, one of gold and two of silver. The gold one in the middle represents the workers, and under its base are the souls of the capitalists. The one on the east, made of silver, represents the peasants, and under its base are the souls of the landlords. The silver one on the west represents the soldiers, and under its base are the souls of the militarists. At night the three pagodas shoot out flames like Roman candles and from the tops of them come clattering great quantities of gold and silver. All this gold and silver comes from the capitalists, the landlords, and the militarists, from whom it has been recaptured by the peasants, workers, and soldiers. That is why the bank is closed at night. They are so busy that they hardly have time to get the gold and silver put away in chests.'

"I did not quite believe what the young apprentice said. But he stated that he had heard it from his sweetheart and that she had it from her brother who had once been an apprentice in the general store across the street but who was now working in the bank. Wasn't it a pity that I did not see the pagodas with my own eyes? Next time I pass through the city I will not miss going. . . ."

After making this speech, the Red Guard glanced up at the sun and then hurried on his way. The peasants stared at one another and did not know whom to believe—the Red Guardsman, the southerner, or some other person.

That was how the story of the gold and silver pagodas, with all sorts of curious and fantastic details, filtered through to every valley, to every farm, to every bamboo copse, and into every peasant's heart.

2

The late rice was already harvested and in the hundred or more peasant families making up the little mountain village, male and female, old and young, were swimming in the delirium of a great ocean of happiness. The poorer they had been before, the happier they now felt. This was joy of a sort that they had never even dreamed about before!

It used to be when the late grain was cut that if the harvest was a good one, they could look forward apprehensively to the visit of the landlord to get his share and any rent that was unpaid. After paying debts and redeeming pawned articles, they could hope, with the help of the idols, to have enough grain to last them until the end of the year. If the harvest were a bad one, they could stare distractedly at the landlords carrying off every grain of rice, and listen to the snapping of whips, the flutter of chickens, and the frightened cries of children.

Now there were no landlords. The peasants had driven them out. Now, when the late grain was harvested, they need only contribute three pints out of each picul for the soviet. There were loads of grain left. After setting aside enough to last them comfortably until the early crop of next year was in, they could go joyfully to sell the remainder, picul after picul. Those who had known only rags now wore newly made clothing, and their pockets were stuffed with the bank notes of the Workers' and Peasants' Bank.

Everywhere you saw new clothes and heard the talk about the gold and silver pagodas. People on the whole hillside and on the farms were talking and the more they talked, the more varied did the stories become until almost everyone had a different version to relate. Some said that the warehouses of the Workers' and Peasants' Bank were overflowing with the gold and silver eggs laid by the pagodas and that the bank was working night and day on the construction of three new buildings. Others said that cash or notes deposited in the bank needed only to be touched to the crest of one of the pagodas and they would also lay eggs—gold or silver, as desired. Everyone talked excitedly, claiming that his particular story was most authentic and that other people were badly mistaken, badly mistaken!

In spite of all the different versions of the story and its many aspects, there was one common core. This was the statement that in the Workers' and Peasants' Bank in the city there were three pagodas, one of gold and two of silver. All agreed on this point and there seemed, therefore, no reason whatever for doubting it. It was enough to keep speculation constantly alive.

Since the last elections and since the two representatives of the rich peasants had been expelled, the village soviet had begun to be a true people's government. All questions, great or small, were taken to the soviet for solution. With such a burning question as this, then, it was but natural that people should be coming daily to the chairman with inquiries.

At a meeting of the soviet the matter was discussed, and it was decided to send a man into the city on an investigation. Lu Kuang-hsing was the man selected. He was not yet twenty, and his father was away with the Red Army. He was overjoyed to be given his passport and to assume the responsibility of this commission, not only because he was the son of a Red soldier, nor because he was a member of the Communist Youth, but because he was a poor peasant who, for the first time in his life, had money in his pocket.

When his neighbors heard that Lu Kuang-hsing was going to the city on his mission, they went joyfully to find him and to hand over money which they wished deposited in the bank. The first to arrive was his aunt, who was about to have a baby. As soon as she came in, she called out, "Kuang-hsing, my good boy! Put these ten dollars in the bank for me. And be sure that you rub them yourself against the gold pagoda so as to make it lay a few golden eggs with which to buy clothes for your new cousin."

Kuang-hsing took the ten dollars and said earnestly, "I hope you won't regret this later, auntie. Things which lay eggs can also fly, you know. 'Don't lose your handful of rice trying to lure a chicken.' If the ten dollars fly away, I won't be responsible."

But the aunt was unmoved. "No, no!" she said firmly, "our luck is in. The Old Man in Heaven is helping the poor now."

That evening Kuang-hsing's grandmother kept after him to take a bath and to put on clean clothes. She said that the pagodas were sacred things and that seeing them was exactly like seeing the gods. One's heart must be sanctified. The young Communist had of course long since abandoned any belief in gods; ever since the land revolution had come into effect and the landlords had been overthrown, the gods also had faded from consciousness. But since he had some new clothes anyway, he changed into them in order to stop the chattering of the old lady.

For this his twelve-year-old sister, an active member of the Young Pioneers, quarreled with him. She railed at him for being superstitious and suggested that he call himself a "god-fearing shock-brigader." The brother was worsted in the argument, but he finally said, "Comrade sister, just wait till tomorrow and see!"

And with this he went to bed.

3

The next day Lu Kuang-hsing rose before dawn. Opening
the door he saw the sky full of stars and a great half-moon
still gleaming brightly over the brow of the western hills. It
was to be a fine day and he was very happy.

Moving noiselessly about, he got himself something to eat.
The little sister had not wakened nor had light come yet in
the east, when he carefully collected his pass and his bank
notes and started over hill and down dale to the city.

It was forty *li* there and back, but it was a familiar road
and he walked rapidly. After all, if a youth of nineteen
could not make speed, who could? Supper had not been
cooked and the sun was still twenty or thirty feet high when
he was back again in the Lu hamlet.

Straight to his home he walked, followed by a few of the
villagers. The aunt was there already, chuckling over some
story with his mother and grandmother. The sister was at a
meeting.

All were in a great hurry to hear the news. Kuang-hsing
was preparing to go the next day to the district soviet with a
report on his investigation so he planned to rehearse his
speech here at home. After wiping his perspiration with a
towel, he said smilingly, "Now you shall hear my 'report,'
but you must listen as though you were at a meeting!"

When they agreed, he took a stand beside his grandmother,
since she was growing a little deaf, and commenced his formal report:

"Acting under orders from the district soviet, I went into
the city to investigate the business of the gold and silver pagodas. On my arrival I went straight to the Workers' and
Peasants' Bank, at the doors of which a large crowd was already gathered. After pushing my way in, I found my eyes
suddenly blinded. Yes, there were gods, after all!

"So vast a heap of gold! Such huge piles of silver! They

were more than gold and silver pagodas. They were mountains of gold and silver. Even the golden *lohans* in the temples were never so broad or so bright!

"On this side of the counter the crowd stood seven or eight deep. Looking over their heads I could make out the upper parts of three large pagodas whose tips reached to the ceiling. I pushed through the crowd and raised myself on tiptoe. The pagodas were really as large at their base as four dining tables, for there were twelve tables placed there side by side, and on them were the three pagodas touching one another. In the middle was the gold one, and on the two sides the silver ones. And in front of the gold pagoda were two golden pillars as thick as a man's thigh which formed a golden arch on top of which a new red flag was flying. There were flashes from the hammer and sickle, done on the flag in gold.

"All of us were dazzled at the sight and there was a tumult of voices. Someone behind me shouted, 'They have even brought out the things from the palace!' 'Has the Red Army captured Nanking?' asked another.

"Suddenly there was a burst of clapping when a man jumped out from behind the gold pagoda."

The aunt could not contain herself. "Did the gods show themselves, Kuang-hsing?" she asked.

"It wasn't a god, auntie, nor was it the Pagoda Spirit. It was a man, not much older than myself, who wore old and ragged clothing. As a matter of fact, he was one of the new members of the provincial soviet who had once been a papermaker. Probably he is the one who makes the paper for the bank notes of the Workers' and Peasants' Bank.

"This man stood high up on a table and patted the gold pagoda. 'Comrades,' he shouted in a loud voice, 'do you know to whom this pagoda belongs?'

"We gave him a confusion of answers: 'The gods!' 'The

communists!' 'The emperor!' 'The Pagoda Spirit!' 'The foreigners!'

"The man beside the gold pagoda kept shaking his head and smiling. 'No, no!' he said, 'Comrades, you are all wrong. These gold and silver pagodas belong to no one but us, the workers and peasants!'

"We all set up a clamor. 'Bronze pagodas are all that we have! Only bronze pagodas!'

"But he went on. 'Bronze pagodas, yes! Each one is a bronze pagoda. And if you take thousands and tens of thousands of bronze pagodas and put them together, isn't that enough for a silver one? If you put hundreds of thousands, millions of bronze pagodas together, isn't that enough for a gold one?'

"We all stood silent as he continued. 'When we are divided, we workers and peasants are only bronze; but when we are united, we are gold and silver. All of this gold and silver belonged to us in the first place, but as long as we depended on Heaven and the gods, it was filched from us by the landlords and the capitalists and we were cheated and plundered. Now we know that it is on ourselves and on our union that we must depend. We have the soviet and the Red Army. So we have wrested back this gold and silver from the gentry, from the homes of the landlords, and from the homes of the counterrevolutionists. There is not a single piece that was not produced by the workers. Much of it came from the grain which the gentry took from the peasants and sold for silver coin and gold bars. . . .'

"Then the representative of the provincial soviet took in one hand a shining silver egg from the tip of one of the silver pagodas, and in the other a piece of gold the size of a sickle handle which came from the top of the gold pagoda. Springing on to the counter, he handed these to us to pass around and examine.

"Then for the first time, we realized everything—it was not a silver egg at all, but a large silver dollar. And when we looked again more closely at the silver pagodas, we found that they were built of thousands of silver dollars heaped one on top of another. The gold pagoda was made of a pile of gold axe handles which they said were called 'gold bars.' The three pagodas were not divinely made at all, but made by men, so we understood why they did not belong to the gods."

"But, Kuang-hsing, if you say that the pagodas do not belong to the gods, then how can they lay gold and silver eggs?" The speaker was one of the villagers, a man twice as old as Kuang-hsing, but a nephew by relation.

"Right! That is what we asked the delegate: 'How does it happen? How is it done?' He told us unhesitatingly. 'You still believe,' he said, 'that the gods are the greatest force in the world. And anything you have never seen before you attribute to the gods. But there are no gods. The greatest force in the world is the union of the workers and the peasants. It is we and not the gods who have overthrown the landlords. It is we and not the gods who have beaten the White Armies. And it is we ourselves and not the gods who have built these three pagodas. We hatch gold or silver eggs by our own efforts. We have no use for gods!'

"Then with a smile he told us how the eggs were laid, and, when we heard it, we all smiled too."

Hereupon, Lu Kuang-hsing of the shock brigade broke off suddenly. He looked about him with a smile and an air of great mystery.

"Tell us, Kuang-hsing, tell us," urged the others impatiently.

The old grandmother had only grasped about half of the story, but as soon as she had comprehended that the gold and silver pagodas actually existed she had taken to saying her Buddhist prayers with great gusto.

Kuang-hsing slowly and calmly drew from his pocket a few booklets and handed them out to his aunt and the villagers. "Be careful of them," he said laughing, "The silver eggs are inside them. That is the truth, auntie. You deposit ten dollars in the bank and the bank gives you this booklet. Next year on this day, if you go to the bank, you will receive one extra dollar. This dollar is called 'interest on savings,' but if you like you may call it a silver egg. . . ."

As they turned the booklets over and over in their hands the villagers began to smile in return.

Only one of them was empty-handed, because he had not produced any money on the previous day. He was leaning up against the door, squinting at what the others held in their hands. "One year?" he said sarcastically. "A year is a long time!"

"Chang Fa-ko," said Kuang-hsing quickly, "A year is a long time and you would be afraid to leave money in the bank, is that it?"

Chang Fa-ko lifted his nose. "I did not say that I would be afraid."

The aunt with the expansive middle had also an expansive temperament. Patting Kuang-hsing on the shoulder with her booklet, she said, "Never mind him! He advised me day before yesterday always to ask for coin instead of notes. But since the bank has these three pagodas, it's all right. Why should anyone be afraid of bank notes? This is a lucky time for the poor! What do you say, grandma?" And she began to talk with the old lady.

Chang Fa-ko lifted his nose once more, but did not open his mouth. After glaring at the group for a moment, he went slowly out of the door.

The nephew who was twice Kuang-hsing's age shook his head and laughed. "I know why he is so angry at Uncle Kuang-hsing. He used to own twenty *mow* of good fields, but that has been divided up now and he has only some very poor land. The fields which were given you belonged once to him. But the division was made by the soviet. We all have better fields than he. Well, why did he engage in money-lending and fleece us all? The gods have eyes. That's a fact. The day of reckoning comes!"

"I used to suffer because of him," said another peasant, "but now—hm—let him. . . ."

Kuang-hsing walked angrily to the door and gazed after the retreating form of Chang Fa-ko. "The kulak!" he said. Then he turned about and said, leaning up against the door, "The reason why we have been given good fields is that my father is in the Red Army. It is not the gods who have eyes, but we ourselves. Tomorrow I shall propose in the district soviet that every man go to the city to see the gold and silver pagodas. Since I have seen them, I realize even more clearly the strength that lies in our union. As a matter of fact, it isn't necessary to leave your money in the bank for a whole year. You can draw it out at any time. But I have no use for money. I shall leave mine there always. Is my cloth pocket safer than the vaults in the bank? The fate of the bank is in our own hands. If we all support it, it can never die. It is our bank, and the gold and silver pagodas are ours, too."

Lu Kuang-hsing spoke with animation, and the aunt and all the villagers began to smile.

The next day, before Kuang-hsing had made any report to the soviet, the news had spread through the whole village. Nevertheless, he offered his report with the suggestion that everyone should make a trip to the city to see the pagodas of gold and silver. And they went in great numbers, not because they disbelieved Kuang-hsing's story, but because it pleased them, it was like a festival, to see their own gold and silver pagodas.

MAO TUN

Spring Silkworms

1

Old T'ung-pao squatted on a stone beside the path which followed the course of the creek. His long pipe lay next to him. It was after tomb-visiting day in mid-spring, and a warm sun was already making its presence felt. It burned against his back like fire. On the towpath a Shaohsing native, his thin blue shirt wide open, was pulling his small craft up against the stream. Beads of sweat as large as soybeans fell from his face to the earth as he strained at the rope. Watching him work so hard, Old T'ung-pao felt himself growing unbearably hot, almost itchy. He was wearing a torn, wadded garment which he had worn all winter long. His only light tunic was still in pawn, for he'd hardly expected it to be so warm so soon after tomb-visiting day.

Even the weather isn't the same anymore, he thought. He spat angrily at the ground. Down there before him the surface of the creek was a shiny green. An occasional boat made little ripples on it, causing the reflected shadows of the earthen bank and the mulberry trees which lined it to blur into an indistinct dark gray mass. But soon the shadows of the trees would take shape again, wavering like drunken men, and in a moment the surface was again smoothly serene, the shadows restored.

The mulberry trees, shaped like human fists, were crowned with finger-like sprouting green leaves. The trees lined the bank of the creek and stood in even rows back into the fields for as far as he could see. Immediately behind him there were many of these short, stumpy trees. The fields were still dried and cracked, but on these trees, basking under the sun's warmth, the little emerald-colored leaves seemed to be growing under his very eyes.

Not far from where Old T'ung-pao sat by the side of the road stood a grayish whitewashed building. It was a cocoon processing shop, but only ten days or so ago it had housed soldiers. The fields around were still pocked with short trenches. Rumors had come flying that the Japanese were about to march on the town, and at this all people of means had fled. But now even the soldiers were gone, and here stood the empty building, waiting for the renewed activity when spring silkworms were brought in.

From the Young Mr. Chen, son of the Second Mr. Chen, Old T'ung-pao heard that there had been trouble at Shanghai this year, that many filatures had ceased working. He had heard too that the cocoon shops here would surely remain closed. But this he couldn't believe. After all, he was a man past his sixtieth birthday and he had lived through many crises and disorders, but never in his life had he ever seen fine green leaves like these left idle on their trees, waiting to be used as dried feed for sheep. Such could come to pass only if the silkworms failed to hatch. This would be the business of Heaven, in any case, for without divine prescience how could any human know such a thing?

"So soon after tomb-visiting day," he thought, "and it has grown so warm." A little amazed, a little stirred with joy, he stared at the budding green leaves. He thought back to a year in his youth, when he was about twenty. Then too it had been warm at this time, and he had changed to his light tunic. That year he had profited greatly from his silkworm crop and on the strength of it had been able to marry. From that time they had been established. His father was a man who could work mightily. His grandfather, whose long struggles had really given the family its start, was already then an old man. He was still vigorous although he had been a captive of the Long Hairs. The Elderly Mr. Chen had just died and his son had not yet become a smoker of opium. The Chen family gave no hint then of becoming the ruin it was today.

Old T'ung-pao had always believed that his family and the Chens were linked to the same fate, although one was a humble peasant family and the other was of great wealth. During the Long Hair uprising, Old T'ung-pao's grandfather and the Elderly Mr. Chen had been taken captive and had spent nearly seven years together. They had made good their escape at the same time, carrying away gold they had stolen from their captors, from the rebels. People still told this story. As Mr. Chen prospered in his silk business, Old T'ung-pao's family made steady progress in raising silkworms. Within ten years they had become the owners of twenty *mow* of rice fields and more than ten *mow* given over to mulberry trees. They had their own house, with three rooms and two doors. His family became the envy of the whole village, just as the Chen family became the number one or number two family in the town. They boasted its only big-door house.

But in the years that followed, both took a turn for the worse. Old T'ung-pao had lost every *mow* of land he had and had accumulated a debt of three hundred dollars. The Chen family had long since gone to ruin. It was whispered that the ghosts of the Long Hairs had complained in the Underworld. Yen Wang, king of that realm, had ruled that they should lose the wealth that they had stolen from the Long Hairs. So the family had gone rapidly downhill and lost all. Old T'ung-pao believed this tale to be true, in some ways, for if it were not the work of demons, what else could have turned so perfect a man as the Second Mr. Chen into an opium smoker?

There was one thing, however, which Old T'ung-pao could not understand. Why should the ruin of the Chen family lead to the ruin of his? He was quite sure his family had not shared in the Long Hairs' gold. It was true, according to his departed father, that while escaping from the Long Hairs his grandfather met one of them on the road and, seeing no other way of escape, had killed him. Perhaps there he had met an eternal enemy. But ever since he'd been old enough to remember, his family had always offered repentance, chanted the sutras, and burned incense for the spirit of that Long Hair. That little ghost should have long since been reincarnated. He didn't remember his grandfather very well, but he knew his father to have been an industrious, economical, and faithful man. This he had seen with his own eyes. He, himself, too, was a good man and had been all his life. Both his son Ah Szu and his daughter-in-law were hardworking and virtuous. Only his younger son, Ah-to, was still foolish, but he was still young and knew nothing of the world. No one could say he would bring bad fortune to the family.

Old T'ung-pao raised his wrinkled brown face. There was pain in its lines as he looked over the creek and across at the rows of mulberry trees. Everything looked exactly as it had twenty years back. But the world had indeed changed. His family ate squash now instead of rice, for the most part, and then there was the three hundred dollars he owed.

A series of shrill, abrupt blasts from a siren broke into his thoughts. They came from beyond a distant bend in the creek where stood another cocoon shop and a well-cut stone dam barely visible from where he sat. A small launch appeared from behind the building, towing three junks behind. It was traveling toward him. The surface of the creek churned and rippled as it passed. The water lapped angrily in waves up the banks on either side. A man in a small open boat in the launch's path barely got to the bank and seized some overhanging reeds in time. Man and boat bobbed up and down in the wake as if in a swing. The puff of the engine and the smell of its smoke spread across the fresh green fields. Old T'ung-pao followed the passage of that motor boat with angry, vindictive eyes. He watched it until it came to the far bend, whistled again, and turned out of sight.

Old T'ung-pao was known as a hater of all things foreign, like steam launches. He'd never seen a foreigner. His father had told him that the Elderly Mr. Chen had seen some once. Their eyebrows were red and their eyes green. They walked straight and never bent their legs. And the Elderly Mr. Chen also hated foreigners. "The foreign devils have cheated us of our last copper," he used to say. Old T'ung-pao was only eight or nine when he saw the Elderly Mr. Chen, and he remembered also what he had heard from his father. Even now he could easily picture him, tugging at his beard and shaking his head as he said: "The foreign devils have cheated us of our last copper."

He didn't know just how the foreign devils had cheated them, but he was certain the Elderly Mr. Chen was right. He could see clearly for himself that strange yarns and cloth and oil had come to the town and steam launches began appearing on the creek, everything produced in the fields was worth less, and everything in the town rose higher and higher in price from day to day and year to year. The little inheritance he had had turned from little to less and finally to nothing in his hands. In the end he had had to borrow money to live. He had good reason to hate the foreign devils. The strength and constancy of his hatred were known throughout the village.

Five years back somebody had told him that the dynasty had been changed for a new one. The new dynasty, they said, wanted to do away with the foreign devils. But he believed none of it. In the town he had seen that many of the young people who used to shout "Down with the foreign devils!" were dressed in the same clothes the foreign devils were supposed to wear. He was sure these youths were in league with the foreigners to cheat the village peasants.

As time passed nobody shouted "Down with the foreign devils!" any more, and his beliefs came true, for everything grew more and more expensive in town and still heavier taxes and other burdens weighed down on the villagers. He was deeply convinced that the foreign devils were back of all this.

But one thing troubled him now more than almost anything else. Last year only cocoons from "new" eggs brought a decent price.* They were ten dollars or so higher per picul. Old T'ung-pao had always lived at peace with his son and daughter-in-law but on this one thing had disputed with them. As early as the year before his daughter-in-law, Mrs. Ah Szu, had broached the idea of breeding worms from the foreign eggs. His younger son, Ah-to, sided with her. Ah Szu, his elder son, of course said no word but in his heart of hearts he also wanted to use the foreign eggs. He was unable to oppose all three of them, and in the end he surrendered.

---

*The "new" egg was an improved product, a result of scientific research. Farmers in the village called it the "foreign" egg.

Now of their three patches of silkworm eggs, two were native and one foreign.

"Things are going from bad to worse. Someday they'll be planting foreign mulberry trees only. Oh, I'm tired, too tired of the world!" said Old T'ung-pao to himself. He picked up his pipe and tapped it angrily against a piece of dried mud next to his foot. The sun shone straight down upon him casting a short, stubby black shadow like a chunk of charred wood. He felt the heat rising within him, for he was still wearing his torn, padded suit. He opened the buttons and fanned himself a while. Finally he stood up and went on his way home.

Back of the mulberry trees was a rice field, now filled only with clumps of mud, dry and half-turned over, set in orderly rows. One or two small patches were planted with other crops, their blossoms fragrant under the sun. Off in the distance stood the cluster of sheds where Old T'ung-pao and his family had lived for three generations. Smoke was now curling up over the roofs. Old T'ung-pao emerged from the rows of mulberry trees and came out onto the rice fields, walking in one of the furrows. He turned again to look at the trees.

"Grandpa! Mama's waiting for you for lunch!" shouted a young lad of over ten who came racing across the next field.

"Hm . . ." said Old T'ung-pao, recognizing his grandson's voice. But his eyes remained fixed on the trees. It was now only just past mid-spring but the leaves were coming out finger-like on the tops of the trees. This he had seen only twice in his life. This year promised to be a good year for silkworms. He thought of their three patches of eggs. How much cocoon would they produce? Perhaps the family could free itself from at least part of its debt if only this year proved better than last!

By now Hsiao Pao reached his grandfather. The boy too

stared at the velvety cover on top of the trees. He gave a shriek of joy and jumped up and down clapping his hands. He began to sing:

"Mid-Spring came but the other day,
  Leaving fingerlike buds on the tree;
  Our silkworm maids are happy and gay,
  And from heart-deep worries are free!"

Old T'ung-pao's wrinkles creased into a smile. The song was a good omen. He put his hand on Hsiao Pao's head and gently rubbed its shaven surface. There was fresh hope in his heavy heart, so hardened by poverty.

2

The weather continued soft and warm. Budding young leaves, nursed by the sun, grew from finger size to the dimensions of a whole hand on the fistlike mulberry trees. All the mulberry orchards around the village were doing well and from a distance looked like a piece of green damask spread flat over short rows of grayish-white bamboo supports. Hope grew surer and bolder in T'ung-pao's heart, as in many others. The mustering of hands for work became the order of the day everywhere in the village. The trays and platters used in raising silkworms were brought out of the old sheds which had hidden them the whole year. They were cleaned and mended. Next to the little stream which cut the village in two, women and boys gathered, moving about, working, humming, giggling, and shrieking with jokes and laughter. They looked thin and meager, these women, boys, and girls. For this year they had lived on little. They were half-fed, half-starved. They were dressed in ragged old clothes. They were hardly better off than beggars. But their spirits were high. They were patient and tolerant and secure in their illusions. Despite their heavy debts, debts growing heavier every passing day, they believed quite simply that if only all went well with the silkworms all else would be well too. They looked ahead a month or so, and in their minds' eyes all this glittering green about them changed into cocoons as white as snow and then changed again into something that clinked, round silver coins. Their stomachs were audibly empty, but they smiled at the bright prospect ahead of them.

Among them were two members of Old T'ung-pao's family, his daughter-in-law and her son, Hsiao Pao. They had just finished cleaning the broad, round, flat bamboo baskets in which the silkworms were to be fed and the bamboo racks upon which they were to be kept. They sat on a stone by the water, wringing out their soaking clothes and wiping the perspiration from their faces.

"Mrs. Ah Szu, are you going to breed foreign eggs?" came a voice from across the narrow streams. Mrs. Ah Szu knew its owner, a girl of twenty, Lu Pao, sister of Lu Fu-ch'ing, who lived just opposite them. Mrs. Ah Szu frowned, as if looking for an argument.

"Don't talk to me about that. Hsiao Pao's daddy's father is dead against it. That crazy old fellow hates everything that even has the word foreign in it as though it were an enemy of seven generations. But you see 'foreign coin' also has that word in it yet he'll accept that without question!"*

The women on the other bank cackled with laughter. Just then a tall and lusty youth came by Lu's paddy and nimbly hopped over the four logs which, flat in the water, formed a makeshift bridge. When she saw him, Mrs. Ah Szu stopped thinking about foreign eggs.

"Brother To-to!" she called to him, "Come and help me

---

*Silver dollars, originally imported into China from abroad, were called *yang chien*, "foreign money."

carry these things home. These baskets are soaking wet and they're as heavy as dead dogs!"

Ah-to reached her side and without a word lifted up six of the dripping baskets and swung them up onto his head where they balanced, the water trickling down about him. He went off, his arms swinging like paddles beside him. Young Ah-to worked for the joy of it. He helped willingly when women in the village asked him to carry heavy things or to scramble into the water for something that had fallen in. But today he must have seemed a little less willing for he carried only six of the large disklike bamboo baskets on his head and nothing in his hands. He took mincing steps up the path, mimicking the walk of town women, turning his waist a little to keep the clumsy load balanced on his head. All the women laughed. Ho-hua, wife of Li Ken-sheng, Old T'ung-pao's neighbor, turned shouting to him:

"Hey there, To-to! Come back and help me carry some too!"

"Call me one sweet name and I'll come running!" he laughed back, continuing on his way until he reached the front of his own house, where he put the baskets down under the eaves.

"I'll call you my foster son!" shouted Ho-hua, bursting into laughter. She had an unusually flat white face, a broad mouth, and eyes so narrow that they looked like two threads. She was a slave girl from a family in town. It was only half a year back that she'd been given to Li, a middle-aged man of solemn mien who used to maintain a funereal silence all the day long. Ho-hua was already notorious in the village for her coquetry.

"Shame on you!" cried somebody in the group of women on the opposite bank. Ho-hua's narrow pig-like eyes opened wide and glinted with anger.

"Meaning whom? Come out if you dare! Don't try to hide!"

"Humph. Kick a coffin and the dead man will feel it. If I mean anybody at all I mean a certain brazen, shameless flirt." The speaker was Lu Pao, who also enjoyed a reputation for boldness in the village. They started splashing water across at each other and in a moment it was a general melée. Trouble-loving women took one side or the other and joined in the fight. The younger ones came in shrieking with glee and laughter while the women continued calling each other names and shouting curses through the spray.

Mrs. Ah Szu was a staid woman. She picked up her remaining racks and, calling to Hsiao Pao not to join in, went on up toward home. Ah-to still stood there under the shadow of the roof watching the scene with smiling eyes. He knew perfectly well why Lu Pao had been trying to pick a quarrel with Ho-hua. He derived a certain pleasure from seeing the sharp-tongued Lu Pao meeting defeat in the squabble. Old T'ung-pao came out of the house, tottering under the weight of a large silkworm rack on which they would soon rest the broad, flat baskets. Ants had gotten at some of its vertical supports and it didn't seem safe to use before it was repaired. The old man saw Ah-to standing looking at the women down at the water. His face assumed stern lines. His son was flighty to be sure. It displeased him most of all when Ah-to indulged in small talk with the wicked Ho-hua. "That bitch is under the White Tiger star. Anyone who meddles with her will surely bring his family to ruin," he often warned his son.

"Are you enjoying yourself here doing nothing?" he growled. "Ah Szu is working the stalks into mounds for the cocoons. Go help him." Old T'ung-pao roared angrily. His bloodshot eyes darted with annoyance as they followed Ah-to into the house. Only then did he turn back to the rack he had brought out and examined it closely. When he had looked it over, he slowly set to work repairing the rotted parts. He had been something of a carpenter in his youth. But he was old now, with no strength left in his fingers. In a few minutes he had to stop and rest. His rising glance stopped at the three pieces of cloth heavy with silkworm eggs hanging on a bamboo pole. Mrs. Ah Szu was out there under the eaves pasting up the trays with paper. Last year they'd been covered with old newspapers to save coppers. Old T'ung-pao believed that was why the silkworm harvest had been bad. So this year the whole family had given up the cost of a whole meal to buy some real pasting paper. Mrs. Ah Szu was carefully and smoothly laying on the sturdy yellow tissue. On top of it she pasted three little sheets covered with a design. Placed symmetrically in the form of a triangle, the upper one bore the image of a vessel in which the treasure they hoped to receive would be duly deposited. The lower two bore a likeness of the "Prince of Silkworms," a mighty man on a horse bearing aloft a pennant.

"Mrs. Ah-Szu," said Old T'ung-pao suddenly, "that thirty dollars we borrowed through your father is enough for only twenty piculs of mulberry leaf. And day after tomorrow we won't have any rice left. What shall we do then?" Old T'ung-pao looked at his daughter-in-law, again short of breath. That thirty-dollar loan had been made at two and a half percent interest monthly. And it was only because the broker was her father, Chang Ts'ai-fa, and because the moneylender, who was Chang's employer, regarded the loan as an act of charity, that he had asked for such low interest. It was to be repaid immediately after the sale of the cocoons, principal and interest together. Mrs. Ah Szu placed the newly covered trays out in the sun to dry. She looked over at her father-in-law.

"Are you going to spend it all on mulberry leaves?" she

asked in sudden anger. "You'll buy too many, like you did last year—"

"Hold your tongue," he broke in, "Your talk will bring us bad luck. Is every year like last year? All we have is about ten piculs of leaf and we have three patches of eggs. How can it be enough?"

"Oh, you're always right. Only all I know is that if there is rice, we'll eat. If there is no rice, we starve," retorted Mrs. Ah Szu. She'd never agreed with him since their argument over using foreign eggs. Old T'ung-pao went blue with anger, but neither said another word.

With the approach of the harvesting time for silkworms, the tension grew. The atmosphere became more sharply charged throughout this tiny village and its twenty-odd inhabitants. Determination, boldness, hope, tempered by fear and suspense. Hunger seemed to be forgotten. Days went by quickly. In Old T'ung-pao's family they lived on whatever scraps they could find, on pumpkins and potatoes. Nor was his family alone in this, for who in the whole village could afford to store two or three piculs of rice? There had been a fine harvest last year but it was hardly off the ground before the landowners, the creditors, and the tax collectors came and their harvest dwindled to nothing. Their only hope now was in the spring silkworm harvest. Every short-term loan they'd contracted in the interim had to be paid back at that time. Everyone was alive with hope and fear, facing the coming battle for the cocoons.

With the approach of Ku Yü, the day of the Great Rain, little specks of stirring green appeared in the black of the eggs on their pieces of cloth. Women talked to each other with joy and anxiety as they compared notes.

"The eggs will soon be hatched at Lu Pao's house."

"Ho-hua said hers will be out tomorrow. How fast!"

"Taoist Huang went to the fortune teller. He heard that leaf would go up to four dollars a picul."

Mrs. Ah Szu studied their egg patches closely. Nothing yet. The hundreds of black dots remained unbroken in color. Not a trace or speck of green among them. Ah Szu impatiently took them out into the light. But neither could he find any sign of moving green. His wife fretted with worry.

"You'd better start trying to hatch them."* He tried to speak reassuringly. "These eggs come from Yu-hang, you know. Maybe it takes them longer." His confident tone made no impression upon her. She made no reply. Old T'ung-pao's dry wrinkled face was long and sad. He said nothing although his heart was heavy with foreboding.

Next morning Mrs. Ah Szu looked anxiously at her piece of cloth and found dots of bright green shining against the black! She ran with them to her husband. She shouted to Old T'ung-pao, to Ah-to, to her son, Hsiao Pao. She tucked the three pieces of cloth to her breast and sat there motionless, hugging them like a mother her suckling babe. At night she kept the pieces of cloth with her, warm under her cover. She made Ah Szu go over and sleep with Ah-to. On each patch the tiny things moved and made her flesh creep when they touched her. But Mrs. Ah Szu was mad with joy and trepidation. She felt as she did when her child was within her, half-anxious, half-relieved when the little being inside her first moved and she felt him. The whole family was uneasy and excited, waiting for the critical days to come. Ah-to was alone unruffled. "Sure, the harvest will be fine," he said. "But getting rich is out of the question. The fates are still a long way off!" Old T'ung-pao raged at him to keep still, but he paid no attention.

*The eggs were often hatched by the women, who would keep the patches of cloth warm between their breasts.

Everything was already in order in the silkworm shed. The day after the eggs began hatching Old T'ung-pao took a large bulb of garlic plastered in mud and set it down on the ground against one wall of the shed. He did this every year, but this time he was especially careful. His hands trembled. The bulb he had set down last year had enabled him to gauge the harvest quite closely. He hardly dared hope for another true forecast this year.

By now every family in the village was wholly absorbed. The paddies and the banks of the streamlet, so often alive with the chatter and laughter of the women, were deserted. By tacit and mutual consent everyone observed the rule of mutual avoidance. There was no visiting, even among close friends, for it was no joke if a guest should frighten off the silkworm god. Most people exchanged only a few whispered words on the threshing ground and then separated. This was a sacred period. In the house of Old T'ung-pao bits of life were already crawling on the three patches of cloth. Tension filled the house. It was but one day before the Ku Yü. Mrs. Ah Szu carefully placed the cloths in the shed instead of under the quilt, for they no longer needed warmth. But when Old T'ung-pao stole a look at his bulb of garlic against the wall, his heart jumped with fear, for only two short sprouts had appeared. He didn't have the courage to look again. He prayed that by the day after next, its leaves would be greener and more plentiful. At last came the day for putting the tiny worms on the trays to be fed.

Mrs. Ah Szu set about cooking rice. She kept looking at the pan uneasily to see if any steam was rising straight into the air. Old T'ung-pao produced the candles and incense he had bought many days before and lit them before the kitchen god in the most pious fashion he knew. Ah Szu and Ah-to had gone out for wildflowers. When they returned Hsiao

Pao helped them cut the *teng-hsin-tsao** into small pieces and crush the flowers. All was ready. The sun was almost directly overhead. The steam rose perfectly straight up from the pan. Mrs. Ah Szu jumped up joyfully, took a paper flower, especially bought for this, and a pair of goose feathers and pinned them to her hair and stepped into the shed. Old T'ung-pao followed carrying a scale and Ah Szu came after him with the torn flowers and the shorn grass. Mrs. Ah Szu uncovered the three cloth patches. She took the flowers and the grass from the hands of her husband and the scale from Old T'ung-pao. She spread the flowers and the grass over the cloths crawling with worms and pulled them over the rod of the scale. Holding them over the trays, she took the goose feathers from her own hair and swept lightly across the cloth. One piece first and then the second, she swept all the tiny silkworms along with the bits of grass and flowers onto the bamboo trays covered with the yellow tissue. The third cloth bore the worms hatched from foreign eggs. These were placed in another tray. At the end Mrs. Ah Szu took the paper flower she had pinned to her hair and tacked it side by side with the goose feathers on the edge of the tray.

The ceremony bore the solemnity of thousands of years of practice. It was like burning incense for soldiers about to leave for battle. It heralded the opening of one month's desperate, restless, sleepless struggle against bad weather, against the demons of ill omen, and against the unknown. The worms—the village called them the Misses Black—crept about sturdily and steadily on the trays. Old T'ung-pao and Mrs. Ah Szu sighed deeply with relief. But when Old T'ung-pao took another stealthy look at his bulb, he paled. Only three or four meager little shoots had grown. Oh Heaven! Like last year again!

*A kind of heavy grass used by peasants as lamp wicks.

3

But the bulb of the Fates did not tell the truth this time, for the silkworms showed great promise. Although it rained throughout the first and second sleep of the worms and although it was now somewhat cooler than it had been after tomb-visiting day, the precious worms were as steady and as sturdy as before. With everyone else in the village things had gone almost as well. An air of excited jubilation pervaded the village. Even the water in the brook seemed to bubble with laughter. For one person in the village, however, everything was ruined. It was Ho-hua. She'd had but one patch of cloth and something had gone wrong with her worms in their third sleep. Many had died. All that were left barely weighed twenty catties. When they entered upon their fourth and final sleep, her middle-aged silent husband was seen one night to hurl three trays of worms angrily into the stream. After that all women in the village observed strict avoidance and no one would pass her door. When they saw her or her husband approaching in the distance, they fled and avoided coming close to them. The fear was in their hearts that to talk or even look at either of the two would bring down upon them a share of their evil luck.

Old T'ung-pao tried to keep Ah-to from seeing or talking to Ho-hua. "If you talk with her again I'll denounce you as a disobedient son!" he threatened one day in the yard, purposely raising his voice in hopes she'd hear him. Hsiao Pao was strictly enjoined not to walk by their door or talk to the Ho family, but Ah-to ignored his father and thought the whole thing ridiculous. He was the only one in Old T'ung-pao's house who believed neither in the fates nor in demons. But as things turned out, he never did speak to Ho-hua. He was too busy.

During the fourth sleep of the worms, the whole family passed two days and two nights without sleep. Even Hsiao

Pao remained awake while the family worked at the worms. After the fourth sleep the silkworms weighed nearly 300 catties. Old T'ung-pao was a man of sixty summers and winters but only twice before had he ever seen silkworms like these, once in the year he married and again the year Ah Szu was born. The day after the fourth sleep the worms consumed seven piculs of leaf. They were all lively, green, smooth, and strong. But even as they waxed well, the members of the family grew thinner and paler, their tired eyes bloodshot. It was clear that the worms would need more feed before they would climb the mounds to begin spinning. Old T'ung-pao talked things over with his son.

"It's impossible for us to borrow from Mr. Chen," he said to Ah Szu, "Let's ask Chang Ts'ai-fa's employer once more."

"We have ten piculs of leaf here. That's a day's food," replied Ah Szu without interest. He was tired unto death and felt as if his eyelids weighed tens of piculs. Old T'ung-pao stormed impatiently at him:

"Don't talk nonsense! Don't you know it's only two days past the fourth sleep? They should have food for even three days more, not counting tomorrow. We should buy another thirty piculs of leaf, yes, a full thirty piculs."

Out in the yard there was a stir when Ah-to came in with five piculs of newly-gathered leaf. This put a stop to their talk and both went out to pluck off the stems. Mrs. Ah Szu hurriedly dropped what she was doing and came over out of the silkworm shed. Lu Pao, the girl from across the creek, came over to help, for there were but few silkworms in her home. It was evening, stars glistened in the sky and a soft breeze was blowing, bringing with it snatches of gossip and laughter from neighboring sheds. One hoarse voice they heard clearly.

"Leaf prices are going up. The market price in town this afternoon was four dollars a picul!"

Old T'ung-pao stirred at this. Thirty piculs would cost one hundred twenty dollars. Where could he get that much money? He began to calculate. They would have at least 500 catties of cocoons. If they could get fifty dollars for 100 catties their lot would bring in two hundred and fifty dollars. These figures relieved him somewhat. From the group plucking the leaves came a soft voice:

"People say the East Market is very quiet. I don't see how the leaf price can go up any higher." It was Lu Pao. Old T'ung-pao looked at her gratefully. The girl stood before a basket of leaves close to Ah-to. They were close, indeed, in the half-darkness of starlight. Under the mulberry branches she felt a hand on her thigh. It squeezed her gently. She stirred slightly, smiled in the shadows and kept silent. The hand crept up to her breast. She jumped away.

"Ai-ya," she cried out.

"What's the matter?" asked Mrs. Ah Szu who was plucking leaves nearby. Lu Pao blushed and glanced quickly at Ah-to. She resumed picking the leaves.

"Nothing," she said, her head down. "A caterpillar, I think."

Ah-to bit his lip hard to keep from laughing. He was thin and exhausted from lack of sleep but still gay and flippant about everything. He shared none of Old T'ung-pao's worries. He at no time believed that a good harvest or even two in silkworms or in grain would get them out of debt or help them recover their lost land. He fully understood that thrift and hard work alone would not tide them over these hard times even if they broke their backs over it. But he worked on with zest, for work was a joy and a game to him, like playing at love with Lu Pao.

Next morning Old T'ung-pao went to town to negotiate a loan for the purchase of the needed leaves. Before going he talked about it to Mrs. Ah Szu and told her that their last bit of land, which could produce only fifteen piculs of leaf, would have to be mortgaged. The thirty piculs were duly bought. When the first baskets arrived, the sturdy little worms—"our darlings," they called them—had already been half an hour without food. Their tiny peaked mouths rose open and swung from side to side. Mrs. Ah Szu sat staring helplessly at them. They scooped the leaves from the baskets and spread them on top of the worms and the shed was presently filled with the swish and the rustle of the worms at their food. Even the voices of the people were drowned out. Everybody worked at fever pace at the racks. Soon the wide trays were white again and another layer of leaves was spread upon them. Just this job of feeding kept everyone busy enough now. In two days the worms would start their "mountain climbing."* Everyone summoned his final energies for the last siege. The end was in sight.

Ah-to was not very tired although he hadn't slept now for three days and three nights. It was his turn this night to keep the vigil in the first half of the night. Old T'ung-pao, Ah Szu, and his wife were to be given a chance to rest. The moon was up and the evening was cool. Ah-to built himself a fire in the shed and kept his watch through the hours after midnight. He had spread leaves on the baskets a second time and was sitting on his haunches by the fire listening to the worms nibbling away. Under the warmth of the blaze his eyelids drooped. He thought he heard a scraping at the door and his eyes opened, but all was silence and they closed again. The sound of the nibbling and scraping grew distant. His head dropped between his shoulder and when his nose struck his knees, he jumped startled awake. He heard a sound behind the reed curtain back of him. He was on his feet in an instant, and he saw what he thought was a hu-

---

*A village term for the spinning of the cocoons on the frames.

man shadow flutter past toward the door. He jumped up and found the door wide open, and through it he saw the shadow racing off. He darted after it, running toward the back of the creek. He rapidly drew up on the shadow, thrust his hand out and, without seeing who it was, grabbed the person and threw him down.

"To-to, To-to, even if you beat me to death I don't blame you, only don't tell on me." It was Ho-hua. Ah-to stepped back speechless with astonishment. He bent down and looked into the narrow piglike eyes close together in that pale, flat face. He saw no fear in them.

"What have you stolen from us?" he asked finally.

"I took some of your worms."

"What have you done with them?"

"I threw them into the water."

Ah-to's expression changed. He saw that she had wanted to spoil their worms.

"You're an evil woman," he said. "We've done you no harm, yet you seek to harm us."

"Oh no? You did, you did. Our silkworms went all wrong although we spoiled nobody's. You're getting on pretty well with yours. Why then do you all treat me like a White Tiger? You all turn your faces away when I come near. You treat me as though I weren't human!"

The woman got up on her feet. Her face was ugly with hate and anger. Ah-to looked at her silently.

"I won't beat you. Get out of here."

He walked toward the shed without looking back. He didn't feel sleepy any more. He made sure no harm had been done to the worms and once more resumed his place by the fire. He saw nothing to hate or pity in Ho-hua, but he couldn't forget what she'd said. He felt something insoluble in the relation of human beings to other human beings, but he didn't know exactly what it was or why. Soon his thoughts drifted from him. All was well. The "darlings" were healthy and eating on insatiably, as if bewitched. The hours passed until dawn. Nothing more happened. Old T'ung-pao and Mrs. Ah Szu came out to relieve him.

They fingered among the worms and picked out some whose bodies had turned white and short and took them to the light to see if that faint line had yet appeared on their backs. Their hearts swelled with joy. But when the sun rose over the hill and Mrs. Ah Szu went down to the stream for water, she saw Lu Pao come running up with a solemn face. She had serious news and was bursting with it.

"Last night I saw the flirt come out of your shed and Ah-to coming after her," she said. "The two of them talked for a long time out there. Aren't you interested in this, Mrs. Ah Szu?" The latter made no reply although her face changed color. She filled her bucket in silence and returned home. She repeated what she'd heard, first to her husband, then to Old T'ung-pao.

"Damn that bitch! She tried to sneak into our shed!" Old T'ung-pao stamped his feet in anger and shouted for Ah-to to come at once and tell what happened. Ah-to just waved his hand. Lu Pao must have been dreaming. She was talking nonsense. The old man went to Lu Pao himself, and she maintained stoutly she'd seen it with her own eyes. Deeply troubled, Old T'ung-pao went back to his shed to look over the worms. They were not a whit less fine or sturdy. But their morning's joy was spoiled. They believed there was truth in what Lu Pao said. They only hoped now that Ho-hua hadn't gotten farther than the door and had talked to Ah-to from the outside.

"And still there are only three or four sprouts on the bulb," said Old T'ung-pao to himself. Things looked dark. Much leaf had been expended on the worms, and they looked richly promising. There was still a chance they might stiffen and die on the mounds. Such a thing was not at all uncommon. But Old T'ung-pao dared not think of it again, for the mere thought itself might bring bad luck.

4

The worms had begun climbing up the straw mounds. Old T'ung-pao and all his family waited in fear and suspense. All their resources had been spent, all their nerves and all their strength. It was impossible to say yet whether their labor and their strength would be repaid. Yet nobody thought of quitting work. Fires were built under the frames. Old T'ung-pao and Ah Szu crouched here and there under them with bent backs. So long as they continued to hear low, swishing sounds, they smiled with pleasure and nodded to each other. If a whole moment passed in silence, they looked at each other in fear and consternation. All hearts worried. For long they dared not even peek at the frames. Sometimes as they tended the fires a drop of urine would fall on them from the frame. Unpleasant as it was, there was cause for joy in this.* They hoped for more.

Three days after the worms started climbing the frames, the fires were put out. Often Ah-to peeped behind the reed curtain to see what was happening. Once Hsiao Pao caught him at it. He grasped his arm and asked if the "darlings" were really weaving their cocoons. Ah-to made a face at him, stuck out his tongue, and said nothing. Mrs. Ah Szu too grew impatient. She looked inside the reed curtain finally one day, and her heart pumped furiously within her, for inside was a sheet of white like fine snow, fully covering the frames. It was the first time she'd ever seen them so splendid as this. Soon the whole family was there looking, and their

*Silkworms discharge urine only when they are fully ripe and ready to "climb the mountain."

faces were beaming. Strained muscles and nerves relaxed, and their hearts were at peace for the first time in a month. The worms had been grateful for their care. Surely they were worth the leaves they'd bought at four dollars a picul. They had not starved and kept their weary vigils for a month in vain. Heaven had eyes!

The same joy came to all the village. The silkworm god had indeed been kind to them! They had managed, these twenty or thirty households, to secure nearly eighty percent cocoons from their silkworms. Old T'ung-pao's family did especially well. The yards and the banks of the creek were filled again with noisy women and boys and girls. All of them looked worn, a good deal thinner than they had been a month back. Their voices were hoarse and rough. But still they were gay and fresh. They talked noisily about their four weeks of tense struggle, and all enjoyed visions of the fruits of their labor. They visualized an endless stream of white silver coins pouring down upon them. Many a heart stirred with the thought of the lined coats and summer clothes pawned away which could now be retrieved. And on the day of the summer festival they could again perhaps taste yellow fish.

The story of Ho-hua and Ah-to was now but gossip. Lu Pao told everybody that Ho-hua was a flirt and offered herself freely to men. But her men listeners laughed coarsely. The women cursed, said a line of prayer, and declared that Old T'ung-pao's family was indeed lucky that their crop was unspoiled by her visit. Heaven had mercy upon them because their ancestors were good. The villagers were much more interested in visiting each other's mounds.

For now the "mountains" were opened to the light, and everybody came to look upon them and congratulate their proud owners. Chang Ts'ai-fa, Ah Szu's father-in-law, came from town to visit Old T'ung-pao and brought his young son

Ah Chiu along with him. For presents they brought soft cake, noodles, plums, and also salt fish. Hsiao Pao danced delightedly, like a puppy dog in the snow.

"Well, old friend, are you going to sell your cocoons or will you weave them into silk?" Chang asked Old T'ung-pao. Chang had led him to a place where they sat beneath an old willow by the stream. Chang was a gay old fellow, his head crammed full of funny stories he had heard from storytellers who used to sit outside in front of the temple in town. He knew all about the romance of the eighteen rebels and the seventy-two uprisings, stories of the Sui and T'ang dynasties. He used to tell the story of the rebel king, Ch'eng Yao-chin, who rose to his royal estate at Wa-kang Se after starting out in life as a vendor of wood and a smuggler of salt. He was a rare old teller of tales. This Old T'ung-pao knew full well. So when Chang asked him whether he meant to sell his cocoons or spin silk thread, he didn't take the question seriously.

"I'll sell my cocoons, of course," he replied.

Old Chang sighed, patted his thigh, and looked unusually thoughtful. He jumped to his feet and pointed to the cocoon shop off outside the village beyond the rows of mulberry trees.

"Old friend, the cocoons are gathered, but the cocoon shops are still closed. None of them will open for business this year. The eighteen rebel kings have come down to earth from heaven, and the leader king, Li Shih-min, has not been born. The world shall have no peace. All cocoon shops shall be closed to business."

Old T'ung-pao couldn't help laughing incredulously. This was obviously nonsense. How could it be otherwise? Was it possible that a whole network of cocoon shops, almost as numerous as privies in the open air, could all stop business? Besides, he'd heard that peace had been arranged with the

Japanese and that there would be no more war. And the soldiers had long since gone away. Chang changed the subject and retailed the local town gossip. He repeated once more the stories of the rebel kings, Chin Shu-pao and Ch'eng Yao-chin, which he'd heard from the storytellers. In the end, almost as an afterthought, he urged Old T'ung-pao to hasten repayment of the thirty dollars he'd borrowed from Chang's employer. But Old T'ung-pao's anxieties were now aroused. As soon as he could, he hurried along the road out of the village. He passed two cocoon shops. Both were shut tight. Not a soul was to be seen. In years gone by they'd have been open by now, with their counters set up and buzzing with activity around the small scales with their black crossbars. What he saw now made him vaguely uneasy, but when he returned home and saw his fine, hard, snow-white cocoons, he smiled. The best of all cocoons! He wouldn't believe nobody wanted them. Anyhow, he had to gather his cocoons and make offerings to the gods. He was thankful to the silkworm god for his generosity. He stopped worrying about the cocoon shops.

But throughout the village smiling faces grew clouded, and gay voices died down to worried murmurs. News of the failure of the cocoon shops to open was brought in from many places and was heard everywhere along the highway. Last year this time the buying agents were running about the village looking over the crop. This year no one came. Creditors and tax collectors alone were on schedule. When the villagers offered them cocoons instead of money, they received hard, sarcastic looks in reply. Men and women cursed and sighed, and none of them understood what had happened. They could hardly believe that they faced still greater difficulties this year when better cocoons had been gathered than ever before. To them it was like a clap of thunder breaking on a brightly sunny day. And for men like Old T'ung-pao, the more silkworms raised, the larger the crop of cocoons, the harder things were to be. He shook his old head. "Indeed the world has changed," he said, bent in utter despair.

They couldn't keep the cocoons at home forever. They had to be disposed of some way. If they could not be sold they could be spun into silk thread. Some of the villagers got out their spinning wheels and repaired them. They hadn't been used for many years. Many of them, Lu Pao's family among them, figured they'd have a better chance of selling the thread. Old T'ung-pao began to think the same way.

"Let's make our own silk," he said, "instead of selling the cocoons. What's the use of selling them? It was the foreigners' idea anyway!"

Mrs. Ah Szu jumped on him. "We have five hundred catties of cocoons here. Just how many spinning wheels do you think you can get hold of?" And she was right, for five hundred catties is no small quantity. Far too much for one family to handle. Get hands to help? That meant more money. Ah Szu sided with his wife.

"If you'd taken my advice and counted on our own fifteen piculs of leaf to raise foreign eggs only, we'd be better off," said Ah-to, who did not like the decisions his father had made.

Old T'ung-pao was too choked with anger and too bewildered to speak. He said nothing.

A ray of hope. Taoist Huang had heard from somewhere that a cocoon shop near Wusih was open for business. He was an old friend of Old T'ung-pao's, a farmer too, not a real Taoist. Old T'ung-pao talked it over with him. The old man came to Ah Szu with the news, and they discussed getting their cocoons to Wusih.

"That's thirty times nine *li* and more by water," growled Old T'ung-pao. "It'll take six days to go there and come back. Damnation! It's like going off to war. But what other way out can you see? We can't eat cocoons like rice. And we've still got those loans. . . ."

Ah Szu agreed. They borrowed a small boat, bought some reed mats, and set out while the weather was still fair. Ah-to went with them. Five days later they returned, but their boat was far from empty. There was one large basket of cocoons they hadn't been able to sell. It had not been easy to do business with that shop so far away. They were very choosy. The foreign eggs had brought thirty-five dollars a picul and the native cocoons twenty. Thin cocoons were not wanted. Old T'ung-pao's had been the best quality obtainable, yet he was left with a basketful of rejects. What he sold had gone for a total of one hundred and eleven dollars. With traveling expenses deducted they returned home with an even hundred dollars, not even enough to pay back what he'd borrowed to buy the last batch of mulberry leaves. Old T'ung-pao came back angry and sick in body and mind.

Mrs. Ah Szu took the ninety-odd catties they brought back and spun them into silk thread. She borrowed Lu Pao's spinning wheels and worked busily at them for five or six days. There was no rice in the house. As Szu took the skeins into town, but nobody wanted to buy them. No pawnshop would take them. Finally, after long negotiations, one pawnshop agreed to take the silk in exchange for one picul of rice which Old T'ung-pao had pawned before the Spring Festival. The village had harvested the best crop of cocoons in the memory of most of its inhibitants. Thanks to it, they all faced the new season with an increased debt. And Old T'ung-pao, because he had had three patches of eggs and had produced the largest number of cocoons, lost his last bit of land and added thirty dollars to his total debt; and for this he and his whole family had also paid with a month of strain and hunger.

MAO TUN

Autumn Harvest

1

It was not until the end of the fifth moon that Old T'ung-pao grew any better. The only medicines he took were the two "divine remedies" of the god Ts'u Shih which his daughter-in-law, Mrs. Ah Szu, had secured at the local temple. He fought his illness with his stubborn old body, which, despite lack of nourishment, seemed to him to grow stronger under the lash of fever. But he knew something was wrong when finally he rose from bed. His legs felt soft, as though he were standing on a heap of cotton. He could not even straighten up. "Have my bones rotted from lying in bed so long?" he asked himself. He refused to yield to the thought and tried mightily to look and act like a strong and healthy man. But when his features looked out at him from the water basin, he sighed softly. Was this his face? It looked more like the mask of a ghost. The cheekbones protruded sharply. His skin was stretched tightly across them, rising over the bridge of his thin pointed nose and sinking into the black hollows of his eyes. He saw his matted hair and his yellow-gray beard, under which his Adam's apple stuck out

like a tiny fist. Old T'ung-pao stared fixedly at this carica-
ture of himself. Tears coursed slowly down his lean cheeks
and dropped into the basin.

These were the first tears stubborn Old T'ung-pao had
shed in years. He had toiled stubbornly for nearly half a
century to establish his home. Through it all he had stead-
fastly worshipped two things only—P'usa, the God of Money, and Health. He deeply believed that without P'usa's
blessing all the money you earned—your effort, cunning,
and shrewdness notwithstanding—would somehow be lost.
But if your health were poor, it mattered little even if you
did have P'usa's blessing because then you could not toil and
seek your living. For forty years on the first and the fifteenth
day of every lunar month Old T'ung-pao faithfully went to
the Money God's shabby little temple at the little bridge beyond the village and there burned incense and kowtowed.
But now he had almost been destroyed by an illness which
struck him more fiercely than the falling price of cocoons.
He felt that the end of his cherished home was near, and he
didn't see how he could save it.

"Ai! How could I have changed so much? I was in bed
only a month!" Old T'ung-pao addressed himself to Mrs. Ah
Szu, who crouched before the stove blowing on the fire. She
made no answer. She blew harder and harder, and her
round head, its hair disheveled, almost seemed to enter the
stove itself. The white smoke filled the room and curled its
way out slowly through the two doors on either side. The
half-green weeds she was using for fuel remained obstinately
untouched by the darting little flames. Thirteen-year-old
Hsiao Pao came running in from the rice paddy for something to eat but started coughing as soon as he got inside the
door. Coughing too, Old T'ung-pao walked unsteadily across
the room to help his daughter-in-law. But just then the stove
brightened up and the weeds began to hum, hiss, and crack-

le. After quickly adding some mulberry twigs to the blaze, Mrs. Ah Szu looked up and rose slowly, her eyes tear-filled. Mrs. Ah Szu, who had always worked more than she'd talked, also shed tears in silence. Old T'ung-pao and his daughter-in-law looked at each other, both with tear-filled eyes. The fire was now burning brightly and licks of flame darted out of the opening, throwing a red glow on the woman's face. But the reflected color which covered her sallow complexion could not change the shrunken lines of her face and figure. Hsiao Pao, a slow child, standing beside his mother, looked like a monkey, all skin and bones. All of this Old T'ung-pao saw now with his eyes. In his dark sickbed he had felt the boy's hand in his and he had sensed how much thinner it had become. But he had never seen it as clearly as he did now. His heart sank within him. "Ai! Ai! What is it, Hsiao Pao?" he almost cried out, "You look as though you had consumption!" Old T'ung-pao forced the words out, and turned his hollow gaze on Mrs. Ah Szu. Still silent, she picked up the torn hem of her jacket and wiped her eyes.

Steam rose from the side of the pan and with it an aroma of something cooking. Hsiao Pao drew near and sniffed.

"Pumpkin again, mama!" he pouted. "Why always pumpkin instead of rice? I want rice! I want rice!" Mrs. Ah Szu drew out a mulberry twig, swiftly as though to turn it on the boy. But she only beat it against the ground, broke it into pieces, and threw it into the stove. She turned her face away and still did not speak.

"Don't cry, Hsiao Pao. You'll have rice when your father gets back." Old T'ung-pao ran his scraggly hand over his grandson's shaven head. "He has gone to your grandfather to ask him to borrow some money for us. With it we'll buy rice and then we'll cook it for you."

He spoke the truth. Hsiao Pao's father had left early in the morning for town to see his father-in-law, Chang Ts'ai-fa. Somehow he would get the old man to act as guarantor for a five or ten-dollar loan from his employer, Mr. Wu, who made it his business to lend money to the farmers in the surrounding villages. But Hsiao Pao did not believe him. For more than a month and a half he had heard his father and mother discuss borrowing money to buy rice. Yet they still had the same pumpkin and taro to eat every day. Hsiao Pao did not mind the taro so much. When it was cooked with some salt, it was quite smooth and rich to the taste. But coarse pumpkin without sugar, how could anybody eat it as a regular food every day? And they'd been eating tasteless pumpkin now without change every day for two weeks. Hsiao Pao's stomach turned at the thought of it. He looked tearfully at his grandfather and his stomach made little noises inside of him. He thought his grandfather and his father and mother were all cruel. The only hope he had left was the return of his Uncle To-to. He was sure his dashing uncle would get hold of some fine cakes for him to eat, as he had done before. But Hsiao Pao recalled accurately that Ah-to had not been back for three whole days.

The pumpkin was getting on now and hissed in the pan. Old T'ung-pao lifted the cover and found it half full, without any soup at all. Indeed, the parts on the bottom and sides were already turning into pumpkin crust. He frowned over his daughter-in-law's extravagance. Before the silkworm time they had also been short of rice and had eaten pumpkin as their regular diet. But then they used to cook two pumpkins in a panful of water. All five of them could have several bowls of pumpkin soup and fill themselves on it. And now he had been in bed for a month and the young people were already growing thriftless. This would never do! His ashen face grew red, and he moved slowly toward the jar to dip some water out and pour it over the pumpkin. Before he reached it, Mrs. Ah Szu hurriedly removed the cover of the pan and started filling their bowls with the thick pumpkin paste.

"Don't add water! Let us three finish it. In the evening Hsiao Pao's father will surely come back with rice. Ai, Hsiao Pao, the pumpkin will taste better this time. It's drier. Come on and eat to your heart's content!" While she spoke, she quickly ladled out the pumpkin and was already scraping out the crust. Old T'ung-pao choked back his anger and walked unsteadily over to the door with his bowl in his hands. He ate slowly with trembling fingers, sitting on the threshold. He felt choked with bitterness. Before him the sun glittered dazzlingly on the rice paddy. The creek lay like a strip of silver next to the field. The water was much lower now, and the willows on the banks were turning yellow. Utter quiet reigned along the water's edge. Not a man or a dog or even a chicken. In former times at midday women and children would be noisily washing clothes or dishes in the water. On the rice field the men would be squatting in the shadow of the trees smoking their long pipes after the noon meal. In the doorways of the surrounding houses there would be men about, talking or eating just like Old T'ung-pao on the threshold of his home. But now, though the sun still shone warmly and the water flowed quietly by, the village seemed as dead as the bare side of a mountain. It had been six weeks since Old T'ung-pao had come outside the house. The village had changed and looked different to him now, like Hsiao Pao who had grown so thin that he hardly knew him.

His bowl was empty. His eyes looked out of their deep black sockets at the creek, at the deserted huts on the far bank. He chewed on mechanically. He did not ask himself why all the people seemed to have left. He only ruminated

over the vast changes that had come to the world since he
had taken ill. First he had found himself so entirely different. Then his family, and now his village which he had
known so well. A strange sadness rose in him. He set the
bowl down on the ground and held his hands to his head
and let these confused thoughts run through his mind.

He remembered how his father and his grandfather, who
had escaped from the Long Hairs, had described villages
which had been destroyed so that not a single shadow of
man, dog, or chicken was to be seen in them. Last New
Year's time, when the little Japanese devils attacked Shanghai, all the villages had been astir over the "second coming
of the Long Hairs." But had he not heard that peace had
been made? No Long Hairs came while he was sick. Yet
how much his desolated village looked now like the places
the Long Hairs used to lay bare! His grandfather used to
tell him that sometimes the Long Hairs did not destroy villages but let all the people follow them and become Long
Hairs too. Then, too, all the villages would be left deserted
and empty. He knew that somewhere far off, there were
Long Hairs disturbing the country, but the people in his village were all peaceful and obedient. Had the Long Hairs really come, then, during his sickness? It did not seem possible.
He heard steps in front of him and raised his head sharply.
He saw a pair of piglike eyes looking at him out of a flat
broad face. He recognized Ho-hua, wife of Li Ken-sheng.
Ho-hua, the coquette! She was also thinner now, but it
made her more beautiful rather than less so. Her piglike
eyes which were looking at him with a mixture of sympathy
and surprise also seemed somehow more pleasant. But Old
T'ung-pao remembered in a flash the hatred which had
come between his family and her during the raising of the
silkworms. He thought it was an evil omen that the White

Tiger Star should be the first person he had met outside his home. He spat angrily and lowered his head to shield his face.

When Old T'ung-pao raised his head again, Ho-hua was before him no longer, but the sun had stretched almost now to his feet. His son, Ah Szu, must just be getting aboard the boat to return from town. The boats always left at this hour. He must have the rice with him too, bought with the money he borrowed. Old T'ung-pao unconsciously licked his lips. To tell the truth, he also hated the pumpkin paste, and the saliva started in his mouth when he pictured having rice to eat.

"Hsiao Pao! Hsiao Pao! Come here to grandpa!" The rice had led his thoughts to his hungry grandson. It was the first time he'd shouted aloud like a hearty man since rising from bed. There was no answer. He shouted again with all his might, even louder this time. He turned sharply with surprise to see Hsiao Pao jump out of Ho-hua's house with a flat little something held outstretched in his hand. The monkey-like boy hopped in front of his grandfather, thrust his hand out, and cried:

"Look, grandpa, look! A roasted bun!" He stuffed it hastily into his mouth. Old T'ung-pao swallowed his saliva hard. His mouth twitched faintly, covetously, then its lines drew down in a frown.

"Who gave it to you, Hsiao Pao? Who gave you the cake?"

"Ho . . . Ho . . ." The boy's mouth was too full for him to speak. But Old T'ung-pao had heard enough and his face hardened. Complicated thoughts came into his head. It was too shameful—that Hsiao Pao should eat the food of his enemies. But how could the Ho family have some to give—where was Heaven's justice in this? Old T'ung-pao was so angry that he stamped his foot, but he could not bring himself to strike Hsiao Pao, who by now had finished and was saying with an air of satisfaction:

"Ho-hua gave it to me, grandpa. Ho-hua is a good person. She's got buns!" Nonsense, thought Old T'ung-pao, reddening and raising his hand, but Hsiao Pao did not appear to notice. "She still has some," he went on. "She got them from town and says she's going back there tomorrow for rice, for rice! White rice, she said!"

Old T'ung-pao jumped up angrily. He had been without rice for a month and a half, and naturally he would envy anybody who had some to eat. But the Ho family which he despised! His face turned blue and he cursed roughly. "What of it! She probably stole it from somebody. Serve her right if she gets arrested and punished!" He spoke his curse but lowered his voice. He stared at his grandson and wondered what he could say to Ho-hua if she came out. No joke to call somebody a thief without evidence to prove it. But nothing stirred over at Ho-hua's house. Nothing happened. Only Hsiao Pao made a face.

"No, grandpa, you're wrong. Ho-hua is a good person. She has cakes and she willingly gave me one!"

Old T'ung-pao turned pale again. Without a word, he fumbled around the water wheel lying under the small porch and picked up a bamboo pole without speaking. Hsiao Pao figured something was wrong, and taking to his heels he made off again for the house of Ho-hua. Old T'ung-pao took a step in pursuit, but his head swirled with sudden dizziness. His legs gave way, and he sank to the ground and sat, the bamboo pole falling from his hands.

"Congratulations! Congratulations! You've come outside today, Old T'ung-pao!" The shout came from a man just approaching the rough plank bridge from the rice fields across the creek. The black spots still danced before Old T'ung-pao's eyes, but he immediately recognized the voice of Taoist Huang from the same village and his heart gladdened. They were great old friends, and Taoist Huang had been one of his most frequent visitors during his illness. The two of them were regarded as eccentrics in the village. Old T'ung-pao was noted for his stubborn hatred of anything with the word "foreign" in it. Taoist Huang was famous for the unusual expressions he picked up in town. Money, for example, he always called "Brother Square-hole."* Whenever he addressed anybody, it was always "your excellent family" or "your excellent self." This reminded people of the manners of Taoists, and that is how he came to be nicknamed "Taoist Huang." But Old T'ung-pao, at least, appreciated his friend's talents, and he often used to say to his son, Ah Szu, that it was nothing short of a shame that Taoist's abilities had to be wasted in tilling the soil.

"You'd choke talking about it, Taoist!" Old T'ung-pao turned with all his troubles to his friend. "I haven't been sick so long, yet the whole world has changed so! The village looks as though it has been destroyed by the Long Hairs, and the bitch, the White Tiger Star, steals some buns from somewhere and makes the brainless Hsiao Pao greedy for them. Would you beat him or not, Taoist?"

While he spoke, Old T'ung-pao picked up the bamboo again and beat it against the ground. Taoist Huang nodded his head, sighed, and shook his shoulders like the old fortune-teller, whose father and grandfather before him had told omens in characters and had lived like him in the Ch'en Huang Temple in the town. At the end, he said quietly:

*"Cash" coins—fractions of a penny—still widely in use at this time in many rural areas, had a square hole in the center.

"The world is in revolt, Brother T'ung-pao, the world is in turmoil. Do you know where the people of the village have gone and for what? Hm, to eat off the rich families and steal the stored rice! This was started by the people of Pai Ch'i Peng day before last and was followed by our own people today. Your excellent son, Ah-to, was also among them. Brother T'ung-pao, you are just rising nobly from your illness. Just pretend you don't know anything about Ah-to. Oh—I'm talking too much today!"

Old T'ung-pao heard the news distinctly. He jumped up, his eyes popping. Almost at once he sank down to the ground as if something had hit him on the head. His lips trembled. Eat off the rich and rob the rice stocks? His heart was both alarmed and comforted. There was a remote kind of satisfaction because Ho-hua's bun did turn out to have a questionable origin. Alarmed, because his own younger son To-to was also involved. Revenge would certainly come down on him too. Taoist Huang watched his friend, his small eyes squinting with fear.

"Sorry, sorry, you should take care of your excellent self. That's the main thing! I see I've done evil with my loose mouth. I've heard that the people up above aren't inclined to be very severe about it, so that's all right. Only warn your excellent son a bit, warn him!"

"Ai-ya!" Old T'ung-pao found his tongue at length. "I tell you, Taoist Huang, I've always thought that little beast didn't behave like a man. I've feared he was the ghost of the Long Hair reborn to take vengence on our whole family, and now it's already done! All right if he doesn't come back, but if he does, I'll bury him alive! Thank you, Taoist Huang, for letting me know! I've certainly been in the dark!"

Old T'ung-pao spoke quaveringly with hate and fear in his

voice. He saw the ghost of the Long Hair standing before him when he closed his eyes. Taoist Huang never thought his friend would take the matter so hard. He was sorry now he'd talked. Old T'ung-pao was even thanking him.

"Never mind, never mind," said he hastily. "Now, I've got to be off. I've got things to do in my humble home. Goodbye. Take good care of yourself. Take care!"

Taoist Huang scrambled up and made off, half-running as though he were anxious to escape from the scene of a newly committed crime. Old T'ung-pao was left sitting there stupefied. The sun beat down hard on his head, but he felt nothing. He was turning over in his mind all the stories he knew about the Long Hairs, stories he had heard from his father and grandfather. The grisly picture of many severed, bloody human heads rose before him when he remembered the sights he had seen with his own eyes during the great Lao Ch'ao, the attack on the royal rice being brought for the Emperor during the reign of Kuang Hsü. His thoughts led him finally to the same conclusion he had long ago drawn from the stories of the Long Hairs. If it were good to revolt, the Long Hairs would have in the end displaced the Emperor and reigned in his stead. But they failed. Didn't that prove that to revolt is evil? But all the world had changed during his illness. That was the terrible thing. And this change had come upon him, upon Old T'ung-pao, who not long ago had been a small farmer with his own land and was now poor. His imagination was still vivid and all of this aroused his greatest fears.

2

Ah Szu got home at sunset. He had not been able to borrow money but he had three bushels of rice with him.

"Wu Lao-yeh scowled and said he had no money. But he finally changed his mind and let me have three bushels on credit. No wonder we've got nothing to eat in the village! In his shop down there he's got more than a hundred piculs of rice. For the three bushels we got today we'll have to give him five bushels of the coarse rice after the autumn harvest. And this he did for us to give us face! You've got to be rich to get richer!"

Ah Szu told his tale gloomily while he divided the rice into two large jars. He gestured to his wife and went back to the old unused pigsty back of the shed where he began whispering animatedly to her. Old T'ung-pao watched them with a heavy heart and turned his gaze back to the two jars. There was something different about Ah Szu too today. Where did those three bushels really come from? He did not dare ask. A few minutes before, he'd quarreled with Mrs. Ah Szu over To-to's bad behavior. She'd called him an old fool.

"Well, go and complain about To-to's unfilial conduct and the yamen will give you a lump of pure gold when you bury him alive!" she'd mocked.

Old T'ung-pao had answered with what he knew from the wisdom of the sages and the hermits. Man's will must be strong despite his poverty, he quoted. But to no avail. Courage isn't edible and is therefore worse than pumpkin! After this Old T'ung-pao fell silent, his heart all the heavier. He knew that Ah Szu had always been upright and honest, but he also knew that Ah Szu was gullible and no match for his wife. Now they were whispering there by the pigsty. Old T'ung-pao looked at them from his distance and felt desolately helpless. His thoughts came to rest on the half-gone pigsty itself. He had built it for himself six years back. It was a good one and had cost him ten dollars for the wood alone. They had not used it last year, and it scarcely looked now as if they would have enough money for a pig this season. He had duly consulted the fortune-teller when he built it, and now so soon had ill luck come upon it! All his feelings of frustrated anger narrowed to a point and drove at the pigsty.

"The Second Mr. Chen once told me he wanted to buy some wood," he said, walking with uneven steps toward his son and daughter-in-law. "Ah Szu! Let's break up the pigsty and sell it to him. What good is the damned thing when we haven't any pigs to put inside and can't afford to get any?"

Ah Szu and his wife turned to him as he came up speaking. Even in the growing dusk he saw excitement in Mrs. Ah Szu's expression. Her face was animated. But now she made an impatient gesture.

"What'd it be worth, the dirty old wood? The Second Mr. Chen wouldn't take it!"

"He'll take it. Depend on me. We've had relations with the Chen family for three generations. How could he refuse?" Old T'ung-pao was thinking of the whole past which seemed so glorious, and so distant, to him now. Because he had shared the dangers of captivity and escape in the time of the Long Hairs with the Eldest Mr. Chen, Old T'ung-pao's grandfather stood well with the Chen family. Even Old T'ung-pao was treated with kindness, and sometimes the young Mr. Chen even called him "Brother T'ung-pao." This served as the basis for Old T'ung-pao's authority.

Mrs. Ah Szu said nothing. She moved away, her face set with displeasure. Old T'ung-pao stared at his son.

"What is To-to doing?" he blurted out finally, "Tell me! You think I know nothing? I can stop being in charge here only when I die!"

A crow came to light on the roof and croaked at them. Ah Szu picked up a piece of broken tile and threw it at the black bird. It flapped off. He spat, shook his head, and said nothing. What could he say and how would he say it? His father said one thing, his wife another, and his brother still another. They all seemed right enough to his simple mind. He was unable to decide.

"It will cost our heads! They'll kill the whole family! I know. I've seen lots of it!"

"Well—can they kill everybody?" As Szu spoke for the first time, faintly, feebly opposing his father's anger. But he changed quickly and in alarm when his father's eyes popped and the blue veins swelled on his forehead.

"Don't worry. Ah-to just went over to have a look. He didn't go down to town today."

"You're mad! Where else has he gone? Taoist Huang told me exactly the opposite!" Old T'ung-pao glared. His son and daughter-in-law both sided with To-to.

"Nonsense! Taoist Huang is confusing the snake-gourd with the beanstalk! They went east today to Yang-chia-ch'iao with the women. The men were only rowing the boats and To-to was only one of the rowers. I'm telling you the truth!"

Unable to resist his father, Ah Szu had actually told the truth, despite his wife's strict bidding not to do so. But two important things Ah Szu did not tell. The rower To-to was in reality the leader of all the people from their village. And he, Ah Szu, had promised his wife that if he did not succeed in raising money to buy rice, he would go off tomorrow and help To-to "row the boat." Old T'ung-pao looked doubtfully at his son. Both remained silent. The evening was growing old. Smoke was rising from the chimney over the house, and they heard Hsiao Pao singing in the house. Mrs. Ah Szu called aloud for her husband. With a murmured reply he turned to go. But he stopped and turned to his father, who was still standing in the shadow of the pigsty.

"The three bushels will last eight or ten days," he said in a relieved tone. "When To-to comes back sometime tonight, we'll tell him not to go rowing for them anymore."

"This pigsty will have to come down," replied Old T'ung-pao. "It'll be ruined this way by wind and rain, and we might as well make something out of it."

He spoke again of the pigsty as a way of saying that they did not have to do anything against the law when they were still quite a way from starvation. He tapped the wood like an experienced carpenter gauging its possible value. Then he too walked into the house.

The rice field was alive with human beings, and the air hummed with voices. All the villagers had come back. Hsiao Pao dashed out of the house like a little mouse, looking for his Uncle To-to. Mrs. Ah Szu hastily threw some mulberry twigs on the fire and followed after him, hungry for news. On the stove the steam was trying to lift the cover off the rice pan, and when it escaped out the sides it brought richly flavored aromas with it. Old T'ung-pao stood within reach of the smell, and the saliva ran in his mouth and his stomach grumbled with anticipation. But while he stood there, his mind was busy with many other things. He thought of how he would bring the unruly To-to to book. He also was thinking about preparations for the forthcoming work in the fields. Of all the folk in the village just then, Old T'ung-pao was probably the only one who was thinking about going into the fields a month hence.

But neither To-to nor their neighbor just across the creek, Lu Fu-ch'ing, was among those who returned. They had remained with the people at Yang-chia-ch'iao for the night. Tomorrow they were going to help "row" the farmers over to Ya-tsui-t'an to gather the peasants in the three villages so that all could go on down to the town together. Mrs. Ah Szu heard this from Lu Pao, the sister of Lu Fu-ch'ing. All the villagers talked excitedly about what was happening, but no one told Old T'ung-pao. They all knew his stubborn character.

"It's good that he stayed there! The scoundrel! I don't recognize him any longer as my son!" Old T'ung-pao shouted and glared at the face of his eldest son. He seemed to read something there. Ah Szu smacked his lips and said nothing. Mrs. Ah Szu glared angrily back at the old man, letting out something like a snort.

Old T'ung-pao scarcely slept the whole night. Whenever he closed his eyes in uneasy rest, he dreamed, and all his dreams were brief. Each time he literally jumped awake as though he had been struck. His eyelids grew unbearably heavy, for he was deeply weary, but still he dared not sleep any more. In his half-somnolent state he heard sounds from the bed of Ah Szu which he dimly supposed came from bedtime intimacies. But then Ah Szu's voice rang out loudly, and the old man sat bolt upright.

"Papa wants to bury you alive, Ah-to! You are right—the old man is too damned stubborn! Yet, in the end the whole thing will fall upon you and the others will get away. . . ."

Old T'ung-pao felt the hair rise along his neck when he realized his son was shouting in his sleep. He leaned over on one elbow.

"Ah Szu!"

No answer. Hsiao Pao laughed aloud in his own dreams. Mrs. Ah Szu muttered curses. Then there was the sound of bodies turning on the flat boards and the sound of steady snoring. But now all sleep was gone from Old T'ung-pao. As he stared into the blackness his mind wandered up the many paths without beginning or end that seemed to stretch from his bed. He thought of the golden days of thirty years back. He remembered the stack of old accounts books they had made when the family was prosperous. Then there was the good mulberry tree land they had lost earlier this spring despite their wonderful silkworm crop. He thought how upright his family had been for generations and how even the Elderly Mr. Chen had applauded their virtue in the days when he still lived. As for himself, T'ung-pao, it had been his ambition ever since he was twenty years old to live in the manner of the honored men in the town. He had always worked with the hoe, but he had not been without ambition. Look now where his toil had brought him. Heaven had no eyes! The thing he could understand least of all was Heaven's motive in giving him an evil offspring like Ah-to. Was it possible for the ghost of the little Long Hair to remain a ghost and find no rebirth during all these sixty years?

Old T'ung-pao broke into a sudden sweat. Heaven! He lay there shivering from head to foot. Ah-to today was just like that Long Hair of long ago! Old T'ung-pao remembered the cry that had sounded throughout the country five years ago. "Down with the rich farmers and the gentry!" More. To-to even then often used to play with the Long Hair sword hidden in their home. It had been carried out of the Long Hair camp by Old T'ung-pao's grandfather. It was the very sword with which his grandfather had killed the Long Hair who tried to bar their way to escape! The threads which bound the sword to Ah-to's life seemed to tighten and trace a malignant pattern in the old man's mind. He thought of all these things, and fear deepened in him.

But of all the pictures that flashed across his brain, there was one he did not think of and could never have imagined. While he lay there coldly sweating and hating his son with a bitter hate, Ah-to and his friend Lu were marching through the heavy mists of daybreak toward Old T'ung-pao's own village, and behind them came the thirty-odd families of Yang-chia-ch'iao. And in the houses all about him, his fellow villagers had passed the night filled with excited dreams and nervous anticipation. Just now, coming back to their own senses from their dreams, they were preparing to welcome Ah-to and the people from Yang-chia-ch'iao.

A stream of light broke through the long crack in the wall. Out on the rice field the sparrows began chirping, and soon the only cock in the village—Taoist Huang's most prized possession—began to crow. From a distance, it sounded like the wailing of a woman. Old T'ung-pao fell into a doze once more, and, half dreaming, he saw flashed before him the Long Hair sword dangling over his head. On its hilt appeared a hand, and his eyes traveled up the knotted muscular forearm and on up to the face above it—the thick brows and round eyes. It was unmistakably Ah-to!

"T'ai! . . ." Old T'ung-pao shouted in anger and fear and jumped from his bed. He stood wide-eyed and a little bewildered in the midst of the dazzling light that poured in the doorway. Mrs. Ah Szu was cooking their morning gruel, and the fire crackled in the stove. Before he could fully pull himself together he heard a subdued murmur of human voices that grew steadily louder. Back of it came the sound of a gong.

"Is there a fire?" He ran out as he asked his question. As soon as he got to the rice field, he understood what was happening. What he saw there was just like the scenes of the troubles he'd seen in the early years of the reign of Kuang Hsü. The villagers from Yang-chia-ch'iao were going by, men and women, old and young. "Come on!" they shouted, "Let's go together!" To-to was one of them. In fact, it was To-to beating the gong!

To-to sprang out of line and stood before his father. Old T'ung-pao grew purple, his eyes hot.

"You . . . you animal! You murdered one!"

"You die only once if you're murdered and we get the same result from starvation! Let's go!" He spoke with a broad smile. "Where's Ah Szu and sister? Let's go together!"

Old T'ung-pao had not heard clearly what was said but he raised his fist to strike his son. Ah Szu rushed between them and hurriedly addressed his brother.

"Listen, Ah-to! You don't have to go now. We bought three bushels of rice on credit yesterday. We have something to live on now."

To-to's thick brows came together, and the expression on his face altered. But before he could speak, a man pushed his way out from behind him. It was Lu Fu-ch'ing. He pushed Ah Szu out of the way and shouted with laughter.

"So, you've got three bushels of rice in your home? Fine! The people from Yang-chia-ch'iao haven't had their breakfast yet. Come on, everybody!"

Ah Szu couldn't believe his ears. They would eat his rice first? But the people of Yang-chia-ch'iao had already brushed past him in a crowd, and with a shout the foremost of them were already inside his house. Old T'ung-pao gave a wild cry as if a piece of flesh had been cut from his chest. His legs gave way, his eyes closed, and he fell to the ground. Ah Szu leaped on Lu Fu-ch'ing like a mad dog. He cursed and he fumed and he sank his teeth into Lu's neck. Lu fought back shouting.

"Are you crazy? What are you doing? Listen to me, Brother Ah Szu! Hai, Ah-to! Look here. . . ."

Ah Szu released Lu from his grip only to seize Ah-to. He struck at him wailing blindly through tears.

"Not even the snake eats the grass by his own nest! You bring people to rob your own flesh and blood!" He held his brother by the head, making him groan. Lu tried vainly to break in between them. Old T'ung-pao sat on the ground and cursed to the heavens. Lu Pao, the girl, finally succeeded in tearing Ah Szu from his brother.

"You have means of borrowing rice. What of the others?" said Ah-to, panting, "You don't want to go because you have some rice. How will we ever get anywhere? If everybody thought the same way as you do, we'd all die! Nobody wants to take your rice without paying you back. Come down to town with us and you'll get your share."

Ah Szu crouched to the ground like a wooden puppet. He said nothing. Lu approached him, with one hand feeling the marks of Ah Szu's teeth in his neck and with the other tapping Ah Szu's shoulder lightly.

"It was decided on beforehand. Anybody in any of the villages with rice would be relieved of it first and then all would go together to town. Brother Ah Szu! . . . This was everybody's decision. You mustn't hate me!"

"Even the Long Hairs were more reasonable! Not so barbarous!" Old T'ung-pao finally realized what was happening. He shook his head and cursed in a low voice, not daring to look up at anybody. His eyes were fixed on the ground. He said to himself, "All right, let them go to town. They'll get their punishment when they get there. Heaven has eyes! There is retribution in this life. Then they'll find that an old man's years are not without meaning!"

Some of the Yang-chia-ch'iao people came noisily out of Old T'ung-pao's house just then, bearing the two large jars of rice. Mrs. Ah Szu, her hair streaming behind her, screamed tearfully after them.

"That's for us! For us! You're robbing food from our very mouths! Robbers! Murderers!"

Nobody paid any attention to her. Gongs were sounding to gather them all together, and the rice jar was deposited in the middle of the field. Lu Pao desperately tried to pull

Mrs. Ah Szu aside and shouted at her, hoping she would hear and understand the better.

"We share what food we have, don't you understand? Live or die together! Who told you to beg for that bit of rice? You can borrow but the others can't. Are you going to live alone and let everybody else starve? Shush! You cry as bitterly as if your father-in-law had died. We eat up your rice, but we will get rice back for you. You have nothing to cry about!"

Ah Szu, still there on the ground like a wooden figure, shook his head, picked himself up, and went over to his wife.

"This was your idea and now we're left with nothing," he said, half comfortingly, half-resentfully. "Let's go with them. The crowd will answer for everything. If heaven falls, everyone will be crushed together."

Two large pans were produced and put over a fire in the field. People from both villages together busily washed and cracked rice gruel. The early morning mist was giving way to the long brilliant slanted rays of a golden sun. Even the pale faces of the people gathered around reddened in this light. At the east end of the creek where the water was deeper and broader, there were five or six boats. There were boatmen too, singing loudly and merrily. Everybody was to go down to town on these boats.

Old T'ung-pao crouched silently on the ground. He looked murderously at the people eating their rice—his rice!—and as if in a dream, he saw them pile into the boats and move away amid much clamor and shouting. He saw Ah-to bending to his oar with all his strength. Ah Szu was sitting in his place with a half-tearful, half-resigned expression on his face. And Mrs. Ah Szu—she seemed to be talking now in friendly fashion with Lu Pao. As the boat swung out into the creek, he saw Hsiao Pao in the stern next to Ah-to, imitating his uncle's broad sweep at the oar.

As if suddenly awakened from his dream, Old T'ung-pao jumped up and began running westward along the bank of the creek. He did not know why he ran. His heart felt blocked and he desperately wanted to talk to somebody, but there was not a single person anywhere. The village was as quiet as the dead. Not even a child had been left behind. He ran back eastward, and there on the other bank he saw a man racing madly toward him. He could not make out who it was because the runner had a white cloth tied about his head. But when he reached the little four-plank bridge, he recognized his friend Taoist Huang. His heart leaped with relief. He stopped short and shouted.

"Even the Long Hairs were more reasonable! Remember, my years have not been lived all in vain! They'll find their punishment awaiting them in town, the murderers!"

Taoist Huang also stopped. He hardly seemed to see or recognize Old T'ung-pao. He stared in front of him for a while then said aloud, "Abominable! Abominable, I tell you. They ate up my old cock! They ate my old cock! It's abominable!"

"The murderers! I see you're talking about your cock. What of it? They'd even kill a man—the murderers!" And Old T'ung-pao turned away and went home leaving Taoist Huang weeping there across the creek.

All the villagers returned safely that night, and each one brought five pints of rice with him. Old T'ung-pao watched them in shocked silence. The officials in town had not acted like officials at all. How could this be possible? A band of about a hundred peasants from three villages had proved so fearsome to them that they hastily agreed to give each one-half bushel of rice! The officials were useless, and because of their betrayal his years were indeed now lived in vain. Surely the world had changed! It had become a world utterly without order or meaning if To-to and those who followed him could triumph!

3

Uprisings for seizing rice stores broke out everywhere. About ten of the small town centers with an area of two hundred square *li* were almost daily besieged by bands of peasants from the surrounding villages. The town gentry thought the peasants ill-mannered and talked harshly about "maintaining order." Announcements in six-character sentences were issued by the district magistrate, the merchant's association, and the local militia, forbidding attacks on rice stores and forbidding peasants to "eat off the rich families." The proclamations promised the peasants that everything would be "talked over" in a friendly way. Some of the gentry, whose own homes had been invaded by hungry men and women, came into town to plead with the pawnshop people and the rice merchants to give up a bit of their rice to tide over the crisis period. Opening up a "door of convenience," they called it. But before the gentry and the tradesmen could decide among themselves just how this door was to be opened, the peasants grew impatient with hunger, and attacks and open seizures increased in number and in violence. They persisted despite the six-character announcements and the warnings of the local militia heads who had become the village heads. By now, there were more than one thousand peasants on the march for rice, and they began to move in the direction of the bigger towns and cities.

At a prosperous center some sixty *li* from Old T'ung-pao's village, the hungry farmers clashed with soldiers and police, who fired several volleys skyward and arrested more than twenty of the peasant leaders. The next day that town was completely cut off from neighboring towns. It was surrounded and besieged by thousands of angry peasants. It was at this town that the "door of convenience" was forced wide open. The gentry and merchants agreed to let the peasants borrow rice for repayment after the autumn harvest, picul for picul. Articles in the pawnshops could be redeemed without payment of interest. Finally, the merchants' association collected one hundred and fifty piculs of rice for free distribution through the village heads. The gentry and the merchants realized that for the present they would best follow the policy of giving a finger to save a hand, and besides, it was understood that all the inhabitants of the town would be made to bear the cost of the one hundred fifty piculs.

The provincial government sent detachments of the "peace preservation corps" to the small towns. Through a combination of threatened force and the gradual opening of "doors of convenience," the rising peasants were ultimately calmed down. It was already the end of the sixth lunar month, and the time for getting back to work in the fields was drawing pressingly near.

But thanks to these uprisings, Old T'ung-pao and his family were able to enjoy one meal of rice and two of porridge every day during those troubled weeks. They incurred no more debts after getting those three bushels of rice. But now they were to get back into the fields. This opened up a dismal prospect for Ah Szu and his wife. They saw in it only another way of increasing the burden of their debt. Old T'ung-pao was angered by their lack of interest. He called it laziness. His dignity had been sorely wounded throughout these past weeks. Now that the rioting was over the soil was waiting to be tilled. He saw it as his duty to bring an end to this period of unthinkable chaos and disorder in their lives. He felt somewhat like a loyal courtier to a deposed emperor. He wanted to reestablish order where all seemed to be ruin. Day and night he lectured them about working the soil. He told them how he had worked diligently in his youth, how his father before him had persisted at his labors and had not failed in the end to put the family on a sound basis. Whenever he came back from the fields, he would half-scold, half-plead with them.

"The shoots must be transplanted tomorrow or the day after. Are you possessed by a ghost, Ah Szu, still not thinking about getting fertilizer?"

"There's still some fertilizer powder left from last year," his son replied listlessly one day. Old T'ung-pao glared fiercely at him.

"What fertilizing powder?" he retorted. "Poison! Foreign ghost poison! I know only the bean cakes used by our ancestors. They do more lasting good! Will the land be of any use any more if it is exhausted by this damnable powder? No, we use bean cake this year!"

"Where are you going to get the money? Even the powder we have is probably no use. They say that if it lies a whole year, it must be mixed with as much new powder again before it can be of any use. But even for that we haven't any money."

"Nonsense! What are you going to do, give up farming then? What are you going to eat? How are you going to get along? How are you going to pay off the debts without working in the fields?"

Old T'ung-pao roared at his son, shaking his lean finger under Ah Szu's nose. Ah Szu sighed. In his heart of hearts he felt his father was right. He knew they could depend only on the soil to raise enough to eat for half the year, to buy clothes, and pay off their debts. Yet their recent experiences had taught him that they were merely pack animals for the creditors. The more they worked the soil, the heavier their debts. Cattle at least were fed. They had to go hungry, all of them.

"What's the use?" Mrs. Ah Szu always would say. They

had become deeply convinced of the correctness of Ah-to's frequent argument:

"Everything is finished for the peasant who gets debts on his back."

Yet what else could they do? They were resolved not to take on any more debts for farming. Yet in some way or other, they had to go on tilling the soil. Ah Szu remained silent in the face of his father's rage. Old T'ung-pao shouted in rage at Ah Szu and his wife.

"I wash my hands of your affairs!"

That afternoon he made off in silence for town. There he saw Old Chang and the Honorable Mr. Chen and told them about his son's misbehavior. They both advised him not to take the matter so seriously. Children have their own blessings, they told him. So Old T'ung-pao found a place to sleep in the town. Next morning he went to call on Mr. Chen, whom he found preparing for sleep after his regular morning pull at his opium pipe. Old T'ung-pao asked for a loan that would pay for a piece of bean cake. Too sleepy to refuse, Mr. Chen promised to get the cake from the guild for him— on credit.

Later that day Old T'ung-pao went along on his way home, his precious bean cake with him. His heart sang and he was cheery. But when he got to his own door, he lay the cake under the porch and with a lengthened face went in to his son and daughter-in-law.

"Only death will make me stop taking care of you. Don't talk about the debt! Just get to work!"

The illusions and dreams he had at the time of the silk-worms were again taking shape in the stubborn old head of T'ung-pao, like tbe young shoots rising out of the field. The sun shone golden every day, and there were cool, gentle, breezes. The slender little greens were coming up so fast, somebody seemed to be pulling them from the ground. The water in the creek dropped daily lower, and before long they had to put the waterwheels on the edge of the field. When Ah Szu grew tired, Old T'ung-pao got on to take his turn, but the wheel hadn't rolled around ten times before he felt a sharp stitch in his side and his legs grew heavy and he grew breathless. He had to step down, and, sighing, he watched Mrs. Ah Szu take his place. The grain grew rapidly and sought thirstily for more and more water. But the creek dropped still inch by inch as if it were being sucked up by the tongue of the Fire Dragon. Everywhere in the village the call came for helpers on the waterwheels. Everyone who could was begged to take a few turns at beating the turgid water up into the parched fields.

Ho-hua had planted only a few rows of miscellaneous grains. She and her silent husband had more time. People readily forgot that she was the "White Tiger Star," and the two were asked everywhere to turn waterwheels. Lu Fu-ch'ing had given up his little plot of rented land, and he and his sister, Lu Pao, came often to help Old T'ung-pao's family. Only To-to was seldom seen in the village. When he did come he helped the neighbors, for Old T'ung-pao would sooner die than see him.

Every morning people looked up anxiously to find the days still brightly blue. Once or twice in the evening they saw a few flaky clouds overhead, and the whole village rejoiced. But the morning brought the same spotless blue-white sky. The old women chanted the names of the Buddha and turned their blurred old eyes heavenward. But it all came to nothing. Four blistering weeks went by without a drop of rain.

Old T'ung-pao's land was higher than the rest, and it soon became almost impossibly difficult for them. The muddy water they drew up from the creek, which was itself now nearly dry, had to pass through a trench almost seventy feet long. Almost half the water was absorbed by the dry earth before it ever reached their field. The strong grain stalks turned yellower every day and began to shrivel up under their tortured eyes. Old T'ung-pao's heart contracted with pain. But he was helpless. Ah Szu's mouth was silent, his face sad. Mrs. Ah Szu complained in a loud voice, now about this, now that. There was no hope for harvest now. Besides all their vain labor, there was the additional debt for the bean cake!

"Wouldn't it be the best harvest you ever saw if only we could get some water?" Old T'ung-pao weakly answered when he could stand it no more. But Mrs. Ah Szu shrieked back at him.

"Yes! Yes! Water! Isn't this little water you want equal to our own blood? There's only Ah Szu and myself and the Lus, whom we could count as another person. Three altogether. How much blood can we afford? It'll dry in our veins before we get done! To-to had so much strength and yet you won't let him come . . . !"

"Sure, let's get To-to! He's as strong as an ox," put in Ah Szu. Old T'ung-pao spat and made no answer.

Next day To-to came pleasantly smiling to help turn the waterwheel. But it was too late. Only a thin ribbon of murky water was left in the middle of the stream. Ah Szu strung out the wheels in three relays in order to reach the water, and even this was possible for only half that day. Despite To-to's strong muscles, they couldn't turn up any water at all. About fifty feet west of their wheel was a place where the creek was deeper, probably up to To-to's waist. But there was no place where they could fix the wheel. If there was no rain that night, their crop was ruined. This went not only for Old T'ung-pao's field; every piece of land in the village would in less than five days dry up like the back of a tortoise. People climbed trees and looked off into the distant sky, but wherever their eyes turned, they saw the same deadly cloudless blue. There was one way out if they acted quickly—they could rent a foreign waterwheel.

Old T'ung-pao hated the word "foreign." Anyway, he refused to believe the wheel was any use. In last year's flood the the peasants in the neighboring village had used a foreign wheel to pump the water away from them. He had not seen it himself, but Taoist Huang, who saw everything, was full of excited praise for it. Then, the problem had been to pump the water *off* the land. Now they wanted to pump water up *on* to the land from half a *li* away. Could that be done? Old T'ung-pao regarded the prospect with suspicion hostility. But before he could comment, Mrs. Ah Szu broke in angrily.

"It's all right to talk about a foreign waterwheel. But where's the money coming from? They say it costs more than a dollar for a single field!"

"Heavens bless us! Everything will be all right if only we have rain tonight!" With new determination, Old T'ung-pao set off in haste toward the poor old temple of the God of Money next to the little bridge outside the village. There he kowtowed and loudly promised P'usa a great offering of thanksgiving after the rain. But there was no water to work on that night. The younger people actually had a night's sleep. But Old T'ung-pao never closed his eyes. Once he thought he heard a little whistling sound along the walls of the house. Rain? Rain? He jumped up eagerly and ran to the door. The sky he saw was gray-black. There were no stars shining, but there was no rain. He still clutched the last faint hopes to him, and he knelt and prayed. The third time he went out to look, the eastern sky was already breaking. He ran down to the field and found his precious grain slightly greener and stronger than it had been under yesterday's sunshine. Dew had helped. But the soil was cracking and felt like rock beneath his touch. Old T'ung-pao's heart beat hard in his chest. He knew full well that with the rising of the sun his paddy was finished for good, and that meant the end of his family. He walked back to his door.

The first rib of red light shed its glow over the whole eastern horizon. Weeds grew out of the creek bed, now dry almost to the bottom. Some of the villagers, taking advantage of the extra space along the bank, had planted corn. This was now almost up to a man's height. Down there a group of villagers were standing talking loudly and animatedly among themselves. Old T'ung-pao walked absently toward them. He stood by and listened. They were talking about renting a foreign waterwheel from town and pooling the cost. One among them, called Li Lao-hu, spoke up.

"We've got to hurry if we want to rent it. The foreign wheel is in use every day. Last night I learned that it is free for today. If we're late it will be of no use." He turned and saw Old T'ung-pao. "Will you take a share, Old T'ung-pao?"

Old T'ung-pao looked blankly at him as if he had not understood. Two things filled his heart so that he could barely open his mouth to speak. He doubted the ability of the foreign waterwheel to help them, and anyway, he had no money. Vaguely he thought he would watch and see the others try it out. If he saw that it did some good, then he'd do something about it. He could manage a loan somehow, he felt.

All that morning Old T'ung-pao and Ah Szu paced up and down along their field as though they were walking by the bed of a hopelessly sick person. The paddy drooped and grew steadily worse. The stalks sagged, first only at the top, finally down to the very ground. The ground cracked. It sounded like sighs. There was no water in the stream to pump, and everywhere the villagers stood around helpless. Some of them gathered at the bridge outside the village anxiously watching for the arrival of their last hope—the foreign waterwheel. When at noon the sun was blazing down upon them and hope ebbing away like the life in their fields, a sudden joyous shout was raised. There it came! A boat with a small black machine on it! It looked so little, but, it was said, it could do the work of eight strong men turning the wheels. The whole village, including Old T'ung-pao and his son, came out to watch the arrival. The boat carrying the machine did not come to shore but anchored in the middle of the river. Several lengths of rubber hose about as thick as a man's arms, scores of feet long, were dragged to the bank and over into the edge of the paddy. Gaping with awe, the villagers watched.

"The water will come into the fields through the pipe," proudly said the newcomer in charge of the hose. The engine suddenly gave forth a groan and began to turn. With a gulp, the pipe spat forth its first mouthful. Then the water came out in a steady stream and poured on into the field without any difficulty. The villagers looked on and cried and laughed with joy and wonder. They forgot for the moment that it was really money which provided the force behind the pump.

Old T'ung-pao stood off to the side watching the scene with wide eyes. He was sure there was some kind of demon inside that thing on the boat making it go around. Probably it was the ghost of Ni Chiu Chin, an eel-like animal that lived in the pool in front of the T'u Ti temple in the town. The water must be its saliva, and during the night it would surely return and suck it all back so that the men from the town could return next day and repeat the hoax. But none of these suspicions could overpower the cool charm of the green water which gushed forth into the fields. When they had finished with the second field, Old T'ung-pao decided that he would seek the help of this ghost and take his chances. He decided to stay in his field all night with a hoe lest the ghost return to reclaim the water.

Without saying anything to his son and daughter-in-law Old T'ung-pao got Taoist Huang and Li Lao-hu to guarantee a loan of eight dollars at two percent a month and secured the approval of the men on the boat. The pipe was duly turned into his field while Old T'ung-pao watched, torn between joy and misgiving.

By sunset Old T'ung-pao's paddy was covered with an inch of fresh green water. When the evening breeze passed over it, the water wrinkled like the face of an old woman. Old T'ung-pao was too pleased to pay any attention to Mrs. Ah Szu. Their new eight-dollar debt! Sure, eight dollars is a great sum—but weren't they going to sell their rice at ten dollars a picul? Last year even coarse rice brought eleven and a half a picul! All of Old T'ung-pao's hopes rose high in his heart once again.

Ah Szu looked on dully with his long sad face unchanged. The stalks were still drooping despite the water. It was too late for water once they had been burned by the sun.

"They'll be all right by tomorrow if we put some fertilizing powder on tonight," said To-to close in Ah Szu's ear. Ah Szu's heart skipped a beat. There was still some powder left, and now was the time to use it! Would it really exhaust the soil? The devil with it! Ah Szu was all for To-to's idea. But Old T'ung-pao had also heard To-to's whispered advice. He ran up to him like an angry tiger and yelled in his face.

"Poison! You grief-laden ghost of the little Long Hair! Murderer! Do you want to poison all of us?"

The others rushed over and urged Old T'ung-pao away

from To-to. Nobody said another word about fertilizing powder. Only Old T'ung-pao continued to rage.

"Wait and see!" he shouted at Ah Szu. "It'll be fine after tonight. Use fertilizing powder, poison! Poison!"

That night Old T'ung-pao would rather have died than leave his field. He feared the return of the ghost of the Ni Chiu Chin. He was also afraid his sons might come with the fertilizing powder. But he imparted his knowledge of the ghost to no one. He simply said he was going to guard his field against the malice of his sons. Everybody knew Old T'ung-pao was stubborn!

The night passed amid utter quiet. The ghost of the Ni Chiu Chin did not come, nor did his sons attempt to carry out their evil intent. But the paddy was still poorly off. In some places it even seemed worse. Old T'ung-pao began again to doubt the qualities of the water pumped up by the foreign wheel. But the grain in his neighbor's fields looked green and healthy!

"He's killed the whole family!" groaned Mrs. Ah Szu. Old T'ung-pao turned dark red. He was worn out with worry and anxiety. Lu Fu-Ch'ing came and advised him to give the powder a try. Maybe it would do some good. Certainly it could do no more harm. Old T'ung-pao stood by in dull silence watching his two sons spreading the powder over the paddy. He turned away nauseated and disgusted.

For two days after that the sun did not shine. Half an inch of water remained in the field. The rice stalks raised their heads, and their rich green color returned to them. Old T'ung-pao denied that this was the work of the powder, but he called it poison no more. A day later there was a drizzle of rain followed by warm mellow sunshine. The paddy grew richer and healthier than it had ever been. Everybody in the village sighed with thanksgiving and relief. They would live on now. Heaven surely had eyes after all!

Then came the autumn breezes, and they wafted the hideous memories of the forty-some days of heat and drought into the past like a forgotten nightmare. Everybody was happy. They looked on their paddies and found them good. They knew from experience the harvest would be full and rich. Old T'ung-pao felt his being reassert itself. His years had indeed not been lived in vain! It would be a plentiful year. He walked among the tall stalks and caressed them. There would be a four-picul harvest! Sometimes when his fingers felt of the heavy, drooping ears, he half-imagined there might even be five piculs out of every *mow*. Every ear was so full! He began to calculate the future. No exaggeration to count on four and a half piculs. Surely not. That meant he would be able to reap forty piculs altogether. Six and four-tenths piculs went to the tax collector. He would still have over thirty piculs. Figuring conservatively at ten dollars a picul, that meant three hundred dollars! That would pay off the best part of his debts. He couldn't imagine a price of less than ten dollars a picul! He and all his neighbors would be relieved of their burdens by one good harvest. Heaven surely had good eyes!

But while Old T'ung-pao contemplated his grain and his rosy dreams, the rice merchants in town, like Heaven, had eyes in their heads, and their eyes were only for their own profit. Before the rice was even cut, the price began to fall. During the reaping—the villagers were cutting down the fruits of months of toil, and piling their grain in neat stacks—the price in town fell to six dollars a picul. While they were grinding out the grain, the price fell further to four dollars. Finally, when they packed their coarse, plentiful rice into market, they could barely sell it at three! The rice merchants looked coldly at their outraged faces.

"That's today's price," they said coldly. "It'll be lower still tomorrow."

Debt collectors were busy in the village pursuing their debts. Would they take rice for the debts? Well, yes. The coarse rice at two-ninety. White rice at three-sixty.

Old T'ung-pao stood confused and silent amid the ruins of all his rosy calculations. His neighbors gathered in angry, excited, bitterly disappointed groups. Their womenfolk wailed. The men cursed.

"Why till the soil any more? You work like the devil and all you get is more debts! I always said so! I always said so!" frothed Mrs. Ah Szu to everyone she met. And she went about the village from house to house like a crazy woman.

What he had gone through with the silkworms brought Old T'ung-pao down in illness. The autumn harvest brought him down to the threshold of death. When he lay there dying and his tongue was already stiff and without speech, his eyes were still clear and were fixed on To-to, and they seemed to say:

"How can it be? How can it be that you were right? Strange, strange. . . ."

Three to Five Bushels More

Open boats, newly arrived from upcountry and heavily laden with the year's new rice, were tied up this way and that at the Wan Sheng Rice Shop landing. A thick white foam clinging to the leaves and rubbish floated like waves in the spaces between the boats. The Wan Sheng Rice Shop stood a few steps up from the landing across a narrow street up which no more than three men could walk abreast. The early sun cast long, slanting columns of light through the slits in the old awning over the shop and shone down in golden bars on the torn felt hats of the men crowded outside at the counter. The boats had barely come alongside and the ropes were scarcely fastened before these men had leaped ashore and rushed up to the shop to learn their fate.

"How much?"

"Five dollars for coarse rice and three for grain," replied the man in the shop, showing no particular interest either in the men or in their rice.

"Eh?" The men in the torn felt caps stared incredulously across the counter. Beautiful, blooming hopes shriveled up inside of them. They stood stupefied.

"Wasn't it thirteen dollars in the sixth month?"

"More, it was fifteen."

"How could it fall so far?"

"Don't you fools know what season it is? Rice is flowing out of the country like a tide. The price will go down still more in a few days' time."

The ready energy with which they had sculled their boats downstream, swiftly as though they were racing a dragon boat, ebbed from them. Blessed by Heaven this year with timely rains and protected against harmful insects and pests, they had reaped a rich harvest of three to five extra bushels a *mow*, and everyone had looked to the future for relief from their many heavy troubles. But now at the last stage of things, they were struck down more heavily than ever before.

"Let's row back without selling!" cried one angry villager.

"Tsi!" sneered the man behind the counter. "You think anybody will starve if you don't sell your rice? There's a lot of foreign rice and wheat everywhere. Before the first lot is gone the great foreign ships come with more."

Talk of foreign rice and foreign ships meant nothing to his listeners. But they knew that to refuse to sell their rice down by the river landing was madness. How could they hold on to the rice? Rent had to be paid. Money borrowed for fertilizer and food and help had to be repaid.

"Let's go to Fan Mu!" Somebody thought they might have better luck there.

"Hmph!" mocked the shopkeeper, feeling his scanty beard. "Talk about Fan Mu! You can go right on down to the city and find the same thing. We've all decided on the price among ourselves. Five for coarse and three for grain."

"We won't get anything by going to Fan Mu," broke in one of the peasants. "There are two tax stations to pass on the way, and who knows how much they'll charge us? And where is the money to pay them?"

"Can't you make it a little higher, sir?" they turned, pleading.

"Easy to say higher. It took money to open this shop. Capital. If we pay you a better price what are we going to get out of it? Who's going to do any such fool thing?"

"We never thought the price would be so low. Last year we sold at seven and a half. This year you sold rice at thirteen. No, you just said fifteen! We were sure it would have to be better than seven and a half and now we find it's only five!"

"Look here, how about keeping the old price, seven and a half?"

"We're poorer than you are. Have pity and lower your profit a little. . . ."

"Don't sell if you don't like the price," said another man behind the counter, impatiently flicking his cigarette into the street. "We didn't invite you here. You came yourselves. What's the use of all this babbling? Others will take our money for their rice. There are two more boats pulling in now." He pointed to the landing.

Three or four men, faces ruddy with hope, jumped up onto the planks and rushed over to join them. The slanting sun was shining on the shoulders of their old padded jackets.

"How much?"

"Worse than last year. Only five dollars," replied somebody in the crowd.

"Eh?" Three or four more men saw their hopes burst like so many bubbles.

But the rice had to be sold, and, as fate would have it, it had to be sold right there to the Wan Sheng shop. The shop had the dollars and the men with the rice had none. The argument lengthened into disputes over the quality of the rice and the fullness of the bushels. Gradually the laden boats were emptied and rose in the water. The scum and the rubbish between the boats slid from view. The men carried their rice into the shop and were given bank notes in return.

"Give us silver dollars, will you? Yuan Shih-kai dollars too—" was this a new trick, these colored papers? They looked suspiciously at the shopkeeper.

"Village bumpkins!" said that gentleman contemptuously, fingering his brush and his abacus. He looked up at them over the rims of his glasses. "One dollar bank note equals one dollar silver. Not a copper less," he said. "We've only got notes here, no silver."

"Then give us Bank of China notes," said one peasant, who could not find the familiar design of the Bank of China on the notes he received.

"Stop being a nuisance! These are Central Bank notes. You refuse to accept them. Do you want to taste the kindness of the law?"

None of them knew why the law should have anything to do with it. But nobody dared ask any more questions. They looked dubiously at the figures on the notes and, with questioning glances at each other they pocketed them in their ragged jackets or tucked them into little pouches hanging from waist bands. They left, murmuring discontentedly. By this time another group of open boats had come up to the landing and the men were jostling and joking over the lines and brushing past them into the shop. The same scene was repeated. The joyous thrill they had known looking at their rich and heavy paddies ever since autumn was dissipated in anger and confusion. But they also, and those who followed, reluctantly poured their rice into the granary of the shop and went off in the end with their notes instead of clinking silver dollars.

The street with its open shops pulsed with the life of harvest time. Back in their fields and on the way downstream the villagers had, with great anticipation, checked off one by one the things they were going to buy on this street. Soap had given out, and they would buy more. They would also stock up on boxes of matches. And oil. They had always lost heavily buying oil from itinerant dealers at ten coppers a spoonful. They figured that if several families could get together and buy a whole tin that would save a great deal. And the women remembered longingly the gaudy cloth in the shops which they heard cost only eight and a half cents a foot. So they clamored to come to town with their men when the rice was loaded on the boats, figuring so much for Ah Ta, so much for Ah Erh and so much for themselves. Some of them dreamed of the shining foreign hand mirrors or of a white towel or of a delicately knitted baby's cap made of real wool. Blessings from Heaven, they had harvested three to five bushels more to every *mow* of their land! Who would blame them for loosening the purse strings a little? If everything went well they would be able to pay rent, debts, and taxes. And maybe there would still be money left after that. Thinking thus, some even planned with a new thrill of expectation to buy a Thermos bottle, a wonderful contraption with which they could keep water hot without a fire. What an improvement on the warmer made of rice stalks and reeds which they used around their teapots! As different as Heaven must be from earth!

But now, like men leaving a gambling house where luck has been steadily against them, the villagers grumbled as they left the Wan Sheng Rice Shop. Lost again. How much they had lost they had no idea. They would not be able to keep for themselves even one or a half or a tenth of one of these bank notes! More—somewhere, somehow they would have to find more to pay what they owed, and other people would dictate how much that came to. But they stood irresolutely on the narrow street. What was lost was lost. They were here in town now. Would it matter so much if they added a little to their burden by making the most necessary

of their contemplated purchases? Almost all of them decided
that there was no use in just getting back into their boats
and rowing away. Instead they walked down the street past
the shops, their short shadows trailing behind them. The
street now took on a lively aspect.

In groups of threes and fives they straggled along the narrow street, going over again and again the money they had
received and cursing the heartless rice merchants. Holding
their children's hands and with baskets on their arms the
women peered into the shops with interest and curiosity.
The children were hypnotized by the foreign dolls, tigers,
dogs, and brightly colored bells and gongs and trumpets of
tin. They dawdled and refused to leave when their mothers
pulled them away.

"Get one for little brother!" wheedled the storekeeper. "Get
a little foreign drum or a horn. What fun! Look!" and he
struck the drum—tung-tung-tung—and he blew on the
horn—pa-pa-pa. . . .

"Tong-tong-tong—this enameled basin of highest quality.
Really cheap at forty cents. Take one home, neighbors!"

"Wei! Wei! Neighbors, here are all kinds of flowered cloth.
Eight and a half cents a foot with a few inches thrown in to
boot! Take some? Buy some to take back?"

The shopkeepers vied for their trade and often they stepped
out into the street and grabbed a "neighbor" by his torn cotton sleeve and tried to drag him inside. Everybody knew this
was one of the rare events of the year—when farmers appeared with money in their pockets! After much indecision
and calculation, what to buy, what not to buy, the notes
were handed over, one by one, to the eager salesmen.
Matches and soap were bought in small quantities. The tin
of oil proved a bit too steep. They would have to go on buying it spoonful by spoonful. If they had planned for two
shirts, they bought cloth for one. If mother and child were

both to get something, the child's was bought and the mother went without. The foreign mirror was handled and looked into, but finally put back with a last, yearning look. The knitted woolen cap was fitted on baby's head but father said no and it was handed back. Nobody dared even ask the price of the Thermos bottle. It would probably cost a whole dollar or dollar and a half. If they bought one, the older folks would frown and scold:

"All that money for such idle things in these times! You'll never know a better life, that's sure! When we were young, did we ever have anything like that?"

But some of the women found it harder to resist their children than to listen to their elders. And they bought small, cheap baby dolls. The dolls' arms and legs could be moved, and they could be made to sit or stand or to raise their hands. Not only did the other children pop their eyes with envy; some of the older people too looked on and even played with pleasure gleaming in their eyes.

The last money they dared spend went for some wine and some cooked meat. With their bundles they went back to their boats, still tied up at the Wan Sheng Rice Shop landing. Taking some salted vegetables and bean curd soup they had brought in bowls, the men sat down in the forward part of the boat to drink the wine and the women busied themselves in the stern with the cooking. Columns of smoke rose from their stoves, one after another, and the breeze blew it into their faces, making their eyes smart. The children tumbled into the empty holds of the boats or picked away in the trash that flowed past, looking for anything they could play with. Only the children were filled with happiness. Among the men, the unaccustomed wine had loosened tongues. Whether they were neighbors or not, here they were at the same place, drinking the same wine and sharing the same troubles. One of them would speak and flourish his bowl of wine in his hand. Somebody would answer, slapping down his chopsticks. When they agreed they shouted "Sure!" When they spoke of their troubles they swore. Bitterness was high in them. They needed outlets.

"Five dollars! The devil's on us!"

"Last year we lost out because of the bad harvest owing to the flood. This year we've had a good harvest and we've lost out again!"

"Lost more this year than last. We got seven and a half last year, don't forget."

"Had to sell the rice kept for ourselves again. Can't even eat our own rice!"

"The devil, what did you sell for? I'm going to hold mine for my wife and family. I'm just not going to pay my rent. I'd rather be put in jail!"

"That's the only way, stop paying rent! Rent means more debts. What do we get by borrowing and paying four or five percent interest a month? Just to have more of a debt to pay off next year?"

"What's the use in working the land?"

"Give up the land and run away like refugees from a famine—that sounds good!"

"Run away from debts and payments. It's a good plan. Let's all go together!"

"Let somebody lead and we'll all take orders from him!"

"Let's go to work in Shanghai. I've heard it's not so bad there. They say in the factories you get fifteen dollars a month! That's worth three bushels of rice according to today's prices! Didn't Little Wang from our village go down to Shanghai?"

"What do you think you're yapping about? Many of the factories have closed down since the fighting with the Japanese. Don't you know Little Wang is a beggar down there now?"

Almost everyone had to have his say and then all fell silent. Little Wang was a beggar now. The sun and the wine deepened the red in their faces until they seemed bloated.

"Whom do we work for anyway, when we work on the land year after year?" somebody finally asked gloomily, sipping some wine.

His neighbor pointed to the shore and the worn gilded characters swayed on the sign over the Wan Sheng Rice Shop.

"Those are the people we work for. We suffer all kinds of hardship, we get ourselves into debt, and finally we produce our rice. Then they—with a silent movement of their lips— just enough to say 'five dollars'—they take it all away from us."

"Wouldn't it be good if we could fix the price ourselves? Eight dollars a bushel. That's all, eight dollars, all I'd ask, honestly, I would not ask for more."

"What are you doing, spinning dreams? Didn't you hear him say he used capital to open the shop and that they wouldn't work for us without a profit?"

"But we've spent money on our land too. Why should we work for them without making any profit? And why should we work for the landlords the same way?"

"When I was up in the granary there," he pointed to the shop and lowered his voice, his bloodshot eyes casting sidelong glances toward shore, "I said to myself—well, let them have the upper hand, taking our rice now. When we have nothing to eat later on, we'll know where to find some."

"If we really had nothing to eat, it wouldn't be a crime, would it, to take some where we could find it?" Everybody agreed in strong voices.

"Didn't they attack the rice stores at Fung Chiao last spring?"

"The soldiers opened fire and killed two men."

345

"Any of us here now might be fired on some day, who knows?"

Nothing came of their aimless talk. When they were done with the wine and the food they took up their oars and pulled away homeward, leaving a gentle wake behind, the dirty, black-green water washing up against the planks of the Wan Sheng Rice Shop landing after they left. More came after them and left the same way in this town and in towns and cities throughout the district. There was nothing at all unusual.

In the cities "Cheap rice is ruining the peasant" became a favorite headline for newspaper editorials. Landlords anticipated tough measures would be needed to collect rents, so they met and issued joint statements to this effect: Good harvest meant surplus rice and falling prices. Farmers would soon experience the pinch and require outside help. Pompous financiers, who would not miss the opportunity to do business in any case, announced plans to "bring relief" to the peasants: (1) Banks and money changers should mobilize capital to buy up rice for stocking up at suitable depots. The following spring, when demand became high, supply of rice would be gradually released to the market so as to insure a stable price. (2) Promote the use of grain as security against payments, thus preventing rice merchants from buying up too much rice for hoarding. (3) Financial circles should raise subscriptions to buy rice for storage, calculating profit or loss after sales were completed. Factory owners made no comment. Lower rice prices brought benefits by cutting the cost of food allowances. Social scientists busily published articles on the subject, saying that neither fact or theory could support the ridiculous argument on a grain surplus. But then, one could hardly say that "cheap rice prices ruin the peasant" either, since without that the peasant suffered just the same under the double yoke of imperialism and feudalism.

These were all speculations in the cities; those who lived in the countryside knew nothing. Some of the farmers sold the last of their own rice or their beloved oxen, or raised new loans at four or five percent a month. Some of them offered themselves to the district prison as prisoners, lamenting the twenty or thirty cents food cost they must hand over each day. Some of them gambled away what money they had left in hopes of winning enough to pay part of their debts. Some begged middlemen to approach the landlords for them and plead for rent reductions. Or else they gave up their land and became half-naked beggars along the roadsides. A few stole arms from the militia and ran away. And still others slipped into fourth class cars on the train bound for Shanghai.

WANG T'UNG-CHAO

Fifty Dollars

He made off, away from the crowd in the field, and walked
slowly along the ditch lined with poplars. The early July afternoon sun burned fiercely down upon his head. Perspiration streamed down his face. An old towel was slung over his
left shoulder and soon was wringing wet, but he did not use
it to dry himself. Actually, he felt no heat outside of him. It
was inside that he felt a blazing ball of fire scorching his
heart so that he could scarcely breathe.

Lao P'u was an honest man of about sixty who had always
been content with his lot and obedient to his betters. He
used to argue with his neighbors over the prospects of the
wheat harvest or about the number of eggs a hen could lay
in a week, but he was almost mute before men in long
gowns. His respectful docility often won their praise.

"He knows his place, he is respectful, sharp as nails. . . .
He's certainly an experienced old servant!" his masters used
to say. But Lao P'u had suffered an indistinct shock at the
meeting he had just left. He walked along, slowly turning
the matter over in his mind and examining it on all sides,
but he saw no way through it.

Fifty Dollars

"Well, well, Lao P'u, where are you coming from? Look how you're sweating!"

At the end of the ditch across an old half-ruined stone bridge came a young man with a bright face under an old torn straw hat. He wore a white cotton jacket, coarse blue trousers cut at the knee, and he was barefoot. Lao P'u looked up on hearing his cheerful greeting.

"Ai-ya. . . . I'm coming from Hsiao Mou's field. They're holding a meeting there. It's about guns."

"About guns? We're not bandits. What do we need guns for?" asked the youth with a smirk.

"Second Brother Wu Teh, don't be a fool. You're always around and you know what's happening. It's a bad business. What are we going to do? The *tuan chang** said that it was ordered by the magistrate personally when he came to town two days ago. The organization of the landholding unions is to be strictly observed this summer. Everyone who has five *mow* of land is going to have to buy a gun, local make muzzle-loader."

Lao P'u stood under a tree frowning. Wu Teh pulled a large rush leaf fan out from under his belt and waved it before him with a flourish. His dark face relaxed and he smiled.

"Sure, the union is for self-protection. You can't protect anything without guns. Good idea! But I guess nobody likes to pay out money unless they absolutely have to!"

"Say, Second Brother, how much does a local-made gun cost?"

"Little workshops with furnaces have already been set up on several farms and they sure have a good eye with them! I've tried them several times and they're almost as good as

*For the organization of the landholders, villages around each town were grouped into *tuan*, or divisions. The *tuan chang* was the division head.

the Hanyang Arsenal . . . straight aim and everything. I
hear they're fifty dollars apiece, isn't that right?"

"Yes, I think so," Lao P'u replied with a worried nod.
"They've fixed up a furnace at San Kuan Temple in town
and three smiths are working there. Fifty dollars a rifle with
some ammunition thrown in. I suppose you're right, it's a
good thing—but still poor people like us have to buy one
too. You see. . . ."

"My good old Mr. P'u! Don't talk about me! I'm not on
equal footing with you. You have land of your own, so you
can pay out fifty dollars for a gun. Anything wrong with
that? Otherwise why didn't the *tuan chang* call me too to the
meeting?" Wu Teh smiled half-maliciously, half-enviously.
He broke up a line of ants on the willow leaves with his fan,
appearing to be quite indifferent to Lao P'u's troubles.

"Hai, hai! There's no justice now! You say I've got five
mow? Well! I've got two and a half *mow* of my own and two
mow more belonging to somebody else and I've pledged the
deed on my own land for the additional two *mow* into the
bargain. Does that help me? Where am I going to get fifty
dollars from? This spring we had a hailstorm, and now I've
got to worry about the autumn tax. Who got them down on
me I don't know, but there I am down on the list for the
cost of a gun to be paid, in ten day's time. Pay out the money and get the gun! Nothing more to it! Can the district
magistrate be disobeyed? Is such a thing possible?"

Lao P'u spoke anxiously and pleadingly. He hoped Wu
Teh would have some sympathetic reply to make, something
that would help him calm down.

"Sure, Mr. P'u, don't I know? You must have gold shining
in your home and your neighbors have lamps to search it
out. In my case, even if I wanted a gun, I couldn't get one.
But you, all these years you've had good harvests and you
worked for rich families. Everybody knows that! And there's

no spendthrift in your home. They must have investigated first!"

Second Brother Wu broke off a green leaf with his fan. It fluttered to the ground, and he stepped on it in the hot dirt with his bare foot. Lao P'u only then remembered to take the towel from his shoulder, and he wiped off his sweat. He felt a little dizzy and looked dully in front of him as he mopped his face and neck.

"Being obedient is better than being short with them! I know they're being strict about it. They've got four people down at the bureau in town now and it's said that if they don't come around, they'll be made a public show by parading them through the streets. Anyway, you'll have a gun for self-defense! If I had fifty dollars, I'd surely get a gun just for fun. But I have no home to protect. Take the long view, Mr. P'u. Aren't you afraid of the bandits?"

"What could I lose even if they do break into my home?" The beads of sweat rolled along Lao P'u's jaw and dropped onto his chest.

"What could you lose? Say, if I were a bandit, I'd certainly put you down on the list. Who cares about rich or poor? It means some money if only you can get at somebody! Do you think they only go for rich men like before?" Lao P'u looked suspiciously at Wu Teh. He was a rascal and a ne'er-do-well, but words like these could not be disputed. He had enough to worry about over the fifty dollars. Suppose the bandits did not think like this rascal did and put him down on their list too? What would he do then? More fuel on the fire eating at his heart.

"Why worry? In this world you're lucky enough to be able to live from day to day. What do you want to do? Save enough so that your two sons can become millionaires . . . ?"

Wu Teh put the fan back into his belt and walked eastward away along the ditch, with light easy steps. Lao P'u turned to watch him go. He lacked the courage to call him back to continue their talk. His feet seemed to be rooted to the ground. His breath came hard, and he kept stretching his neck with a sharp movement of the chin. The sharp face of the *tuan chang* was before him again. They all knew each other in town, and this one wasn't even his own equal, thought Lao P'u angrily. Everybody knew he was only the idle son of a once prosperous old family. His chief talents were carrying his bird cage around to the teahouses, drinking tea with big leaves, and looking over the shoulders of the cardplayers. Who didn't know about it? Then he became *tuan chang*, and he forthwith assumed new dignity as an official! He was even more severe than the district magistrate who used to come around to the village sometimes to inspect dead bodies. Now the *tuan chang* spoke the word of law in the fields.

"Fifty dollars in ten days' time. If this isn't paid in and I must do my duty, don't say I'm acting in an unneighborly fashion! Public affairs must be dealt with in an official way. I can take no other responsibility. . . ." He slashed the air with his arms as he spoke like an executioner beheading his victims. Lao P'u became immersed in his mental rehearsal of what had passed in the field. For the moment, his anxiety over the fifty dollars and the bandits receded, and his eyes remained absently fixed on the western sky where the sun was dropping and shedding a blood-red shower on a huge jagged cloud high in the heavens. Continuing on the way to his home, one and a half *li* out of the town, Lao P'u kept looking anxiously across at the red cloud, wondering fearfully if it weren't an evil omen. The sun seemed like an enormous projection of the ball of fire beating against his heart.

Lao P'u lived outside the town, not in a village but on the

border of a grove which had formerly been the burial ground of one of the bigger families in town. Lao P'u's father had promised that he and his descendants would look after the tombs if they permitted him to build his house on their grounds. Three generations of them had lived there now, but during that time the town family had gone to ruin and the grove had been thrown open as a cemetery for others as well. Inroads had been made on the trees, and there now remained only a few scraggly cedars and one or two poplar trees which had been planted later. Many of the older graves had disappeared into the surrounding earth. The tombstones were broken, and grass and weeds overgrew everything. Lao P'u was still supposed to be the caretaker, but there were no valuable trees left for him to look after and there was nobody left to care for the rest of it.

His house was made of mud with a roof of thatched straw. A crude fence closed in a good-sized yard entered through a gate fashioned of broken boards. Just inside was the grain stack and beyond was the hay used as fuel. During the summer and autumn evenings Lao P'u and his family would gather, seated around the big flat stone in the middle of the yard, and talk over the day's doings. Sometimes they would just sit and smoke and listen to the rustle of the old cedars and poplars back of them. People in town always used to say there were ghosts in the grove and advised him to leave, but Lao P'u paid no attention to them. He had too great an affection for this bit of land which had cost him nothing. He had no place to go and, even if he had, there was no way of taking his house with him. Lao P'u refused to recognize the presence of the spirits of the dead. His children, who used to clamber up and around the grave mounds, knew no fear of them.

This evening when Lao P'u got home, he had no stomach for supper. He sat silently and watched the others with a vacant expression on his face. His eldest son knew him well and readily guessed something wrong in the wind when he saw his father's frown and heard his oft-repeated sighs. He saw no use in asking about the meeting. If there was to be any trouble, he would wait for the old man to speak. But after two bowls of millet, his second son grew impatient.

"What's the matter, father? What's it all about anyway? There's always something new to plague us!"

Tapping his pipe against the leg of his stool, Lao P'u shook his head.

"What can they want now out of a poor family like ours?" persisted the younger one. "There's no army passing through town now."

"Hsiao Chu," said Lao P'u slowly, looking at the broad bare shoulders of his sons, pale in the light of a sickly moon, "You're still young. Your brother knows more than you do. You're too blunt and too forward. That's no way to be. You'll get into trouble. You know that your grandfather and I worked our whole lives—two lifetimes now—and I can continue because I've taught myself to obey others. Does it occur to you that if anything had ever gone wrong, we wouldn't be here now?" Lao P'u grasped at the chance to lecture his son. It put off having to talk about the meeting, the fifty dollars, and the gun.

"Me? Blunt? Why I've never touched anybody or said anything to anybody. I just do my work on the land and gather dry grass, and that's all." Hsiao Chu was indignant. He was a tall broad youth of twenty. Unlike his brother, who had acquired his father's capacity for docile obedience, Hsiao Chu was vigorous, assertive, and ready to help people who were in trouble.

"Well, don't go on thinking everything will be all right working on the land and picking grass. With things the way they are now, nothing can be done, absolutely nothing. I've lived this long and I can speak for myself. But who knows what's coming afterward. You, Hsiao Chu, what's going to come of you? I'm worried, worried. . . ."

Both sons stared at their father. This unprecedented outburst frightened them and made them uneasy. The elder, whose name was P'u Kuei, knew of little beyond the boundaries of their little field and the work that had to be done on it year in and year out. He rarely ever went into town. Since Lao P'u worked most of the time as a servant for some big family, practically all the work on their land fell on the shoulders of the elder son, who was much like his father and was now nearing forty years of age. Hsiao Chu had gone to a primary school until he was past ten, but after that they had no more money to pay for his schooling, and besides they needed him at home. Since he was sixteen, his life had followed the pattern set by his elder brother. But he remained strong-spirited. He had acquired some knowledge of the world about him, and, although he lived exactly like his father and brother, he could see beyond them. He had no use for their cowardly docility and always spoke his mind forthrightly. Lao P'u often secretly quaked with worry for his future. He deeply regretted ever having permitted him to spend four years studying "foreign books."

His deep anxiety for his son made Lao P'u, who had been accustomed to the life of a slave, rule him with a rigid hand. He was never allowed to have dealings with any people outside the family. Hsiao Chu liked to talk—and that was the whole trouble. Lao P'u had served masters of official rank for two generations, and he had learned perfectly well that most troubles started through talking. Life now was not the same as it used to be. There was often forced labor for the soldiers and there were bandit attacks. These could easily smash your home and bring an end to your family. The officials in town were far more powerful even than the militia head in the days of the Lien rebels,* and the young men in the villages with their guns were hard to deal with. Hsiao Chu was direct in his manner and always ready to enter an argument. Lao P'u's fear for his future had been heightened by the events of the day.

Hsiao Chu sat in the shadows of a tree, out of the light of the moon. He tapped his foot with annoyance on a bulging root.

"Worry, worry, only for me! Three years ago I wanted to go off to the Northeast but you wouldn't let me!"

"Hsiao Chu—" broke in P'u Kuei, who feared his father would grow angry. But he stopped short. Hsiao Chu turned to him a moment in silence, then went on:

"How good you are, Brother P'u Kuei, your quiet honesty has won the applause of all our neighbors as well as father. But I! I'm not a thief or a bandit, yet all the worrying around here is done for me! What I have to say, nobody wants to hear. What would be more welcome—to bow my head, lower my voice everywhere, and stuff my mouth with 'your honors' and 'your excellencies'? I haven't got that kind of mouth. Is it my fault I can't do that?"

Hsiao Chu's voice rose to a high pitch of impatience and discontent. Ordinarily Lao Pu would have reproached his younger son by tapping his knees and pointing out the error of his ways. But this time, he sat silently drawing on his pipe, the sparks in the bowl glimmering in the darkness after Hsiao Chu had finished.

The women of the family were sitting in a group over by the door of the central room of the house. There were Hsiao Chu's sister-in-law, his twenty-year-old sister, and his little niece. Together with the three-year-old nephew already

*Reference is to a post-Taiping peasant uprising in the northwest.

asleep on the *k'ang* inside, they made up the rest of the household.

"Listen, Second Uncle," said the sister-in-law. She was a clever and hard-working woman who had taken care of the household since the death of Mrs. Lao P'u some years before. "Listen," she said, "Isn't it a good thing that father thinks about you and worries for you? He wouldn't have said anything if it were your useless brother. But you, Second Uncle, you read and write. In the future we'll all be depending upon you. Father has worked his whole lifetime now, but you're young. Things are different now and Father only wants you to get more experience. He's lived long and he means you no ill!"

"Chen's mother, you're clear and right," Lao P'u nodded his head vigorously. "I always say I have an excellent daughter-in-law. Certainly, Hsiao Chu, do you think I'm talking only for the sake of calling you down and picking on you? Everything is upside down. You think I can't see things straight. I know young people like you despise a useless old fellow like me. Well, I've eaten bean cakes for tens of years more than you have. You think you want to go to the Northeast. Look, I'm so old, and still I have to work for people in town, and there'd be only your sister-in-law and your brother home. We've lived on farming for generations. Do you suppose that after two or three years, you'd be coming back bursting with gold? Not so easy! Don't take things so lightly as all that! You know as well as I do how expensive labor is. In the busy season even a short-term hand will cost us about a dollar. What would we do if you went to the Northeast? I haven't got any money. Well, go on with you, act as you please . . . act as you please. . . !"

Lao P'u beat his pipe against a stone at his feet. Hsiao Chu looked up at the cloud-hidden moon in stubborn silence. P'u

Kuei said nothing. A sudden breeze whistled softly through the tops of the cedars. It was cool and pleasant.

"I'm not out for trouble just to please myself, Hsiao Chu," the old man went on. "You must understand. I'm so worried I couldn't even eat tonight. You, you youngster, you jump at me before I can even begin to talk. You're ready to quarrel before you know what it's all about. What's the use of my worrying about it?"

The wife of P'u Kuei filled a jar with rice gruel from a large kettle and placed it with three bowls out in the yard. She filled one for Lao P'u.

"You're right, father," she said. "Don't bother so much with brother over here. Tell us what you heard in town."

"Ai! Everything would be all right if we could find fifty dollars," replied Lao P'u wearily.

"Fifty dollars! Can anybody ask us for fifty dollars? Are we listed by the bandits?" Hsiao Chu's sister-in-law leaned against a small tree, her mouth open with amazement.

"That's the new rule. The *tuan* has given us only ten days. Even stricter than the tax collections."

Lao P'u slowly unfolded the events at that afternoon's meeting in Hsiao Mou's field. He told them how the group of villages dependent on the town had been divided into divisions under the landholders' association and how they were now under Mr. Leng's *tuan*. When he finished, he stuffed some tobacco into his pipe and lighted it as if he hoped to consume his sorrow in its ashes.

"This is an outrage!" cried Hsiao Chu. "Whom are you going to talk reason to? Never mind the size of our land and the money—but about this gun! You say I can't think straight, father. Look here, we live by this grove. If the bandits come, can we fight back with a single gun? We'd simply be planting it here for them to take—" His voice rose to a shout.

Fifty Dollars

"Not so loud, not so loud, somebody may be near . . ."
from the ever-cautious P'u Kuei.

Lao P'u was unable to deny the justice of Hsiao Chu's outburst. He had not been thinking of this angle of the matter
at all. All he was concerned with was the fear of being made
a public show of in the streets if he failed to get the fifty
dollars within ten days. But the boy was right. Through all
the years of his life by the cemetery grove, all had been
peacefully quiet. Even during the last few years, with more
bandits than there had ever been, they were never touched.
Lao P'u had never had to seek refuge or defense. Everybody
knew that he had but two *mow* of land and that the deed to
them was pledged for the additional two and a half *mow*
which he rented. But now if they had a gun, wouldn't it be
like asking for trouble? Not because of money, maybe, but
because of the gun. A bandit values one gun more than he
does ten human beings. The fifty dollars would be like a
sign up on his fence inviting the bandits to come in. This
was a damnable thing! Lao P'u remembered Mr. Leng's final words at the meeting.

"Everyone who receives a gun must put his seal in town to
a promise that nobody else will receive the gun as a gift or
be permitted to use it. Whenever the association calls, you
must come out with your gun. Be careful, because if you lose
the gun, it will be the same as betraying us to the bandits.
Even if it is not intentional, it will arouse certain suspicion."
Mr. Leng spoke these words at the end. Everybody in the
crowd was somewhat preoccupied with the new money problem just laid before them. They were too worried about getting the money to listen to the rules for keeping the gun.
But Lao P'u remembered it all now. He nervously filled his
pipe, lighted it, refilled, and smoked some more. He made
no reply to his son.

"You've worked so long in town and you know so many

people there, father, can't you beg off somehow?" asked the
wife of P'u Kuei. "Plead with Mr. Leng or, better still, the
head of the association himself. Suppose we pay eight or ten
dollars to get free of having to buy the gun. Can that be
done?"

"Ai, I did think of that," replied Lao P'u, "I'm old now
and I have some standing in town. People see that I'm old
and honest and it's easy for me to talk. But I've already
tried this."

"You asked the association head?"

"Who else? He's a generation younger than my master, he's
young and easy to talk to. In fact, I watched him grow right
from his amah's breast. I went right to him . . . but what
he said was reasonable too."

Hsiao Chu, who had been thinking along a far different
line, asked suddenly, "What did he say?"

"He's the head of the association. The order for the guns
was referred to the division heads. Since the magistrate was
being so strict about it, nobody dared give any favors to his
own friends. That's what he said."

"Hm . . . he's not responsible. But let them show us our
five *mow* of land. If they can, we'll buy the gun according to
the regulations."

"I said that. I told that to the division head. He said that
he had made a clear investigation and that everybody said
that things had been well with us these years. So even if we
didn't have that much land, we would still have to get a
gun."

There were no more tobacco leaves left in the torn blue
cloth pouch, but Lao P'u kept digging his pipe down into
the bottom of it, scraping for leaves where there were none.

"Why are they so hard and unreasonable on old neighbors
like us?" sighed P'u Kuei's wife. Her husband echoed her
sigh from the flat rock upon which he sat.

"Nobody could manage better. It's not only us. Anybody who doesn't obey the rule will suffer for it. They've already got several in prison in town. What I can't figure out is who was hardhearted enough to put us down on the list. I've always been careful. I've never bragged in town, yet this is what I get. If it were you, Hsiao Chu, with your blunt speech, we would have had trouble long ago!"

"Then I guess we've got to borrow the money," said the woman finally. "Don't keep nagging Brother any more. He's also feeling bad about it."

She was going to say more but Hsiao Chu stood up with a sudden movement.

"We've got to get it? Well, let's pawn our land and stop eating and get it! What's the use of begging around? Who can't shoot a gun? Let me have it when we get one. It'll be fun to be sent out to shoot people! Rich or poor, what's the odds? What do you think, father?"

"—And the money?" asked P'u Kuei feebly. Hsiao Chu turned on him with a sneer but said nothing.

The moon was covered now with a broad sweep of black clouds, and the breeze had been whipped up into a wind that brushed swiftly overhead. The night gave promise of rain. It was pitch black. Lao P'u beat his pipe against the gravel in the yard. Soon all was silent.

And so, a month afterward, Lao P'u borrowed the fifty dollars and brought home a locally made rifle.

After the organization of the landholders' association, there were many guns on hand, and the people were divided into watches to stand guard by turn. The leaders received frequent praise from the magistrate, and since there had been no disturbances of any kind during the month, everybody was quite pleased. On the Autumn Festival there was a great feast and everyone drank heavily of wine. After that, there was gambling the whole night through and singsong girls to entertain. All the members of the militia were rewarded with wine and food, and everyone was satisfied. Several nights later, one of the lesser leaders invited the union head and the division head to his house to continue the day's merrymaking. The place was only a few steps away from the house in which Lao P'u worked. There was a great movement of men and much noise. Such excitement had never been seen before in their street. The women stood outside their houses and passed envious comments on the appearance of the leaders and their militia followers. The children ran after them in crowds and even the dogs darted around excitedly. Lao P'u remained in town that night so he saw all that happened.

Two turns down from the street was the watchtower where there was supposed to be a permanent guard. The bodyguards of the leaders, who were left out in the lane while their masters made merry, went to the tower to pass the time drinking tea and gambling. From the house came the sound of several instruments and the hum and laughter of the feasting and singing. The door was wide open and the men in the tower could hear.

It was already after ten when Lao P'u went to the little room he lived in as a servant and prepared to go to sleep. But after he had blown out his lamp and lain down, no sleep came to him. Ever since mid-July he had suffered from sleeplessness. It was an affliction he had never known before. He felt his age coming upon him and an abiding sense of disquiet. Because of his standing, he had been able to borrow the fifty dollars without interest, but it had to be paid back by the end of the month. The harvest was not a good one, and it was still doubtful whether they would be able to pay their taxes when all their expenses had been paid. His elder son and daughter-in-law had toiled day and night, yet what seemed to be the use of it? Where would he get the money to pay the tax and his debt? Meanwhile Hsiao Chu had learned how to handle the rifle, and this added to Lao P'u's fears. Turning these matters over and over in his mind in recent weeks had made it impossible for him to sleep. His graying hair turned perceptibly whiter every day.

The moonlight came in through the torn paper window and made it more difficult for him to sleep. Through the few thin walls that separated him from the house of the merry-makers came the noise and the clatter and the chatter of the many guests. Lao P'u unbuttoned his jacket and felt his old bones. He looked down on the dirt floor, and a sudden dizziness almost caused him to fall off the *k'ang* to the ground. He pulled himself back and tried to calm his nerves. He had just stretched out on his back when the splutter of rifle fire coming from a southerly direction brought him bolt upright. Dogs barked loudly outside and there was shouting and the noise of men running through the street. Lao P'u jumped from bed and ran out the door.

"To the watchtower! To the watchtower! It's coming from the south!" shouted some militiamen on the street. People came tumbling from their houses into the streets to find out what was happening. At the tower some of the more hardy clambered up to the top and peered into the night to see if they could discover what was up. The more fearful remained below and shouted up questions or waited for information. It was clear now that the firing was directly south. It was not a continuous stream any longer but cracks of rifle fire every few minutes. The listeners could vaguely hear shouting. The people in the streets replaced fear with curiosity as soon as they realized that there were no bandits this side of the tower and that everybody was up and out and prepared to repel any attack.

Only Lao P'u's heart burst with fear as he rushed to the

tower and stood watching from the upper wall under which
crouched several militiamen. The moon cast a pale white
light over the field and the scrubby trees beyond the town.
But a thin, sheetlike cloud crossed the moon's face, and
nothing emerged in distinct lines from the scene which
spread itself before his anxious eyes. Dogs barked. Over to
the south and a little west a burst of flame severed the blue-
black blur. It blazed upward in long licks. The crack of fire-
arms continued. There were spluttering volleys punctuated
by replying shots which seemed to come right out of the fire.
From the wild shouting, it seemed that the attackers were
present in considerable strength. Lao P'u stretched out over
the wall, straining his eyes. Right there! There where the
fire roared was his home and the cemetery grove! He almost
fell over the wall.

One of the crouching militiamen pulled him down by the
leg.

"Hey, old uncle! Get down! Bullets have no eyes!"

"But that's my—"

"Your home? You're right, it is. I saw it when the shots
first started!"

Lao P'u looked about him like a madman.

"Help! Oh, help! Honorable brothers, there are two children there! Save them! Oh heaven! . . ."

"Shut up!" snarled the militiaman, pulling him down from
the wall. "Quit your screaming. Do you want them to start
firing over here?"

"Guns, the guns! Look, you're just watching it like a show!
Shoot at them! Shoot and drive them off! Drive them off!!"
screamed Lao P'u.

"Impossible, Uncle P'u. You hurry over to the association
head and we'll wait here for orders. We don't know how
many they've got there or anything. You go find somebody
who can make a decision. Are they still there feasting?"

Fifty Dollars

The distraught old man found new life in this suggestion. All his strength flowed back into his legs, and he rushed down to ground level and off to find the leaders. Before he reached the house, he met a group of them, all carrying arms. Lao P'u danced around them, begging them to hurry, to give orders to fire on the bandits, to drive them off and save his home. They climbed up the tower, Lao P'u at their heels. They surveyed the scene and everyone agreed the fight was taking place around the P'u home. The fire and the sparks were certainly shooting into the sky from the old cedar and poplar grove. Somebody suggested that ten men be sent out to the rescue. But one of the leaders objected:

"It's almost midnight now. Do you know how many they have there? Wouldn't it be a trick just to get the tiger off the mountain?"*

"If they were ready to attack so boldly, they must be watching the road," said another hesitantly. The rest of the men stood around listening, their eyes wide with fear. Lao P'u got down on his knees in front of the little knot of leaders.

"Sirs! Brothers! Save us! Think of my two children! What's the use of an old bag of bones like me?" He dropped flat on the stone and sobbed tearlessly.

"Can't be done! This is no time for sentiment. Can you be sure that the bandits won't rush in on us when we open up the gate? Are you going to play around with the lives and guns of everyone in town? Save you! You must have lost your senses. Who's going to take the responsibility? Go and look for the association head. He's still down at the house. See what he says."

"Let us go together quickly, this is no joke," said Mr. Leng.

"Please . . . please, sirs . . . when Mr. Leng organized the

---

*That is, to lure the militia away.

association, didn't he say when there's trouble outside, help
each other? I bought a gun and I've got it in my house!"
Fear found a new boldness in Lao P'u.

"Hurry down. Who wants to talk about rules now?" Someone pushed Lao P'u down the steep steps. The flames now
cut a deeper swath into the darkness. The guns continued
crackling and the men on the tower could plainly hear the
whistling bullets. In between they could hear the snapping of
the dry wood and hay going up in flames.

"They're finished! The P'us are finished!" Some of the militiamen showed impatience and concern. But they dared not
move or shoot. The fire was now blazing brilliantly and the
whole tower was bathed in red. By the time Lao P'u got
back with the division head, the fire was raging like a small
volcano.

"Shoot from the tower, but don't move out of it!" shouted
the puffing leader.

Glad of a chance for something to do, the militiamen started firing aimlessly at the dark splotches of shadow around
the fire. Lao P'u came up and saw his home standing like a
slack shadow in the midst of the flames. He collapsed blub-
bering to the ground. Somebody grabbed a horn and blew
the alarm call. Almost immediately the firing died down.
The bandits seemed to be retreating, fearing an actual attack. It was about one o'clock. The fire over in the grove
slowly died down.

Lao P'u awoke in the darkness not long before dawn. After
long pleading, he persuaded the men to open the gate of the
tower and let him go home. Wu Teh went with him. The
fence around his home and the gate were burned to the
ground. The ox shed was a smoldering ruin. The roof of the
house had been burned out and yawned open to the sky. In
the room lay Lao P'u's eldest son stretched flat on the
ground, his eyes and mouth opened wide and a gaping blue-

black hole just above his left temple. Hsiao Chu lay groaning on the *k'ang*. The fleshy part of his leg was shattered into a bloody pulp. The rifle lay by his side, his hand clutching the stock. The bullet bag lay on the floor next to him, empty. In the next room were the womenfolk, unwounded but unconscious with fear and exhaustion. Whimpering on the floor was Lao P'u's grandson. A bullet had grazed his little rump, but the blood had already clotted and he had cried himself into exhaustion. In the back they found the ashes of Lao P'u's haystack and his rice store.

That morning the town buzzed with excitement over the fate that had come to the household of Lao P'u. Some said that Lao P'u had always tried to appear very poor but in reality had acquired sufficient riches to lure the bandits to his home. Others thought that it might be an act of revenge, but most of the people agreed that the bandits had come for the rifle.

Lao P'u and his family had their dead and their wounded. They did not stop to wonder why the bandits came.

The association head and the young men in the militia had high praise for Hsiao Chu. With one rifle and only one hundred rounds of ammunition he had been able to stave off the attack of the bandits. Who could blame the association now? Lao P'u hadn't wanted to buy the gun, but look how useful it had been! Wouldn't they all surely have died but for that? Some of his family might have been carried away, and that would have cost Lao P'u still more money. The leaders were also gratified by the rifle's performance. It hadn't split asunder after heavy use. Their locally made product was almost as good as the rifles put out by regular factories! An informal meeting was held and a report drawn up to send the district authorities. It was also decided to grant Lao P'u some tens of dollars by way of compensation for his losses. Affairs resumed their normal course in town, and before two days had passed, people found no more to say about the incident. It became a dim memory for all but Lao P'u and his family.

The house by the cemetery grove in which Lao P'u had lived, and his father and grandfather before him, had to be given up now. Lao P'u could not afford to rebuild it, and he dared not risk another bandit attack. The old man went to the town elders and, after long, anguished begging, won permission to live in an empty shack located on a field inside the town. Within the next month, Hsiao Chu recovered from his wound. But Lao P'u's grandson grew worse. His little rump grew red and swollen and began to fester. They found that the bullet had lodged in the flesh and not just glanced by as they thought at first. It took three incisions by the village druggist to extract the lead. But it cost the child too much blood. After thirty-five days of pain, the little one followed his father in death. The wife of P'u Kuei lay ill in bed all this time, but the doctors assured Lao P'u that there would be no third death in his family. Meanwhile new debts were added to old. The medicines and treatment cost Lao P'u heavily. He mortgaged away his little plot of ground to pay off what he could.

The association had voted a grant to Lao P'u, but he never received any money. Friends urged him to go to the leaders and ask for it. "I sacrificed two lives," he would say listlessly. "Can they pay me back for them?" His anger simmered and boiled now only when his eye fell upon the rifle standing behind his door. One day, finally, with Hsiao Chu shouldering the gun beside him, he went to the *tuan chang* and asked him to take it. He wanted no money. But let them keep the gun. He had no more use for it now since they lived in town and had no more land.

"Impossible!" said the division head. "We can't set any such precedent. If everyone turns his gun in, what will be left? Our association would be finished. Even though you live in town, you're still required to be on hand with the rifle when we demand it. You old fool, if not for the gun, would Hsiao Chu still be alive? Get along!"

So Hsiao Chu shouldered the root of all their troubles once more, and they went back to the house.

The autumn lengthened toward winter. Lao P'u could work no more. Nor could he eat. He looked skyward with dimming eyes and murmured to himself. He grew deaf and only with the greatest difficulty could he hear words shouted into his ear. Hsiao Chu was idle now since their land was gone. He had been proudly congratulated for his defense of their farm, but it did him little good. Things became more and more difficult, and often they could barely scrape together a meal a day. Hsiao Chu could not stand the idleness and the bleakness of his home and his old father, and he was often away for long periods. He used to spend much time in the company of Wu Teh, who had carried him out from among the ashes and ruins of their old home by the cemetery grove. People looked on Wu Teh as a worthless rascal, but Hsiao Chu began to discover his virtues.

Early one morning when the dew was heralding the imminence of day and the streets of the town were still unpeopled and silent, somebody whistled outside. Hsiao Chu emerged soundlessly from the door of their little shack.

"Ready, Wu Teh?" There was a trepidation and uncertainty in his voice.

"You're a green youngster," whispered Wu's voice in reply. "Could anything be easier? I know them all so well that I often join them to fight just for fun. Always can use more. Here it is." He pulled a long black object out from under his torn jacket and brandished it bravely.

"Bullets, too. Get it quickly, we've got to get going."

Hsiao Chu crept back through the door and emerged in a minute with the rifle in his hands. He faltered.

"Only . . . the old man. . . ." He looked back into the shadows under the doorway.

"Can you feed him? Best to go away. When you return, they'll probably want to make you head of the militia," mocked Wu Teh. "Hurry, everything's set. We'll be caught if we hang around. I've got the rope here. Let's move, otherwise we won't make it. . . ."

Hsiao Chu walked on out into the oncoming dawn. Next day it was learned that a revolver and considerable ammunition had been stolen from the watchtower. From Lao P'u's house, the rifle, which had cost fifty dollars and brought so much grief down upon the heads of his family, was gone too. And Hsiao Chu never returned.

CHENG NUNG

On the Threshing Field

1

Gråy white dawn was just turning the cracks in the straw
wall into slivers of light when T'ai Sheng jumped suddenly
awake. Rubbing his eyes, he was out of bed and making for
the door. Was the weather changing? When he opened the
door he saw a heavy white mist which shrouded the whole
world in its moist translucency. The air was heavy with dew
that was not quite rain. As T'ai Sheng stood there peering
skyward with a farmer's eyes, it sent trickles of moisture
across his forehead and down his lean brown cheeks. In the
growing morning he saw flakes of white clouds against the
gray chasing each other lightly across the heavens. In the
farthest east he saw the clouds bend over and a long, narrow
strip of shining silver, like a man opening his mouth to
smile, and he knew that this smile was a harbinger of fair
weather. The tensed muscles of his face and his whole body
relaxed. He sighed softly and turned back into the house.

  The woman was standing listlessly in the center of the
room, lazily stretching, still dull with sleep. He stared at her.

  "Hurry up with the rice gruel," he commanded roughly.

She seemed not to hear him.

He did not bother to reply. He rolled his cloth girdle around his waist and gathered together his sickle and his carrying pole. Filling his long pipe he struck a flint, drew heavily, and then turned to her.

"Bring the gruel to the field when it's ready," he said. "We'll have to eat there. The harvesters will be on the field this afternoon. We've got to get everything in shape before then. Understand? Bring a pile of straw with you."

He went out and felt the mist swirl between his legs. An autumn breeze pregnant with moisture chilled him. Plodding along he frequently raised his eyes to the eastern horizon where the clouds had now cleared and the smile had broadened into a bright expanse of morning light. As he anxiously watched the skies opened above him, and the mist and its moisture retreated before the clearing blue. Wholly certain now of a fair day, he hastened his steps. Fields lay richly content on either side of him, thick with grain, the drooping ears sending a golden sheen along the lower layers of the rising mist. His heart swelled with gladness. Through several years of drought, flood, and pestilence they had reaped no harvest. Another failure in the autumn crop, the only crop in this region, would have meant the end of himself and all his neighbors. Hunger, beggary, death. He shuddered and wondered bitterly again to himself why he should be living in such low-lying country. Everywhere else in springtime there was tilling and sowing, but here the land was still mostly under water. They could plant only a late crop. Moreover, none of the land was his own. It was all rented from the landlords, and he and all his neighbors in their village and in all the villages of the district were condemned to chronic poverty tempered by hunger and toil. Two out of three years were hungry years. How could it be otherwise?

These late-crop fields were not like the early-crop land elsewhere, which could be rented in small pieces. Here the land-lords divided their land into broad lots, rich fields mixed with poor ones. If you wanted to rent, you had to take the bad with the good. Water buffalo, tools, seed—who could buy these for himself? Everything was leased from the land-lord. Even a good harvest, netting, say, fifty or sixty piculs of rice from thirty or forty *mow* of land, would be divided, item by item, and most of it dumped into the landlord's granary. And the last few years! He drew a long, angry breath.

"I've already worked my old black bones in these fields," he thought bitterly. "What am I going to do? The only oth-er way is to stop working the land. Who would keep on doing it anyway?" But as he thought his eye wandered over the full fields. It was a one hundred percent harvest this year. The thick golden gleam revived new hopes. Heaven is not entirely closing its doors on people, he thought, and looked eastward again where streaks of red were breaking through the silver gray. He cast his thoughts from him, and breaking into a trot he ran down to his own land. He had forty *mow*. It was very large. The landlord said it was good land. But he had worked it now for three years and never had a fair harvest. Each year he thought he would let it go. And each time he held on, bound to it by some intangible hope. They had said it was good land. "If I don't get a good harvest out of it, I'll never die peacefully," he used to think with angry determination.

Setting down his sickle and his carrying pole he walked along the narrow pathway bordering the field and looked searchingly along the rows of ripened grain. He saw—indeed he had seen it long ago—that the ears in his fields were not so smooth or abundant as on neighboring land. In some doz-en *mow* he could really count on no more than a fifty per-cent harvest. The weak stalks, wavering more like weeds in the morning breeze, compared to the heavy golden bunches drooping over the fields of his neighbors, pierced his heart sharply. The crop had evidently suffered from lack of water. But by whose fault? So broad was the field that when water had to be pumped into it day and night the strength of one water buffalo proved insufficient for the task. He had long ago asked the landlord to get another buffalo to help but he had never done so. And now his crop was the poorest of them all. Anger mounted in him.

"Damn!" he muttered. "And he blames me for laziness. He says I waste his land. Bah!" In any case he knew that even if the harvest were good, it would benefit him little. Yet a sense of loss stabbed him deeply.

He walked back to where he had left his tools. He lit his pipe and stared unseeingly in front of him, smoking. Coming slowly out of his reverie he saw the field before him, and comforting thoughts came to him afresh. It was better than before anyway. He picked up his sickle and with swift movements he knelt to work. One row after another he cut. His mind no longer functioned. Mechanically he swung back and forth, slashing through the rice stalks and leaving them cut and in disarray on the ground behind him. Once in a while he straightened his back and stretched his neck looking skyward. How long would it take to finish these six-odd *fen*?* He had no thought for time but cut on. At last he finished, and when at the end of the last row he lifted his head he saw that the sun had come up and driven away all the clouds and all the mist and hung there brilliantly shining in the eastern sky. He began to feel hungry and looked along the path leading from his home.

"What the devil's the matter? Still not coming. What's she doing?" he growled.

He squatted on the narrow path, lit his pipe again, and, to

Fen = one-tenth of a *mow*.

fill in for his impatience, he began to think of the new day's toil. But he was unable to concentrate upon it and instead grew increasingly impatient. He glanced repeatedly down the road and irritably cursed his wife's tardiness. If anything went wrong with the harvest, he began to think, the responsibility would be hers. Angrily he threw his pipe to the ground, jumped to his feet and stared unblinkingly down the road. He seemed to be trying to suck the woman out of empty space with his glare. Then he would seize her by the hair and beat her solidly for the delay.

At last she came in sight. Two huge bundles of straw bunched on either side concealed her almost entirely from sight. The straw seemed to be walking by itself along the narrow path, coming slowly toward him.

"Damn you, why don't you get a move on?" he shouted. But his anger had cooled.

She crept up to him, finally, and dropped her load of straw at his feet. He saw then that she was also carrying a covered pail of rice gruel with half a bowl of salt cabbage on top of it. How could she have walked fast, he asked himself with a quick pang. She came up to him with the food. She was breathing heavily, and large beads of sweat ran down her face. Sitting down on the edge of the path she picked up a corner of her skirt and mopped her forehead and cheeks. T'ai Sheng watched and his irritation faded from him. Remorse and sympathy replaced it, and it was in a soft, distracted way that he asked:

"Why didn't you come sooner?"

"I haven't got three hands," replied his wife calmly, taking in huge draughts of the free, open air.

T'ai Sheng was silent. He sat down and uncovered the pail.

The meal through, T'ai Sheng took a few hasty puffs at his pipe, tapped it on the ground, and without further delay set to with his sickle once more, his wife along with him. Silently the pair of them worked like machines, rising and falling, moving forward and back. The swish of their sickles on the dry stalk was the only accompaniment, a productive symphony as the golden stalks fell about them. So too had worked their fathers and grandfathers and their ancestors before them. They handled their sickles with an instinct of thoroughness bred of generations. After cutting they piled the stalks and began to set up the rough framework of a shelter and filled in the skeleton with the straw. At last it was complete, and T'ai Sheng paused for a smoke. Both of them stood panting a moment.

"I am going to bring the master down," said T'ai Sheng. "Have to borrow money from him too. We'll need it tonight. You stay here and even off the threshing field."

The owner of their land was a man named Cheng who lived about five *li* away. He was the biggest landlord in the village and owned almost all the fields around T'ai Sheng's plot. T'ai Sheng set out for his big house with trepidation. Who in the whole district was not terrified by Mr. Cheng's iron ways? This year T'ai Sheng had been reproached any number of times because his fields were too dry. Now he had to borrow money from him again. Although it was in the landlord's own interest and would be repaid almost immediately, yet it was the way of Mr. Cheng to sneer and insult anybody who came seeking help, as if Heaven had given him the right to scold anyone who came to borrow money from him, something he thought of as a sin of the poor. T'ai Sheng knew he would not escape the master's wrath.

"Master . . ." he began. His extreme discomfort drove the words back down his throat.

"Hm . . ." said Mr. Cheng.

"I've come to invite the master to come to supervise the reaping and the threshing," said T'ai Sheng at last, forcing a smile to his lips.

"Hm . . ." sniffed the master contemptuously. T'ai Sheng stood there feeling ashamed and awkward. But Mr. Cheng ordered him to sit down.

"You people seem to have forgotten all the rules. Why didn't you inform me yesterday? You know I have other land to care for and I have to engage men to watch the reaping and threshing. You know that, don't you? Do you think I can keep armies of men here waiting on your pleasure?"

"I know, I'm sorry," fumbled T'ai Sheng. "I'm singlehanded. I really couldn't find time yesterday."

"Busy? So busy as all that? Then you shouldn't have come even now!"

T'ai Sheng did not know how to answer. He trembled with anger and humiliation, but he set his teeth and said nothing. Mr. Cheng was also silent. The thought of the money he wanted to borrow had been driven from him by fear and hatred of the man before him. But how was anger to help him? The thing was to find a way to break this intolerable silence. Yet T'ai Sheng could not find a single word that seemed appropriate.

"It's nearly noon now. Have lunch here and we'll go." Mr. Cheng was now being generous. His scowl gave way to an expression that was supposed to be both benevolent and overbearing. This was what he used to tell his friends was the policy of being hard and kind at the same time. T'ai Sheng felt relieved, tried to think of something to say but could only shift uneasily. The work yet to be done on the threshing field made him feel like saying "No." But the word came up in his throat, revolved around his tongue, and retreated.

"The threshing field isn't ready," he faltered.

This unleashed a new stream on the hard side. Mr. Cheng sneered, telling T'ai Sheng that his show of industry was a sham, that he was lazy and useless, that he never had anything ready on time. He, Master Cheng, had to suffer because T'ai Sheng was lazy.

"You can't go on like this," he concluded. "That lot of land is good land. Many tenants have fought to have it. I gave it to you because you've been working on it for several years. But now it's no better than if it were fallow. Who would be willing to let the land lie fallow year after year?"

T'ai Sheng said nothing. He only wanted to finish the food and get off as quickly as possible.

"Call Mr. Fan!" shouted Mr. Cheng to a servant after a short period of silence.

Mr. Fan was a private tutor specially engaged by the land-lord. Just under thirty, he was said to be a graduate from a certain school. Besides being a teacher he was one of the lo-cal gentry. Presently he appeared and the master smiled at him.

"I'll have to ask your help again," said Mr. Cheng. "Will you oversee another harvest for me? Truly, I haven't anybody else. The work is simple and quiet. All you have to do is sit by the hut."

"Quite, quite, I understand," Mr. Fan replied quickly.

"You must start right away. The tenant is here now. You'd better take your bedding with you."

"Good, I'll go back and get ready."

When Mr. Fan had gone the master sent his servants scur-rying for the various things he had to take along, especially the seal box.* T'ai Sheng stood by, his stomach now full and his mind wholly preoccupied with the question of the loan. Every so often when Mr. Cheng seemed unoccupied he tried to bring up the subject. Every time he waited too long and something else distracted the master's attention. His hes-

---

*A device for branding lime impressions on the rice mounds.

itation and timidity apparently communicated their purpose
to the landlord, who busied himself about the courtyard and
gave T'ai Sheng no chance to speak. They would be leaving
in a minute. But the more urgent the thought, the less able
he was to bring it up.

"What are you waiting for, T'ai Sheng?" His master's voice
jerked him up. "Pack up that stuff."

He did as he was ordered. When he had finished he stood
again like a log. The master gave some detailed orders to
the tutor and then turned icily to T'ai Sheng.

"Packed? Where's your pole?"

As if in a dream, T'ai Sheng mechanically took up his pole
and inserted one end of it under the ropes which bound the
tutor's bag. The other end was attached to a package so
heavy that at first try he was unable to lift it from the
ground. His heart tightened and stopped. He turned to Mr.
Cheng.

"I . . . I . . ." he began. Everybody looked at his burning
face.

"What is it?"

"I want to borrow a few more dollars from the master."

"Borrow again! You're always like this—do you think I'm
your private bank?"

"What can I do? I haven't been able to get everything I
need for the supervisor."

"You're a great planner, aren't you?" sneered Mr. Cheng.
"When you need anything, you always come to me. Do you
think life is easy?"

T'ai Sheng summoned all his control and forced himself to
smile.

"I'd like to be a tenant myself. It's easier," added Mr.
Cheng. But now he decided it was time to temper hardness
with kindness so he took five dollars out of his pocket and
handed them to T'ai Sheng. With that painful, difficult

smile on his face, T'ai Sheng shouldered the pole and made off through the gate carrying the bedding and the suitcase of the tutor Mr. Fan.

2

A hubbub of sound throbbed over the countryside. A new world of life and activity pervaded the silent fields. Each straw hut represented the holdings of a tenant, and from the bank of the canal looking up and downstream on both sides many of the crude straw structures could be seen rising over the sunken level of the paddies. In all of them men and women were doing exactly the same thing in the same way and in the same order. Except when brief time was taken out for eating they bent over their work, a man to each *mow* of land according to custom. During the day the fields were dotted with toiling men and women, working swiftly and seriously and intent upon their task. In the evening, however, it was quite different. The sounds of the threshing and folk tunes harmonized into a rural symphony, beat by beat. In it they seemed to be relating their woes and their hardships, consoling each other, and in their harmony their weary hearts seemed to beat with a common pulse keeping time for all. Here and there oil lamps flickered in the darkness.

T'ai Sheng needed six reapers to help him cover his plot of ground. The day after Mr. Fan arrived T'ai Sheng led his helpers out onto the field at the first break of dawn, and like the tenants and laborers in all the neighboring fields, they set to work cutting down and stacking the golden grain. Only his wife remained behind at the straw hut, cleaning out the rice bowls and washing off the chopsticks with a clatter and splashing of water. She was not entirely alone. There was Mr. Fan who was just now sticking his head out from under his bedding. He blinked his eyes and looked around.

"Mother's——! Not a man around," he thought as his eyes rested on the sturdy, broad back of T'ai Sheng's wife. "Too stupid, too ugly . . . otherwise what a chance it would be!" Nevertheless he coughed and noisily cleared his throat. The woman went on washing her dishes without turning around. "Stupid!" His eyes were still fixed upon her hips. "Not too bad if you look from the back," he reflected. "Quite passable, in fact, but how stupid!" He laughed to himself.

Mr. Fan was famous as a "lime tub"—he left his impression on any woman he met. It was his practice to disregard no woman who was passable. Moreover, as a graduate of a modern school, he deemed that he was thereby practicing the new freedom in love. He jumped out of bed, assumed a masterful expression, and shouted:

"Washing water!"

The woman looked at him over her shoulder. Lifting her arms out of the tub in which she was washing up, she dried them off on her hem and went slowly over to the water jar. She poured some into a basin which stood on a table specially placed there for the honored guest. This done, she silently and mechanically returned to her work.

"Just like a log," observed Mr. Fan and dipped his hands into the basin.

After she had finished the bowls and chopsticks, T'ai Sheng's wife, without waiting to be asked, cleaned out Mr. Fan's pipe, set up a cup of tea for him, and tidied his bedding, doing everything she knew to be necessary for the comfort of their master's harvest representative. She went about it with a face frozen by a lifetime of hardship; she was conscious of nothing but her work. She appeared to the eye so utterly without sensibilities that even Mr. Fan, a self-fancied master at the art of starting flirtations, did not know how to speak to her.

"You'll find boiling water in the kettle over there," she

said. "I have to go home for some rice," with which she turned and walked down the path.

"A log! A lump!" Mr. Fan stared angrily after her retreating back. After she had gone from sight, Mr. Fan felt inexpressibly lonely. There was no life around the hut, and the gentle morning breeze only made him drowsy. He walked part of the way into the field. The sun was just beginning to break over the tops of the hills far away. Near him, across the waving expanse of ripe grain, he saw the heads and shoulders and chests of men at work, moving along and swinging their sickles. But this held no interest for him. He had seen too much harvesting, be it early crops or late ones, they were always the same. He walked slowly back to the hut.

"Tiresome business, this." He sat trying to find solace in smoking. "And that damned stupid woman! Impossible. Do these people think I'm a green outsider to this business? I bet they do. And they think they can cheat me." His face grew more animated. He had new thoughts to play with. "I'll show them. I'll show them who's master. . . ."

And so he ruminated until the long paper roll he used to light his pipe burnt down to his fingers and brought him up with a start to the realization that the sun was high overhead. It was time to eat. At this point, Mr. Fan purposely took on a heightened air of importance. This was how his plan took effect:

It was the traditional custom that the master and the tenant eat at separate tables and that among the master's dishes there was to be at least one of meat. Actually Mr. Fan knew nothing of this custom when he sat down to his food. Busy in the fields, neither T'ai Sheng nor his wife had made the trip down to the market to get the master's meat. They themselves always used eggs instead, and they thought now that eggs might this one time prove acceptable to their master's deputy. T'ai Sheng himself served Mr. Fan, setting the dishes before him, filling his rice bowl, and generally looking after his comfort. When all was done, he stood next to the table and with his best smile said:

"I'm sorry, Mr. Fan. I didn't go to market this morning."

Mr. Fan dropped his chopsticks. His eye ran quickly over the dishes, and he guessed there was something amiss with them, something injurious to his dignity. He glowered at T'ai Sheng.

"I don't want to eat," he said abruptly. "Pack my things. I'm leaving."

"Why, master?" T'ai Sheng was aghast.

Mr. Fan's outburst brought all the hired help to their feet. They crowded around the master's table.

"Nothing, nothing, pack up my things to take home."

"What is it? What's the matter?" they asked.

"This is an outrageous insult!" shouted Mr. Fan.

Everybody turned to look at T'ai Sheng who stood there dazed and wide-eyed.

"Look here," continued Mr. Fan, "I'm no glutton and I've eaten the best foods there are. But he should certainly have known how to treat me sitting here. I am the same as the master himself in these fields!" He pointed to the dishes.

The crowd began to understand. Some cried, "Oh! Oh!" and made faces. Others tried to be helpful.

"Sure, he's wrong, but forgive it this time."

T'ai Sheng also found words. He bit back his sick anger and spoke gently.

"I have already asked your pardon. I asked you to forgive me this time."

"You think that's enough? I tell you, insulting me is like insulting Master Cheng. Of course, maybe I don't count for much, but you still want to work on Master Cheng's land, don't you?"

"Please don't be angry, master," broke in T'ai Sheng's wife, thrusting herself before him, her face cold as ever. "Forgive us this once. We will acknowledge we were wrong. But how could we dare insult the master?"

"That's right, that's right," came voices from the crowd. "Let's laugh about it and sit down to eat."

Mr. Fan began to feel satisfied with the demonstration of his power of these people. To make it complete, he added a long chapter of complaints about the hut, the cold toilet water, and the lack of water to drink.

"I'm ready to overlook anything I can . . ." he said finally, mollified, and sat down again at his table.

"Good, let's eat," said the others and all went back to their places.

Mr. Fan's arrogance did not affect his appetite, for very soon his dishes were wiped clean. Before long everybody went back to work in the fields. Mr. Fan did not remain in the hut, but several times during the course of the afternoon, he strode manfully back and forth along the paths lining the fields. His authority expanded in all its majesty when he came upon the many women who were gathering up stray fallen ears of rice left behind in the field by the cutters. He shouted at them, forbidding them to pick any more. They paid him no heed. This had ever been their traditional privilege and they depended on their pickings to fill out their family rice stores. Like sparrows, they descended upon the reaped fields each year with their baskets. No one, not even a Mr. Fan, could hinder them. But Mr. Fan grew furious when he saw his orders ignored. He rushed into the field, fell upon an old woman, seized her basket, emptied it on the ground, and walked back up to the pathway with the basket in his hand.

"You'll know I mean what I say next time!" he said.

The old woman followed at his heels. She begged and

wept. Other women followed her off the field. Some joined
in her pleading. The rest stood around and watched and listened.

"What a devil of a master!" said some. "We're not robbing
you. This is the custom. Can't we pick up the stray ears?"

"Have pity, give her back the basket."

The woman crowded around the tutor, who felt himself
mightily exalted. His heart expanded with pleasure. He felt
strong and powerful and pleased. He felt like smiling expan-
sively, but with an effort kept his face severe.

"She tried to cheat me in my very presence!" he shouted.

"No, sir, not at all! We're just picking the stray ears. She's
so old. Please return the basket to her!"

The crowd of pleading women about him had for the moment satisfied his sense of power. Now he looked around at
their faces with a new and more concrete interest. His gaze
soon concentrated on a few younger girls.

"Why do you people come here to pick these leavings?"

"What are we going to eat if we don't pick?"

"Young and beautiful girls like you, wouldn't you do better
at something else?"

"We're very stupid," they replied, slyly giggling. "We don't
know about anything else."

"Where do you live? How many in your family? You
should. . . ."

"Why so many questions, are you looking for a wife?"
asked one girl, bolder than the rest.

"Yes, yes, that's just what I am looking for, a wife," he
laughed.

"But you masters are rich men!"

"What's that got to do with it?"

"What's that got to do with it? And you even forbid us to
pick stray ears of rice!"

"Oh, I'm not so mean as all that," he waved his hand

deprecatingly. "Wait and after a while you can have a few armfuls of stalks," he said grandly.

He looked from one to the other like a hungry eagle, annoyed that he could not possess them all at once. What pure delight! Among these women he felt like an emperor. They all tried to please him. They all admired him and he could have any one of them he liked. Before them he shed all his dignity. He used all the phrases he knew to produce the desired effect. As for the girls, what did they care so long as they could pick some rice or perhaps even get hold of some of the reaped rice? What harm in a little flirting if it proved worthwhile? Most of them went back into the field, some picking the fallen ears, but some stealing from the harvest proper. The young ones remained, ogling at him. "We have to go now," they said. "If we don't get any rice, we'll be scolded when we get home."

"Don't worry," said the tutor, "each one of you can have a stalk." He pointed to the newly cut stalks strewn on the field.

"Oh, good!" and with an eye on Mr. Fan and smiles for him, they went over and started pulling away the stalks, sitting down to rub the rice into their baskets. Fan sat down beside them, and on the pretext of helping them with the rice he began to fondle them. The girls by now had taken over the entire field.

Nearby T'ai Sheng was at work. Hearing the laughter and the tiny shrieks of the girls, he looked over and saw them taking the stalks.

"Damn it!" he dropped his sickle, scrambled up into the path and ran toward them. "Are you a bunch of thieves . . . you. . . ." Like sparrows the women scattered before him. The girls with Fan picked up their baskets and ran off, leaving the emperor without his court.

"Ma-ti, they have. . . ." T'ai Sheng was looking at the

field and trembling with angry excitement when he saw the
tutor Mr. Fan pick himself up at the spot where the girls
had been sitting and stared after the departing women.

"Damned pig of a schoolmaster," growled T'ai Sheng.
"Our blood and sweat for his fun!"

He felt like running over and beating Mr. Fan to a pulp.
But he could not even say a word in reproach. He simply
stood and stared at the man who was still looking after the
fleeing women and who turned finally until his eyes met
T'ai Sheng's. Mr. Fan remained as calm as an autumn evening. As if nothing had happened, he strolled back and forth
along the path.

"He should be beheaded, the dog!" Angrily T'ai Sheng
turned away and went back to his work.

In the evening the threshing began. T'ai Sheng and his
wife were both busy tying up the stalks and raking in the
husks. Mr. Fan sat once more in the hut and was again feeling lonesome and impatient. He was thinking about a rosy-
cheeked girl of the afternoon who had giggled more than the
others and who had let him hold her hand. At night after
work, she had told him, many of the harvest workers would
come to her place to play and gamble. Would he come too?
This girl would be easy, he felt. He tingled with impatient
anticipation. Why didn't they finish? The sound of the
threshing rang like an angry discord in his ears. He walked
out into the field and saw the shadows of men there at work.
He hated them. He thought of T'ai Sheng and his wife and
the day's events. They were intentionally trying to make a
fool of him, especially that wife, with her face stiff as a
corpse all the day long. And now they were spoiling his
good time. Well, it was the easiest thing in the world to be
revenged on a tenant! Nursing his anger and his impatience
he made the round of the threshing field. Mr. Fan stopped
in front of the mound of husks. He thrust his hand into it at

several places. He turned to T'ai Sheng and with seeming negligence he said:

"Don't be too greedy. It looks as though you've raked in all the rice with your husks."

"There's got to be some husk, sir," said T'ai Sheng, startled by this unexpected remark. "If there's any rice there, we didn't take it in intentionally."*

"Husk!" said Mr. Fan. "I don't think Mr. Cheng will be entirely blind."

When the work ended, Mr. Fan took out the seal and ceremoniously branded a dozen lime impressions around the rice mound. This done, he went off with the harvesters for an evening's play. Nobody knew when he got back that night.

Next day when Mr. Fan rose, he discovered that some of the rice had been stolen. It was obvious, for almost all of the lime impressions on one side had been obliterated.

"T'ai Sheng! Come over here and look at this. This is serious!"

T'ai Sheng was stupefied and could make no reply at all. In truth, he was more at a loss and pained than Mr. Fan was.

"Look at it!" Fan glared at him. "What do you see?"

"I never stirred from the place all night. I'm the one who takes the loss."

"Loss? Don't think you can pull the wool over anybody's eyes about this."

Each word stabbed at T'ai Sheng, who could only reply: "What do you mean by that?"

"Hm," sniffed Mr. Fan. "To play a cheap trick like this—"

"You can't accuse people like this!" cried out T'ai Sheng.

"And why not accuse?" sneered Mr. Fan. "Am I to suppose that the rice flew away by itself?"

---

*It was the custom for the tenant to keep the husk as a bonus.

T'ai Sheng bit his lip and watched Mr. Fan bend over the ground away from the rice mound. He saw stray grains of rice which seemed to follow a definite trail.

"Look here, it was carried along this way!" Mr. Fan looked triumphantly at his victim.

"What can I say?" cried T'ai Sheng in despair. "If you say I took it then I must take the blame for it!"

"I'm not saying you took it," replied Mr. Fan. "What do I care about it anyway? If Mr. Cheng doesn't bother about it, it's all right with me. But anyway, T'ai Sheng, you can't expect to be entirely free of suspicion. Maybe you don't know anything about it at all. But how about your wife? She has such stealthy ways. Can you vouch for her?"

T'ai Sheng's wife fell to her knees. "I stole it? I stole it? Heaven only knows," she cried, "whoever touched that mound."

"Go ahead and tell them anything you like!" shouted T'ai Sheng, staring straight ahead.

Mr. Fan sniffed indifferently and walked back into the hut.

"No use worrying now. Let's hope Master Cheng won't pursue the matter," he said.

3

Came the day of the final accounting. Master Cheng came to the home of T'ai Sheng and brought two friends with him. For this most important day of the whole harvest season tradition dictated that the tenant prepare a fine feast for his master. Before they sat down Mr. Fan led the visitors around the field and told them all the bad things that had happened. He laid heavy emphasis on the robbery from the rice mound. Together they estimated the quantity of rice in the piles and also took a guess at the amount of rice mixed in with the husks. Master Cheng nodded solemnly each time

Cheng Nung

and appeared to have made up his mind already about everything.

"Let's settle everything after eating," he said.

When T'ai Sheng invited them to the table, Mr. Cheng looked at the dishes spread there, meat, fish, vegetable, but no chicken.

"Say, T'ai Sheng, have all the chickens around here died of plague?"

"I beg your pardon," said the tenant humbly. "We really couldn't get any."

"Certainly, I can forgive anything," said Mr. Cheng with a snicker to his friends.

After they had eaten, they began measuring out the rice. Altogether they measured fifty-five piculs. They divided it, thirty percent to the landlord and the remaining seventy percent to the tenant. That seemed excellent. But of the tenant's share half again was taken to cover the cost of renting the water buffalo. That left T'ai Sheng nineteen piculs. Two more were deducted for rent of tools and waterwheels, three piculs for seed and a bit more for other incidentals. T'ai Sheng looked on with blinking eyes. His pile was now reduced to twelve piculs.

They finished with the rice and turned to the stalks.

"Master, let the stalk go, won't you? Leave us something for our year's work," pleaded T'ai Sheng.

"Things are not that simple, you know," replied Mr. Cheng.

They divided the stalk in half and turned to the husks. They thrust their hands into the pile speculatively. T'ai Sheng watched them uneasily. "There's not much there," he said, "not more than a picul."

"I'm not blind," retorted the landlord. "More like twenty piculs. You're just too satisfied with yourself, aren't you?"

"Twenty piculs!" T'ai Sheng froze. "Surely the master is joking!"

"Who's joking? Not twenty piculs? Well, then, let's separate it with the wind box."

"It can't be twenty piculs," begged T'ai Sheng. "Have pity, master. There is no need to separate it."

"Then it counts for twenty piculs!"

"Then let the master take the whole thing!"

"Separate it!"

"It's our bonus. Are we going to work the whole year for nothing?"

"You can't expect to get away as cheaply as that."

It looked as if the husk was going to be separated after all. T'ai Sheng sickened of begging. He decided to say no more and just stood by silently. At this point the master's two friends relented and intervened.

"Forget it, let it go," said one.

"Let it count for six piculs," said the other to T'ai Sheng.

"All right, six piculs." T'ai Sheng's heart felt as though it were splitting into a thousand pieces. They took three more piculs from his share and dumped them on the landlord's much larger pile. Everything had now been divided, but as they turned to go into the hut, Mr. Cheng pulled out an abacus and called T'ai Sheng to him.

"T'ai Sheng, you borrowed twenty dollars this year. Ten during planting, five during weeding, and five more a few days ago. Right?"

T'ai Sheng nodded. Mr. Cheng flicked up a few beads on the counting board.

". . . And also three bushels of rice during weeding time."

T'ai Sheng nodded again and a few more beads went into new places.

"What are you going to do about it, T'ai Sheng?" asked

Cheng Nung

Mr. Cheng. "To be perfectly frank, I'm not going to rent this land to you next year. Think it over. During the year you're lazy and the crop goes to pieces. When harvest time comes you try all kinds of tricks. I know all about it. Land as good as this—how come only fifty-odd piculs?" Cheng's eyes shifted with cunning as he said this.

During this speech, T'ai Sheng's eyes remained fixed on the landlord's face and in him his slow rage, compressed into his most profound depths, bubbled up and burst forth.

"This is the meanest. . . . You damnable greedy—" The cords in his brown neck stood rigid and he could say no more.

Mr. Cheng toyed with his abacus and pretended not to see.

"Murderer!" burst out T'ai Sheng.

"Counting the interest from the beginning," went on Mr. Cheng, "it comes to thirty-four dollars plus three bushels and six *sheng* of rice. According to the present market price you owe me eleven piculs more," he calculated calmly, pointing to the total on his abacus.

"Damn you, I'm not going to pay a single cash! Try and collect!" shouted T'ai Sheng in the master's face.

"What kind of fart is this?" shouted Mr. Cheng getting to his feet and slamming his hand on the table.

"To hell with you, you murdering thief! I'm not afraid of you," cried T'ai Sheng.

Mr. Cheng's face went blue with anger. He made as if to jump forward and strike T'ai Sheng. His friends held him back. He sat down again, breathing hard. "This is an outrage, an outrage!"

T'ai Sheng stood flatly in front of him and pointed his finger at his face. "Come on, damn you, come on! Mother's——! You think I'm afraid of you?"

Mr. Fan and the master's friends grew frightened. It was evident to them now that T'ai Sheng would surrender no more because he had nothing left to give them. They persuaded the master to leave and pass on to the next tenant's hut. Mr. Cheng left finally, muttering under his breath. T'ai Sheng watched them go.

"Rape of their mothers! Robbers!" he shouted hoarsely.

"Heaven, poor people cannot live!" cried the wife of T'ai Sheng, beating her breast, stamping her feet furiously.

The fields again grew quiet and almost deserted. Only on the road to the landlord's house the squeaking of the carts laden with rice cut sharply into the silence. The bitterness of a year's toil had again been converted into wealth for others. Not only T'ai Sheng but all the tenant farmers listened with contracting hearts and, seeing the harvest shrink before their eyes, followed the rasp of the cartwheels down the road to the horizon away from them.

The Courier

A giant lemon tree grew before the door of Lin Chi. Under it in June they had shot an obese rent collector. He lay sprawled across the roots that showed overground. After those who shot him had gone, his lips moved and he groaned faintly. Onlookers pointed to the holster strapped around Lin Chi's waist.

"Well, come on. Your gun hasn't been used yet. Don't you know how?"

The shock went up Lin's arm and into his body. But the fat man was silent now and the people around nodded and shook erect thumbs from their upraised fists, signifying approval. Ever since then, Lin Chi had stood high in his neighbors' estimation.

Lin Chi was seldom home after he became courier for the Chiang-p'ing district. He was constantly on the run and got back now and again for a meal, or at best to spend half a night with his wife. The neighbors often used to come and watch him eat, but he sat on a broken stool at his meal and paid no attention to them. There was only one other stool in the room so most of them stood awkwardly silent against the door. Sometimes they would cough to attract attention, but it was Lin Chi's wife, piling fuel on the fire or filling her husband's rice bowl, who would turn to greet them.

"Have you all eaten?" she would say sometimes. Or, "Good morning." Then she would step lightly past them through the door and rest against it, her hands folded behind her and her eyes fixed on the slender bamboo pole on the hill yonder. If the pole was down, it meant the enemy was coming. Inside the neighbors began plying Lin Chi with questions.

"Somebody said that the fifteen automatic rifles buried by Yeh Ting's bodyguards at Chieh Shih when he sailed for Hongkong were dug up by our people and, much to everybody's surprise, were found to be in quite good condition—not a bit rusted. Have you heard about it?"

"Have you ever passed the Ts'ui Po bridge at the foot of Fa Liu Shan? There are two tea shops there on this side of it. There's a crooked-nosed woman always walking back and forth. (Pei! His spit hit the floor.) And you call yourself a courier! Lots of sedan-chair men wait there to pick up fares going over the hill. And under the stall there are a lot of broken white cups, the kind used on the telegraph poles. I bet you didn't see those either! Well, about fifteen days ago, a regimental commander went there."

"That's right! From Tung Hai. No question about it."

"Ai, and how unlucky it was for him to get there just when our people had finished a meal in the village. Ha, ha! What worm can survive a night in a chicken coop? They forced them out of the bamboo grove. They took him and all his men and all their horses too up Fa Liu mountain. We cleaned them out of ten revolvers, no less. He had eight guards and an orderly. There were twelve of ours. Three of them had nothing, two had hoes, and six carried spears. One of them had a homemade revolver which couldn't even be fired. I've seen it. Not as good as yours. Yours is German, automatic, isn't it?"

Lin Chi spat fish bones onto the floor and smiled. He hardly ever talked. He filled his bowl again from the big copper pan on the stove, and with a preparatory tap of his chopsticks on the broken board table, he set to eating again. He knew how his neighbors liked to talk.

"I wanted to ask you, Lin Chi. They say that three whole letters can be carried in one ear. Can that be so? The letters sure must be small. They also say letters are carried under the eyelids. What do you do, pretend to be blind when you meet up with the enemy?"

"How can you just say you're blind?" put in another, scornfully. "No cloth bag, no gong. Do you think they'd believe you?"

"Much more important to study the characters *chia-tzu, yi-ch'ou**—the cloth bag and the gong don't matter a damn. . . ."

Lin Chi laughed too. He filled his bowl again.

"Lin, you wouldn't tell us anything, would you? You can't give away any secrets. But look, for instance, suppose I were the courier instead of you—I say just for instance. Then, suppose I have to pass a guard station like the teahouse at Huang T'u Tun. What trick do you suppose I'd use to get through there? Guess. Why nothing but a sedan chair. Too big, you think? What's a messenger going to do who had to carry not only letters, but manifestoes and leaflets every day as well? Hm. Don't forget a sedan chair has several big bamboo poles. Suppose I had something even bulkier than leaflets, like a revolver. Do you think it could be found? I

*Referring to a system of fortune-telling based on year, month, day, and hour of birth, often used by blind men in the villages.

suppose it would work well the first time and not so well the
second. Easy to be a sedan chair carrier. We can pull our
rear ends around pretty easily, can't we? Ha, ha, ha! La, la,
Lin, these things all depend on us, don't they?"

After a long, slow smile, Lin replied: "Of course."

On the road, Lin always dressed in ordinary clothes, the
same that everybody wore—a blue jacket and black-striped
trousers. It was always his habit to roll one trouser leg up a
little higher than the other. This time it was his job to conduct a young man from Chiang-p'ing to Mei-leng. The
youth was engaged in political work and liked to talk a
great deal. Lin Chi cautioned him. Night walking must be
done in utter silence. Not even the sound of footsteps was allowed. With ears to the ground, the sentries of the enemy
could sometimes hear steps coming half a *li* away. Kept
from talking, the boy would cough. To get to Mei-leng, they
had to pass through a dangerous valley, watched at both
ends by the enemy. Lin Chi planned to get through there
before daybreak. He grasped the hand of his companion and
pulled him close.

"You walk like a clodhopper!" he hissed into his ear. "You
haven't got the slightest idea of how to go about it. Suppose
you stepped into a hole, do you think a fall is all you'd
get?"

The young man opened his mouth to reply but Lin Chi
flattened his palm against the young man's lips. Thereafter
the youth stepped carefully behind Lin Chi. The moon set,
and under the stars the woods cast a faint shadow on the
hillside opposite them. The stolid, silent Lin Chi changed
into a cunning, wary wolf, and the young man saw the head
in front of him turn this way and that, cocked to listen.
Sometimes he stopped short in the middle of the path and

the young man would barely catch himself up in time, and would always jerk back in fright.

"Listen, you. . . ." Lin Chi's lips were against the young man's ear again. "Get down."

He crouched behind while Lin Chi lay out his full length on the ground. The trees ahead rose clearly in the starlight and Lin's eyes measured all the shadows. Everything seemed to have died with the end of the day, and Lin strained all his senses to penetrate the dark silence before them. After a long moment, he touched the young man with his foot. They rose and set out again as before, Lin Chi leading and the youth following behind.

"Password!" The word lashed out at them like the roar of a beast. They stood stock still. It came again, a sullen challenge.

"Password!" The forest became even more still.

Lin Chi stepped back. Just as he was about to crouch down and freeze he heard *kerplunk*. The youth behind him had slipped off the path into the stream to his left. In front of him, at the very spot Lin Chi had left, flashlights and bullets played along the path. He immediately flattened himself on the ground and inched his way to a crevice.

The niche he found himself in was very close to the place where it all happened. He could see all too clearly what happened to the youth after his capture.

About eight o'clock the next morning, Lin Chi arrived back in Chiang-p'ing and reported the death of the young man. Death was an ordinary sequel to the dangers all of them ran daily. Lin's superiors recorded the matter in the course of their busy routine. But for him, things had changed. A steady pain drummed in his heart. He tried to find out the name of the young man. He asked everyone he met. People began to think him a little odd.

"Look here, brother," he asked the armed guard in front of
the district party headquarters. "You must be his friend, you
know, the boy I took to Mei-leng. Can you tell me his
name?"

"You must be mistaken, comrade. You're confusing me
with someone else."

"Mistaken? How am I mistaken? I asked you for his name.
Can't you tell me that?"

It never occurred to him that the guard could become angry so suddenly. The guard brusquely pushed him aside, put
on a scowl and cursed him.

Lin Chi felt the painful grip of remorse on him as he
weakly slumped to the ground for reflection. His head felt
like a great weight on him and his face seemed burning hot.
Sitting with his head on his knees, he realized that no matter what, he could still hear the last cries of that young man.
And dimly at first, but then with urgency, it came to him
that it would always be like this, that there would never be
any way he could stop remembering the whole painful business.

"Password!" and everything became silent. "Password!" He
took a step backward. Just as he was about to crouch down
and freeze, he heard a splash. The youth behind him had
slipped off the narrow trail into the water. The flashlights
and the rifles opened up instantly. Could he have remained
there even a moment longer? He had already flattened himself out on the ground and had begun to inch his way toward a small gully.—"Could I have jumped into the water
after him? And if I had, how could we have gotten away—
But I ran away myself first. . . ."

When his thoughts reached this point, Lin Chi jumped to
his feet. Then he sank back down again against the wall.
After awhile, he rose and walked off. After that he stopped
everyone he met to tell just how it had happened. When he

got to the point in his story where his young friend was dragged from the stream and killed, he would call himself a pig. Using his arm as if it were a butcher's cleaver, he would strike again and again at his own chest and then with an awful cry fall writhing to the ground. At first people in the street gathered around him, as they would around a story-teller. But their interest soon flagged and before long only children stood around him. He's mad, the people said, and, shrugging, went off.

". . . On this side was a copse and on the other was a stream . . ."

One of the little boys rapped Lin Chi's head and shouted at him as loud as he could:

". . . And then someone yelled 'Password!' " The boy flattened himself on the ground and inched up to Lin Chi and crawled around him squealing: "But then I ran away myself first! I ran away myself first!"

And all the other children laughed.

Lin Chi lay sick in his bed at home. Several of the Chiang-p'ing comrades came to see him. His once pleasant brown face had grown lined and thin. Every time a new caller came, in the same voice and with the same words, he began his story, shaking his head. At the end, he would always ask his caller, with tears in his eyes:

"The older one ran away and the younger one died. Tell me, can that be right?"

"Nonsense! How can you think that way?" Someone asked once. "Let me tell you a story about a doctor, Lin," the visitor continued after a pause. "A doctor went to examine a patient once who was by that time beyond any possible help. The doctor looked at the suffering man and there was nothing he could do about it. 'I'm a doctor,' he said, 'but even the best I could do wouldn't cure you. I'm sorry you have to

die, but I can't follow you into the grave, can I?' Tell me,
Lin, do you think any man could blame the doctor for not
having gone to his death together with his patient? See what
I'm getting at?"

But no matter what the caller might have added, there was
nothing he could have said that would have made any difference. Lin Chi lay back on the pillow and closed his eyes.
Turning his head from side to side, he said again in a weary
voice, "Tell me, the elder ran away and the younger died,
can that be right?"

To tell the truth, what he wanted now was some form of
punishment as a kind of medicine. To the guilty, comfort is
useless.

Lin Chi grew steadily worse. After days of effort his wife
learned the young man's name and secretly she went to the
spot where he died. She burned incense and sacrificed paper
money there. She called out the name of the young man
and begged for the return of her husband's lost soul. But Lin
Chi grew no better and the neighbors often gathered around
him with stories they hoped would comfort him.

"Hah! Lin, old friend, what do these students think they
know anyway? I tell you, learning to follow the trail at
night is no simple thing." The speaker's intense loathing for
the students who came to lecture him and the others on politics was plainly visible. Mentioning this led him to ridicule
the young man who had lost his life with Lin Chi.

"Say, did you ever hear the story of Wu Shih-ling of Yen-
chow? Huh! So he's read a book or two—no more than a
showoff, I'd say, and what use is that to anyone? On the
night I'm talking about a courier that went out with him
came pretty close to catching it. How'd it happen, you say?
Well, Wu Shih-ling was saying how brave he was—what can
you do with someone like that?—and so he had the courier
walk behind him—he was the one carrying the documents.

Well, it was that place where they put a watch out. Where you get the road to Tung Hai crossing the road we take from Chiang-p'ing on into town. There's that hill there—just a rise, really, but it's right there at the crossroad, and since it's all flat paddyland around there anybody on top can see all around him. The enemy is no dummy, you know, so they put a watch up there first thing. Now that kid Wu Shih-ling—no more than a pink-cheeked baby he was—but he was pretty smart, too. He says, 'It's too risky for the two of us to go together here.' Oh, he was showing his courage all right, so he tells the courier, 'I'll go on ahead first through the crossroad.' That courier—you know him, don't you? Name was Li, Li T'an-shui. From the foot of Mt. Chiang-chun. Spindly-legged fellow. Broken nose. Tell him to do anything and you don't have to tell him twice. Go through fire, he would. He was no coward, that's for sure, but if you want him to go through last, well, that's fine with him all right. It was past midnight, maybe one or so in the morning, and Wu Shih-ling gets through all right. You have to hand it to him, he had the legs for this work all right, no question about that, but after he got through and waited for a bit he began to worry. They had agreed to go on ahead to an old tomb and to wait there for each other, but Wu Shih-ling, he couldn't wait any time at all—a kid like that, hardly more than a baby yet.

"When he got to that old tomb all by himself, he was scared out of his wits and Li T'an-shui hadn't showed up yet, so first thing you know he gets excited and starts shouting, 'T'an-shui! Oh T'an-shui!' like that.

"Li T'an-shui was just then making his way over the rocks that cross the stream at the foot of the hill there. When he heard the shouts, *clunk*! he stepped on the wrong rock. The sentries were spread out on patrol all over the little dikes between the paddies, and they opened fire right away."

"Then what happened?" one of his listeners asked.
"What happened? Well, it was a tight spot, wouldn't you
say?" He paused a bit here, then went on with his story,
"Well, funny thing, but it was that wretch Wu Shih-ling
who got him out of it."

"When Wu heard the rifle fire he took off on the run. The
fields were flooded all around there, and Wu made like a
mud turtle and dived right in and crawled as far away as he
could get. He went about four *li* and was just about spent
when he came to . . . what was it now, Hsin-liao? Or was it
K'ung-tzu Chai? I've forgotten now which village it was, but
anyway, during those days the enemy hadn't yet got all the
villages under their control so the villagers had patrols out
every night on the watch for spies. Every place had its own
password, but Wu Shih-ling was so scared he couldn't remember what it was.

"Password!" When he heard that out in front of him he
panicked and slipped down into a pond. The villagers began
beating gongs and gathering their militia around the pond
with spears and swords. Thinking that Wu Shih-ling must be
an enemy spy they sent someone into the water to find him
and stab him to death. All their shouting and gong-beating
roused the other villages roundabout so that in all four di-
rections the alarm was sounded. Now the enemy couldn't
have been anything near a whole company in strength and
couldn't hold the hill if they had to. Lose their ass if they
tried. In all the commotion Li T'an-shui got out of there.

"Did they kill Wu Shih-ling in the pond with their
spears?" someone asked.

"Oh no, what a laugh that was! Where do you think he
hid? He got in under the waterwheel at the edge of the
pond. They didn't find him. When finally Li T'an-shui
came up and told the whole story, the villagers saw they'd
made a mistake. Standing by the waterside, Li called for

Wu to come out. Hmph, called him! If I were Li, I'd have run a spear through him. What was the use of saving him?"

Stories like this only increased Lin Chi's agony. He tossed from side to side in his bed while his visitors were talking, or he closed his eyes tightly, or even slept through their tales.

"Why didn't you shoot at them, Lin?" asked one of his neighbors one day. "Isn't your gun for use on the enemy?"

Lin Chi's face brightened and he lifted himself up. "You're right, you're right!" He grasped his friend's hand and beat it against his own head. "Come on, beat my brains open with your fist! I'm a fool. . . ."

His friend tapped his head lightly to humor him. "I told you to break my head open!" shouted Lin Chi angrily. He fumbled in the box next to his bed and pulled out his gun. His frightened visitors ran toward the door. Lin Chi's wife, startled by the commotion, ran toward the room, but as she entered the door, she was thrust back by a terrific explosion, and she saw both her husband and the gun fall to the floor.

Land of Snow

1

This is the Minya Konga. The people call it the "Mountain
of Many Ghosts."

The snow is like silver. Its whiteness is terrifying. Immense,
lumplike mountains are entirely covered with a single unbroken canopy, stretching off to infinity beyond the sky like
so much smooth white flour. These mountains are so barren-
ly white that not a single speck of color, much less a tree,
breaks the bright monotony for as far as one can see. When
you look up and around, the giant peaks stare back at you,
a quiet, deadly white stare. You can only breathe a sad sigh.
Standing among them, you seem to be in a chasm rent in
the snow, for, where the mountains tower, the sky becomes a
narrow patch overhead. Often you will see no sky at all,
only white mist swirling in the air currents up above you,
like white smoke coming from a burning building. Densely
the mist descends sometimes until, fully enveloped, you can
barely see your companions in front of you and in back. A
companion ten feet away begins to fade into the ghostly
white shadows. You are aware of those beyond him only by

the sound of feet tramping on the hard snow. The peaks rise endlessly before you. Not a single shadow of brown or green breaks the glare. Only the damp white mist and the deadly brilliant snow. It pierces your eyes and dims them and makes them ache. But you have to struggle to keep them open lest you fall from the trail into one of those yawning chasms opening thousands of feet below you.

A column of men tramped on into this boundless world of dead, dazzling whiteness. They marched quietly, each man following in the footsteps of the man in front of him. It was so cold, so terribly white, and the air so thin, that the men panted at every two or three steps. Their feet, heavily encased in coarse felt, stepped warily forward, sinking at least two feet into the snow at every step. The snow came up to the thigh. Each man had to steady himself on one foot while he pulled the other free, the way farmers do when they plant winter rice in a field of mud. So he stepped, pulled, stepped, pulled, and thus he and his column climbed and descended and climbed again. No matter how strong or bull-like the man, he would never dare take six or seven steps in a stretch. If he did, he would certainly faint and sink into the snow like a lump of ice. According to custom, the column advanced three steps at a time. Then the men would pause briefly. They would raise their heads to look up at the white mist and the silvery mountainsides, and their hearts would ache and they would shudder involuntarily.

Their felt puttees, woven out of untreated, coarse, poor wool by the natives of Sikang, did not look like the puttees of ordinary soldiers. But although their legs were thus covered by so heavy a material, they were soon soaking wet inside and out. From thighs to toes there was an unbroken sensation of wet, icy coldness. Their feet were already numb although occasionally a sensation of prickly pain would rise in their toes. Their straw shoes were entirely covered with hardened snow which had turned into blocks of ice, contracting in the process and causing heavy pressure on the feet. Efforts would be made to loosen them every once in a while, but it was impossible to stand on one foot or to thrust one's hands down into the snow. So one walked on as best one could.

The men wore uniforms of the same white felt, only now it was black and foul-smelling. Rifles and ammunition belts were slung over their shoulders, and blanket rolls and other equipment were lashed to their bodies. Yet they were cold, so cold they could not even tremble, for their bodies were numb. Their fingers were numb, like pieces of ginger, and they could not even lift them to wipe their beards. And could they have done so, they would have felt no beards, for in these icy mountains the hair on their faces dropped off at the root, congealed into heavy ice by the breath that came warm and hard from their mouths. It was in this way that old Chang Chan-piao lost his beard, brushed off clean. It was damned funny.

The exertion of walking and shortness of breath caused perspiration. When the beads of sweat fell onto the felt, they froze immediately. When one sweated and panted, one's heart contracted painfully. The stomach too felt strained. One felt hungry, yet had no desire for food. For four days these men had been climbing the Mountain of Many Ghosts. They were continually hungry, but they could not eat. A full bag of *draba** still dangled at each man's side, little lighter than when they had started. Still every day they had to force some down to fill their stomachs, because they could not climb at all when empty. More than twenty of them had lost their fingers. They did not know that numbed

---

*A Tibetan word for a common native food made of barley or corn flour, prepared by mixing with milk fat and rolling into a lump.

limbs should first be warmed by curling in a blanket to re-
vive the circulation. As soon as they stopped, they heated
their hands at the fire. Next day their hands would turn
black and dry up and the fingers would fall from the knuck-
les as if cut away. Now they could not use their guns nor
prepare *draba* for themselves. Such were the fruits of their
frontier service! Returning homeward to rotate patrol, those
who could not use their rifles were given the job of carrying
them, so every one of those men bore five or six which
swayed in the mist as they tramped. "Hai-yo! Hai-yo!"

When they had gone out to the borderland to fight back
the invading Tibetan rebels last spring, there had been a full
battalion of them. On the way out two platoons froze to
death on this same mountain and a third became ineffective
after their toes rotted off from the cold. Considering that
these men received wages amounting to forty or fifty cents a
month, everyone should have deserted. But where to? Into
these weary cold mountains on all sides? If he did not freeze
or starve to death, a man was certain to be caught in the
end and shot. So, although all of them wanted to desert,
none actually did. Except the men who died, they all went
out and saw service in the Gantze district where they remained a few months and engaged in the campaign against
the Tibetans. At the end there were only fifty of them left,
including the score without fingers. However, there were still
a battalion commander and three company commanders as
before. Of the four platoon commanders, only two were left,
but the number of upper-class people remained the same
since the battalion commander added two native concubines
to his family. Now that they had been recalled, everybody
thought there was some chance of returning home alive.
Sometimes they thought of their comrades who had frozen
or been killed in the fighting, but these were only passing
thoughts. They were glad to be returning. But all of them

were changed. They hated, but could not speak out their hate. It weighed on their minds.

Li Te-sheng was hungry. But he had no more fingers with which to prepare the *draba* and stuff it into his mouth. His stomach grumbled for food and made him even shorter of breath. He felt faint and asked Wu Chan-ao, the man in front of him, to help him. Together they stood for a few minutes and Wu began to knead the *draba* for him.

Crack! Crack! With a hiss and a slap the commander's whip landed twice. "Rape of your goddamned mothers! You sons of bitches! Leaving your column, eh, swine?"

The blows of the whip utterly dumbfounded both men, who stood staring at the commander like vacant idiots until the meaning of his words sank in. Then they hastily started off after the disappearing column. The commander who watched them go was a truly imposing sight. He was a major. He wore a uniform and overcoat of heavy leather and a fur cap, and he rode a hardy pony. Every soldier who saw him was scared of him. His eyes were covered by a pair of yellow goggles, and it was impossible to judge his expression, whether it be angry or pleased, making him seem a mysterious figure. But none of them liked him, and the column up ahead grew curiously agitated when the word spread:

"The commander is using his whip again!"

"The commander is using his whip again!"

Like orders being passed on, the word passed up the line from the last soldier to the first.

"God damn it! What's all the howling about?" shouted the commander.

Silence immediately descended upon the column, and every man stepped warily forward after the man before him. There was only the sound of tramping on snow, crunching, crunching, and the flat noises made by bayonets bumping against men's sides combined with the tinkle of the bells and the ponies' necks. As if advancing to a surprise attack, the column marched forward.

The battalion commander not only had his fur cap, leather uniform, and overcoat, but his two native concubines and four *ulags** carrying first-class Yunnan opium, but his heart was full of hate. He was bitter because he was not a kinsman of the brigadier. He had been incorporated with his men into the brigadier's army from the old frontier forces, and he belonged to a different military clique. He hated the brigadier for treating him badly.

"Damn his hide!" he thought. "Why didn't he send his own brother-in-law out as battalion commander? My battalion's pay has been regularly discounted fifty to sixty percent. He said we must resist the British imperialists, so he sends my battalion out to die while his brother-in-law sits back there and enjoys himself. And now more than two companies of my men are gone. Damn that swine of a brigadier! He's trying to finish me off!"

While he sat there on his pony, his hatred and rage mounted as he again went over the bitter ground in his mind. It meant the loss of his strength. He was afraid his very position would totter from under him. In his fury he lashed his whip to the pony's flanks. The animal leaped forward at the sudden onslaught. The snow flew from under his feet and landed in a flurry on the backs and heads of the soldiers just ahead. The pony lurched forward and drove head on into Hsia Te-hai, who was carrying five rifles. Hsia fell into the snow, the rifles on top of him. Their weight deadened him, and the snow filled his mouth and eyes. Suffocating, the soldier fainted dead away. The commander still sat safely on his pony, for the snow was too thick, too heavy to let the animal bolt. The commander held his reins tightly and calmly

*Tibetan pack animals.

410

ordered some of the men to pick up Hsia. It was some time
before the soldier revived. The commander gave him permission to come up behind more leisurely and distributed his
load of rifles among five other soldiers. The column resumed
its march.

Complaints again traveled up the ranks, rear to forward.
Hsia was staggering alone far behind them. Each step was
agony, and the sweat poured from his face and body. He no
longer seemed to possess lower limbs. He was afraid and angry, and his hatred mounted within him. He could walk no
faster and the column was already out of sight up ahead.
Tears froze on his cheeks. He tried to raise his hand to
brush them off, but he had long since lost his fingers. He
had only a stump like a wooden club. His misery was beyond bearing, and long sharp arrows pierced his weakening
mind. He could only roll his stump helplessly across his eyes.

"Old Hsia! Come on, I'll help you!"

Hsia raised his head and saw Liu Hsiao-erh walking toward him and his heart eased off, as if relieved of a great
burden.

"Did the commander tell you to come?" he asked.

"Damn him, no. He forbade me to come. A whole battalion and only fifty or sixty left. I was afraid the tigers would
take you if you were left alone, so I wanted to accompany
you. That damned pig forbade me to come. I was furious
and argued with him. If it weren't for Lieutenant Chang, I
could never have got here."

"Rape his whoring mother! Rape his concubines! He
knocked me down, the swine!"

"Damn him! We die and he wears his leather coats and
buys concubines, and squeezes us to buy opium. Now he's a
damned big shot, but when he saw that English officer during the fighting, what a coward he was. I saw his face go
blue. And that other time when the Tibetans charged us, he

trembled from head to foot and he hid himself back of the mountain. Now, comrade, let me tell you frankly—we've been through fire and hell and I'm not going to say anything now. But wait until we get back. We'll have our accounting with him then!"

Hsia began to see a focus for things he had not understood. "You're right, damn his hide. We'll have a final accounting!"

Suddenly pony bells tinkled at their backs. "Why are you lagging? Trying to desert?" It was the harsh voice of the lieutenant-commander. The two soldiers walked on as if they had heard nothing. They did not answer and did not turn. The tinkling grew louder until they could hear the pony's breath at their backs. The lieutenant-commander seldom had contact with the soldiers. When he had, he could only be harsh and arrogant. That these two soldiers did not stand to attention and salute and failed even to answer his question infuriated him. They were insulting him before all the adjutants, quartermasters, and orderlies. He pulled out his whip and laid it across their backs.

"Do you want to desert? you . . . you. . . ."

Liu Hsiao-erh's anger mounted with the pain in his back. Yet no matter how great his anger, still his years of submission to officers proved the greater force. With his back aching almost beyond support, he stared dumbly up at the officer for a long time before he could finally explain why they were behind the column. The adjutant laughed aloud when he heard the story through, not because it was so funny but because he grabbed at anything to relieve the monotony of the long ride through the mist and the snow. Soon the lieutenant-commander and his staff passed them, all on *ulag*s. There were even five orderlies on mounts, guarding a few *ulag*s carrying ammunition and other supplies. Gradually men and ponies drew farther and farther away, disappearing

finally in the white mist. After them, the tinkling of their
bells died away.

"———! Rape of their mothers!"

"Dogs! Sons of dogs! Rotten eggs! We fight with our bodies
and they advance in power and wealth! Even those damned
dogs of orderlies ride ponies while we walk. We fight and
die—for what? If there were land to till only the son of a
dog would become a soldier!"

Hsia wanted to say something in agreement, but he felt so
cold, so sick, so hungry, that his words fell back in his throat
and made him feel the more sickeningly nauseated. The two
men looked at each other wearily, too wearily for more
words. Leaning on each other, they resumed their slow progress forward.

The white mist thinned. The sun gleamed fitfully over the
top of the peak. The rays struck the snow and rebounded
into their faces and burned them like scorching, searing
flames, even though they were smeared with grease.* The
two men were afraid to open their eyes beyond the narrow-
est slits. The column of fifty was already far ahead of them
threading its way along a narrow ledge. One of the concubines on her pony crowded the soldier, Chen Chan-k'uei, to
the edge of the precipice. Instinctively the man thrust in-
ward against the pony, drove it against the sheer wall, and
knocked the concubine off her saddle into the snow. She
shrieked. The commandant immediately called a halt and
rode over to where his favorite lay in the snow. He kicked
viciously at the soldier with his boot, and in an instant Chen
Chan-k'uei was over the edge and rolling frighteningly down
the steep slope, down, down, a thousand feet into the chasm,
leaving in his wake only a flurried path of disturbed snow.

*The crude milk grease mixed with the *draba* was also smeared on their
faces as a protection against the heat of the sun reflected from the snow.

The mist had thinned, and almost everybody saw what h p-
pened. There was an uproar of voices. The company and
platoon commanders went pale as corpses. The men shouted,
but so great was their anger that none of them said anything
coherent. It was a blind roar of hate. Still in his saddle, the
commander trembled. He pulled his revolver from its holster.
Its blue barrel wavered in his uncertain hand.

"You goddamned rebels. '. . . Who dares make trouble? I'll
shoot anyone who moves!"

Standing directly by his stirrups was the soldier Li Te-
sheng.

"The commander . . . goddamn him!" shouted Li. The officer swung his revolver on him and pulled the trigger, the
shot echoing back from the great white walls around them.
Nobody was hit. His boot flashed out and Li Te-sheng followed his comrade down the slope, rifle and man falling to a
white death in the silent snow deeper than any of them
could see.

His last cry was drowned in a mighty roar that rose from
the soldiers. "Watch yourselves!" shouted Captain Li. His
voice thundered over the rest. What might have happened
then did not happen, for, while the thin air in the enveloped
valley reverberated with the din of echoes, the mist thick-
ened and rushed in upon them. The sun disappeared. Man
was concealed from man, and the mountains and the trail
from all of them, by the dense white thickness which enclosed them. No man could even see his own hand before
him. From the slope above, great chunks of snow came tumbling like monster hailstones. Everyone sought his own shelter from the sudden storm. Nature stepped in and with a
thunder of its own silenced the voices of the men. The falling snow and ice fell more heavily and more fiercely, and
the anguish and the misery of the men were already beyond
the limits of ordinary endurance. But they could not stem

nature's attack, they could only cower beneath it. Finally it grew silent, and there was nothing to do but roll up in blankets in the snow, covered from head to foot. The officers dismounted and slept in the same way.

All was quiet and calm.

2

Next morning the waking men found themselves covered with a foot of snow. When they laboriously dug themselves free and rose, they felt chilled to their bones. It was warm sleeping in the snow, but when they emerged to meet that cold white mist, they shuddered. The snow had ceased falling, and the mist was not as dense as it had been the day before. But still they could not see the sky nor even the summit of the mountain. They were hungry, but their nausea prevented them from eating. Their legs were still buried in the freshly fallen snow and remained there as if they were no longer parts of their bodies. Nobody had the slightest desire to budge an inch. But in their hearts there was bitter, angry hatred. Every man cursed his fate and his life, but nobody spoke. Somebody was tramping in front of them, crunch, crunch! A question followed.

"Who are you?"

"Chen Ta-ch'üan," a soldier answered. They made out the face of Captain Li, who walked along asking each man his name. "Who are you?" Li's peaked mean face always made one long to punch him square in the nose. But somehow or other one always answered meekly.

"Yang Fang."

The captain walked past him. Yang Fang thought of raising his leg and kicking the hated Li down the abyss. But his leg was numb, and he could not move it. He heard the captain calling out a name, but there was no answer.

"Yang Fang!" It was Li's voice.

"Yes, sir?"

"Come here!"

He could not have explained how, but his numbed legs moved directly in response to the captain's order. His legs seemed to belong to the captain. Li pointed to a mound of snow.

"Pull out Wu Lai-tou!"

Yang Fang looked at the captain but said nothing. He bent down with Wang Kang, and the two of them started digging the snow away with their hands. It cut them like burning needles, and the pain ran through their bodies like electric currents. Wu Lai-tou was frozen stiff. His lips were contracted into a grimace, as if he had died smiling. His body was like a block of ice. Li ordered them to take the dead man's rifle and ammunition, the rifle to Yang Fang, the cartridge belts to Wang Kang. In Yang's mind there was misery, disgust, and revolt. But he did as he was ordered. The captain walked on as if nothing had happened.

"Damn the———!" said Yang.

Wang Kang smiled a frozen smile.

The mist thinned and an order came down the line. "Get ready to move! Get ready to move!" The order was passed on down. Nobody wanted to move, but nobody could refuse to go. So those who could hurriedly shoved some *draba* into their mouths and smeared some of the grease on their faces. "Come on, let's go. In the city we'll have our accounting!" In many minds this thought stirred as they started out. Crunch, crunch, on through the snow, and the bayonets clumped again against their sides. The pony bells again tinkled.

The mountain pass was far behind them now. At last, one evening they could see the familiar north gate of Ta-chien-lu. Smoke rose from hundreds of chimneys, and they saw sparkling streams and brown hills, llamas and tradesmen.

Surely the Minya Konga with its many ghosts was far behind them now. When they came out on the street they already felt at home, and their minds eased and they sighed. As soon as they had topped the mountain and begun the descent, they had all tacitly marched as fast as they could despite their aching, frozen feet. Now that they were within the shadow of the old gate, they could not step another inch forward. Their legs felt as if they were going to break and fall off. When they came upon a patch of honest earth, uncovered by snow, they wanted to stretch out upon it and hug it close and sleep. Some of them sat down on a stone by a paddy.

"How heavenly it would be to have a field like that to till!" thought Chang Chan-piao to himself with an infinite pain of longing.

"What are you sitting here for?" The captain rode down on them roaring.

"We're only taking a little rest, sir."

"Eh?" Captain Li dismounted and walked toward them with his whip. The men did not stand up.

"Sir, our legs have given way."

"Damned dogs . . . you and you. . .!" He lay about their backs with the whip. "You're trying to make trouble, even here. Get up and get going even if your legs break. Go!" His last word was thundered at them. The soldiers dragged themselves and pulled their insensible limbs forward. They finally arrived at brigade headquarters. A machine gun squatted ominously at the gate. There were a dozen or so men lolling around, some of them with familiar faces. They greeted the weary column.

Hsia Te-hai stretched out his fingerless hands. Others did likewise. "This is what you get out there." The men stared at him and shook their heads sympathetically.

A squad of armed soldiers came by rushing two others

bound in heavy rope before them. "Deserters," said somebody. They were like pigs going to the slaughter. It was
drawing toward dusk. Squads of soldiers drove long lines of
conscripted coolies through the gate. They said the Third
Battalion was going out to the frontier. The newly returned
men felt lucky that they had gotten back alive. They desired
only to sleep. They wanted nothing but rest. None could
think of anything beyond that. Their thoughts were only for
the remains of their shattered bodies. They were billeted in
an old deserted temple near East Gate. The commander, the
lieutenant-commander, the adjutant, and the two captains,
of course, went to much better quarters. When roll was
called, it was found that three more men were missing.
Somebody said they had died in the storm, but nobody
cared. As soon as this last formality was over, the men simply dropped where they were in the great temple hall. Soon
there was a chorus of sonorous snoring. The gods sat there
watching them silently.

3

On the third day, before the first bugle call was sounded, a
soldier ran in and out among the rows of sleeping men,
bending over, shaking shoulders, and whispering. One by
one, they sat up still groggy with sleep. They watched the
fellow, some of them coughing and spitting. What was it all
about? Listen. What was he saying?

"Our commander was detained by the brigadier last
night."

"Detained?"

Even those still asleep or dozing rose at this. Their legs
were still like logs and every bone ached as if they had been
severely beaten. But they all rose at this news. They began
to gather in knots. Heads were moving. Words flowed.

"Detained? How about our pay?"

"The commander said we'd be paid when we got here. He said he'd give us several months' pay altogether!"

"The brigadier said he'd embezzled our pay."

"Let's go to the brigadier!"

"And he got four *ulag*s loaded with opium, mind you, four—look there!"

They pointed to the boxes of opium piled up in the corner of the hall. The crowd of men broke into excited little groups discussing the new situation. First call had sounded long since, but the roll call had not followed. The officers were running in and out, back and forth, and seemed upset, too upset to remember the roll call. Somebody ran down to the captain's window and listened.

"The commander's trouble is luckily settled." It was the captain's voice.

"Is the brigadier letting him get away with the embezzled pay?"

"The commander asked the chief of staff to mediate. He promised the brigadier one *ulag* load of opium. The brigadier ordered him to clear out quickly so that there would be no trouble from the men."

"But what are we going to do about the men?" asked Wang.

"They're going to be reorganized today. Whoever starts trouble will be shot," said the captain raising his voice.

The listening men slipped away and the news quickly spread. The groups coalesced and everybody was talking at once.

"The brigadier has betrayed us!"

"The brigadier has betrayed us. . . ."

"Those goddamned officers always help each other. . . ."

"They're all the same. . . ."

"Damn their hides, we risked our lives for a few dimes. . . ."

"Let's go and sweat it out of the commander. . . . Come on, let's everybody go! Anyone who doesn't is a dog!"

A soldier named Wu Kuei was a well-known deserter. He had been a soldier since he was fifteen and had been in and out of about thirty units. Earlier this year when his unit was in the mountains beyond the pass, he dared not escape. He thought he'd never get back this time to mingle with people again. He left the crowd and crept up toward the window to eavesdrop on the officers. He heard nothing and raised his eyes slowly to a level with the window sill. Suddenly he felt a scorching pain across his back. Before he had time to turn, two more blows rasped across him. He wheeled around and found himself looking into the face of the platoon leader Chang who roared at him:

"What are you doing here? Trying to start a mutiny?" Wu bent his arm around to feel his sore back. "Stand to! You dog, don't you know how to stand at attention? You scum, get out of here!" Chang went off toward the captain's room. The soldiers hissed after him, but he pretended not to hear. Presently the captain and the other officers walked to the big hall. They ordered five orderlies and the others to remove all but two of the cases of opium to the house where the adjutant was staying. The two cases they ordered carried to the home of the brigadier. A lieutenant went with each party.

"Fall in!" shouted the captain. His whistle sent a long piercing streak of sound through the hall. Wu Kuei went slowly past him to his place in the ranks. The captain struck him a solid blow on his back. "Hurry up, you corpse!" The ranks lined up. Roll was called. The captain swept the line with hard eyes.

"Listen!" he roared. There was a shuffling of legs as they came to attention. "What's the matter with you? No rice? Smarten up there!" He swore in a stream at the men, his face red. The ranks still stood dully under his lashing. Their legs hurt.

"Listen! We are going to be incorporated into the Third Battalion by order of the brigadier. Our commander is leaving for army headquarters today. Spruce up and put your arms in order. We're going to give him a send-off. Did you hear?"

Heads bobbed in the ranks. The men looked at each other. Only a few halfhearted *Yes, sir*'s.

"Well? Well?" the captain's eyes ranged up and down the line of men, spitting hatred and anger. With vicious eyes, he seemed to be looking for a victim to vent his spleen on. "What kind of soldiers do you call yourselves? No discipline. Anybody that wants to make trouble, step forward!"

The ranks calmed down. The captain was looking for a victim, but he was distracted by thoughts of himself. He stood to lose his own job, perhaps, when the reorganization took place. After a brief pause, he raised his voice and spoke again.

"Get ready at once! Clear?"

"Yes, sir!"

"At ease, break ranks."

The men rushed back into the hall amid a confusion of talk.

"Into the Third Battalion! . . ."

"It means we have to go out again! . . ."

"Rape their mothers, they want to murder us. . . ."

Everybody knew that the Third Battalion was headed for the frontier and for death.

"Listen, men, let's go and demand our pay! If we don't get our pay, we won't let the commander leave!"

"Good idea!" said Hsia Te-hai. "Let's demand our pay. I want to ask for my fingers back too!"

Everyone was talking amid noise and confusion. Bayonets

and rifles clattered. The captain in his room heard them, but he was afraid of what the day might produce. He remained where he was.

Fall in again. No man was permitted to carry a rifle. They marched to the city gate, stood in ranks, and waited a long time. From far away, pony bells began to tinkle. Before long the orderlies rode past with the pack animals. The lieutenant-commander and the concubines followed them. After a brief pause came a platoon of armed guards, and immediately behind them, the commander of the battalion. The chief of staff and some officers from brigade headquarters accompanied him.

"Stop him!" shouted somebody in the ranks. There was an agitated movement among the men. Deadly pale, the captain shouted, "Attention!" Nobody paid any attention to him. The soldiers broke ranks and surrounded the commander. "Give us our pay!" they roared at him. "Pay us or you don't leave!"

"What's this, a mutiny?" thundered the chief of staff. "Lieutenant Wu! Arrest the ringleaders! This is an outrage! Captain Li, order the men back! Fire if they resist!"

Hsia Te-hai stood at attention. "Sir, we want our pay!" he said.

"So you're running this, eh? Lieutenant Wu, arrest this man!"

The armed guard closed in on them. Hsia Te-hai and Wang Kang were arrested. The men were enraged but felt lost without their arms. At gunpoint they sullenly fell back into line and were marched to the temple by Captain Li. They were dismissed and crowded into the large hall, everybody cursing.

"Why not use our bayonets? Afraid of their goddamned rifles?"

Everyone stood about wringing hands, excited, upset, and

cursing. Two brothers were arrested and they did not know
what to do. They were certain it would be futile to make demands. Everyone waited and waited, but they knew nothing
hopeful would come out of it. The sky was dark. Snow was
falling again. They milled around in the hall without knowing what to do. Every man looked to the next for a plan, a
suggestion, but none was forthcoming. Suddenly they heard
a bugle sound mournfully coming through the temple door.
"They are taking them out to be shot!" somebody cried. Everybody was frightened and they rushed to the gate. Their
hearts were beating hard, not from fear but out of an un-
speakable tension. Their eyes were burning like fire. Two
lines of armed men were marching by and snow was falling
on the bare bodies of the tightly bound prisoners.

"Two of them are deserters!"

"Too bad, there's Hsia, he's tied up too!"

"What is their crime?"

The men nearly went mad with anger. They wanted to run
out and rescue Hsia and Wang. Every man waited for the
next to lead. Everybody was confused and no one took the
lead.

"We escaped from the mountain pass. Who counted on
meeting death here!" It seemed that everyone shared these
thoughts, as if they all knew who they were. "That's right,
our lives are worth no more than those of chickens!"

Suddenly the brigadier came haughtily toward them. Four
bodyguards with drawn Mausers accompanied him. Just
then Captain Li came out from behind and the men cleared
the way for him to come through. As soon as the brigadier
entered the temple door Captain Li roared:

"Salute!"

Mechanically every hand went up. The brigadier's face was
fierce-looking, his lips quivered as if to scold. Finally he ordered the captain to have the men fall in. He had some-

thing to say. Everybody knew what was coming. They roused themselves as though they had forgotten how fatigued they were. Ranks formed in the courtyard. Snow was falling upon them, but they forgot the cold. Their hearts were tight with tension, like fuses waiting to be lit. The captain stood with the petty officers behind the brigadier.

"You are heaven's special army, aren't you?" He stood in the falling snow and spat his words out contemptuously at the men, his eyes moving along their ranks. "Just because you've been to the frontier, you're untouchable, aren't you? Do you know what a soldier is? It's his job to obey. Obedience without question. You know that! Now you have openly assaulted an officer. You held him up and blackmailed him. You're mutineers! You're not fit to be soldiers!"

Their hearts quivered and their burning eyes stared straight ahead.

"You all aren't soldiers! You're bandits! We of the revolutionary army. . . ."*

"Your 'revolution' only means murder!" muttered somebody at the end of the line.

"Who spoke?" barked the brigadier. "Captain, pull him out!"

The men turned their heads ever so slightly. They watched Wu Kuei being dragged from the ranks. Tension rose even more.

"Shoot him, Captain," said the brigadier firmly.

"Shoot?" Someone cried out from the ranks.

The men forgot everything else except that their enemy stood in front of them. They charged forward like cornered beasts and flashed their bayonets in their hands. The brigadier and the captain made for the gate. The four bodyguards opened fire with their Mausers, sweeping across the

---

*The Kuomintang regarded itself as "revolutionary."

424

soldiers as though they were wild beasts. Several men fell. But before they could fire again, they were transfixed with a dozen bayonets, and four bodies went down under the feet of the men. The brigadier and the captain did not run far before they were met by two sentinels at the gate rushing in with their rifles. The two officers fell back and were cut down by the men pursuing them.

"Let's go, men!" The men poured into the hall. Arms were flung up and in utter disorder they made for the East Gate, as if their feet had suddenly grown wings. They brushed through the thickly falling snow but nobody felt it. Now they felt their legs were again part of their bodies. They wished they could fly; they were all able to press ahead. Their days in the snow-filled mountains were forgotten. They felt good. They were free. They laughed and talked and shouted, their saliva running. "Where are we off to, men?"

"Where do we go? To fight this man-eating world!"

Death

"Sister Lin! Sister Lin!"

She opened her eyes, wide and startled, the call still sounding in her ears. It was the voice of Ah Mao, a young girl worker she had recently come to know. But no Ah Mao bent through the blackness over her. Her whole body and her arms and hands burned with pain against the damp chill of the cement floor on which she lay outstretched. Her hair lay in matted disarray, damp against her forehead. Her blouse was torn from one shoulder and the underthings had been ripped away with it. An icy wind fanned her bare flesh. She raised her hand to cover herself and instinctively tried to pull her torn clothes together. Faintly her senses registered a small square shaft of gray night light. Her eyes finally took in a tiny window up near the ceiling. She was in a cell less than twenty feet square. Next to the wall was a plain board table and two benches. Across one of them lay a cane whip. Now she remembered. This was the reality, Ah Mao's voice was a dream. Could it all have happened just a few hours ago?

She had jumped off a number eighteen trackless tram and found herself staring into a pimpled face half-covered by a black felt hat. The man was standing under the street lamp. A shock went through her, she lowered her head and started off away from him. Too late.

"Ah, Miss T'an!"

The voice reached out and clutched at her. Her steps and her heart quickened. There was no doubt about it, this was Wang. She had only to hear him call her name and she knew it was Wang, horrid, treacherous Wang.

"Hai, Miss T'an!"

It was closer now, and she heard his steps just back of her. It was already half-past eleven. Tibet Road was almost empty of pedestrians. She cast about for a refuge, but along the full length of the street to the west was the jet blackness of the foreigners' racecourse. A soft spring breeze blew across the open space. Across the street were the lights of the Chueh Lu Hotel Cabaret, and she could hear the music. The lights of the moving electric signs flashed by.

"Hai, don't you recognize your old friend?" A heavy hand tapped her shoulder. She turned around angrily and cried out,

"You must be seeing things! I've never seen you before in my life!" She saw, terror-stricken, that there was another person there, a tall man in a dark gown standing beside Wang. "That's it," she thought. "Finished." Her heart jumped and she tried to run. Wang twisted her arm behind her and after a short struggle she knew escape was impossible. "You mean you don't remember an old friend of four or five years?" Wang said laughing. "Come on, we're going to have a little chat, aren't we? Tell me, now, how have things been with you lately, busy?"

She struggled vainly to free herself, but soon saw she had no chance. She stood still and stared with hatred at Wang.

"You're a little thinner now," he cackled. "Are they keeping you a little too busy?"

The black gown came up and took her other arm.

"Ah yes, permit me to introduce our Comrade T'an, a real heroine. . . ."

She spat directly into his pimpled face. With a negligent gesture, he wiped it off with his free hand and went on.

"Well, let's get a car. Let's go." The man in the black gown went off down the street.

All this could have been only a few hours ago. It all came back so clearly now, yet it still seemed unreal. The small electric bulb had shone down from the ceiling. Wang had grinned at her from that bench over there and Black Gown's heavy boots had crushed her ankles. Her back felt as though it had been fearfully burned. She felt it gingerly with her fingers. The whip had raised half-inch welts. But the pain in her fingers was even greater. Huge wet and sticky blisters had appeared in the joints where a third man, a long-faced person with a crooked nose, dressed in an open shirt, had burned them with his cigar.

"I know you're still living with Li." Wang fixed his red eyes upon her. "Just tell me where you live now."

The same Wang. He hadn't changed any. The same coarse voice and loose mouth full of revolutionary talk. She felt as if somebody had inserted needles into her heart.

"My name isn't T'an and I never saw you before!" Li must have gone by now. It must be after one. Surely he'll know there's something wrong!

"Snap into it! Where do you live?" Black Gown slapped her along the side of her head with the flat of his hand. She went sprawling, her temples ringing. Long Face laughed loudly. Puffing vigorously at his cigar he leaned over and mumbled something into Black Gown's ear.

"Yes, yes," he nodded and turned back to the girl.

"You still won't talk? What's the use of it? We're all out of the same crowd and nothing can escape us. These past three months we've raided nearly three hundred places here in Shanghai. How many more can there be? There's nothing you can do alone to save anything and you ought to be glad of the chance to get out of it. If you use your head, there'll be no more trouble. You'll be free and, what's more, under our protection—nothing to be afraid of. . . ."

—And Li, will Li understand by now? It was the usual thing to get away if any comrade failed to get back by twelve. But you could never tell with Li. He might go on writing—

She looked at the whip, the edge of Long Face's cigar, and the rope on the bench, and at the three faces under the dim light. She clenched her teeth tightly. All she could remember after that was screaming, feeling her clothes being ripped away, needle-sharp pain in her heart, the men grunting. Surely by morning he'll have got away, she was thinking at the last. Now she was regaining consciousness. There was no telling how much time had passed. Some time before dawn yet, it seemed. The three of them had given up and left her to herself in this cold and dark room. Terribly alone, she felt like the only person left in the world.

"Ah Mao!" She wanted to call out to Ah Mao, she was so sure she had just heard her voice. Can Ah Mao be here in this very room? No, it was not possible. She put her hand to her forehead. It was burning hot.

I must be delirious, she thought to herself. Her mind was slowly clearing. She knew Ah Mao could not be here, that she had to be in her cramped little attic room with the low ceiling, sleeping there beside her poor old mother, sick with yellow jaundice. She would be disappointed about their meeting for tomorrow at half-past eight. Too bad, Ah Mao would be waiting in vain for her there behind the shed. She might run into more of those hoodlums who hang around the factory. Ah Mao had told her once that they had chased her down the street while a policeman there had just laughed. A poor vulnerable working girl, everyone ready to bully and exploit her, no one willing to protect her. She had just finished her three months' apprenticeship, twelve hours a day in the heavy sticky air of the factory with the thundering shafts and belts overhead. She stood in the narrow lane between the long lines of spindles watching the slender yarn. She got nothing for this. She had to pay her introducer. This month she could handle the machine herself, but according to a new rule there were to be two girls to each machine instead of three. From the first of next month they were to be cut down to five days' work with only one girl to each machine. She'd get only eight dollars for that and she had to give two dollars to the head foreman. And her mother was ill with jaundice.

She had first met Ah Mao not long before in a Japanese-style house in Yangtzepoo. Her pallid, lined face made her look older than she was. Someone brought her over and introduced her and after that they talked together. Ah Mao was very shy and kept her head down all the time. So young, and yet she seemed to understand everything. Strength and determination showed in her eyes. It seemed true of all the young factory girls; no matter how thin and sallow they became from all the bloodsucking of the exploiters, they all had this strength. Ah Mao had it too, and for some reason, she found herself liking the girl.

"Sister Lin, they say the five-day shift will begin on May first. Everybody's worrying about it. What shall we do?"

They all called her Sister Lin. No one knew her name was T'an. They looked on her as a kind of goddess of mercy and wisdom. Whenever she came, they would ask her endless questions and talk about their problems. May first! Her pain was forgotten and so was the dark cramped cell. She thought of all the arrangements made for today's meeting, so much started. And now, just for lack of those last few steps. . . . She moved impatiently, but stinging pain reminded her where she was, and she lay quiet.

She stared up at the tiny window opening and her eyes traveled along the walls until they reached the chained door. She wondered if she could shrink into a tiny insect and slip out through the crack. But this was doubly an illusion, for there was no crack. This was probably just a dream. Hadn't she seen herself this way a hundred times in dreams? Always she had jumped awake with her heart pumping and relaxed with relief to find it only a dream. But everything now was too hard and real, the cold cement floor under her and the pain of her lacerated flesh. It was never like this in the dream.

—Why should I be afraid of something I've been prepared for? I'm a weakling. 1927 . . . 1928 . . . 1929 . . . now 1933—not a day without its fears and risks. I was not afraid to run from my father's house with nothing, yet I still know fear—

Five years ago her husband had been shot. Weak with grief and despair, she had almost taken her baby and returned to the home she had fled from years before. Six months old, a fair and fat and laughing little bundle. She had carried it to a hotel. She couldn't go back to their place. She had sat on the bed and tried to find a way through her agony. A burst of lewd laughter had come from the next room. She remembered what she'd read somewhere in Dostoevsky.

"Only the shedding of pure blood will rid the world of its filth."

Friends took her baby far away to another world. A year ago she received a picture of a sturdy little lad in the arms of a white-clothed nurse. He must be much bigger now. Her

baby was being well cared for. How about all the others—
the abuse and hunger and the pain of the mothers and the
death all around them—what awaited them for their pains?

"Miss T'an, get wise to yourself." The door had opened
and the three figures reappeared. The yellow light went up
again and they stood staring down at her. "We've been
friends for years. Do you think I like to see you suffer?
There's no use, I tell you. Everything's shot to hell and
there's no hope for China anyway. I've been to Russia.
More to eat there, true. But no chance for that in China.
You know as well as I do. Years of struggle and no results.
Lots of talk and dispute about this line or that line, but
when you get right down to it, they're just fighting for their
own power and it only costs the lives of others. I can't see it.
Everybody with eyes in his head has come around now.
Look at Feng K'o-sheng whom you worshipped like a god.
Are you any better than he? He's now up in Nanking. He's
got money, women, and protection. You speak out and everything will be all right. Just one word, Miss T'an, just one
word and your troubles are over."

She dragged herself up into a sitting position against the
wall. Her face was pale and swollen. She stared back at
Wang and said nothing.

"It's clear as a bell. You've got two choices. . . ."

She bit her lower lip hard. Black Gown hung a heavy rope
on a hook in the ceiling.

"What are you still bothering with her for, Wang? I'll
teach her to speak!"

Wang sat down scratching his head. Long Face laughed
loudly and whispered into Black Gown's ear. That worthy
nodded vigorously.

"So you won't talk?"

"I haven't got anything to say." She looked up with a
quiver at the rope.

"Well, you'll get what you deserve!"

Two rough dark hands grabbed her body. The end of the rope was lashed around her slender wrists. Long Face put the cigar in his mouth and pulled heavily on the other end of the line. She was dragged up to her knees. Black Gown picked up the whip and swung back.

"You won't talk?" With a savage swish he brought it down on her body. "Pull her up higher!" Her arms were pulled toward the ceiling and her thin body dangled under them, her toes barely touching the floor. The whip flew back and forth in Black Gown's hands.

"Ai-ya!" exclaimed Wang. Her screams ended in moaning sighs. "What do you want to suffer like this for? Come on, out with it!"

"Let's rest a minute—" Black Gown stopped, panting. He gestured to Long Face to make his end fast on a nail. They sat down and lighted cigarettes. Her limp body hung suspended. She felt no pain. Numbness crept up her limbs. Long Face again whispered into Black Gown's ear. The latter's square face bent, listening, then he shrugged his shoulders.

"So you're tough, are you? We'll see how tough you are! Wang, strip off her trousers!"

Wang looked from Long Face to Black Gown and back again. He didn't care for this part of the job.

"Well, get on, get a move on . . . !"

"Speak out!" said Wang. "Women like you can't stand this."

Nerves twitched in her body. Other faces and names and places rose before her. She could tell all about them and this would stop. She could bear no more of it.

"I can't stand any more!" The words formed in her mind. She tried to get the words out.

"Look, she's coming to her senses now!"

She opened her eyes and with all her strength she spat in Wang's face.

"See what you get, Wang. Still want to help an old comrade?"

Her last ounce of resistance was used up. She felt her clothes being jerked from her with a rip and a tear. Her legs felt as though they had been immersed in icy water. Inadvertently she kicked her dangling legs. The rope cut her lacerated wrists like a sharp knife. The whole weight of her body hung from her wrists now. Her blood rushed downward, draining from her arms, her face and neck to her naked limbs.

"To judge from the face, you'd never think she was as fair as all that!" Long Face laughed aloud. "There are a few good-lookers among these bastards and the men soon gobble them up. Is this hot enough for you?"

He held his cigar against her flesh. She screamed. Wang looked on in silence. It seemed a long time since they came back to the cell. House numbers and street names tumbled in a crazy way through her brain.

Long Face's laugh was louder. Her cries dropped into groans.

"Let her hang there a while. It'll do her good. Come on down and have a drink."

They left the light on. Her white body looked grayish yellow under it. She dimly felt as though her skin were covered by a thick sticky covering. Her sense of feeling came and went. Her arms seemed to be breaking above her. Through her numbness the pain advanced like the passage of a slender knife through the flesh. Let somebody come! Anybody. Even Long Face. She'd tell them anything they wanted. Only let her lie down. She fixed her eyes on the door. Open, open, open. . . .

Death

It opened.

"You'll talk now?"

The voice belonged to Black Gown. She saw three splotches in front of her. Three faces, one long, one square, one red. She was dizzily faint and scarcely felt the pain any more. Her eyes closed and other pictures took shape before her. Ah Mao and the five day shift and the face of her dead beloved, and the flag, their flag, unfurling in a breeze. For them, she thought, for them, all this despicable torture and outrage, not for me alone, for them, for our group. . . . She fell unconscious again and felt nothing, not even when they cut her loose from the rope. Wang dashed water in her face. Her eyes blinked open. Pimple face again. Also Ah Mao, her miserable work at those machines, her mother, jaundice.

The three men stood looking down at her body, at a loss. Her eyes opened again. You have destroyed my body, she thought, but not us. I have defeated you after all. These were her thoughts, but she could speak no more. Slowly consciousness ebbed away. Through the tiny window the gray morning came and the light softly caressed her still body.

YIN FU

Words of Blood

Written in blood, the giant words lie
Sprawling across the face of Nanking Road.
This is the day unforgettable,
That paints its lurid colors once each year.

Written in blood, the giant words engrave
The cries that come from a million throats.
This is the day unforgettable,
The day of anger for a million hearts.

Written in blood, the giant words record
The history of struggle and of clash.
This is the day unforgettable,
That casts its shadow on rebel souls.

May Thirtieth! May Thirtieth!
Arise and stalk abroad on Nanking Road!
Let the color of your blood light up the sky
Your sturdy form the Whangpoo River reflect
Your bell-toned prophecy rouse the world!

"Today they have their Paradise
Tomorrow comes their Hell!

Translated by George A. Kennedy.

436

Today they write in letters of our blood,
Tomorrow we shall bathe in their tears."
I am Rebellion's opening page!
I am the first child of History!
I am a herald of a new season
I am the sharp edge of a new era!

Then "May" (五) shall be a shackle around their necks,
And "Thirtieth" (卅) shall be bars to cage our foes!
Then "May" shall be the sickle and the hammer,
And "Thirtieth" shall be shells and broken chains!

It is enough! Four years the blood has smeared
On those two bloody words that must no longer gleam,
A thousand hearts and voices are resolved:
This day shall pass, wiped out for evermore!

Notes on Chinese Left-wing Periodicals (1934)

Sun (*T'ai-yang*), a monthly, was issued for the first time in the spring of 1928 and ceased publication a year later. Its editors were Chiang Kuang-tz'u (who later left the Communist Party and died in 1931), Ch'ien Hsing-ts'un, and others. This magazine began with the slogan "revolutionary literature" but lacked a clear proletarian standpoint. It mainly published creative pieces, most of them consisting of immature sloganizing. There were a few critical essays which claimed to base themselves on a Marxist view of literature, but their theories were almost purely idealistic in character. The magazine did not attack feudal literature, which was still extremely influential at that time. On the whole, this magazine started out to be the pioneer of revolutionary literature but was guilty of an extreme left infantilism and reflected far more petty bourgeois romanticism than revolutionary realism.

Culture Critic (*Wen-hua p'i-p'ang*), a monthly, was also inaugurated in the spring of 1928 but was suppressed after about one year. (The same magazine appeared two months later under the name *Thought* (*Szu-hsiang yueh-k'an*) but was banned again after four months.) It was edited by the leaders of the Creation Society, founded in 1921, most prominent among them being Kuo Mo-jo, Yü Ta-fu, and others. Before 1926 this group had pursued a romantic notion of "beauty" but in 1927 it absorbed newly emerged people like Li Ch'u-li, Chu Ching-wo, Feng Nai-ch'ao, P'eng K'ang, and others and drastically changed its character, launching its advocacy of proletarian literature. The magazine was general in nature. It published essays on dialectical materialism, on political and economic subjects, although its leading articles dealt with literary matters. It had many of the faults of the *Sun*, although the two groups often attacked each other. *Culture Critic* had the virtue, however, of offering a lead to Chinese youth taking the first steps toward dialectical materialism, although it did not do so without many mistakes.

Creation (*Ch'uang-chao yueh-k'an*) was another monthly issued by the same society. It appeared first in 1926, lapsed for more than a year, was resumed, and then closed down again when the Creation Society itself was suppressed in 1929. It was similar to *Culture Critic*, only larger in size and number of pages.

The Rushing Tide (*Pen-liu*) had a brief career in 1928 under the editorship of Lu Hsün. It never actually advocated proletarian literature but was clearly left-wing in tendency. It published the works of Jou Shih and others who later became heroic martyrs and also published translations (done by Lu Hsün) of articles about cultural and literary policies of groups in the U.S.S.R.

Sprout (*Meng-ya*), a monthly, was published in 1930. Following official harassment, it appeared after its fifth number as

New Earth (*Hsin-ti*), an underground publication which put out six issues. It was edited by Feng Hsüeh-feng. It strongly attacked the Crescent Moon group led by Dr. Huh Shih. This group got its name from its magazine *Crescent Moon* (*Hsin-yueh*) which opposed proletarian literature and indirectly defended the ruling classes in China. *Sprout* appeared at the time the League of Leftist Writers was organizing. The mistakes of *Sun* and *Culture Critic* were being corrected and a new school of left-wing literature was coming into being. Most of the contributors to *Sprout* became key figures on the staff of the League of Leftist Writers. *Sprout* brought the weapon of Marxist criticism to bear on the Chinese literary world and also published translations of famous proletarian works of foreign countries, among them several Russian stories translated by Lu Hsün. Lu Hsün's translation of A. A. Fadeev's *Razgrom*, a novel, first appeared in this magazine.

Cultivator on Barren Land (*T'o-huang-che*) appeared as a monthly in the spring of 1930 and lasted for three numbers. It had a close relation to the League of Leftist Writers. Members of the *Sun* and *Creation* groups worked together for this magazine. Its contributors were mostly members of the League of Leftist Writers. This magazine worked in close cooperation with *Sprout* in the work of the League but was under the influence of the Li Li-san line in the Communist Party. It paid little attention either to the Crescent Moon group or to feudal literature.

Partisan (*Pa-erh-ti-san*), a weekly, was issued as the formal organ of the League of Leftist Writers in 1931. It was secretly printed and circulated. The first number was a special issue dedicated to the five writers murdered by the Kuomintang on February 7 of that year. To get it printed after that, its name had to be changed, and it next appeared as *Litera-*

ture Leader (Wen-hsueh tao-pao). Under that name it continued, despite the most intense terror, from August to November 1931, publishing eight issues. It was a peak time of the white terror, when the Kuomintang clamped down hard on all leftist publications and at the same time arranged the appearance of a "nationalist literature" as a foil to the leftists. *Literature Leader* used its editorial weapons on two fronts, against the left adventurist tendencies in the Communist ranks and against the right opportunism which followed the liquidation of "Li Li-sanism" in the Communist Party. In addition, the magazine attacked the Kuomintang's "nationalist literature," opposing to it the slogan "people's literature." All the important resolutions of the League on political and literary questions were published in the *Literature Leader.*

The Big Dipper (Pei-tou) appeared as a monthly in August 1931 under the editorship of Ting Ling and continued until the spring of 1932, nine numbers in all. During that period it was the only open (legally published) left-wing literary magazine and was directly under the leadership of the League of Leftist Writers. It also included among its contributors liberal writers who tried to take a nonpartisan view of politics. Left-wing magazines had been closed to these neutral liberal writers, but *The Big Dipper* took the stand of encouraging and guiding them. In addition to creative works (of which, unfortunately, only a few were good), the magazine published essays on literary theory and criticism. It exercised considerable influence among the youth. It was finally suppressed.

Crossroads (Shih-tzu chieh-t'ou) appeared on December 1, 1931 and was suppressed after its third issue. It was a general periodical with special emphasis on literature. It was edited, published, and circulated by the League. It was noted for its discussion of translations and its defense of direct translations against those who attacked this method because it made the translation of left-wing literary works into Chinese so difficult to read. It also published sharp essays attacking the Nanking Government and the Kuomintang for submitting to the Japanese imperialists.

Literature Monthly (*Wen-hsueh yueh-pao*) appeared in June 1932 and was suppressed in December that same year. It was an open left literary publication directly sponsored by the League of Leftist Writers, similar to *The Big Dipper* but of far better quality. All the left-wing writers as well as the best of the neutral liberals also contributed to this magazine. Its six issues contained discussions of important topics such as the problem of literature for the masses and the problems of translation. One of its issues was in honor of Gorky. It carried on polemics against the so-called "third group" who tried to be fellow-travelers of the revolution without doing any of the revolution's dirty work. *Literature Monthly* was chiefly distinguished by the fact that it introduced many new writers to the world of Chinese letters.

Literature and Arts (*Wen-i*) appeared as a monthly in October 1933. It published the works of some of the best of the younger left-wing writers. It was suppressed in December 1933.

Spring Light (*Ch'un-kuang*) appeared in March 1934. It also devoted itself mainly to the creative writings of the younger authors.

Poetry (*Wen-hsueh ts'a-chih, shih-ko*) was brought out by left-wing poets as their own organ at the end of 1933 and at this writing (March 1934), its third number has appeared. Formerly all poetry had been included with other work in the general literary magazines and had largely been buried there. This periodical is the first to devote itself exclusively to poetry. It publishes much work by Chinese poets, many translations, and articles on poetry.

All of the magazines mentioned so far were published in Shanghai. There are many others, large and small, published elsewhere. I can note here only the few I have seen:
Literature Magazine (*Wen-hsueh tsa-chih*) was a monthly published in Peking in 1933 and suppressed after two issues. It was similar to Shanghai's *Literature Monthly* and it was the only left-wing literary periodical in the north at that time. It was succeeded by *Literature and Arts Monthly* (*Wen-i yueh-pao*) in June 1933, which disappeared under the terror after three issues. *Northern Youth* (*Pei-fang ch'ing-nien*) appeared as a weekly almost immediately after the taking of Mukden by the Japanese in September 1931. It was devoted to short criticisms and stories. It published essays attacking the Kuomintang's surrenders to Japanese imperialism. It also published correspondence about life under Kuomintang and imperialist oppression and numerous reports on the student movement. Many of its editors and contributors were arrested and it was finally suppressed in May 1933 after appearing under six different names. It had the longest consecutive publication of any of its type and had great influence not only among students but among workers and soldiers as well.

Other northern publications were *Science News* (*K'o-hsueh hsin-wen*), a weekly which appeared in June 1933 and was suppressed in July after five issues, and *Pomegranate Flowers* (*Liu-hua*), published in Taiyuan, Shansi, which appeared for the same length of time. In Amoy, *Lu ha*, a monthly, appeared on November 15, 1933, and lasted for a short time, taking its name from a publication which had appeared once in a while as a newspaper supplement in 1928.